NATIONAL HEROES

Also by Alexander Walker

The Celluloid Sacrifice
Stardom
Stanley Kubrick Directs
Hollywood, England
Rudolph Valentino
Double Takes
Superstars
The Shattered Silents
Garbo: A Portrait
Peter Sellers
Joan Crawford
Marlene Dietrich
Rachel Roberts: No Bells on Sunday

Alexander Walker

NATIONAL HEROES

British Cinema
in the Seventies and Eighties

'Nothing has changed.'
— Alan Parker, 1982

HARRAP · LONDON

For
SAM GOLDWYN, JUN.
— now read on

First published in Great Britain 1985
by HARRAP LIMITED
19–23 Ludgate Hill, London EC4M 7PD

© *Conundrum Ltd* 1985

ISBN 0 245–54268–X

Designed by Mike Sedgwick
Typeset by Spire Print Services Ltd, Salisbury
Printed and bound in Great Britain
by Biddles Ltd, Guildford and King's Lynn

CONTENTS

ILLUSTRATIONS

Note: The first company named after the caption is the film's
original distributor; the second, its production company.

Between pp. 44 and 45
Sunday, Bloody Sunday: Peter Finch, Murray Head, Glenda Jackson (United
    Artists: Vectia Films for United Artists)
Michael Caine in *Get Carter* (MGM-EMI: MGM)
A gaunt Richard Burton in *Villain* (MGM-EMI: Anglo-EMI)
'Carcasses' in *The Long Good Friday* (HandMade Films: Calendar Productions
    for Black Lion Films)
David Essex and small friend in *That'll Be The Day* (MGM-EMI: Goodtimes
    Enterprises)
. . . and as the man in the white suit in its sequel, *Stardust* (EMI: Goodtimes
    Enterprises)
Oliver Reed burns merrily at the stake in *The Devils* (Warner Bros: Russo
    Productions/Warner Bros.)
Roger Daltry as Liszt in *Lisztomania* (Columbia-Warner: VPS/Goodtimes
    Enterprises)

Between pp. 108 and 109
Man about town: Malcolm McDowell in *O Lucky Man!* (Columbia-Warner:
    Memorial/Sam)
. . . and—without his pin-stripe suit—in *Britannia Hospital*
    (Columbia-EMI-Warner: Film & General/EMI/NFFC)
Ben Cross racing Nigel Havers round the college quad in *Chariots of Fire*
    (Twentieth Century-Fox: Enigma/Fox/Allied Stars)
'Nowhere to go' for Del Walker, Anne Gooding and Sam Shepherd in *Bronco
    Bullfrog* (British Lion: Maya Films)
Bully-Boy (Ray Winstone) in a Borstal scene from *Scum* (GTO Films: Berwick
    Street Films 'A')

The hopelessness of unemployed youth, depicted by Ray Gange in *Rude Boy* (Tigon Films: Buzzy Enterprises)

'Black encounter' in *Babylon* (Osiris Films: Diversity Music/NFFC/Chrysalis Group)

Punk Britain—from *Jubilee* (Cinegate: Whaley Malin Productions)

Tight spots for James Bond—Sean Connery in *Never Say Never Again* (Columbia-EMI-Warner: Woodcote/Talia Films)

. . . and Roger Moore in *Octopussy* (United International Pictures: Eon Productions)

Between pp. 172 and 173

The Monty Python team in *The Life of Brian* (Cinema International Corporation: HandMade)

A 'Homoclinch' from *Sebastiane* (Cinegate: Distac)

Teeny-Toughs in *Bugsy Malone* (Fox-Rank: Bugsy Malone Productions/NFFC)

Julie Christie in *Memoirs of a Survivor* (Columbia-EMI-Warner: Memorial/EMI/NFFC)

Anthony Higgins in period piece *The Draughtsman's Contract* (BFI: BFI Production Board/Channel 4)

An oversize bear-hug—from *The Company of Wolves* (Palace Pictures: Palace Productions/ITC)

Table for two: Jonathan Pryce and David De Keyser in *The Ploughman's Lunch* (Virgin: Greenpoint Films/Goldcrest/Michael White)

Between pp. 236 and 237

Dee Hepburn in *Gregory's Girl* (ITC Film Distributors Ltd: Lake Productions)

Julie Walters and Michael Caine in *Educating Rita* (Rank: Acorn Pictures)

'An unusual love story': Phyllis Logan in *Another Time, Another Place* (Cinegate: Umbrella Films/Rediffusion Films/Channel 4/Scottish Arts Council)

Jeremy Irons, as an exiled Pole, in *Moonlighting* (Miracle: Michael White/NFDF/Channel 4)

Rupert Everett in *Another Country* (Virgin-Twentieth Century-Fox: Goldcrest/NFFC)

Miranda Richardson (portraying Ruth Ellis) dancing with Ian Holm in *Dance with a Stranger* (Twentieth Century-Fox: First Film Co./Goldcrest)

Ulster terrorism: Stephen Rea in *Angel* (BFI: Motion Picture Co. of Ireland/Irish Film Board/Channel 4)

Oscar time: David Puttnam has something to smile about—for *Chariots of Fire* (Oscar © Academy of Motion Picture Arts and Sciences ®)

. . . and Richard Attenborough with a brace for *Gandhi* (Oscar © Academy of Motion Picture Arts and Sciences ®)

PREFACE

In 1974 a book of mine appeared under the title *Hollywood, England*. I can best describe it by quoting what I wrote then: 'It is an attempt to illustrate the diversity of talents and motives, economic changes, historical accidents and occasional artistic achievements making up what was called the British film industry during a brief, turbulent part of its existence — the Sixties.'

This present book attempts to take the story up to date — a different story, of course.

The Seventies, and what we have seen up to now of the Eighties, have their own heroes and non-heroes, plots and counterplots, success stories and disasters. I am frankly surprised at how few of the cast of *Hollywood, England* re-appear in *National Heroes*. (The title is, in part, ironic.) But a different diversity has produced its own dynamic: its own set of forces that form the entity we call the 'industry', though that very word 'entity' recalls the mutating monster that thrives on chaos in the more pretentious class of horror film.

I hope the study will illuminate, even at a lower intensity, the correlation between a society and the films that mirror change or occasionally effect it. The Sixties, though, was a unique period: a decade in which a nation's collective energies found release in an increasingly feverish 'vitality fantasy', to use Christopher Booker's handy label, as our films (and we ourselves) passed through the stages of youth-cult, affluence, permissiveness, etc., until the only outcome was an 'explosion into reality' with the Seventies.

This present account begins in 1970, on 'the day after', to use a phrase that the fashion in 'post-holocaust drama' has made grimly appropriate.

It is a highly personal account: some would say a partisan one. I have known personally almost all the huge cast of characters, viewed (and reviewed) their films, interviewed many of them (re-interviewed the key ones for this book), and been an engrossed spectator of their successful or calamitous policies. Some few among them have my admiration: mostly for survival, sometimes for achievement — in both cases, against the odds. Sam Goldwyn, jun., to whom this volume is dedicated, came late to its predecessor and read it, I think, by way of a lightning guide to the diversity of an industry which his own compatriots had largely invigorated by their finance, if not their talent, in the Sixties.

He flatteringly called it 'history in human terms'. I hope he will find humanity here, too. He certainly will find diversity again: for another reason for attempting an overview of the period is to illustrate the vanity of believing there is a clearer purpose in popular culture than human motive can lend it. There are certainly patterns in the politics of film-making: but, as I have said elsewhere, they tell one more about the nature of the people who make the films than about the films themselves. This is another reason for writing about the industrial process in its human form, however worthy of praise, doubt or condemnation the form proves to be.

The structure I have adopted is roughly but not scrupulously chronological. I have used the privilege of hindsight to know when to advance and retreat in time. Some characters appear in others' stories as well as their own; ambitions are made to pause at the natural break; comeuppances are recorded in their due place; and all against a background of changing Britain, apparently as powerless in asserting its own destiny as it is inept at sorting out its film industry's. Being of a cynical disposition, I am neither surprised nor unduly dismayed at the enormity of the mess which this country has made of its recurrent attempt to sustain a film culture. Some few hardy souls manage to make pictures that will tell posterity what we were like: but most of the characters in this drama are like those in the Alan Price song from *O Lucky Man!*: 'On and on and on and on we go/Round the world in circles turning/Earning what we can.' (You will notice, I hope, that almost no one in the story comes out of it a poor man.)

Hollywood, England dealt in large measure with the young creative film-makers of that marvellous decade; *National Heroes* places the emphasis on the people with power (producers, financiers, entrepreneurs, corporate bosses) and the ways they have asserted it through the films they made or caused to be made. Creative endeavour is still present, like Hope in Pandora's Box. But I am well aware that its success stories were achieved 'despite' rather than 'because of' the character of the era.

I have erred on the side of generosity where dates are concerned: for in surveying such a packed period of events, one has to keep one's temporal bearings — and, in any case, I find it revealing to check my memory against such and such an event. (All important films, at their first mention, are accompanied by their year of exhibition: those dealt with in any detail carry the date of their London premiere: a selective industry chronology is included.) For reasons that are all too obvious, I have had to abandon any attempt to translate Sterling into its dollar equivalent (or vice versa): but there comes a point towards the end where there is not much difference.

My gratitude extends to too many people to name here: but I am especially indebted to those I interviewed for this study, and I hope the footnotes signifying their first appearance in the narrative will be compensation for their time and frankness. The debt is easier where my publishers are concerned. I express my warmest thanks to Simon Scott, editorial director at Harrap, for making this book possible and for putting its predecessor back into print after a period of 'scarcity' caused by its being out of print. Gratitude, too, to my editor, Ian Hyde; and, of course, to my agent, Carol Smith.

To Charles Wintour and Louis Kirby, editors of *The Standard* during the period covered, I express my indebtedness for the opportunity this newspaper gave me to acquire the raw material for the present study.

As these words are being written, an event called 'British Film Year' is beginning. I cannot honestly call this book part of the celebrations: but I hope it will stand as a memorial, of some kind.

Davos, 1983 London, 1985

ACKNOWLEDGMENTS

The author wishes to acknowledge his indebtedness to the writers and publishers of the following works quoted in the text: *Dancing Ledge*, by Derek Jarman (Quartet, London, 1984); *The Grades*, by Hunter Davies (Weidenfeld, London, 1981); *Life of Python*, by George Perry (Pavilion, London, 1983); *Me and My Brothers*, by Charles Kray with Jonathan Sykes (Everest, London, 1976); *Notes for a Life*, by Bryan Forbes (Collins, London, 1974); *O Lucky Man!*, by Lindsay Anderson and David Sherwin (Plexus, London, 1973); *Peter Hall's Diaries*, ed. John Goodwin (Hamish Hamilton, London, 1983); *The Seventies*, by Christopher Booker (Allen Lane, London, 1980); *The Seventies*, by Norman Shrapnel (Constable, London, 1980); *Stardust Memories*, by Ray Connolly (Pavilion, London, 1983).

Grateful acknowledgment is made of quotations from articles, interviews and reviews in the following publications: *AIP & Co.*; *Daily Express*; *Daily Mail*; *Encounter*; *Evening Standard*; *Film Policy White Paper*; *Film and Television Technician*; *Financial Times*; *Fortune*; *The Guardian*; *Los Angeles Times*; *Marxism Today*; *Monthly Film Bulletin*; *Ms. London*; *National Film Finance Corporation Reports*; *Newsweek*; *The New Yorker*; *The New York Times*; *Nova*; *The Observer*; *Screen International*; *Sight and Sound*; *Spectator*; *Stills*; *The Sunday Telegraph*; *The Sunday Times*; *Time*; *The Times*; *Variety*; *Vogue*; *Western Mail*.

In addition to those named in the Preface and credited elsewhere for the interviews they granted him, the author wishes to express his gratitude to the following staff and institutions for the professional assistance given him in his research: the staff of the British Film Institute Reference Library; the staff of the National Film Archive Stills Library; the chief librarian and staff of the British Museum Newspaper and Periodical Library.

CHAPTER ONE

State of Change

(The silent majority) represents a process which is as good as inevitable, given a sufficient degree of sexual jealousy, unemployment and social conflict. It is not, nor does it have the makings of a political party. But it is the authentic voice of the British backlash. — Nova *magazine, 1972.*

The first few years of the 1970s brought home to British cinema and society just what bad times lay ahead. Nothing seemed to be moving. The Americans had cut back on making films in Britain. Hollywood's own financial panic, caused by over-costly films and overstocked inventories, had subsided in 1971; yet the film capital was left breathless by the accelerated transience of social change in America and its films panted to keep up with the booming sexual permissiveness and escalating violence just as the ones produced in Britain had done in the 'Swinging Sixties'. But British cinema now, in contrast, looked like the country itself: it had a residual energy, but in the main was feeling dull, drained, debilitated, infected by a run-down feeling becoming characteristic of British life. Christopher Booker diagnosed the 'unwelcome explosion into reality' when he came to cast a backward look at the Seventies. 'One of the main reasons why (the decade) had such an air of hangover, of aftermath,' he wrote, 'was that a psychological climax had been passed which could never be worked up to with the same frenzied excitement again, simply because so many of the "kicks" had come from the very act of "pushing back frontiers" dismantling "taboos" and flouting conventions which could never again, in the same way, be re-erected.'*

Maybe so: but it was only half the truth. The other half was that, as

*Christopher Booker, *The Seventies* (Allen Lane, 1980), p. 32.

the decade advanced, the dissipated energies collected themselves, but now began to be exercised by and on behalf of those who were bent on re-erecting all the constraints that had been demolished. Only the pattern of prejudice changed, not its ultimate power.

For the moment, though, the mood of exhaustion was brilliantly evoked by a film already mentioned in *Hollywood, England*, which deserves more than passing attention. *Sunday, Bloody Sunday* (1 July 1971) was a transitional film embodying a terminal feeling. It was (as we can now see) the only major film of the new decade with principal characters drawn from the newly beleaguered middle class whose confidence and savings were to suffer such fearsome erosion in the inflation that set in from 1974 on. It was located with some precision in the London of 1970, a city (as I wrote in 1973) already 'sliding from its "swinging" euphoria into its "hangover" period — from "What's it all about?" to "What will you settle for?" '

Penelope Gilliatt had based her screen-play upon a random observation John Schlesinger had made to her. What clinched the modest budget he eventually pried out of a dubious United Artists was the huge transatlantic box-office his first American film, *Midnight Cowboy*, was then generating. (Film companies like to preserve a 'relationship' with directors who can deliver.) On the face of it, the two films could not have looked more different. *Midnight Cowboy* was a New York film about a sexual mercenary's itinerary through high and low life. It began like an East Side Sodom and Gomorrah: it ended, as Jon Voight and Dustin Hoffman jointly discover that the wages of sin is love, like a Skid Row account of David and Jonathan. *Sunday, Bloody Sunday* was pre-eminently a London movie: it dealt in mood and nuances, it ended in quiet understatement and desperation. What linked the two films was Schlesinger's view of life as something to bear with rather than manage, something to live through and (if one was lucky) survive rather than dig into and enjoy.

It was to be his last British film that decade. For much of the 1970s he worked in America with American stars and on American subjects. Even *Yanks*, the film he shot in Britain in 1979, had American-West German money behind it! Although it was about the 'friendly invasion' of the GIs, Schlesinger had been unable to find a penny of British finance for it! He kept on his home in South Kensington; but as taxation put the bite on him and other highly paid British artists, he spent more of his time in a house high up in the Hollywood Hills that had belonged to Michael Butler, producer of *Hair*, who had had it decorated in the style of the stage show; so it was now an extraordinary depository of all the psychedelic tints and artefacts associated with the once trendy but now increasingly slummy London alley-way, Carnaby Street.

The title of Schlesinger's very first British feature was implicit in the theme of *Sunday, Bloody Sunday*. It, too, was about 'a kind of loving'. It was a triangle story in which only two of the angles ever got to meet at any one time. The title had the extra '*Sunday*' added as a prefix because the backers feared that Penelope Gilliatt's choice, *Bloody Sunday*, would connote the sectarian violence then rife in Ulster.

The film's characters resemble the capital city they inhabit: apprehensive people undergoing a state of change, uncertain of the next move. A motif in the film was the telephone answering service, staffed by a gimlet-eyed Bessie Love, which sustains the illusion that people are in contact with each other. The joyous abandon of the Sixties has been overtaken by the sheer uncertainty of living — and soon with the arrival of London's first letter bomb, in September 1972, a new physical hazard would be added to the destabilized feeling that *Sunday, Bloody Sunday* already so brilliantly conveyed. It was also the first major film to give a glimpse of the drug scene as a 'problem', not a 'kick', in the opiate loneliness of the all-night pharmacy in Piccadilly where addicts waited in turn for their 'fix' on a National Health prescription.

The economic essence of life is also being devalued, much like the inherent worth of the Sterling currency in the news bulletins incessantly infiltrating the quiet desperation of apparently well-ordered middle-class households. Some people can still hedge their bets, protect their assets: the heroine's father breaks off his dinner to check on the Wall Street closing prices. (Not too many years later, one British film-maker would sigh and say how much he wished he'd listened to 'that *Bloody* film' and switched into American equities before the British stock market began its hectic mid-decade plunge.)

For most people, though, getting through to life's values is already hard enough without having to fight the falling value of money. As someone in the film says, leafing through an illustrated album of Church martyrology, today one has to be bludgeoned into feelings.

Peter Finch's homosexual Jewish physician, excluded from orthodoxy on the twin grounds of sexual deviancy and lapsed faith, knows all too well the limited application of medicine to the soul sickness of the times. He gets small joy out of his aberrant affections, though Schlesinger gained due credit for this early view of homosexuality as simply part of a conventional and contributive life-style. Odd to remember that it was also Finch who, ten years earlier, had risked presenting a full-length sympathetic portrayal of a homosexual on the British screen in *The Trials of Oscar Wilde*. He was to die of a massive coronary seven years later, the most sorely missed of actors, even though the parts that required his warmth and intelligence were by then precious few.

Luciana Arrighi's production design for the film showed the 'Playtime' delights of the Sixties turning into the cast-offs of the Seventies. Finch's home is silting up with all manner of once trendy and pricey bric-a-brac, lying around now like consolation toys abandoned when they did not prove the cure for loneliness. His boy-friend, played by Murray Head from *Hair*, is a kinetic sculptor whose neon-lit pieces resemble his own limited nature — they emit a charming illumination, but little body warmth. The character is coolly disengaged, but he retains that elixir of the Sixties — *youth*. He can still choose. And he does, simply walking away from entanglements, opting for the vitality he presciently senses in New York: a forerunner of what many of the talented Sixties people would soon be doing, too.

Surprisingly, perhaps, what motivates these characters isn't sexual jealousy. Maybe if sex had played a more decisive role, the film's box-office fate would have been brighter. As it was, its exhibition was half-hearted, its audiences were small. Schlesinger's frustration, compounded by the adverse effect its poor showing had on his efforts to raise the money for *Hadrian VII*, was one reason why he opted to work in America. The man and woman in the film are almost maddeningly sensible about sharing their mutual boy-friend in their respective beds. What comes between them is an intangible discontent with life rather than any competitive tussle for love. For such people, says the film, the stock of Sixties' options has been drastically reduced: better now, as Finch says, to settle for half a loaf than no bread at all. Billy Williams's camera circles round the resigned doctor, then turns sympathetically towards him as he starts speaking directly to us film-goers. The physician has imperceptibly turned into the patient, explaining his malaise. And we have become the actors in 'one vast play', as Christopher Booker saw daily life becoming in the Seventies, wishing perhaps we could leave the stage, but not quite knowing how. *Sunday, Bloody Sunday* ends on a mellow note as Finch — stoic, muted, touching — asks for our understanding. As an epilogue for Sixties' People, it was kinder than many of them deserved. At long last, someone in *Sunday, Bloody Sunday* has made a connection with life, though, in truth, the news he brings holds little enough comfort and no joy at all. That was the mood as the new decade started.

THE UNROMANTIC ENGLISHWOMAN

The woman in *Sunday, Bloody Sunday* was played by Glenda Jackson. Just as Julie Christie's 'Golden Girl' had given a characteristic burnish to the Sixties, Jackson's articulate, pragmatic, rebarbative nature seemed in tune with the raw new decade. Her agreeing to be in the film helped Schlesinger find the money: for she came to it with the 'Oscar' she had deservedly won for portraying the sexually liberated but still unfulfilled heroine in Ken Russell's film of D. H. Lawrence's *Women in Love* in 1970.

This time, too, she played a woman who was too intelligent for her own emotional comfort: a divorcée who, typically, has first salvaged her books from the ruins of her marriage. Equally typical of the times is her ex-husband's complaint, which is not about his wife's leaving him, but about the spaces she left on his library shelves. More and more as the decade advanced, the Seventies defined themselves by what they *lacked*, by what was missing.

As Penelope Gilliatt drew her, the character is near to emotional burn-out — soon a common affliction among the doers and movers of the Sixties. She works as a management consultant, resettling sacked executives in new jobs, but never fully salving their pride nor enhancing their lives. Again, Gilliatt's screen-play is ominously exact: as unemployment became *the* endemic social disease of the Seventies, even the professional classes were ravaged beyond moral repair. Yet there was seldom a time in the years ahead when Glenda Jackson was not in demand. Unlike Julie Christie, she did not exhibit any of the physical withdrawal symptoms that may have been due to over-exposure and mistrust of the media; unlike Vanessa Redgrave, her politics were a sort of diffused feminism, militant up to a point, but not calculated to frighten the bankers in their counting-houses.

She remained, as they say, 'bankable' — almost the only female British star with that rating on either side of the Atlantic. At first sight, this is odd: for she is not cast in the conventional plaster of stardom. She is well aware — and probably not a whit displeased by it — that some men admire her without actually liking her. Men in particular seem to be made uneasy by some of her stances *vis-à-vis* their sex. Her former husband was once quoted as saying: 'If she'd gone into politics, she'd be Prime Minister, if she'd taken to crime, she'd be Jack the Ripper.' Until a woman did become Tory Premier, both occupations were historically male preserves.

Jackson does not make it easy for anyone to pigeon-hole her. She is neither glamour symbol, nor yet strident drudge; her looks have more to do with elbow-grease than facials; she is raw-boned and angular, as if shaped by the same biting winds of her birthplace, Merseyside, that threw up the flinty Beatles. Her genetic inheritance is physically visible in the hands of her bricklayer father. She was the eldest of four children whose mother, a one-time barmaid, raised them by kindness backed up by a loud voice: a discipline Jackson says she dreaded, though her voice is a considerable part of her own arsenal. Appropriately, she was named after Glenda Farrell, a Hollywood actress best remembered for playing hard-bitten women reporters.

She did a stint in Boots the chemists' chain stores, and maybe her down-to-earth manner goes back to those shop-counter days of dishing out aspirin and laxative to the public. Her own approach to stage acting sometimes seemed to treat it as a necessary purgative: if the audience suffered, so much the better for their souls and bowels. Many of her movies, in contrast, she must have regarded as akin to undergoing an enforced but well-paid spell of constipation. In one particular case, when cast as Lady Hamilton to Peter Finch's Nelson in a film that displayed them both like historical table cutlery, she overstepped polite conventions (and probably contractual obligations) and told the world what she thought of the production even before it was screened. 'Culture' was not much talked about in her childhood, lest the neighbours thought one was stuck-up: but she hankered after a job in the local lending library so as to 'better' herself. She grew up ill disposed to the commercial hustle of show-business 'culture' and today bears it on sufferance. She found her perfect role almost first time off — which can sometimes be no help at all in later developing one's patience with the less-than-perfect. This was when she played Gudrun Brangwen in *Women in Love*. Her no-nonsense Northern upbringing verified the nature of a woman both sensual and practical: she struck a feminist note that continued to reverberate through the roles that engaged her intelligence.

But Glenda Jackson's star-power resides in her emphatic use of her gender, which is not at all the same as saying she is 'sexy'. Indeed the sexual charge she packs can sometimes blow apart a man's *amour propre*. I know (male) film-goers who cannot watch *A Touch of Class* (1973), the film that won her a second 'Oscar', with any degree of comfort. 'Screwball' is one thing; 'ballbreaking' is something else again . . .

Of men, Glenda Jackson has been quoted as saying: 'One heck of a lot of outlay for a very small return from most of them.' In nude scenes she has always found men to be the vain partners: but they never manage to turn her into the sexual object that other actresses use as an excuse not to play the scene. Few other stars can display their own nudity so candidly — or would care to. It goes a long way to redress (if that's the word) the vulgarity of the scenes in Ken Russell's *The Music Lovers* (1971) which required her to turn her naked body into a terrifying battle-engine for an assault on her husband Tchaikovsky's virginity. A nude Jackson gives an impression not only of contours, but of a constitution.

The actress she most closely resembles in temperament is Bette Davis. Both are known for the formidable 'put down'. It is no accident that both have played Elizabeth Tudor, a role renowned for the chance it offers to reprimand, sometimes in the most terminal fashion, uppity male courtiers. Davis boxed one upstart lover's ears in a showdown at Court: Jackson, playing Elizabeth 1 to Vanessa Redgrave's *Mary, Queen of Scots* (1972), went for another unlucky suitor's solar plexus, probably as near the mark as producer Hal Wallis would prudishly permit. But when it comes to listing the 'Royalty' of the English theatrical establishment, Jackson registers as a republican. 'That doomed dump!' she reportedly called London's newly built National Theatre, the plosive consonants echoing Bette Davis's dismissal of a locality that incurred her displeasure in *Beyond the Forest* — 'What a dump!'

Talking about a role, Jackson sometimes reveals more about herself than she would consent to do in a 'straight' interview. Thus when she said of the poetess Stevie Smith, whom she played on stage and screen, that she 'stood four-square and looked the big things straight in the eye', it's a reasonable assumption that this is the martial stance she, too, prefers. Confrontation becomes her: but she must be evenly matched. With partners who are a dramatic pound or two underweight, she is liable to sound short-tempered and even a mite shrewish.

What finally gives Glenda Jackson's career its modern ring is her impenitent dislike — so characteristic of the Seventies — of what being a star involves. Without being a groupie or a zealot, she creates an impression that the job of acting is simply not a big enough Cause — not worthy of her total commitment. Reportedly, she has vowed to give it up altogether as if it were a bad habit, like smoking, contracted casually, guiltily indulged in, overdue for replacement by some more socially approved alternative. Such as . . .? Well, such as the 'social work' which, throughout the Seventies, she has persistently envisaged herself doing. In 1970 she was quoted as saying: 'I'd like to do something socially useful or adopt lots of children.' In 1971: 'I'll probably give it all up in three years and take up social work.' In 1972: 'I'll probably give it all up quite soon.' In 1973: 'I feel (all the energy) should be channelled into something more worth-while, helping the homeless and the handicapped.' in 1976: 'I sometimes feel I'd be better employed getting into social welfare work.'

Stars of an older generation than hers sometimes criticized their employers for good professional reasons, usually to do with the bad roles that the studio handed them to play. A star like Glenda Jackson, shaped in the social retrenchment of the Seventies, seems to experience a need to lay a moral foundation under her rejection of the extravagance, egoism and hypocrisy that comprise much of the movie scene. When she appeared as the eponymous heroine of *The Romantic Englishwoman* (1975), Helmut Berger, who played her lover, delivered the ironical judgment: 'The English woman is the most romantic — she wants everything.' One feels that Glenda Jackson applies a similarly 'romantic' rule to life: it must be all or nothing. Hence, perhaps, the discontent that underlies her acting with rasping effectiveness. Perhaps thinking of what the film industry would do with her if she let it, she is wont to quote Bette Davis to the effect that, 'I'm so sick of always having to apologize for being intelligent.' 'So true,' Ms Jackson is apt to add, with a smile that would have cut tungsten.

VILLAINIES

Sexual anxiety in *Sunday, Bloody Sunday* was so quietly pitched, so stoically endured that the film could scarcely have been conceived as a high-tempered sermon to the multitude on the state of change in mid-Sixties life: rather, as an elegiac mediation. But other films in the following months were not so reticent — and nothing like so well bred. British cinema in the early 1970s began to focus on the nature of what we were increasingly to have dunned into us in editorial platitudes, namely the 'Violent Society'.

Organized and even individual crime was not a strong feature of British movies in the Sixties: there was so much else of a permissive nature to captivate the novelty-hungry generation. Things were changing by the end of the decade. *Performance*, with James Fox as an East End criminal on the run seeking sanctuary with Mick Jagger's reclusive Pop idol, joined two of the tributaries of British life, the trendy and the trad, into sinister confluence. But the film's delayed appearance on the home screen made it feel like an obituary notice when it finally appeared, rather than an omen. Other real-life 'performances', as the criminal class called their business, had already seized people's horrified fascination. They would have been familiar enough to the characters played by Fox and Jagger.

'The most gripping entertainment in London,' was how the 'star' of one of them later characterized the events that occupied the Central Criminal Courts, the 'Old Bailey', for an unprecedented 'run' of eight weeks at the start of 1969. There, the three Kray brothers, Reggie, Ronnie and Charles, along with seven other 'supporting players', had been variously charged with murder or complicity to murder. The victim was one Jack McVitie, nicknamed 'The Hat' in the best criminal tradition, because of his cinematic habit of keeping it on his head indoors as well as out. McVitie was 'a nothing man', as Charles Kray called him in an autobiography published seven years later, 'a small-time villain with a high forehead — due to shortage of hair, not surplus of brains — who was used as an errand boy'* in the Kray twins' extortion racket. On one October night, in 1967, McVitie was repeatedly stabbed in the face, neck and body. In Charles Kray's vivid phrase, which would have lent distinction to an author's camera directions in an otherwise impersonal screen-play, his blood sprayed the furnishings as well as the people present 'with dreadful impartiality'.

The sentences passed on the accused two years later by Mr Justice Melford Stevenson were, to say the least, more discriminating. Reggie and Ronnie Kray got life, with a recommendation that they serve a minimum of thirty years: as these words are being written, they are still behind bars in spite of periodic attempts to muster public sympathy for a parole. Charles Kray drew ten years: which allowed him, after full remission, to be set at impenitent liberty in 1976 and tell the story in *Me and My Brothers*. It is one of the decade's most extraordinary books: a mixture of family loyalties and filial pieties of the sort that, in much more

*Charles Kray, with Jonathan Sykes, *Me and My Brothers* (Everest, 1976) p. 197.

law-abiding hands, helped establish some of the West End's great show-business empires before and after the war, including one that was shaping a part of the film industry at the very time Charles Kray published his memoirs.

The Krays' trial lasted from 7 January to 5 March 1969, kept twenty-three counsel (including nine QCs) gainfully employed and cost upwards of £150,000. As well as securing a place in the *Guinness Book of Records* — for the time spent, not the blood spilt — it worked its way deeply into public consciousness by saturating the media before and during it and for years afterwards. Even in recent times, the baleful stardom of the still imprisoned Krays bathed such events as the funeral of their devoted and doughty mother with a glamour not quite welcomed, but not rejected, either, by the actual stage and screen personalities impelled by kinship or simply East End loyalty to attend. At the time, the trial imparted a darkening coloration to the end of the Sixties. It matched the moral disintegration of Swinging London's good-time fabric represented by *Performance*.

As the Seventies advanced, the feeling of revulsion for the times was articulated even by a man who was inclined by temperament to private effacement, not public prophecy. Perhaps Sir Alec Guinness was over-anxious in that summer of 1972 to explain why he should be wearing the uniform of the Fuhrer in an Anglo-Italian co-production, *Hitler — The Last Ten Days* (1973), being shot in London by Ennio de Concini with sets designed by Ken Adam. But his words only paraphrased what editorials and columnists were putting into equally concerned if less colloquial prose. 'The situation in England', said Sir Alec, 'strikes every month a decadent, yes *decadent* note. All these depressing things. People say, why not get someone else to sort it all out for them. In situations like this, it is always possible for a strong man to appear and be welcomed by so many people.'*

The sentiments did indeed anticipate the 'Hitler Wave,' as it was called: first editions of *Mein Kampf* fetched record prices at auctions in Brussels and Vienna in 1973; and the Guinness film created a stir, though it was not 'welcomed by so many people' as had perhaps been hoped due to Bernard Delfont, head of EMI's film division, who banned it from his cinema circuit on the ground that he could not reconcile himself to making money out of a subject so abhorrent to his Jewish co-religionists, and no doubt other faiths, too. But there was already a British-made documentary, *Swastika,* in production, a third of it comprising scenes from the Fuhrer's home life, shot by Eva Braun, which had recently been unearthed in the unlikely archives of the US Marines and Signals Corps. It was being assembled by a new company, Visual Programmes Systems, whose executives numbered Sandy

*Time, 28 August 1972.

Lieberson, who had produced *Performance*, and a youthful advertising executive turned film-maker, David Puttnam.

All in all, the early 1970s saw a disturbing agglomeration of ill omens. Though not exactly Hitlers in stature or scale of crime, some domestic monsters of evil had already been exhumed by British film-makers sensing the way that the public's imagination had been stimulated by the Krays' trial and the proximity of the criminal underworld it disclosed. Considering that British society has been customarily well-stocked with murderers, it is surprising how few real-life crimes reached the screen until one remembers the libel laws and the film censorship board's distaste for even indirectly incurring their penalty by passing a film devoted to the misdeeds of identifiable people. At least *10 Rillington Place* (5 February 1971) could persuasively present itself as a case against the restoration of the death penalty, which sections of the media had been demanding, by showing how one man's crimes resulted in an innocent man's execution.

Richard Attenborough, bald, asthmatic and meek-mannered in a way that recalled his hen-pecked husband in *Seance on a Wet Afternoon* seven years earlier, played John Reginald Christie who, from 1944 on, murdered seven women, including the pregnant wife of his lodger Timothy Evans. Evans was the one to be accused of the crime at the time and hanged. He was played with intensely convincing pathos by John Hurt, an actor who then took out his patent rights (which he still holds) as the British cinema's favourite victim-figure. Directed in London by Richard Fleischer, who had exposed the split-minded pathology of *The Boston Strangler* in 1965, it owed its limited success to the way Hurt's performance verified the anti-hanging polemic of Ludovic Kennedy's book on which it was based: without a word spoken, his handkerchief-pale features as he went to his death in a daze of confused innocence said everything.

For all the lurid expectancy its multiple murders aroused, *10 Rillington Place* looked like a humane society's pamphlet compared to the moral void opened up within weeks of its appearance by two other British-made movies. These owed something to the New Violence of Hollywood films (such as *Blind Terror* or *Pretty Maids All in a Row* that same year) which fed off the gruesome public interest aroused by the so-called Labianco and Sharon Tate killings by the 'Manson family' in 1969. Nubile victims were disposed of as if they were used cosmetic tissues and their life-style was played up for all its hedonistic truths and inventions in order to stoke up the anger of the social have-nots to a homicidal intensity. This had become a commonplace of American cinema since *Bonnie and Clyde*: but the emphasis on the criminal, rather than the Law, was a new note in British movie-making, which had traditionally glamorized the police thanks to a long line of stalwart and much-loved leading men of cinema and television.

Public terrorism came to London in the first years of the Seventies, with Pakistani dissidents being shot dead at the Indian High Commission's premises, machine-gun attacks on various Middle East embassies and letter bombs disseminated to prominent addresses all over the city, so that the 'Affluent Society' of the Sixties quickly came to be called the 'Violent Society'. As violence grew more perceptible, it was reflected in films which put the emphasis of interest on the criminal anti-hero, stripped of political motives, of course, but rooted very precisely in the London underworld of the Krays, and demonstrating his ugly skills with the verisimilitude of the psychopaths nurtured by Hollywood.

Both *Get Carter* (11 March 1971) and *Villain* (12 August 1971) borrowed from the manners and 'verbals' of the South London working-class world and the picture painted by witnesses at the Krays' trial of 'malevolent monsters who held the East End in terror', to quote Charles Kray's recollection of those bits of Old Bailey testimony that fell sadly short of his own affectionate view of his siblings. Both films were brutal, hard-edged, Anglicized versions of the American gangster genre. The transatlantic influence was marked in other ways, too.

Get Carter was one of the four films that MGM's British production company had rather hastily agreed, in July 1970, to co-finance with EMI, in order to temper the hostility of the British film unions to the closure of the Hollywood company's British studio at Borehamwood, just down the road from EMI's Elstree lot. It was produced by Michael Klinger, a most capable and unsqueamish film-maker, well equipped to emulate the realism that American films were now flaunting with the disappearance of the old 'Morality Code'. Mike Hodges wrote and directed it. He had been the author of a recent TV play, *Rumour*, about an English provincial crime reporter trapped and destroyed by malevolent real-life figures lured out of the underworld by his hyper-active imagination. It had revealed a vividly conceptualized view of life as a state of constantly impending doom only tempered by periods of grievous bodily harm.

The permutations forced on British cinema of the Seventies in its effort to repeat the successes of the Sixties were revealed at their starkest in Michael Caine's brutal portrayal of the title role. Carter is the 'hard man' who might have had Alfie as his weakling brother. A tough London racketeer devoid of self-pity, or mercy towards others, he travels North to Newcastle to avenge his brother's death at the hands of the local heavy mob whose ice-cube cool boss is none other than that 'angry young man' of two decades earlier, John Osborne, now adorned with an Edwardian beard, ensconced in a gaming club, and looking for all the world like a Teddy Boy made good (or gone to the bad, according to one's generational sympathies).

Get Carter was not the only film of the time to create the impression that the leading characters in Sixties cinema had simply turned round in their tracks — as if the people we had got to know in the good times were using the other half of the ticket they had carefully preserved against the evil day to return to their origins and establish their validity all over again. It was a reversal of a trend which had transformed Billy Liar's girl-friend from the Midlands into the jet-set's Darling by putting Julie Christie on the train south; or Rita Tushingham's unmarried mother in *A Taste of Honey* into the dolly-bird of *The Knack* by packing her off to London and 'the smoke'.

Caine's example had been preceded by Nicol Williamson's portrayal of another hard man compelled to return and seek his destiny back where his origins lie. In *The Reckoning* (15 January 1970) Williamson played a back-street yob from Liverpool who has got on so fast in a big London business and raised himself so high on the bodies of his victims that he is only one floor below the boss — as he coolly reminds the boss. As in *Get Carter*, a violent death in the family summons him back to his provincial birthplace, and filial piety of a type that the Kray household would have found familiar impels him to an act of violence that differs from the mayhem committed in the parallel world of big business only by its bloody directness. Rachel Roberts, mascot of everything that was provincial, repressed, suffering yet sensual in Sixties cinema, reappears in coarsened form as a randy housewife with poker-work eyebrows and a bawdy glance. Jack Gold, who directed *The Reckoning*, gave it a realism that was all the more astonishing because economy had forced him to re-create the ambience of Bingo halls, beery pubs and smoky wrestling stadiums entirely in the studio — itself a reversal of Sixties' preference for locations. Like *Get Carter*, it took a breath-takingly cynical view of an entrepreneur acting out his imperatives in response to the tribal law of the fittest man's survival.

Once again the cinema was in tune with the predominant mood of British society, though this time it lasted for a shorter spell than a whole decade. For when Edward Heath became Prime Minister in June 1970, after the Tories' surprise victory in the General Election, the machinations of big-business entrepreneurs had already caught the national imagination. A TV series entitled *The Plane Makers*, originally built around factory workers, took off, and swiftly gained height in the ratings, only when its drama was moved off the workshop floor into the executive suites and the boardroom under a new title that replaced the notion of measurable output by one of unrestrained ambition: it was renamed *The Power Game*.

If any title were symptomatic of the Seventies, it was this one. True, the 'power game' had begun to be played with feverish intensity in the property market during the last year or two of Harold Wilson's Labour Government in the Sixties; but under Heath, all kinds of dubious operators and brash speculators specializing in take-over bids and asset stripping stepped brazenly out of the shadows to set off a merger mania and a banking boom which had its apocalyptic outcome before the decade was half over. Even earlier, the business community was brought into such disrepute that Heath had to denounce 'the unattractive and unacceptable face of capitalism'. If he had sought one representative face, he could have done no better than identify Nicol Williamson's finger-snapping executive, swallowing aspirin on the run and manifesting his aggressiveness with a suicidal foot on the accelerator in the early-morning rush-hour or a murderous hand in the plotting of boardroom vendettas.

Caine's Carter was a more down-market example of the same sort of entrepreneurial Tory energy. In his case, though, the body-count is higher. *The Reckoning* showed big business as a corrupting experience: but *Get Carter* has a total moral vacuum at its centre. Early on, Caine is glimpsed with his nose in *Farewell, My Lovely* on the train ride to Newcastle.

But if the intention is to establish a fraternal link with Chandler's hero who went down mean streets without contracting their moral taint, then it backfires. No chivalry, no sympathy, no mercy is shown by this human killing-machine. He pushes a knife through one man's heart; tips another over his penthouse wall to crash down on a passing car; batters a third to death and sends him out to sea in a shale-dumper; merely shoots a fourth in a ferry-boat ambush; locks one girl in a car trunk — where she gets drowned by accident — and drowns another on purpose after drugging her to the point of insensibility.

Sex was absent — but it was represented in atypically sterile fashion by Britt Ekland, in a curiously masturbatory scene, talking over the telephone. Its sexual impact was diminished beside the explosion of aggression which showed that British cinema could compete all too effectively with Hollywood models directed by men whose credo seemed to be: 'Don't defuse it, detonate it; don't distance the audience, rub their faces in it.' Jonathan Miller, physician as well as stage director, inspecting the burst arteries, broken skulls, blown-off faces and all the rest of the horrid anatomical realism created by the make-up men, coined the term 'medical materialism' to describe this characteristic of the Seventies: an unhealthy preoccupation with the damage people inflicted on each other and with a society self-destructively bent on inflicting the maximum damage on its own living organs.

If *Get Carter* were grist to the medical mill, *Villain* (which opened a few weeks later) could have kept the libel lawyers busy, although, to be sure, the Kray twins were in no position to allege that 'Vic Dakin', the character played by Richard Burton, had been constructed out of their composite features. They might even have been a little proud of the unexpectedly good job Burton made of it. The role is not often mentioned among the few to which he *did* lend distinction in a career that was blemished by many more ill-chosen and ill-played parts. But his is exceptional acting, totally self-sacrificing, conscripting a lot of the self-disgust that Burton felt for wasting his talent in films whose only reward was written in appropriate zeroes on the cheques he received.

In *Villain* he looks, simply, godawful. His face is like an old glove that does not quite fit and has had to be pinched in here and there. His eyes are pebbles. The voice that had too often sounded self-enraptured in roles where, admittedly, listening to himself was the only compensation, is now hard and cheapened. And the immense dramatic 'weight' he carries, to the point of seeming overweight in commonplace films, is this time a bonus, not a burden. It reinforces his epic contempt for the tawdry ordinariness of the world that Vic Dakin seeks to dominate.

The trick of getting two notable comedy writers, Dick Clement and Ian La Frenais, to give a guignolesque turn of phrase to Vic's repudiation of every decency in life gives the film a macabre life-in-death vitality typical of the born East Ender who is never so grim as when he is jesting. One recalls Ronnie Kray, in good voice, challenging (successfully) the notion that he and his fellow-accused should be identified in the Old Bailey dock by numbered placards — 'Not a bleedin' cattle market, is it, your Honour?' Burton, when bespotted by some scarlet droppings from a balcony where a badly carved-up body has been dumped, croaks 'Bleedin' pigeons' in just the same tone of voice.

The movie was another of the MGM-EMI British co-productions, though it was made by the same all-American talents of Elliott Kastner, Alan Ladd, jun., and Jay Kanter, who had been associated with quite a few of Universal's British-made productions of the Sixties whose long run of honourable failures has been already examined in *Hollywood, England*. Yet *Villain* was not only outstandingly successful at the British box-office, but a British film to its back teeth — which were not even Hollywood-capped. Under Michael Tuchner's direction, it studied the British villain in his native habitat. And it showed how it is enlarged by fear, sustained by vice, entrenched by profit and only marginally diminished by the force of law. Violent though the film is, its true focus is on terror. Terror backed by force, of course; all the same, terror which the film traces responsibly back to its source in the deep conservatism (with a lower-case 'c') of gangsters who resist any change in the society they plunder so brutally.

These villains have to suffer the irritations of traffic jams like all of us; they run to ulcers; they decry the work-shyness of factory clerks whose lightning strike jeopardizes a pay-roll snatch; they lament that the Army draft has been abolished for the kids; and deplore the vandalism that puts a pay-phone out of action and upsets their carefully synchronized plans. Burton is devoted to his mother (played by Cathleen Nesbitt) and gets his private kicks from 'a nice Jewish peasant boy' whom he regularly beats up and then beds down. By not being depicted in any detail, however, this kink suggests the huge volume of psychotic power held in reserve under the criminal surface. There is a perverted sense of moral ascendancy in his dealings with 'ordinary' humanity. 'Disgusting . . . disgusting' he hisses at a terrified Member of Parliament (Donald Sinden) like a sergeant-major barking at a rookie with a dirty cap badge; 'Puts up your widow's pension', he cynically congratulates a newly promoted policeman; 'Don't collect from him for a week . . . reward for initiative', is his sneering pat on the back for a tip-off. *Villain* ends with Burton cornered but not cowed, swivelling an angry eye around the witnesses to his latest enormity and uttering a maniac bellow which are the last unanswered words in the film: 'WHO DO YOU THINK YOU'RE LOOKING AT?'

The question was answered in Charles Kray's book six years later: 'My brothers . . . whatever crimes they had committed, were men of generous impulses who were always ready to help those in need and never raised a hand against the innocent, whether man, woman or child, which is more than can be said for bomb terrorists who received a lighter punishment for more serious crimes. Let me say that I know nothing of the Irish problem,' his apologia continues, 'and have no comment to make on the methods adopted by those who think the solution lies in bombs, bullets and bloodshed, but I am comparing the sentences passed on my brothers with those recently passed on men who were responsible for the wholesale slaughter of ordinary people.'*

Ironists might relish this defence: but it is one which (with a few rougher locutions) could have gone straight into *Villain* had Ulster-born terrorism then impinged on the English consciousness by virtue of the bombs that were later to go off on the English mainland (sometimes right beside the Krays' old stamping ground in Knightsbridge). As it happens, the 'Irish dimension' was available to John Mackenzie when he directed *The Long Good Friday*, exactly ten years after Michael Tuchner's film, in which another East End villain (Bob Hoskins this time round) who has benefited, as Charles Kray put it, 'at the expense of those who could well afford to part with money', now finds the IRA moving on to his hallowed turf. But this was one change still in the future. *Villain*, in 1971, was a film that threw into relief the permanency of indigenous violence.

TABOO OR NOT TABOO

Other factors were already influencing the permissive attitudes fostered by Sixties cinema. What was or was not 'permissible' became more and

---

*Charles Kray, op. cit., p. 224.

more frequently a subject of hot, sometimes litigious debate as the
increasingly explicit scenes of sex and violence, mostly in films from
Hollywood, began to provoke a backlash against the 'liberating'
consequences of broken taboos. For a time, though, morality followed
trade.

It was in an effort to reduce the numbers of films falling into the 'X'
Certificate category — i.e., out of bounds to children under sixteen —
that the British Board of Film Censors, in November 1969, proposed a
'deal' to the distributors and exhibitors. In return for agreeing to raise
the 'X' rated age-limit to eighteen, an 'AA' Certificate would be made
available for what were borderline 'X' films. This would bar children
under fourteen, but allow the 14-to-18-year-olds to see movies that
would formerly have been restricted to the smaller audience of
older adolescents. What this manoeuvring really meant was that the
fifteen-year-olds, who formed the most reliable box-office group, would
now be admitted to the more explicit movies; while the moral quid pro
quo was to put the *most* explicit movies theoretically out of bounds. In
practice, of course, it did nothing of the sort: admittance to the films that
rated an 'X' was easily gained by determined children of the 16-to-18
stage of adolescence. Everyone was kept happy, including (one must
suppose) the parents, who preferred to remain in ignorance of what their
children saw. Where the moral line wavered, British hypocrisy could
still be relied on to hold it steady.

But there were also early signs of the way in which the media coverage
of controversial films had begun to affect the attitude of the law which,
up to then, had been tolerant or else preferred to turn a blind eye
towards what was on the screen. This changed almost overnight early in
1970. On 3 February no fewer than thirty-two policemen, led by a chief
inspector, suddenly descended on the Open Space Theatre where Andy
Warhol's *Flesh* was being shown to club members. They halted the
screening, seized the film (along with essential parts of the projector),
took the names and addresses of everyone present, confiscated the
membership list, the box-office records and even the programmes. If
proof were needed of how different the then film censor, John Trevelyan,
was from the stage censor, the Lord Chamberlain — whose office had
been abolished when his functions absorbed into the Obscene
Publications Act of 1959 — it was to be found in the fact that *Flesh*'s
distributor, an engagingly ebullient Anglo-Asian called Jimmy
Vaughan, immediately telephoned Trevelyan's office for help.
Trevelyan called the police action 'unjustified and preposterous'.

The media played up the affair for all it was worth. It soon became a
hot political issue. The raid was raised in the House of Commons on 4
February; a screening of *Flesh* was held at the House of Lords on 24
February — on which day in New York people able to produce British
passports were admitted free to the cinema showing *Flesh*, where the

movie was being described as 'Busted in London'. On 27 February Vaughan Films were told they would not be prosecuted: but the cinema was convicted of some minor infraction of club membership rules. Even that was not the end. On 11 March an embarrassed Home Secretary, then James Callaghan (who was to become Prime Minister six years later upon Harold Wilson's retirement) had to explain the police action — and, of course, was at a loss to explain it at all. 'There is a great deal of pornography about that is causing a great deal of concern to many people in this country,' he said, exposing the weakness of his position by the vagueness of his language. He added: 'It is the general desire of the average person in this country that it should stop.' This was purest Establishment waffle: the average person had expressed no such desire at all and, in any case, *Flesh* had not been deemed pornographic in any British court. In the end, Trevelyan prevailed upon Andy Warhol to pay the £200 fine levied on the theatre — and the newspapers, unconscious of both their inaccuracy and their irony, reported that Warhol had done so in the fight against film censorship.

Flesh went back on the bill at the Open Space, where it was joined by *Lonesome Cowboys*. This theatre, along with the Arts Laboratory, were London's two avant-garde venues in the early Seventies. ('Laboratory', 'space' and, very shortly, 'workshop' were the new decade's most over-worked words.) Neither was a hearth of exactly glowing rebellion. The Open Space featured an upstairs 'People Section' where the food and the members were brought into 'creative relationship', and a downstairs 'Viewing Area' where (when I visited it) in addition to Warhol's camp Western being projected in the half-light, a yellow Japanese moped was being dismantled in the adjacent 'Conversation Pit'. The stripping down of the machine ultimately absorbed more of the small audience's attention than the stripping off on the screen. *Flesh*, being a marginally more solemn work — after all, hadn't it been seized by the police? — was taken more seriously and even enjoyed: an art critic's analysis of it in one of the three 'quality' Sunday papers applied the physical criteria of Michelangelo's sculptures, in all solemnity, to the nudity of Joe D'Allesandro's phlegmatic stud.

Though the police raid endowed them with a notoriety they in no way merited, such films as these were still regarded as esoterica, safely corralled in out-of-the-way intellectual venues. More publicly available sensations arrived in London in March 1970, with Antonioni's *Zabriskie Point*. The British censor requested MGM to make ten cuts in it — mainly to sunder the threesomes of young lovers participating in a dusty love-in in Death Valley. Unexpectedly, MGM's British company appealed to the Greater London Council, which was the court of last resort for a distributor with a film that had been turned down by the censorship board.

Ironically, it was this elected body, whose power to issue licences to cinemas compelled the distributors to apply to the censor for certificates, which now began to surprise everyone by showing itself more liberal-minded than even Mr Trevelyan dared be — thought perhaps he, being the acute politician he was, had had a word in someone's ear. For the GLC's public services committee passed *Zabriskie Point* uncut with an 'X' Certificate permitting its screening in the London area. (The new eighteen-year-old rating was not due to come into force until July 1970: so this meant that sixteen-year-olds were admitted to *Zabriskie Point*: like the orgiastic young in the movie, it was this age group's last official fling.) However, public reaction to the film was sluggish; Press interest drooped; and it was eventually given a general 'X' Certificate in the belief that what lacked attractiveness could scarcely spread corruption.

But the incident had again focused attention on the films that were actually to be seen on the metropolitan screens; and this issue was seldom off the news or feature pages of the British Press in the months ahead. It was always a good circulation-builder. Self-interest dictated public interest: in much the same way, the cynical said, that the GLC's distaste for enforcing morality on those whose 'right to view' certain films was, so far as age was concerned, not unconnected with their 'right to vote' in municipal elections.

The feeling of a crisis a-building was sharpened when John Trevelyan returned from a convention of American theatre owners held in Washington DC in the early spring of 1970 and announced: 'The porn market in America has almost completely replaced the nude market.' As well as its weather, Britain was now taking its porn from across the Atlantic. Film-goers in London and, increasingly, in the provincial cities were being offered the delights that Americans could now see freely at their neighbourhood cinemas thanks to the courtroom battles that had been won by lawyers guilefully putting old Constitutional guarantees of free speech to uses undreamed of by the Founding Fathers. *Variety,* a trade paper that not long before had been wont to refer coyly to 'bosoms' and 'derrières', was now candidly rating movies for 'the stag market' or 'the dirty old man trade'. 'Plotwise,' wrote one *Variety* reviewer of such a film, 'the total box-score is two straightforward couplings, a fellatio or two, an Arab sheik's romp with two playmates, an incestuous masturbation, a rape immediately followed by a criminal abortion, and a lesbian coupling.'

The movie in question was rated 'an innovative advance in erotic film-making'. Mainline studios, envious of the profits being made in back-streets, were following suit: Russ ('King of the Skin Flicks') Meyer had actually been hired by Twentieth Century-Fox to film a sequel to *Valley of the Dolls*. As this turned out, it was an inspired parody of the genre: but that wasn't how it appeared at the time of the announcement to the concerned students of a radically altered market-place, where a 'sex flick' like *The Techniques of Love* could take $43,255 in one week at three mini-cinemas, or the equal of what one major Hollywood production had taken in four weeks at eighteen cinemas. The rest of the world was seen as additional gravy: hence the boom in London's cinema clubs (which could play uncertificated films) that occurred over the 1970–1 period.

The official censor was not the only one to feel embattled. The London Airports Customs officers, who had up to now found their 8mm. and 16mm. projectors sufficient to cope with the dubious 'home movies' which they confiscated from travellers, were having to install 35mm. equipment to handle the steep increase in 'big budget' porn. The Press compared the situation to the cynical flouting of the Gaming Act which, in its early days, had promoted the London casino boom. 'There are men', said Mr Trevelyan, 'ready to move in on the sexploitation scene — ready to have front men to take the rap, pay a fine, even go to jail — for the sake of the vast profits to be made from screen porn.'

The concern was fuelled anew in October 1970, by the denial of a Certificate to Joseph Strick's version of Henry Miller's *Tropic of Cancer*. An appeal was immediately made to the GLC: as a result, it gained a London-only Certificate, opened at four screens in the same cinema complex, and thus enjoyed 'freedom of expression' without offending too many people and upheld its maker's 'artistic freedom' without earning him too much money. This was what the English meant by a 'workable compromise'.

The censor who had said often enough that his job was to decide 'what the public will stand for' was discovering by the end of 1970 that the public would stand for anything that the law did not actually step in and deny them. Trevelyan at least drew the honest conclusion from this untenable state of affairs and, in December 1970, he announced his retirement after twelve years in the job. 'I am simply sickened by having to put in days filled from dawn to dusk with the sight and sound of human copulation,' he said.* Then, lest it be supposed that it was simply an excess of anything so 'natural' that had provoked his decision to quit his job, he added, '. . . plus a wide variety of other sexual activities, real or simulated'.

Trevelyan's retirement did not take place until well into 1971, when a successor had been found, and one of his decisions taken soon after he had make it plain that he had had enough demonstrated that, for all the negative aspects of his job, he still rated freedom of expression considerably higher than some of his predecessors. He gave a general 'X' Certificate to the Warhol film, *Flesh*, which had been the subject of contention not long before. It happened that this unexpected dispensation coincided with a major retrospective of Warhol's art at the

Evening Standard, 9 December 1970.

Tate Gallery: it was presumed that the 'coloured stills' extended a protective licence to the artist's moving pictures. It may possibly have been a coincidence that Trevelyan's retirement was not marked by the knighthood which it had been expected he would receive for the years he had put in guiding film-makers to a greater degree of responsible freedom more often than warning them off the public demesne as unwelcome trespassers. He had done the State some service: he had also caused it some embarrassment. He received a 'CBE' — and that was all. He was never asked to serve on any other Government-appointed body. In a way, that was perhaps a greater honour.

EXIT OZ, ENTER LONGFORD

The capacity of events to change the prevailing climate of opinion was tested even more publicly in the summer of 1971, in one case with a tragic outcome, in the other with a comic but none the less influential accompaniment. The first refers to the 'The Trials of Oz', as Tony Palmer dubbed them in his invaluable book,* one of the earliest (and still among the best) of the 'instant histories' which came to form a sub-genre of the publishing business from this time on. The *Oz* trial was the longest obscenity trial in British legal history, dragging on over six weeks from 23 June 1971, until the three accused, Richard Neville, Felix Dennis and Jim Anderson, were found not guilty of conspiring to corrupt public morals, but guilty of publishing an obscene article, sending it through the post and doing so for profit and gain. The article in question was the twenty-eighth issue of the radical-satirical magazine *Oz*, called 'The School Kids Issue' because the trio had aimed it at young people; and contributions from some twenty boys and girls, all under eighteen, had been printed in its pages. The young writers had vented their opinions on school, drugs and sex — one of them, a boy of fourteen, drawing a picture of a woman having intercourse with an animal. The generational passions roused by the trial and reported in inflammatory (often inaccurate) detail by sections of the Press could not have been more harshly exemplified than by the penalty inflicted on the trio of defendants after they had been found guilty, denied bail and sent to Wandsworth Prison before being returned to Judge Argyle for sentencing on 5 August 1971. When they re-appeared, it was seen they had suffered what the *New Law Journal* called 'a monstrous violation of the individual's personal integrity' by being given a close haircut of a type usually reserved (in earlier decades, too) for convicts suffering from lice.

Their jail sentences were ultimately suspended upon appeal. But, by

*Tony Palmer, *The Trials of Oz* (Blond & Briggs, 1971).

this time, what had been written and broadcast on radio and television about the affair had polarized public opinion. Not for the last time, the impression that, rightly or wrongly, children were at risk had contributed to a feeling that unconstrained freedom of expression such as the Sixties had encouraged was now something much more than a wavering battle-line between the Establishment and the artists: it was interpreted as a frontal attack upon hearth, home and family. It promoted a feeling that an already uneasy compromise had broken down and it gave fresh impetus to those who were emboldened by the verdict to seek more evidence of national degeneracy.

Later in 1971 the police were active again, this time seizing copies of *The Little Red Schoolbook*, a primer on revolution intended for circulation among sixth-formers. A sex-instruction film made for schools was also the subject of criticism, though its pathetic intentions seemed all the more necessary following a debate on pornography in the House of Lords in which one Peer told a touching tale of an uninstructed youth who had tried to penetrate his girl-friend through her navel. But another, the Bishop of Lichfield, said that he tried to keep himself 'unscathed' by avoiding all films with an 'X' Certificate. A third noble Lord referred to the cinema as the 'non-patrial in the woodpile' of the arts: 'non-patrial' had recently been coined as a euphemism (mostly employed with sarcastic emphasis) for a Commonwealth Briton: i.e., a 'nigger'. Old fears and taboos were certainly restive.

It has to be admitted that the cinemas had contributed to lighting a fire under the woodpile by aggressively flaunting the shabbier range of 'X' Certificate films, thus making it difficult for people who might seek to reassure Bishops by reminding them that the letter 'X' also covered a multitude of virtues. The indignation of the public moralists, who were increasingly conspicuous in the aftermath of the *Oz* Trial, was three parts against the lewd 'sell' for certain films on public exhibition, one part against the contents which (if viewed at all by the complainants) were generally tedious and had been prudently disinfected upon legal advice even before being screened.

The *Evening Standard* published an important survey of fifty cinemas in the Central London area between 22 and 29 April 1971, and tried to relate what film-goers were being offered to the changing social and sexual mores of society. Subjective though the conclusions had to be, they are worth quoting as a mark of how high the tide of Sixties permissiveness had risen.

Of the 60 films viewed by two dozen researchers, 31 had 'X' Certificates (banned to under eighteen), 12 had 'AA' (14–16 year-olds), 5 were 'A' (more suitable for older children) and a mere 12 were 'U' (general audiences). The cinema's meagre contribution to so-called family entertainment was soon to be made part of the broader attack on those who were out to destroy the basis of family life: hence the outcry against the sex-instruction film mentioned above, since its view of what was 'natural' did not fit easily into what was conventionally regarded as 'familial'.

Of the 'X' films, the following conclusions were advanced: nudity had become commonplace, full-frontal female nudity was almost so, full-frontal male nudity becoming so; homosexuality was implied in the theme or depicted in the act in just half the films; masturbation, in about a quarter. These proportions, though, must be qualified by the inclusion of no fewer than four sex-instructional films in the cinema bills, only one or two of which could have convincingly pleaded a case for instructing the public in anything other than expanding their range of possible perversions.

Again it is significant that the outcry against pornography was intensifying at a time when those who advertised that they wished to help people achieve sexual fulfilment were being matched by the multiplying numbers of deviant practices deemed to threaten 'normal' family life. 'Bad language' was reported to have become so familiar to cinema-goers that when Barbra Streisand in *The Owl and the Pussycat* — one of the films surveyed — actually said 'Fuck off!' in the most ladylike accents she could manage to a carload of harassing youths, it simply got 'a big laugh' from the audience. Physical violence occurred in more than half the films; violence with sexual or sadistic overtones in about a quarter: but again the quantitive approach has to be qualified by the validity of the violence in the context of the scene.

The survey's commentary, necessarily adopting a neutrality that ill became the author, in order to avoid any suspicion of a newspaper 'crusade' for or against the 'explicit cinema', concluded with these words: 'At its worst, the survey indicated a society where sex is mechanistic, violence is regarded as the norm and perversions are simply the things one hasn't done oneself, yet. At its best, it reveals a cinema more truthful as well as more candid about hitherto forbidden areas of life and more self-fulfilling in the way it lets its responsible artists portray them.'* Whichever way the cinema moved in future months depended on the way society itself moved — 'something, thankfully, that our survey did not set out to ascertain'.**

The Business Section of *The Observer*, in August 1971, devoted the top half of its front page to calculating the current value of the wages of sin in

Evening Standard, 29 April 1971.
**The films in the survey were: *Deep End; I'm an Elephant, Madame; Red Beard; Little Big Man; Tales of Beatrix Potter; Paint Your Wagon; Beyond the Valley of the Dolls; Myra Breckinridge; Investigation of a Citizen Above Suspicion; Anatomy of Love; Wild, Willing and Sexy; Dad's Army; Gallery Murders; Love Is a Four-Letter Word; The Great White Hope; Song of Norway; Guess What We Learned in School Today; There's a Girl in My Soup; Hands Off, Greta; Lawman; Sextrovert; The Railway Children; I Had My Brother's Wife; Alyse and Chloe; Husbands; Without a Stitch On; The Owl and the Pussycat; Scrooge; Ryan's Daughter; Butch Cassidy and the Sundance Kid; Get Carter; Flesh; Portraits of Women; Frankenstein on Campus; Language of Love; My Swedish Meatball; The Last Valley; The McKenzie Break; Sabata; Waterloo; Women in Love; Patton; The Music Lovers; Cromwell; Soldier Blue; Anne of the Thousand Days; Five Easy Pieces; The Wanderer; Love Story; Elvis, That's the Way It Is; The Aristocats; Performance; Zeppelin; Death in Venice; The Red Balloon; The Great Adventure; Seventeen; Hombre; Vixen.*

Britain, concluding that in a £10 million business 'the last thing the British pornographers want is a . . . relaxation of the lubricity laws', lest it result in a slump in trade. It is worth recording that at this time the West End of London contained some 30 porn shops; there were estimated to be another 20 in the suburbs; about 50–60 in the provinces; and 50–80 firms were running a profitable mail-order business in 'sexual aids'. Clearly, a market glut was in the making: no wonder such 'businessmen' wanted the laws retained, not relaxed. Any anti-porn crusader would be sure of a welcome.

Such a friend, some of the pornographers imagined, they had in Frank Pakenham, seventh Earl of Longford, though he certainly would not have seen it this way. The sixty-five-year-old Peer, a Roman Catholic convert, who had just been made one of the twenty-four Knights of the Garter, stepped into the middle of the censorship issue in 1971 to announce a private investigation into pornography, including illustrated magazines and live strip shows.

Lord Longford, inevitably nicknamed 'Lord Porn', may have cut an eccentric figure; but he had the redeeming and rare gift of being able to look totally unembarrassed by the public ridicule he received as well as the ability to let simplicities fall from his lips as if they were words of received wisdom. The vague brief that he drew up for his 52-member inquiry into pornography was widened to include the issue of violence only when he heard about some of the films then on view. By one of those creative accidents that sharpen issues without clarifying them, an 'X' Certificate trailer for the realistically violent Western *Soldier Blue,* depicting an Indian massacre in one of its scenes, found its way into the programme of a Saturday morning's film club for children. The father of some of the children who had been exposed to it, Peter Thompson, was sufficiently stirred to exercise his considerable skill as a consultant to a pressure group known as the Festival of Light which came into being around this time. It was dedicated to campaign with religious fervour against what were identified as Britain's declining moral standards.

By being thrown into high relief by the media, even when it was ridiculed, such a campaign contributed to a sense of all-enveloping moral concern. Lord Longford became a totem figure as he and his self-appointed committee members — they were often mistaken for an official Government commission — roved far and wide, at home and abroad. Eventually they turned in a report that surprised no one at all by its conclusions, even though these ran completely counter to the far more searching report of President Johnson's Commission on Obscenity and Pornography which had been published in America at the end of September 1970. It had generally concluded that pornography had no deleterious effect on society and actually recommended the repeal of dozens of anti-obscenity laws.

Since films alone among the arts in Britain were still subject to censorship, Lord Longford's report predictably settled like a swarm of indignant bees on them. It concluded that pornography created an addiction; recommended strengthening censorship; found the censorship board too closely linked with the film industry; believed that the Home Secretary, not the industry, ought to appoint its officials and these should include lay members. In short, it pretended that democracy would be the gainer if the board were reconstructed, though many doubted if this would do more than provide a more representative selection of sectional alarms, hatreds, prejudices, ignorance and vested interests far more amorphous than at present existed on the board.

The *Longford Report* also advocated bringing films into line with a new definition of obscenity — substituting the notion of 'outrage' for the legalistic notion of 'corrupt and deprave', even though it was commonly known to be part of human nature for someone, somewhere, to be outraged by something or other virtually every day in life. The transient state of 'outrage', if the Longford committee had its way, would be judged as serious a danger to the human condition as the permanent state of 'corruption and depravity'. An Obscene Publications Act rewritten on these lines could well result in easier convictions: but then having more stumps and a bigger ball could well result in more 'Outs!' at cricket matches.

The *Longford Report*, published in September 1972, had a great deal written about and around it: then it was pigeon-holed. It had served its turn: the media were on the scent of other sensations. But twelve years later, anyone who blew the dust off it and compared its tone and contents with that later exercise in repressive absurdity, the 1984 Video Recordings Act, would have been struck by the sinister similarities between the vague and all-embracing nature of the noble Lord's proposals for the betterment of his fellow-men and those which had been passed into law by the considerably more devious creation of a 'moral panic' over so-called 'video nasties'. Lord Longford may have simply started marching before the signal was given.

By 1971, though, the numbers of those beginning to fall in behind him were being sensed, if not yet counted. Such repressive events, and their media coverage, were a focus for what *Nova* magazine, itself a pace-maker in the permissive revolution of the Sixties, was soon to describe as representing 'the mass rejection of sex by those who doubt their ability to cope with it; the imposition of authority by those who have had to stifle every anarchic impulse years back; the sweeping of violence from the screen and television set by those who know the effect it can have on them personally . . . It is the authentic voice of the British backlash.'*

Nova, June 1972.

CHAPTER TWO

Putting the Clock Back

Everyone is going through changes,
No one knows what's going on,
Everybody changes places,
But the world still carries on.

Love must always turn to sorrow
And everyone must play the game.
It's here today and gone tomorrow
But the world goes on the same.

Alan Price, in O Lucky Man!

Early one evening in July 1971, four men met for supper in the Veneziana, a Soho restaurant, to discuss the hard-drugs scene. The scene, that is, as the cinema screen presented it. The actual scene on the streets in and around Soho had not at this time been very deeply investigated by the media; but the four were worried at the possibility that an American film, if shown, might be accused of encouraging the abuse of addictive drugs. They were meeting to decide what to do about it. One of them was Jimmy Vaughan, the distributor who had done spectacularly well out of *Flesh*, and had been pressing the British Board of Film Censors to certificate this other Andy Warhol film, *Trash*. If passed, it would be the first film dealing with heroin to be screened in a British cinema. The censorship board had so far refused to pass it. The board's president, Lord Harlech, was another of those around the table; the third and fourth members were the retiring film censor, John Trevelyan, and the man who had been appointed his successor in March 1971, and had assumed his functions that July, while retaining his predecessor in a consultative and advisory capacity for the first month. His name was Stephen Murphy.

Murphy was a forty-nine-year-old Scot from Glasgow who had given up his job as senior programme officer at the Independent Television (later Broadcasting) Authority to become the BBFC secretary — the man popularly referred to as 'the censor'. He was a florid-faced individual. He chain-smoked almost as addictively as his predecessor. His white hair stuck out in spikes and gave him an apostolic appearance which contrasted with the lean, leathery, saturnine features of Trevelyan. There was a more vital difference between the two: a difference that was to be a crucial factor in the awesome controversy into which the unhappy Murphy found himself precipitated almost as soon as he had moved into the pleasant, bow-windowed office overlooking leafy Soho Square. It had to do with publicity. Trevelyan manipulated the publicity that his job inevitably attracted with dexterity and frequent gratification. (Had he followed his brother, Lord Trevelyan, into the Foreign Service, there is every reason to believe he would have given his sibling a good run for the Moscow posting: it had analogies to his dealings with the film community.) Murphy, on the other hand, came from the back rooms at the publicity-shy ITA. He hated publicity and found it unpleasant stuff to have on his hands. Trevelyan lovingly moulded it: Murphy couldn't wait to shake it off.

Over supper that night, however, the censors found agreement easy. They reiterated their refusal of a certificate to *Trash*; then, in keeping with time-honoured 'compromise', they encouraged Jimmy Vaughan to apply to the GLC for a local *nihil obstat*.

To everyone's surprise, the GLC turned the film down flat. The chairman of the GLC's 22-man viewing sub-committee was Dr Mark Patterson, a haemotologist by profession and a parliamentary candidate by ambition — he unsuccessfully stood as Tory candidate for North Ealing in 1974. His influence was considerable and, as his sub-committee was the 'court of last resort', a distributor could not appeal against its decision elsewhere. Dr Patterson's blunt view of the film was that it was a 'drug addict's charter'. 'Anyone knowing nothing about main-line addiction could find out everything by seeing *Trash*,' he said, 'When we vetted it after the censor's rejection, we found it completely unacceptable.'

More important than this particular verdict, however, was the GLC policy which he indicated was going to be applied to films. 'We are probably going to be more independent of the censorship board in future.' This was interpreted as taking a harder — i.e., less liberal — attitude to controversial films. In other words, confidence was withdrawn from the board at the very moment a new censor had taken over. It was much in line with the way opinion in the country was felt to be moving during the first year of Edward Heath's Government.

It wasn't long before Murphy discovered to his cost one of the built-in contradictions of the British film industry in which the censor is supposed to protect the public from the excesses of the film-makers and the film-makers from the intolerance of the public. With the appearance of Ken Russell's *The Devils* (22 July 1971), the cordon sanitaire between the two was badly, indeed irretrievably, breached.

Russell's film claimed to be based on the seventeenth-century demonology trials at Loudon, events that had already served Aldous Huxley and John Whiting as the basis for a book and a play respectively: but as Russell portrayed the events, they seemed more inspired by memories of De Sade and the folklore of Dachau. Warner Bros., the producers, may have felt this, too, judging by the pretentious (and vain) attempt they made to put a self-protective wrapper around the film by distributing to critics, and other likely sources of trouble, a booklet filled with scholarly glosses on the religious heresies and State politics of the time. It looked less like a political-ecclesiastical crib than a worried distributor's alibi for a movie that was a garish glossary of sado-masochistic practices and used serious issues of conscience or conviction as opportunities to flaunt its director's striking flair for portraying pain and suffering. In fantasy, Vanessa Redgrave's perverse Mother Superior licks the stigmata of her lover who is represented as a crucified Christ-figure; impromptu medical examinations are performed on the altar table; nude nuns massage phallic candles with lubricious relish; hot-water enemas are applied in a brutal pantomime of purgation; and the vomit of those accused of being possessed by the devil was picked through in the hope of discovering a crumb of undigested demon. In short, the drama's analytical function was persistently subjugated to the anatomical embarrassments of the martyrs.

Passing such a film for public exhibition had not been Murphy's responsibility. Before he took over, Trevelyan had given it an 'X' Certificate after requesting minor deletions: a pectoral cross employed as a dildo had proved too unorthodox, an inquisitor's reference to 'other means' of persuasion was not now followed by specific details — for such relief, many felt, much thanks. But the terminal convulsions of Oliver Reed, who was burned at the stake, still far exceeded anything to which even the 'medical materialism' of Hollywood violence had accustomed British film-goers. After a few quiet reflections on celibacy versus marriage had been permitted Reed's renegade priest, he was subjected to a process of literal physical disintegration during which his head was shaved, his tongue stretched, his testicles were pierced, his lower limbs split with wedge-like logs of wood, and his body was flambéd over a quick flame — not so quick, though, that one might miss every boil and blister being raised on his blackening flesh.

On the very night of the première, Russell followed the example of his film's inquisitors in expelling the devils and, live on BBC TV (in the accidental but bemused presence of another interviewee, a former Minister of Defence), he drubbed a film critic over the head with a rolled-up copy of the newspaper in which the movie had been condemned that very afternoon. If viewers relished a critic being on the receiving end, their response instantly turned to displeasure, even protest, when Russell suited the word to the action — the word being the same four-letter one that Kenneth Tynan had been the first to use publicly on television in the Sixties. The calls that jammed the BBC switchboard proved that the expletive had lost none of its primal power to give offence.

It was one of those moments, insignificant in themselves and certainly provoking no enduring enmity between the hurt party (who happened to be this writer) and his assailant, which nevertheless reveal how the intolerance of the normally passive majority can be exploded by a spark. The private dispute between the film director, the critic and even the TV moderator (none other than the same Ludovic Kennedy who had campaigned against institutional violence in his recently filmed book *10 Rillington Place*), rumbled on for weeks in a diminuendo of accusations of collusion, threats of libel and eventual qualified apologies. The public indignation roused by the film seemed better orchestrated. Some of the 450 local authorities who generally accepted the censor's ratings were warned against the film in remarkably similarly worded letters from people posing as public moralists; a significant minority of the authorities 'called in' the film to view it themselves. In some towns it was banned. The GLC's viewing committee decided against a ban by a bare three votes.

Such scattered evidence of an increasingly intolerant attitude to the 'anything goes' position of recent years was a sign to law-makers as well as film-makers that the mood of the country was changing — and fast. And hardly had *The Devils* been exorcised from the West End cinemas than another major row broke over Murphy's head of white hair — this time a film he had passed for exhibition.

Sam Peckinpah's British-made melodrama *Straw Dogs* (20 November 1971) had been intended (Peckinpah said) to reflect the anarchy of society. Many felt it simply displayed the imbalance of its maker's own appetite for violence. Perhaps if it had been set in some isolated Western homestead in the 1880s, the terrorizing of two newly-weds (Dustin Hoffman and Susan George) might have fitted into the traditional expectations of the genre: but the contemporary setting in the West of England invaded by the sort of yobbos who materialize like folk devils to terrorize the local residents and appear on the next day's front pages and in courtroom docks, seemed like putting on indecent display all the nightmares that could affront the British bourgeoisie. Murphy's office had made one or two cuts in the double rape Susan George suffers: but the unintentional effect was to turn an act of 'orthodox' assault into what appeared to be an additional act of sodomy. The critical furore provoked a consensus of opinion that not a single point which one might have expected it to make about violence breeding counter-violence, or about the immorality of seeking to opt out of one's social responsibilities by retreating to a reclusive hideaway, was credibly presented in the welter of mayhem and salaciousness.

Pressed for a public statement, Murphy (who hadn't been two months in his job) rashly committed himself to the view that he though *Straw Dogs* 'a brilliant but brutal film that says something important'. Then, even more imprudently, he confessed that he himself had been surprised to find his examiners emerging from a screening of it at the board's headquarters brimming over with the same enthusiasm. It transpired that Murphy had earlier and unofficially viewed the film and told the makers that he could not possibly pass it uncut. Deletions had been made: though the unfortunate impression one of them created has been mentioned. Murphy had held his president, Lord Harlech, in reserve to support him in passing the film if his examiners opposed it. Faced with no opposition, he had given it an 'X'.

The reviews in the British papers were all the sharper because it appeared to critics that mainline violence was permissible in a big-budget picture like *Straw Dogs*, which had the muscle of a major distributor behind it, whereas a small-budget underground movie like *Trash*, the bread-and-butter of an independent distributor, continued to be banned. The savage notices of *Straw Dogs* were cynically exploited by the distributors, one of them being blown up to the dimensions of a cinema wall and put up on show outside the West End theatre.

The result was an unprecedented letter to *The Times* (17 December 1971) signed by thirteen leading critics. While carefully refraining from saying that any film should be banned, they deplored the escalation of sex and violence in films generally and criticized Murphy for the double standards which they alleged the board was operating and called for clarification. 'This could be the end,' said an obviously distressed film censor who was appearing on the day of the letter in a TV pilot programme about the arts being recorded in Granada's Manchester studios. Some comfort came when the audience, which had been picked to be representative, appeared less hostile to *Straw Dogs* than the film critic who was confronting Murphy in the programme — until it was discovered that a few of them had seen *Godspell* by mistake and were confusing the two films!

As Murphy was flown back that night to London in Granada's executive aircraft, the film censor launched into a deeply bitter attack on critics whom he deemed to be out of touch with the public — and also unburdened himself of yet another threat to his board's authority. This was an article he knew was going to appear in one of the following Sunday's tabloids, an interview with Adrienne Corri who was playing a rape victim in *A Clockwork Orange*, the film being made in Britain by Stanley Kubrick and due for release early in 1972. Murphy was right to feel apprehensive. Having missed the boat where the indiscriminate

violence of *Straw Dogs* was concerned, newspapers, pressure groups and
the legion of all-purpose commentators were now set to turn *A Clockwork
Orange* into a *cause célèbre* and make it the scapegoat for the wave of
violence they now saw everywhere in daily life, no less than on the
screen.

ORANGE ALERT

A large part of the outrage in Britain that greeted Stanley Kubrick's *A
Clockwork Orange* (13 January 1972) can only be explained by the fact
that sections of public opinion were 'waiting for it', ready and indeed
willing to be outraged, and express their outrage in terms that showed
how totally they had misread the film's essential theme. It was the rage
of Caliban seeing his own face in the mirror.

Kubrick's film is a bold, forceful, imaginative allegory of the power of
society to contain the non-conformist individual. Couched in terms of a
horror-comic, the film expands into an infinity of terrifying implications
for society in the mid-Seventies. After the multitude of films that
exploited the 'Permissive Society', it was the first landmark study of the
'Violent Society'. It is true that *A Clockwork Orange* is set in the near
future. But Kubrick insinuates contemporary apprehension into our
minds the way that his ur-punk hero (Malcolm McDowell) has
electrodes inserted into his frontal lobes to purge him of his original sin
by indelibly branding the consequences of his anti-social behaviour on
his understanding. The film is charged with the feeling of present fears
made manifest and of a future which has invaded our consciousness
before we are ready or able to absorb the shock of it.

For the first time in a Kubrick film, the native accents and urban
landscape are recognizably British, though they have a relevance to a
wider world that has lost its humanity and retains only a baroque
eroticism, a proletarian ghastliness and an institutionalized callousness.
Sexuality has been robbed of freedom; procreation has become simply
the 'old in-out, in-out'; politics are totalitarian poles apart; and there is
no middle ground for men of good will. Adults get by on tranquilizers:
society's vital energies are the property of violent teenagers.

The lord of these droogs is Alex, played by McDowell with the face of
a perverted Candide. In the opening close-up, he resembles a fallen
angel: but not when he rears up on his toes to bludgeon one of this gang
with a sword-stick and Kubrick's slow-motion photography delineates a
prehistoric savagery, a primal past that our smooth skins and so-called
reason have deceived us into believing had died with the Ape Men of
2001's barbaric overture.

It isn't a new generation which *A Clockwork Orange* shows: it is a new
genus. The 'tribes' of Punk Britain who were to make the cover of *Time*

Seventies hangover: The 'get-away people' of the Sixties found life in the new era something to live through and survive rather than dig into and enjoy. Peter Finch and Glenda Jackson, in *Sunday, Bloody Sunday*, 1971 (above), with Murray Head, their shared lover. He went to America: British film-makers soon followed suit.

Medical materialism, Pop classicism: Oliver Reed's terminal convulsions at the stake, in Ken Russell's *The Devils*, 1971 (below, left), was shocking even in the New Violence of Seventies cinema; Roger Daltry, in *Lisztomania*, 1975 (below, right), also underwent a test to destruction.

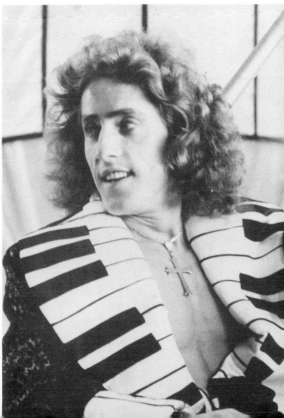

British villains, American glamour: Michael Caine, in *Get Carter*, 1971 (above), and Richard Burton, in *Villain*, 1971 (opposite), brought transatlantic brutalism to life, death and the pursuit of illegal profit in Britain. Bob Hoskins, with henchmen and hangers-on in *The Long Good Friday* (below), proved that by 1981 the natives had learnt the lesson.

Pop revisionism: By 1973 the post-Beatles generation had begun to look back, not in anger so much as cynicism as the dream fell apart. David Essex, in *That'll Be the Day* (above), prepared to walk out of family responsibilities and the rock 'n roll era into Pop-star success in a white suit in the sequel, *Stardust*, 1974 (below). Despite appearances, the result was exhaustion and burn-out.

magazine twelve years later, in 1984, just as their 'Swinging' ancestors had done in the same magazine in 1967, would have recognized the origin of their species in Kubrick's gangs whose language is a boastful stream of slang called Nadsat which connotes a sense of future time and conveys their zest for anarchy. It endows these young bloods with the verbal swagger of Mercutio and company during their nocturnal sprees to stir up the old 'ultra-violence'.

Public criticism of the film was correspondingly violent — unprecedently so. It was vented with particular fury on the sequences that threatened people's security in the home or family. Alex's murder of a prurient recluse in her own domestic museum of erotic objects, battering her to death with a grossly outsize phallus, came in for the sort of vituperative reaction usually reserved by the Press for public exhibitions of such 'way-out' art. The 'perversions' roused more anger than the fate of their collector. The critics, not in the main professional ones, seemed determined to read into such sequences all the outrage — and then some more — that rape and murder had provoked in *Straw Dogs*.

For in Kubrick's film violence is stylized rather than realistically presented: the gang rape is done to Rossini's *Thieving Magpie*; the mugging of a householder is turned into a surrealistic soft-shoe shuffle and Alex puts his not-so-soft boot in to the lilting rhythm of *Singin' an' Dancin' in the Rain*; and even the grotesque killing of the Cat Woman simply shows that those who live by the erotic symbol die by it, too. Music is a part of the masque of death: it leads the *Comus*-like rout. It also underscores the retribution doled out to a captive Alex who regains his liberty by volunteering for shock therapy, having his criminal will replaced by conditioned servility, exchanging his pagan revelry for Christian guilt and suppressing his capacity for choice by letting society install in him the clockwork mechanisms of the conditioned reflex.

The fatal kink in this conditioning incorporates a musical reference: Alex's alienation from the only piece of man-made culture he appreciated, Beethoven's Ninth Symphony, commonly known as the *Hymn to Man*. It was in line with the prophetic ironies of Kubrick's earlier films, *Dr Strangelove* and *2001: A Space Odyssey*, that this same piece of music was soon to become the official anthem of the European Community into which Edward Heath, at that very moment, was planning to lead Britain on 1 January 1973.

Coming at a time when 'Law and Order' was to the forefront of the Tory Government's policy, no official welcome could be expected for the scene in which the Minister of the Interior's exultant cry, 'It works', was presented as morality enough for clamping new restrictions on human liberty by suppressing freedom of choice itself. Political opportunism could scarcely have been conceptualized more hilariously than when the Minister (played by Anthony Sharp in the manner of that erstwhile apostate angel of permissiveness, Malcolm Muggeridge, who had emerged in the Seventies as its retributive Jehovah) literally spoon-feeds a convalescent Alex into making an unholy pact with the State machine — brute force in alliance with its sophisticated reflection.

As Home Secretary succeeded Home Secretary throughout the Seventies, whether of the Right or Left, each came more and more to resemble the haughty politician of the film until in William (later Viscount) Whitelaw, even the office-holder's manner of speech assumed the clipped, semi-coded vocabulary of Anthony Burgess's dialogue as it was flicked off Sharp's tongue. In short, the film made enemies all round it with its forecast of a Britain squeezed by reactionary forces until the bourgeois pips squeaked.

Malcolm McDowell had been made a generational ikon by his star role in Lindsay Anderson's *If . . .* in 1969; once again he gave a human face to a force that was now travelling under its own inhuman power to create terror and havoc. He was a juvenile Satan whose clearly articulated gloating over the evil he did was found by many to be the film's most upsetting feature. They could not cast it out of their thoughts. It was central to their own violent attempt to cast out the devil by casting up all kinds of dire warnings about the film's anti-social effects. McDowell's performance (the best he was to give in a career that shortly afterwards took him to Hollywood, with only subsequent 'guest' appearances in British films) was in the line of descent from Milton's Lucifer who swore that 'to do aught good never will be our task, But ever to do ill our sole delight'. He represented a generation that had grown up since 1969 and taken leave of their parents in the most extreme way possible — by denying the hope that humanity places in its posterity. The belief that our children will reproduce ourselves is one that has kept the human race going. *A Clockwork Orange* not only intimated that henceforth we would bring forth monster-children only, but that the progeny in turn would be worse than unforgiving. Whether or not they were able to articulate their feelings, many left *A Clockwork Orange* with fear in their hearts that their offspring would up and murder them, too.

It was no comfort at all to such people that a film which opened on the very same day in London as *A Clockwork Orange* said exactly the opposite. *Family Life* (13 January 1972) was a dramatic illustration by director Ken Loach and producer Tony Garnett of the fashionable and vastly influential theories of R. D. Laing which held that families were 'the slaughterhouses of our children'.

Family Life asked for (and received) compassion for its afflicted heroine — a tribute to Sandy Ratcliff, playing a girl whose mental depression reduced her mostly to the state of a mute object. But many interpreted the movie as yet another attempt to undermine the family unit which, the authors alleged, had driven the girl mad in the first place.

David Mercer's screen-play faithfully followed Laing's case studies as reported in *The Divided Self* and *Self and Others*, but fleshed them out with a view of how suburban conformity, repressed sexuality, middle-class genteelness and the deadening environment of sterile prejudices as catching as a flu bug, have reduced the daughter of two uncomprehending parents to a state where she could be said to have had no mind of her own. Her efforts to reassert her 'self' are mistaken for wilfulness, then condemned as wickedness; and she enters a mental hospital for treatment.

The film at this point becomes unashamedly schematic, portraying the Laingian analyst as the humane and permissive head of a loose 'household' of patients, but presenting his opposite number as the collective institution which sees the girl as an object whose nuts and bolts need to be tightened by electro-shock treatment. Viewed retrospectively, the dialectic has a glaring weakness: but then, in the mid-1980s, there is much less sympathy for the devil than could still be mustered in the early 1970s, which had not quite surrendered its Sixties nostalgia for people 'doing their own thing'. To view madness as a form of sanity now appears as extreme as to view the family as the parade ground of debilitating constraints. But like the efficient polemicists they were (and are), Loach and Garnett allowed no one any choice but to see things as they persuasively suggested they could be happening to people whose behaviour looked realistically observed, whereas in fact it was the product of many hours of improvisation and editorial selection.

If its moral seems in doubt today and the Laingian treatment as extreme as some of the methods it condemned, that was not how it appeared in 1972. Then it looked like a warning that parents' neuroses could be passed on to their children just as casually as the plates of traditional bread-and-butter are passed around the tea-table. Opposition to it was uncomfortably reminiscent of, but more ineffectual than, the undertow at the *Oz* trial, where it was alleged that children had been recruited by the magazine to help demolish the basis of the very family life which gave them birth. It was yet one more incitement to 'respectable society' to turn on those who assailed its sanctity and adopt a far more aggressive posture to protect what they saw as the morality of existence. The Holy Communion for the cast of the hedonistic musical *Hair*, which had been celebrated on the show's third birthday in 1971 by the Dean of St Paul's, now seemed to have been superseded by the need for a service of exorcism to cleanse the land and mind of all the evil spirits that had taken up squatters' rights. Public alarm was coupled with a call for a new sobriety.

A Clockwork Orange became the focus for this newly aroused 'moral opposition'. It was denounced over the next year or so, in features and editorials, on radio and television, even in the courtrooms, where at least one defendant found guilty of the manslaughter of a tramp pleaded that witnessing an attack on a hobo by Alex's droogs in the film had predisposed him to behave in the same way. Respectability had been lent the backlash even before the film opened.

Caught off-guard in a newspaper interview, the then Home Secretary, Reginald Maudling, declared his intention of vetting the film for himself before the première. It may have been meant as simply a public relations exercise — to demonstrate Maudling's concern with violence in the community. Instead, he was seen as leading the attack on the 'violent cinema'. Chase its devils off the screen, went the belief, and peace will be restored in our streets, safety to our doorsteps, rectitude to our children. Wardour Street people, a craven lot at the best of times, were consternated. The Home Secretary actually making an inspection of their wares! And before they had even put them on sale to the public! 'Does Mr Maudling wish to lend support to this pernicious brand of post-censorship activity by those people who are least well-equipped for the job?' asked the *Evening Standard*'s editorial on 14 January 1972, and left no doubt that, if so, he was going about it the right way. To Warner Bros. and Kubrick, it was a serious matter to have to face the prospect of their film being banned, or, at the very least, prejudiced by the Minister principally responsible for law and order who would see his fictitious counterpart in the film acidly and justly lampooned for just such opportunistic politics.

It would have been an appropriate rebuke to Maudling — a man whose own probity in financial dealings came under police inspection before he retired from politics — if he had been told to buy a ticket and view the film along with the rest of the public. However, he was given a private screening: any opinion he expressed has gone unrecorded. But the damage had been done.

Local authorities up and down Britain now began clamping down on *The Devils*, *Straw Dogs*, *A Clockwork Orange*, and any other movies with a high quota of violence, delaying their provincial openings, requiring local cuts, sometimes imposing outright bans. Alas, it was not every town councillor who was prepared to dress down the petitioners from his local church as roundly as a member of Chatham (Kent) local authority. When *A Clockwork Orange* was called 'offensive to Christians' he replied robustly: 'I think we must accept that Christians are now in the minority in this country.' Even the GLC, formerly a 'court of appeal' against restrictive censorship, now came out and declared that 'a marginally harder line' should be taken. How wide the margin? How tough the line? Consensus censorship was visibly in ruins.

The film was even linked to the darkening political mood of the country as a coal strike precipitated energy-saving power cuts and an IRA bomb exploded at Aldershot barracks betokening the fact that violence, the long-term curse of Ulster politics, had now an unpleasantly long reach into English communities. Dr Mark Patterson, of the GLC viewing committee, said of *A Clockwork Orange*: 'Personally, I thought it a

superb piece of cinema which had an important message.* This was a
surprise, coming from someone who had recently spoken so censoriously
of *Trash*. Then he added: 'But in the context of the violent times we live
in, it was unsettling.' He disclaimed any desire for 'political censorship',
but left his interviewer with the impression that films which reflected
anarchy — even if they didn't incite it — and provided no 'answers'
would get a rougher ride from his local authority and others, too, maybe.

A scapegoat was needed to propitiate the wrathful gods; and it wasn't
hard to tell across whose neck the sacrificial knife might be drawn.
Throughout March 1972, the British film-trade paper, *Cinema TV Today*
(which became *Screen International* on 6 September 1975) reported
demands from exhibitors and others for Stephen Murphy's resignation.
'We've got the wrong man for the job,' was the common assertion. Even
The Times asked 'Is Censorship Breaking Down?' and answered: 'The
only realistic alternatives . . . are a new statutory system of censorship
. . . or the development of a closer understanding between the board and
local authorities.'

Lord Harlech, who had been out of the country during this period as a
member of the commission trying to patch up the even more intractable
problems arising from Rhodesia's unilateral declaration of
independence, returned to London and, on 15 March 1972, issued a
statement affirming his 'complete confidence' in the censorship board's
secretary. He then went in to a meeting with the principal film trade
bodies, the apparent upshot of which was that he himself would deal
with local authorities if they queried censorship certificates, while his
board's secretary would preserve a discreet silence.

Stephen Murphy, who had once been driven to seek sanctuary in the
Roman Catholic church in Soho Square by Pressmen 'doorstepping' his
office, lived to breathe again. But for how long? *The Guardian*'s editorial
on 22 July 1972 declared: 'Film censorship, as now practised, is not
going to survive much longer.' In a sense this was an accurate enough
prediction, though Murphy's troubled term had a bit longer to run than
some of his critics were prepared to credit at the end of this first year
when violence came of age in Britian — and when British society seemed
to be keeping up with the worst that the screen could show.

To chart the turn of the tide, except where individual British films
contributed to it, is beyond the scope of this study. The economic crisis
of 1974 played a great part in changing the moral outlook. Stephen
Murphy, however, played little part in the latter. At the start of 1975, he
resigned: he had lasted four years in the job compared with his
predecessor's thirteen. He returned — thankfully, one imagines — to the
back rooms at the Independent Broadcasting Authority where his
decisions were far less likely to have to undergo public scrutiny and

Evening Standard, 29 February 1972.

criticism. James Ferman was appointed his successor in June. 'I've never heard of him,' Lord Longford was quoted as saying. 'But I hope that he's a Christian . . . or even a Jew, or Muhammadan. But whatever, a man of strong moral opinions.'* Actually, he was a television producer who had been born in New York and had worked for ITV and BBC TV. When Lord Longford was acquainted with this and told that one of Ferman's TV productions, about an elderly sex offender, had won even Mrs Whitehouse's praise, he commented: 'He sounds very promising.' Ferman has lived up to this blessing; it is to be hoped that his office will one day receive the detailed attention it deserves.

LUCKY STRIKE!

From the end of March 1972 until midway through July, Lindsay Anderson was engaged in making *O Lucky Man!* It was produced by Albert Finney's Memorial Films for Warner Bros., the American major's first British film for several years. It was premiered in London on 2 May 1973, then screened two weeks later as the British entry at the Cannes Film Festival. At the main evening showing in the Palais des Festivals, a posturing starlet, delaying the film-goers filing in to take their seats by her antics, suddenly felt herself chastised by an indignant Anderson who slapped her bottom and cried, 'Get inside and see the film. This is a degenerate festival. I remember it when it was a fine one. Now it's cheap and disgusting.'

As a means of giving starlets a 'sense of enlightenment', it is doubtful if this technique was as effective as in the film itself, when Lindsay Anderson, in person, smacks Malcolm McDowell over the head with a rolled-up film script. The 'meaning' of this transcendental moment has been many times discussed. It's an important one, to be sure. For in a film that dealt with Britain's 'state of change' as Anderson saw it, it came to signify Anderson's own 'altered state' ever since he had seemed to stamp the international student revolt of 1968 with his own jubilant seal of approval in the film *If. . . .* That film had ended with McDowell straddling the old school ramparts with a female guerrilla and mowing down the headmaster and representative Establishment figures with a sub-machine gun. What did the vastly less bloodthirsty gesture at the end of *O Lucky Man!* portend?

The director never gave his imprimatur of approval to any of the interpretations his critics ventured to make. What follows is based on a serial version of the story prepared for a newspaper, but this in turn was based on Anderson's tentative glosses in half-a-dozen different interviews. It has not been disavowed by him.

*Lord Longford, quoted in *The Guardian*, 18 June 1975.

Mick Travis, as the McDowell character is again named, has his head smacked, and then . . . 'For a second there was a blackout. And in that second a state of waking alertness seized me. Like having your head cleaved spiritually. And I saw that the world I had travelled through was incomprehensible, that I wouldn't ever understand it, that I wouldn't ever unravel its secrets, that the things people did in it or had done to them would never be more important than the fact of the world. I knew in that monumental jolt to my consciousness that it was wrong to think of changing the forces of the world. One must use them to re-direct oneself, to bend to their bidding. The path of knowledge is a forced march through the world and I had had beginner's luck.'

Writing in the Summer 1973 issue of *Sight and Sound*, a periodical usually unsympathetic to Anderson's work, David Wilson connected this moment of perception with what he termed a 'conflict of opposites' in Anderson's oeuvre. 'In critical terms, the need for commitment on the one hand, and on the other what, writing in *Sequence*, (Anderson) described as "the willingness to jettison our own prejudices and viewpoints and accept those of the artist".' *O Lucky Man!* certainly seems to signify a resolution of such irreconcilables, even though the director made it plain at the time — and reiterated it in other interviews — that acceptance is not the same as surrender. An inability to change the world doesn't cue a withdrawal from the obligation to criticize its follies. *O Lucky Man!* exemplifies Anderson's undiminished zeal and his satirical amplitude, somewhat more generous in spirit as well as target area than Wilson's description of it as 'comprehensive spite'.

The brief that David Sherwin was given for writing the scenario — as he described it in the published text* — started off as the episodic 'Adventures of a Coffee Salesman', based on Malcolm McDowell's own trainee experiences in that line of business. It was then expanded in Sherwin's mind (and on his typewriter) by Anderson's sympathetic re-direction of it into the epic mould. *Heaven's My Destination*, *Amerika* and *A Pilgrim's Progress* were mentioned in script discussions, raising the sights rather than inseminating the subject. Anderson at one point said: 'Our character . . . perhaps he should just want to be successful. I mean to . . . give it an epic quality, a view of society, it ought to be quite separate things he tries, thinking that each time this is going to be marvellous, this is the answer, then when it collapses he tries something new — so each time we see a completely different section of life.'

Combined with McDowell's 'aside' in chatting with Sherwin that 'I always believed I would be lucky,' this became both the film's energizing force and its almost random sense of construction. I Ching, the Chinese technique of allowing destiny to select one's moves in life, was applied at several points in the production. Anderson, for example, used to 'create'

O Lucky Man!, by Lindsay Anderson and David Sherwin (Plexus, 1973).

the various radio newscasts he needed for the film simply by taping whatever the BBC put out over 'the haunted air'. In this way, a talk on Zen Buddhism was provided 'by the magic intervention of choice' only a few days before he was due to dub the particular reel. The talk is heard being delivered on the sound-track just before Mick is arrested outside a secret Government establishment and taken off to be interrogated, not about the state of his soul but about the State's atomic plans. 'Every day', it goes, 'should be looked upon as living in the moment rather than in the past or the future — and this is what Zen is really all about — living now.'

It's the parallel sense of 'living now', in Britain's present, 1982–3, that *O Lucky Man!* is all about. It is a contemporary Morality play constructed out of Dr Johnson's 'grand overview' of life as well as Ben Jonson's narrower humours of individual character. The form allows for parody, pastiche and even pert references to other films: not only Anderson's own films (Rachel Roberts re-appears as the self-punishing houseproud widow of *This Sporting Life*) but also Kubrick's *A Clockwork Orange* on which McDowell had worked immediately before being 'inherited' by Anderson. (The sequence where a tramp falls into his own bonfire and one where the derelicts vociferously resist Mick's appeal to the 'brotherhood of man' were mischievous glosses on Kubrick, somewhat dourly received by that director.)

But it is the comedy of private corruption in public life which really animates the 'Royal Court stock company' who are cast as ruthless tycoons, hypocritical town-hall worthies, venal policemen, perverted judges, fascist mercenaries, two-faced PR people, tyrant rulers from Black Africa, sin-obsessed do-gooders and of course the intolerant down-and-outs. In such a world, Anderson asks, is it really unthinkable for a loony man of science to be experimenting on people in the hope of turning them into more adaptable pigs? Since pigs have a better survival value than humans, is it really blameworthy?

O Lucky Man! takes a far more bilious view of life than was visible on the horizon when Mick and his gun-toting girl-friend enacted their symbolic slaughter at the end of *If. . . .* To a certain extent, it is a revisionist film: the ending of the earlier film no longer feels like a call to arms. Its terminal violence appears to have been simply a grand but futile anarchic gesture. The 'writing on the wall', as Anderson once called *If...*, now figures literally in the second film as disenchanted graffiti proclaiming: 'Revolution Is the Opium of the Intellectuals.'

But if Mick Travis is no longer a rebel, he is still 'his own man'. His fiery independence has been gentled into a hardy innocence by experience of the world and it is this that protects him in a Vanity Fair society bent on seducing, exploiting, punishing and even experimenting on him. Ultimately, he is left undefeated, but far more aware of how completely he is a part of all that he has known. 'I think what the film shows is the way that Zen has supplanted Marcuse,' says Anderson. 'When I read a Zen work today, it honestly seems to me the only way of looking at the world. One just has to accept things — that certainly doesn't mean one has to throw in one's lot and conform. I think the difference between the Sixties and now is that picking up a protest manner at every pretext can now be seen as only a sentimental gesture. The attitude of the film, though, still allows one to carry a banner *when* one thinks it proper and timely.'*

Alan Price's music and lyrics, cut directly into the story as he and his group comment on the action, or prepare us for the next rise and dip in Mick's progress, emphasize the lyrical heartbeat that still pumps the blood through Anderson's chastisement.

Extraordinary confirmation of his vision of public life reduced to a capering fresco of boobies was offered the very month that *O Lucky Man!* opened in Britain. For, in May 1973, one of Edward Heath's ministers, Lord Lambton, who was Under-Secretary of State at the Ministry of Defence, resigned office after his name had been linked with a Maida Vale prostitute. Lord Jellicoe, the Tory Leader of the Lords, resigned too, in circumstances which were erroneously linked in the media with Lord Lambton's peccadillo. (A perfect vignette from *O Lucky Man!* — one wondered if I Ching had anything to do with it!) Exactly a decade earlier, the Profumo scandal had coincided with Joseph Losey's survey of the rotten fabric of English society in *The Servant*: no wonder, as Norman Shrapnel succinctly remarked in his book on *The Seventies*, 'Time marches back'.** The scandal elicited some interesting Press reactions to the current state of the country's morality, official and unofficial. 'It is not the conduct itself,' said *The Guardian* cynically, in a line that would have fitted easily into the mouth of one of the VIPs in *O Lucky Man!* 'but the fact that it is publicly known that apparently unfits (public men) for their work.'***

But it was J. W. M. Thompson, Editor of *The Sunday Telegraph*, who took to his own editorial pages and deciphered the moral omens of the affair in a most discerning way — one that shed retrospective illumination on how the influence of the Sixties was waning. 'The new morality of sexual free-for-all has been assiduously propounded and it has had its effects in innumerable directions. These are to be seen as part of the fabric of every-day life, transforming the general idea of what is fit for public consumption by way of entertainment or information. . . .' Then he suggested, shrewdly in view of the gathering backlash, that 'the full gale of permissiveness still belongs only in the realm of the media, or among that minority of the population who constitute the fashionable consensus. The tolerance (of the majority) does not imply anything

---

*Lindsay Anderson, interviewed by the author at Cannes, 21 May 1973.
**Norman Shrapnel, *The Seventies* (Constable, 1980).
*** *The Guardian*, 25 May 1973.

approaching unqualified approval when the new morality is translated from words (or pictures) into action.'* In other words, in Thompson's opinion, the media were largely responsible for creating a sense of excitement and manufacturing the permissiveness that was becoming less and less representative of the country's real opinion whenever it was put to the test.

Poor Lord Lambton had done nothing as dishonourable as lying to Parliament (as John Profumo had done). But he had shown himself unpardonably out of touch with real life (if not cinema satire) — and had had to pay the penalty. It is time to beware when the media suspect that the public has dropped behind them in the race towards the next sensation, or is even moving in the opposite direction. Then editors and others who influence the content and presentation of trends, attitudes and events begin to search for the 'line' they feel their constituents to be treading. The same entrepreneurial skills that once sold permissiveness now began to turn censoriousness to commercial advantage. By 1973 there was plenty of evidence of this change in the making, though it was hardly to go by the name of 'enlightenment'.

THE LONGEST-RUNNING FANTASY

Even James Bond was not invulnerable to change in the Seventies, though admittedly his licence to kill had been passed on to a new Bond in 1968 after Sean Connery firmly indicated his desire not to renew it. He was tired of being increasingly subordinated to production hyperbole, proxy stunt men and scene-stealing gimmickry. There was an additional irritation. Connery was already a very rich man: but he was aware of how much richer the Bond cycle had made others. His bosses, naturally, were modest men discreet about the division of the spoils: but Connery's laconic nature was not deceived. 'They're not exactly enamoured of each other,' he was reported as saying of Harry Saltzman and Cubby Broccoli in 1973. 'Probably because they're both sitting on 50 million dollars and looking across the desk at each other and thinking, "that bugger's got half of what should be mine".' He soon realized that his own estimate probably erred on the low side. When he heard that CBS had offered his producers $20m. for television screenings of the first five Bond films he had made since *Dr No* in 1962, *and been turned down*, Connery gained an 'enlightening' insight into how much the continuous world-wide re-issue of the films must be worth.

This is not to imply he had been badly done by. Quite the reverse, perhaps. It is usually impossible for anyone not privy to a star's accountants to know the extent of his good fortune; but thanks to a

The Sunday Telegraph, 27 May 1973.

recent development in the off-screen saga of James Bond, an accurate picture has emerged of the rewards and power that accrued to Connery as his popularity in the role reached global proportions.

On 20 June 1984 Connery filed a $225m. law suit in the US District Court against MGM/UA Entertainment Co. (distributors of the Bond films) and Cubby Broccoli (by this date the series' sole producer). Connery claimed he hadn't been paid all the money due him on the five Bonds he had completed after *Dr No*. In support of his claim, he was compelled to reveal the details of how his business deals had been structured and these give an unprecedentedly candid view of the relationship between the biggest British star of the Sixties and the phenomenon that helped make him so. They also show the fiscal pressures that the British Treasury put on a super-star like Connery, forcing him to take avoiding action worthy of some of the ingenious escape devices he had manipulated in the movies. Every time he made a film, he set up a 'loan out' company ostensibly to supply his services to the production. On some occasions he used two companies, one covering his services in the USA and Canada, the other for the United Kingdom. How much he was paid for *Dr No* is not specified: but it did well enough for Connery to be guaranteed one per cent of all gross monies in excess of $4m. received by United Artists in the USA.

In 1964 Danjaq (the Swiss-based holding company for Broccoli-Saltzman's Eon Productions, named after their respective wives, Daniella and Jacqueline) undertook to pay Connery five per cent of the profits from all the ensuing Bond films he starred in, after deducting the production cost and distribution fees — the standard net-profit deal that may or may not enrich the participant, since his share depends on what's left after others over whom he has no control have added up the production-distribution bill.

But things apparently went very well for Connery. Immense popularity may have had the effect on his financial muscles that spinach had on Popeye's biceps; for during the making of *You Only Live Twice*, in 1966, he was rewarded with five per cent of Eon Productions' net profits *and* five per cent of all profits the film made in the rest of the world outside the UK and the USA. Even this was probably dwarfed by an arrangement that gave him 25 per cent of all profits received by Danjaq from the merchandising of the Bond character and his 007 logo. Broccoli, Saltzman and United Artists have always — and rightly — been jealous of the merchandising potential of their films: even designer Ken Adam has been denied permission to reproduce his production sketches, while books about the Bond films, with certain copyright exceptions, have been forced to use location shots in place of stills from the films in order to illustrate their hero's predicaments: presumbly there is an *Official James Bond Handbook* in the merchandising works somewhere.

By the time he made *Diamonds Are Forever*, in 1971, Connery was getting ten per cent of the gross from the first dollar the film earned. But with a separate agreement applying to the United Kingdom, he got an additional 2.5 per cent of the gross receipts from *Diamonds Are Forever*! In the (highly unlikely) event of any one Bond film making a loss, the producers agreed not to deduct it from the profits of another. It was an enviable example of how a super-star, once he's been taken into bed with the producers, gets away with a larger and larger share of the bedclothes. The fact that the company charged with collecting Connery's money — Inforex by name and incorporated in the Dutch Antilles for the slenderest of scenic reasons — was actually suing for a dollar fortune which it alleged the actor was still owed, is proof enough of the fabulous lode that the Bond films struck from those hesitant and hard-won beginnings recounted earlier in *Hollywood, England*.

Freed from Bondage after *You Only Live Twice*, in 1967, Connery became one of the six directors of Dunbar & Co., a private bank in Pall Mall, which appealed to the self-protectiveness that years of aggressive exposure as James Bond had ingrained in him. His Celtic nature, which had helped make Bond reasonably classless (or at least without the emphatic Anglo-Saxon vowels that might have grated on the sensibilities of other parts of the world), now asserted itself and, as if to emphasize his liberty, he espoused the cause of Scottish nationalism — though an absence of 'suitable scripts' warily deterred him from playing a role in the upper-case Nationalism of Scottish politics. Connery's native temperament had never quite made him feel at ease in the life-style that Bond was supposed to revel in; and it became a matter of conscience, as well as cash, when the producers begged him to return to the role two years later. This is no bad strain to be under — particularly if the outcome leaves the conscience clear and makes the cash grow.

What renewed the need for the old Bond was the comparative disappointment of the new one, George Lazenby, who inherited the licence but, alas, not the *élan* in *On Her Majesty's Secret Service* (18 December 1969). Lazenby was unlucky. He had the looks, but was not allowed the time to acquire the pedigree. It was more than a little unfair, when one recalls that Ian Fleming's Bond had begun his literary life as hardly more than a bundle of snobbish brand-labels; Lazenby's pre-Bond experience had been mainly acquired in television commercials for some of the same goods. But Bond had outgrown his status symbols; and now there was only one name associated with him — Sean Connery's. Another actor who had 'paid his dues' in the same sort of adventure genre as the Bonds might — just *might* — have graduated to the prime role: but the public perhaps resented being asked to accept someone who had neither earned his right to be a contender, nor possessed enough distinctiveness of his own to dim the memory of his predecessor.

Lazenby never won that precious favour, *time*, to ease himself more comfortably into the tailored shoulder-holster or turn his tongue more casually round lines like, 'Ah, Royal Beluga caviar from the *North Caspian*.' Carrying 'Big Fry', a brand of cheap chocolate, in an outsize pack on one's shoulder in his best-known commercial offered him a poor chance for acquiring such discriminating tastes. However, he could have passed for what Richard Maibaum's witty script called 'the other fellow' on the shady side of the casino — and when it came to doing battle there was nothing to show which Bond had the better stand-in. Sartorially, Lazenby could fight his way into a dress shirt as effectively as Connery.

One load he didn't have to carry in *O.H.M.S.S.* was the one Connery laboured under, namely electronic gadgetry: this time Bond depended on what God had given him, not IBM. The producers had also discovered a reassuringly sentimental streak in him: when Bond's new wife (Diana Rigg) got shot dead before the confetti had blown off her going-away outfit, the chap actually grew moist-eyed! Above all, the direction of Peter Hunt — an editor on earlier Bond films — brought a cutting-room crispness to every set-up, though even he was not able to truncate a film that feels as if it is ending four times before it actually does so. John Glen, not only this film's editor, but its second-unit director (and later a Bond director in his own right), gave *O.H.M.S.S.* a completely different feeling from any earlier Bonds. Using the discontinuity of a cartoon strip (what would soon be called a 'video clip'), he made fist-fights look like the splitting of the atom, had blows boomeranging in from off-screen and bodies flying apart as if released from a spring-clip. All of which was vivid enough, but won Lazenby no public affection at all. He retired from the series and was only to be seen in spasmodic action films which impressed whatever virtues they had on the public by reminding them that George Lazenby WAS James Bond — once.

It was David Picker, president of United Artists, who enticed Connery back into the films. After three days' haggling with lawyers and accountants, he laid the world (or what it was *then* worth) at his feet: a $1.2m. cash fee, ten per cent of the gross, overage arrangements that would have earned him $150,000 a week if shooting exceeded the schedule and — most important to Connery's peace of mind — the right to pick two additional non-Bond projects which United Artists agreed to finance up to a million dollars each. It was a shrewd deal: it paid fair tribute to Connery's value, it underwrote his talents over and above the ones that Bond employed; and since he invested his fee in a Scottish education trust, it satisfied his Celtic itch to make his money work as well as to put himself to work.

Diamonds Are Forever (26 December 1971) revealed a Connery who was now packing flab as well as a Walther PPK. His style resembled an elder statesman of espionage with an implanted pace-maker. But his independent attitude to the role which these traits betokened showed up to advantage. The public loved him all the more now that he had a veteran's licence not to take things too seriously yet still give a stylish reading to a line like that when his love-making is interrupted: 'You've caught me with more than my hands up.' After completing the film and collecting his (pro tem) winnings, Sean Connery, aged forty-one, terminated (with extreme relief rather than displeasure) his connection with the role that had made him a hyper-star. 'Never again', he swore. The vow would return, like a golden boomerang, in the film that called itself, with a helpless shrug, *Never Say Never Again*. But that was twelve years away.

Meanwhile, Broccoli and Saltzman had to find a new Bond, urgently. Ten years earlier they had made a short-list of possible contenders. As well as Patrick McGoohan and Richard Johnson, it featured Roger Moore. Moore was then a leading man in television series like *The Saint* which, while not denying him the right to swing a useful fist now and then, more often than not required him to lead with his smile and make a romantic pitch to the female viewers. Moore was actually two years older than Connery. But by this time — he was appearing in *The Persuaders* that summer of 1971 — he had acquired experience in internationally distributed television series without acquiring the handicap of any single high-definition role which might have caused viewers to identify him with *it* rather than with the one he was now offered — and accepted. The reported fee of $1 million was to rise steeply and quickly if the box-office indicated that the public accepted him as Connery's legitimate heir.

The contrast between the two stars was piquant — it was the substitution of the head prefect for the school bully. Moore looked such an essentially *nice* lad; Connery had brought with him a hint of macho relish. The retiring Bond had learnt to wear his wardrobe as if he had grown into it; the new man at first carried *his* with the slight self-consciousness of someone in uniform. Connery was a hairy man, though the growth was mainly on his chest; Moore was a smooth man, and his growth appeared at first glance to be mainly on his scalp. Both men, in their different ways, were virile specimens — and patriots. Roger would have gone all out to win the race for the school; so would Sean, but probably by nobbling his competitor in the locker room.

The replacement of Sean by Roger came at a propitious moment in the series. For the producers had been feeling that a new man should have a new attitude to women — not *too* new a one, however, not so radically new as to accord them sexual equality with him. The Women's Lib movement was well under way in the United States, though not yet so influential as to cause the happy (male) fantasists who were Bond's fans any guilty *frisson* about their sexist satisfactions.

But the new James Bond in *Live and Let Die* (5 July 1973) seemed at times to believe in the possibility of true romance (or *True Romance*, to judge by bedroom dialogue that could have come off that magazine's pages), which reminded one that the old Bond, not to put too fine a point on Fleming's mechanistic prose, often didn't look further than a good bang. 'I think we can lick you into shape,' Moore says to one of the Bond girls: a line like that couldn't have been risked on Connery's Bond. In short, Moore lightened the sexist element by adding his own alloy of jokey comedy. Female film-goers, as has been noted, sensed that Connery's Bond would be kind to them, but wanted him to be a tiny bit cruel first. Moore looked as if he knew his way about when both were in bed, but he gave reassurance that he was in it for their mutual pleasure rather than for putting the woman where she belonged — which, in a phrase John Osborne once used with great effectiveness and offence, was 'on her back'.

This timely lightening of the character sometimes imparted a light-comedy style to the adventures, while the huge budgets that were now the order of the day still allowed film-goers to be enjoyably overwhelmed by fantasy effects and stunts that imitators without the 'Bondian formula' (or cash) could not bring off. The new Bond had a nod-and-a-wink collusion with film-goers which pre-empted the growing Seventies tendency to throw the trendy Sixties fashions — like the Bond mystique — into ungrateful discard as the harsher facts of every-day existence began to shape and limit people's daily expectations.

Moore's nimble tongue could defuse the films' tendency to treat human life as continuously expendable. He not only stylishly exterminated his enemies: he simultaneously purged the act of offensiveness. 'Only being disarming', he quips, as he snips the cables controlling the fearsome metal claw which the villainous Tee Hee wears in place of a hand. In the same dexterous way, he snipped any connection that some people might have attempted to establish between the popularity of the Bond films and what was now being publicly labelled in the United States as 'The New Violence'.

Yet the Bond series did not quite avoid some of the other hazards of the changing times. Roger Moore's success in the series has tended to make people forget how harshly this first film starring him as Bond was received by sections of the media in America. Not because of its excessive violence; still less because of its sexual chauvinism. But on the grounds of its allegedly racist bias.

Seeking to capitalize on the healthy box-office returns of the current genre of black exploitation films in America, the Bond producers provided 007 with a black adversary, 'Mr Big' (played by Yaphet Koto), a Harlem-bred and Moscow-backed criminal whose mission was to prepare the USA for a Russian take-over by turning it into a nation of junkies. *Time* magazine's critic, Richard Schickel, identifying Bond as 'The Great White Hope', reprimanded the film for depicting blacks as either stupid brutes or superstitious primitives and for using miscegenation as a continual sexual turn-on. 'Both novelties are deplorable,' Schickel rapped, categorizing the film as 'the most vulgar addition to a series that has long since outlived its brief historical moment — if not, alas, its profitability'.*

Strong words, that others echoed; but, alas, a case of wishful thinking on both counts. *Live and Let Die* confirmed Roger Moore as Connery's accepted successor and the Bond saga as the only one of the main three strands of fantasy — the other two being the Beatles and the 'Swinging London' life-style — to continue running potently through the Seventies and even into the Eighties.

Times, 9 July 1973.

CHAPTER THREE

A Boy Called Enigma

The trouble with film-making is that it never allows you a moment when you feel you can go out and celebrate.
                              — *David Puttnam*

'This boy', David Puttnam's headmaster wrote in his school-leaving report, 'is a total enigma.' It was a verdict that the sixteen-year-old took to heart. It shines today on the brass company name-plate beside the highly polished front door of the South Kensington mews house which serves as office and home for himself and his family, including his wife Patsy whom he met at Minchenden Grammer School when she was barely twelve and he was just four years older. Just to add another riddle to the 'Enigma', he has turned the terminal letter 'A' upside down. The word also appears on his writing paper, superimposed on one of the best-known English landscape paintings, John Constable's *The Hay Wain*, which has had the horse and cart deleted to make room for it. Such clues entice one to read them, and inevitably one reads back into them what one now knows of the 'enigma' who was being called by almost everyone in the early Eighties a 'one-man British film industry' and christened 'Cinepa' — how he must have gritted his teeth over that! — by *Reader's Digest*, which was paying him the ultimate compliment by holding up his life-story as an example of self-endeavour and success.

If there is any enigmatic element surrounding David Puttman, it surely lies in the slightly bemused attitude taken to him by many commentators. How could someone so unostentatious in his behaviour, so modest, so *ordinary* get so far — and so fast? As far as most of the printed media were concerned, he had hardly been heard of till the Seventies were half over. There are signs that he has a twinge of ironic regret at not living up to the legend of moguldom. 'I'm not very smart, but I'm sensible,' he told Aljean Harmetz in 1983, with a little moralistic nod at the awful difficulties which Francis Ford Coppola had then landed himself in as a result, it was implied, of overweening ambitiousness. 'Films that get messed up are examples of people not acting sensibly,' he continued, then added a trifle wistfully, '. . . because acting sensibly is not equated with creativity.'*

Now this is not the sort of quote which makes the kindling to set a reputation on fire overnight. Interviewers have always entertained more hospitable thoughts about destructive — better still, self-destructive — geniuses than the man whose talents keep the show going from behind the scenes. But Puttnam is not playing it cool on purpose: that style of trendy self-confidence simply isn't part of the nature of a profoundly un-trendy individual. Even in his mid-forties he retains a boyish figure, an impression reinforced by his modest stature and not at all dispersed by a beard he grew in the hope that it would counter the advantage he once had (and used, where girl-friends were concerned) of looking, without it, like Paul McCartney's double. Friends, though, have noted that Puttnam began growing his beard at the same time as he noticed one on Stanley Kubrick, whose independence he holds in awe, though the reclusive Kubrick's totality of control over his films is still beyond Puttnam's grasp: in this, too, he remains a *sensible* obsessive. He is usually tie-less — which is rather the rule than the exception in movie circles — but again the impression is one of a college kid, not a whizz-kid: he is not laid back or cultivating a studied inelegance: he is probably quite genuinely expecting his mother to tell him to put on a tie and, while he's about it, button up his school blazer. After *Chariots of Fire* carted off four 'Oscars' in 1982, the papers were casting Puttnam as the prince whose hour had come to fit the glass slipper on the shrinking foot of the British film industry and claim the girl as his own. But *The Observer* cruelly referred to him as Buttons, the page-boy in the run-down household of Cinders's father, the appositely named Baron Stoneybroke, who brings the girl all the aid and comfort he can, but never gets to marry her.

The truth about David Puttnam always seem to contradict the image. This entirely conventional-looking boy was unconventional enough at the start of the Eighties to have beaten Hollywood's biggest and best on its own award-winning territory — and this was only part of it. He was being hailed as doing more to promote the essentially British nature of his country's films than anyone since Sir Michael Balcon; a trustee for future talents as a governor of the National Film and Television School; a strong voice on the board of the National Film Finance Corporation; a profitable part of Channel 4's television output; an active contributor to the fortunes of Goldcrest, the front-runner among the newly formed film companies of the late Seventies; and a persuasive member of Sir Harold (later Lord) Wilson's Interim Action Committee on the Film Industry,

New York Times, 3 May 1983.

whose meeting he once stunned into momentary silence by proposing to
have all films and drama removed from the TV screens and making the
public pay a realistic price for the privilege of seeing them on cable.
Though a Socialist (or on the way to being a Social Democrat), he was
also a confidant of Mrs Thatcher and striving to make her put patriotism
(at least as far as financing the film industry was concerned) before the
market forces of a free economy; and he was the recipient of a sovereign
honour when created a CBE in 1983. Yes, there is an enigma here.

Puttnam has got farther than most — and will get farther still — by
upholding convention rather more often than breaking rules. Everything
he has achieved is very closely related to his upbringing. His
film-making experience has been a sort of 'extension course' of his
boyhood and working youth. His background, as he is fond of saying,
was one of 'almost mythic ordinariness'.

He was born in London in 1941 into the very middle of the middle
classes. His father was a photographer in a Fleet Street agency, where he
used to bring young David on Saturday morning, thus possibly
accustoming the child to seeing the world in pictures, rather than words.
('Words are not David's strong point,' said Mark Boxer, who later
employed him briefly on a short-lived trendy magazine in the Sixties.)
'My mum', says Puttnam, 'was an ordinary mum, serving slices of cake
and pots of tea.' One wonders if the walls of their suburban home
aspired to 'good' reproductions of artists of the accepted schools, such as
Constable's *Hay Wain*. If so, it would be a sentimental link with 'Enigma,
jun'. Little else is ever explained by Puttnam about his family: it is
somewhat odd that where one would have expected the background to
reflect the customary middle class ambition for a child to go on to higher
education and a 'good' job in the professions, David was allowed to leave
his grammar school and go straight into a job as a messenger boy for a
West End advertising agency.

But if the traditional education pattern was broken, that moment
launched his strong self-improvement drive, matching himself now
against the demands of an actual job rather than a distant goal: 'I
bought a stop-watch to see how many seconds I could cut off my delivery
times going up and down the escalators in the London Underground
couriering copy from the agency to the client.* Such zeal got him
promoted to an office job, with a rise in salary from £8 a week to £16. He
quickly moved through several agencies, using them as stepping stones,
until, in the impressionable part of his teens, he fell under the influence
of an executive at Collett, Dickinson and Pearce. 'Colin Millward taught
me that competence is not a point of arrival: it is only a point of
departure. It was crucial advice in film-making. Some other producers
can't wait to get going once they have a perfectly satisfactory script: but

---

*David Puttnam, interviewed by the author, 28 March 1984. Unless stated otherwise, all subsequent quotations
from Puttnam come from the same source.

I plough through as many drafts as I feel is necessary till the germ of the idea is developed to perfection. Or else I don't make the picture.'

Proof of this is Puttnam's postponement — to date, anyhow — of *The October Circle*, a novel he bought in the mid-Seventies whose subject is a Bulgarian family which is divided over the Soviet invasion of Czechoslovakia in 1968. What has delayed the project is not just the fact that the hero is a Communist who does not lose his faith despite the historical events: this has certainly made it more difficult to find finance than if the story had ended with a conversion to Western ways of thought (and capitalism). But, by 1981, the project was in its sixth year, its fifth draft and its fourth writer; and a data bank of professional and non-professional actors who might fit the eventual roles had been built up on video-tapes. Despite the sizeable investment all this represented, Puttnam wasn't satisfied that he had reached 'the point of departure'.

Colin Millward would have approved. He saw young Puttnam as 'a boy with a mission'. He was persuasive. Once he had convinced himself — and this is still the thrust that powers Puttnam — he could sway others. He was 'good at making things happen'. In short, Puttnam had found a talent for 'hustling': the technique of setting up a buyer for a deal by convincing him that he needs what one is trying to sell him. It is not quite the same as 'dealing'. What distinguishes the hustler from the dealer is 'expediency'. The hustler has to resort to it more frequently than the dealer who tries to base the relationship on reciprocity — though of course the film business is by no means as clear cut as this implies.

Puttnam found himself developing talents that later made him slightly ashamed. 'I wouldn't like to meet the man I was then,' he says today. Probably it was the reflex action of an idealist discovering his touch as a pragmatist, profiting from the result, but not seeing it enhancing his self-image however much it contributed to his status.

He was now on £4,500 a year — a high salary in those days for a youth just turned twenty. He was working with copywriters who included Alan Parker (later a film director and Puttnam associate) and Charles Saatchi (later a partner in the agency which promoted some of Britain's biggest institutions, including the Tory Party) and was handling major accounts after cutting his teeth on such tasks as writing the two-inch single-column advertisement taken by the Victoria and Albert Museum in the BBC publication *The Listener*. He built up a huge network of contacts in the world of display advertising, among them the brightest talents then working on television commercials who wanted to make a wide name for themselves but were not yet ready to leave the well-paid, if (to the outsider) anonymous, world of advertising for the lonelier, chancier reaches of feature film-making. When they discovered that they *were* ready, Puttnam was there to welcome them.

He left Collett, Dickinson and Pearce rather than work on a cigarette company's advertising campaign. He was then in his mid-twenties. He worked briefly, and none too happily, on Mark Boxer's *London Life* magazine, then borrowed £3,000 and started a photographic agency with clients who now sound like a roll-call of the brightest and best of the Sixties: Bailey, Duffy, Avedon, Richard Montgomery . . . 'All we had in common was limitless energy and the urge to risk failure.' But he later admitted to a friend and associate, writer Ray Connolly, that he 'only ever saw it as a means to an end'. It was the high noon of 'Swinging London', a phenomenon that was promoted (indeed often created) by the vivid picture-spreads of newspapers and magazines which gave the young and affluent the pattern for their life-styles.

But it was not as satisfying as Puttman had hoped: after all, setting up a picture-spread with a magazine allows an entrepreneur less leeway (or satisfaction) than the man who sets up his cameras and makes it all happen. The pictures did not move, either, and few of the photographers he handled were equipped by temperament to go into the world of movies. One or two of them may have resented a bias they detected in Puttnam: for films to him meant far, far more than entertainment.

Growing up into his teens in the mid-Fifties, Puttnam belonged to the last generation to whom the cinema was far more of a reality than television, whose capacity to expand and fill up people's leisure hours did not really take off till ITV arrived as a populist rival to BBC TV in 1955. Moreover, the sort of film that Puttnam saw as a boy deeply influenced the sort that he himself would make as a producer. 'They were the films of Kazan, Robert Rossen, Zinnemann and Stanley Kramer. Films that were deeply thematic, but easily accessible to popular audiences. They dealt with big issues and recognizable areas of life and people's troubles, but always in an entertaining way.' To Aljean Harmetz, he admitted: 'Any ethical basis in my life was implanted by (these films). I wanted to be Montgomery Clift looking after that boy in *The Search*, I wanted to be James Dean in *East of Eden*.'

His debt was wide and permanently acknowledged; but it was a debt to a cinema that was itself coming to an end as power passed to a younger generation of film-makers who were devoid of the shaping experiences of the Thirties that influenced the above-mentioned director-producers: the new ones were more self-interested and callous of human values. 'The films I saw in my impressionable years', Puttnam adds, 'were critical of society all right, but showed the Americans' capacity for infinite hopefulness. You had to admire America in those days. There was a basic decency to its films then. I think this influenced me when I came to shoot subjects of my own finding, which, you'll note, are not usually adaptations of books or plays, but based on true events or, let's say to be safe, "news stories". Just like a lot of those post-1945 films from America.'

In the late-Sixties and Seventies, young people in Britain began

receiving quite a different view of the States — it was the amorality and
viciousness of life there that Hollywood films now disseminated,
disposing audiences to expect the same kind of life for themselves.
American films narrowed their breadth of vision and shortened their
focal length till they embraced only self, self, self. 'Films should be used
to show what is best in society, or what can be so, given the exceptional
man or woman with vision and will-power,' says Puttnam. 'Movies
influence too many people's attitudes to life for us to be indifferent to
what they're presenting on the screen.'

There is a strong evangelical thrust to Puttnam: indeed were he not so
skilful in wedding treatment to subject, one might accuse him of
censoriousness. Decency, no more than patriotism, is not enough for
survival. He has several times said that the man he most admires, Sir
Michael Balcon, simply couldn't survive in the market-place of today's
film culture: it is too squalid, there is no room for decency. Puttnam's
reply to a query about why he had not up to then tackled a topic like
juvenile delinquency is probably very close to the one Balcon would
have given. He told Roy Lockett, deputy general secretary of the
ACTT,* the principal film union, that he had 'sat down with Pete
Townshend and Alan Parker with the specific intention of making a film
about football hooliganism'. He hoped it was going to be a multi-faceted
film dealing with a lot of social ailments. 'Very early on Pete
Townshend brought up the fact that we couldn't find a way of doing it
that was going to be attractive and get people to come and see the film,
without, to some extent, glorifying racism or violence for at least half of
the very people who would form its natural audience.'**

It was the old problem of the artist's responsibility to his subject, he
said, and quoted the example of Leni Riefenstahl and her film of the
'Nazi' Olympics in 1936. Even if she had been a Marxist, he said, her
talent wouldn't have allowed her to make a very different film. The
excitement of one's technique may betray one's purpose.

It was, in a way Puttnam may not have consciously recognized at the
time, the problem of the advertising man who ignores the dilemma of the
moral purpose to which he puts his selling skills because there is no
realistic way of solving it and remaining in the job. Puttnam had 'solved'
it by resigning from the job when he was asked to advertise
cancer-causing cigarettes. But the moral problems of film-making would
sometimes sneak up and take him unawares, and there was nothing he
could do about it then.

In 1968, after about two-and-a-half years running his photographic
agency, Puttman yielded to the pull of feature films. Along with Sanford
(Sandy) Lieberson, an ex-agent and American-in-London who was then
putting together the film that became *Performance* for Warner Bros., he

*The Association of Cinematograph, Television and Allied Technicians.
**David Puttnam, interviewed by Roy Lockett, *Marxism Today*, February 1982.

formed the eupeptically named Goodtimes Enterprises. (To be on the safe side, though, he 'sensibly' retained a 60 per cent interest in the photo-agency.)

Both producers had a nose as keen as the Bisto Kids in the seasoning ads. for catching things on the wind. It was too bad, though, that they held out their plates for a helping before the kitchen was ready to deliver. They had also formed the bulkily titled Visual Programmes Systems to catch the audio-visual revolution; but the revolution came late (if indeed it is here yet) and video-cassettes, which would have made it viable, did not become commonplace till nearly ten years later; so that some of the early VPS productions with a factual basis and an educational bias, like *The Double-Headed Eagle* (director, Lutz Becker, 1972) and *Swastika* (director Philippe Mora, 1973), both successful studies of Nazism, only showed there was no market in programmes that the TV could do more cheaply. Feature films became Goodtimes's mainstay.

Luck was with them, at first. For £500, Alan Parker, Puttnam's companion in copy-writing, wrote a script 'on spec', a story of a schoolkid's love-affair, which was read by the producer Ron Cass when he was showing *The Stud* (which starred his wife Joan Collins) in the Cannes Film Festival market-place; and he passed it on to Seagram's, the American distilling giant, which he had heard wanted to get 'into films' for their fiscal attractions. Edgar Bronfman, Seagram's boss, who later tried to buy MGM, disliked it, but asked his sixteen-year-old son to give his opinion. The boy liked the youth angle, the Pop connections and told his Dad he should be making 'movies aimed at kids' and not investing in million-dollar would-be blockbusters. Result: Seagram's put up $400,000; The British distribution company Hemdale, added another $200,000. The money was actually riding on two juvenile stars, Mark Lester and Jack Wild, who had been Oliver Twist and The Artful Dodger respectively in the 1968 British musical *Oliver!* 'I always think of it as the *Jules et Jim* of the nappy set,' Puttman says, a trifle shamefully perhaps, although he is generous enough to concede that 'for a long time afterwards it was a cheque from *Melody* that kept Sandy and me going'.

Melody (11 April 1971: later re-titled, nauseatingly, *S.W.A.L.K.*, after a schoolkid's mnemonic for 'Sealed With A Loving Kiss') was held to be well-timed, for its release coincided with the furore over *The Little Red Schoolbook*, to which reference has been made, though its romantic fantasy defused any possible charge of corruption of the innocent by turning pupil-power into pubescent love.

It was a romantic fantasy, produced by Ron Cass and directed by Waris Hussein, heavily interspersed with numbers by Crosby, Stills, Young and Nash and the Bee Gees. It was largely set in a South London comprehensive school and is notable for the feeling of early autobiography which Puttnam and Parker put into its story. One of the boys is an obstreperous extrovert rather like Parker was: the other, quieter, lonelier, the child of comfortably off but none too understanding parents, is a Puttnam-figure. The latter develops an instant crush on the eponymous heroine (Tracy Hyde), an eleven-year-old, much as Puttnam at the age of fifteen took an immediate fancy to the twelve-year-old girl at their co-ed school whom he later married. In the film, the couple 'elope' and are 'married' by their pal in a makeshift chapel.

Characteristic of its makers' advertising experience was the way the movie used its music like 'commercials' in order to 'sell' the mood: a technique not so common at the time, but which quickly became one of the decade's stylistic cliches. The movie got a surprisingly warm welcome from some American critics, particularly in *Newsweek* and *The New York Times*, which may be put down to the goodwill generated by *The Graduate* and other youth-oriented movies which followed it. The British critics were altogether cooler: but the film did quite well in America and very well in the Far East (which hadn't yet been hit by 'Swinging Sixties' hangover). *'Melody'*, says Puttnam, 'gave me confidence in myself: my next film, *The Pied Piper,* taught me the dreadful risks I ran.'

The Pied Piper is the 'forgotten' film in the Puttnam canon; and Puttnam prefers it that way. Even how much it cost cannot be accurately verified, since the financial records which were then kept at the merchant bank financing Goodtimes have been mislaid. But the point is, as Puttnam says, 'it didn't work. And a film that doesn't work teaches you a hell of a lot very quickly about the movie-making business.'

It was to be a musical version of the Pied Piper story and Puttman got it into his head that he wanted a 'different' feel to it — not an Anglo-Saxon one, but, if possible, a Continental one, an East European one. He had just seen Jiri Menzel's *Closely Observed Trains*, which had won the 1967 Foreign Language Film 'Oscar', and felt that its 'tone' would transplant perfectly into the lyrical pathos of the Pied Piper tale.

But the Czech bureaucracy refused to 'release' Menzel to direct an 'outside' film. Menzel suggested his countryman Milos Forman, who had finished his first Hollywood film, *Taking Off*. Puttnam saw it, reacted enthusiastically, and all looked set — until, to boost the confidence of Seagram's, which was putting up half the budget, Puttnam showed its executives the still unreleased Forman film. This tale of comfortably-off American parents 'losing' their children to the radical-hippy-protest movement was a 'Pied Piper' fantasy far less acceptable to the backers: it came too close to home and they hated it. 'They told me I could use anyone but "that Czech",' says Puttnam, who had to choose quickly — and chose Jacques Demy on the strength of his bitter-sweet 1964 musical *The Umbrellas of Cherbourg*.

But what should have been a sweet deal, was soon an embittered one. 'Demy had his own particular approach, which he didn't believe could be done on our budget. He favoured camera takes lasting four or five minutes, which enormously complicates editing.' Donovan, the tender-toned Pop ballad singer cast as the Pied Piper, had composed eight songs for the film: Demy preferred to use only four. Puttnam admits, 'I was in awe of Demy, intimidated by his reputation.'

It was a painful early lesson: if the producer is dominated by circumstances, or the adjacent talents of director or stars, the film suffers. Puttnam prefers not to go into details about *The Pied Piper*'s resounding failure (one gets the impression it was written off), but the fact that he had started off 'on the wrong foot', so to speak, convinced him he had sacrificed the producer's 'precious ability' to oversee the picture objectively. He was to allow himself to ignore similar danger signals on two future occasions: but for the moment, formidable compensation was to hand.

STARDUST MEMORIES

'David said, "Do a film for me," and *That'll Be the Day* (12 April 1973) was planned that same afternoon.'* Ray Connolly, in 1971 a feature writer on London's *Evening Standard,* had called to offer Puttnam the opportunity to rebut some of the uncomplimentary comments of the British critics on *Melody.* 'We got on so well,' Connolly says; 'then when he said, "Let's do a film about ourselves, our age group," I jumped at the chance. At that time there hadn't really been any films about "us", about "the post-Beatles generation". We put a lot of autobiography into it. The title comes from a Buddy Holly song; but I had some lines from a Harry Nilsson hit floating through my head: "In 1941, a happy father had a son . . . In 1944, the father walked right out the door." I recalled my own Dad going off to war, David recalled his coming home from it. We'd other things in common, too, like the grammar schools we'd gone to. One of the characters we invented did all the sensible, respectable, "wet" things: he was very much based on me. Another one broke with school and threw away his books: that was how David tended to see himself. Not that it was *that* cut-and-dried in the film. . . .'

David Essex, fresh from his stage success in *Godspell*, who played the boy who turns his back on school in the 1950s and becomes an early drop-out, expressed Puttnam's envy of the 'might have been' possibilities that he himself could have embraced, given just a slightly different life, temperament and opportunity. (In the sequel to *That'll Be the Day,* Essex becomes a celebrity, grows a beard and turns into a virtual double for Puttnam!)

That'll Be the Day was set in the Fifties when the reigning sound was

---

*Ray Connolly, interviewed by the author, 3 August 1984. Unless stated otherwise, all subsequent quotations from Connolly come from the same source.

rock 'n roll and parents were growing worried at the rebellious rhythms coursing through their children like a secondary and alien bloodstream. It was the story of one such kid (Essex) who tears off his school tie and throws away the chance of university 'qualifications', the shibboleth-word beloved by the middle classes. ('David's mother, and mine, too, were always saying, "You need qualifications",' Connolly recalls, 'so we made sure *that* went in!') Neither rebelling nor seeking a cause, Essex drifts around beach fronts, fun fairs, holiday camps in a Britain not yet transformed into a youthscape by teenage affluence. The movie proved a very good vehicle for permitting now ageing Pop idols to 'cross over' and become character actors — and *Stardust* would prove an even more effective one. Ringo Starr had imagined he was a natural comic who could make other people laugh without really trying — he had found out that he wasn't and couldn't.

'We wanted to draw on the experience of an actual Fifties beginner who became a Sixties star,' says Connolly, 'so we made an appointment to see Ringo at the offices of Apple' — the Beatles' short-lived entrepreneurial enterprise where it seemed every caller cheerfully ripped off the Fab Four. 'Our talk went so well that David said to me: "Let's offer Ringo a part." At first he was considered for the role of Stormy Tempest. (the Pop singer later played by Billy Fury): but I said; "Let's give him a bigger part." — "Could he do it?" — "Well, let's find out." So he did two weeks, and worked really hard though things got strained — Ringo's attention span is limited.'

It was the best film performance Ringo has ever given. Playing a tougher, more well-worn teenager who initiates Essex into casual sex, he got his thick lips round Connolly's flat, sarcastic dialogue and made a funny, unswaggering, honest impression. The movie was notable for the way that the characters had change built into them. Essex coarsens with sexual competence — 'Been doing some gardening?' Ringo quips, after his pal's now nightly return from his date on the waste ground. Change even affected Essex's modestly ambitious school chum, based on Puttnam and Connolly as their respective mothers saw them, who sports evidence of his exposure to university radicalism in his Trotsky-ite beard. Small touches, but they paint living people as life is constantly remodelling them. Especially effective in its sad, wise-after-the-event way is Essex's visit to the students' union where Trad rules the dance floor not rock 'n roll and, without a word being spoken, he experiences the galling guilt of the educational chance he threw away.

That'll Be the Day was exactly the kind of film that two middle-class boys would see as making amends to their parents for their generational transgressions!With Essex's return home and temporary settlement into stifling domesticity — which he will walk out on at the end of the film as his own screen father does at the start — his story begins to run into the life-with-mother suburban trap so freshly analysed by John Schlesinger in *A Kind of Loving* some eleven years earlier. But it never loses sight of the truth about the seduction of the fifties generation, the emergence of a new beat among British kids and the siren song of the new rich Pop idols, like the one amiably parodied by Billy Fury, squawking into the microphone like a demented parakeet in gold and silver plumage or swivelling his scarlet-suited pelvis *à la Elvis*.

George Melly praised its 'amazing period accuracy . . . a great treat for all us nostalgic scelerotics of the Fifties. Everything from the Festival of Britain-style wallpaper in the coffee bar to the jiving girls' flash of stocking-tops is right. The gulf between working-class rock 'n rollers and the CND badge-wearing university students is nicely demonstrated. Even the language of lechery is completely of its time.'*

But if nostalgics found it appealing, the movie didn't pitch any specific appeal to them: in fact, it signally avoided the scrapbook exploitation of the past it could have so easily enlisted. It was fresh-looking and all of a piece; and though it appealed, like the recollected sweetness of the first drink, to Melly's generation which now found itself with a hangover, it served early notice of David Puttnam's view of movies as exemplary illustrations rather than inflammatory invitations to imitation.

Puttnam had tried to get Nat Cohen's Anglo-EMI company to put up all of the budget. Failing, he made an agreement with Ronco Records, a small American recording company. 'In return for part of the financing, I think we promised to work a 44-track album into the story!' Connolly says, a bit awed even ten years later at the undertaking. 'It meant finding (or creating) openings for about fifteen seconds of music. We'd scratch our heads and say, "Where can we possibly put three more songs?" That explains why the Essex character spent so much time wandering around the beaches or fun fairs — so that we could lay down a few contractual seconds of Pop music!'

FLEURS DU MAL

Although it was not appreciated by its makers at the time, *That'll Be the Day* marked the start of a revisionist view of the Sixties. Instead of being caught up in its excitements, helping to manufacture more of them and formulate the life-styles to go with them, film-makers like Puttnam and Connolly, fresh from jobs in advertising and journalism, both cynical trades, were now edging more and more to one side and viewing their generation with a still entertaining but increasingly moralizing eye. Connolly was slightly more of a moralist than Puttnam. His later columns in *The Standard*, as the newspaper was renamed in the 1980s, were to exhibit some of the revisionist if not actually reactionary features

The Observer, 15 April 1973.

that other journalists of his generation had developed with the loss of illusions or, at any rate, of youthful acceleration.

The claim made by the Pop stars of the late-Sixties and early Seventies that their music was a life-style as well as an art form was being challenged in the most unrefutable way when the celebrated names started dropping dead — Janis Joplin, Jimi Hendrix, Keith Moon, Jim Morrison among them. Others who didn't succomb fatally to drug abuse became reborn Christians. Mick Jagger took a wife and had a wedding that was as bourgeois as any middle-class boy's, though it was held in the south of France with considerably more flash than suburbia would have thought it prudent to display. As George Melly pointed out sardonically, the 1968 demos in Paris simply toughened the Establishment's resistance to any repetition once the barricades had been dismantled.

Lindsay Anderson's *O Lucky Man!* has already been mentioned as a symptom of the cooling of youth. The times, they were a-changing all right: now running against the old, strong, seductive pull of Pop rebellion. 'Instead of changing the world,' George Melly observed, 'musicians now settle for exploiting it . . . No one thinks of Pop music as a call to arms any more . . . Musicians have joined the acceptance world. Where *did* all the flowers go?'*

Some of the flowers, Connolly realized, were dead blooms that he had helped cultivate in scores of journalistic interviews that now read like obituaries. There is nothing like death to create the sense of a definable era out of generational confusion. In 1983, when he reprinted fifty out of seven times as many 'star' profiles he had written for a variety of Sixties publications along with brief postscripts, their cumulative mentions of death, self-destruction, drugs and related disasters of fortune or flesh cast the same kind of baleful retrospective illumination on the period that one perceives was inherent in David Bailey's *Box of Pin-Ups* nearly twenty years earlier. The hero of *That'll Be the Day* had yet to meet his doom; but at present he remained in the tradition of working- or lower middle-class lads from *Room at the Top* onwards: in other words, a bit of a bastard, but basically forgivable. He leaves his home, a wife and a newly-born baby at the end of the film and goes off with a second-hand guitar he can't even play properly to follow the music that's been coursing through his impressionable years. *Time* magazine's critic, Jay Cocks, recognized that 'the movie has learned from its predecessors in the school of angry British realism how to deal with the social milieu. Industrial Britain is presented with fierce but never condescending accuracy.' He called it an 'unassuming and pleasurable' movie and hinted that its sequel, which had been finished but was as yet unseen in America, 'may be something more'.** It was.

The Observer, 7 October 1973.
**Time*, 16 December 1974.

The idea for a sequel had been in the minds of Puttnam and Connolly even before director Claude Whatham had finished shooting the last scenes of *That'll Be the Day*. 'The feeling around the film had been good;' Connolly says, 'you *knew* it was something special. Even so, when David kept saying, "They'll *demand* a sequel," I wasn't too sure: but that's my downbeat nature. David wanted to do the early Sixties. I wanted to bring it up to date, to spill over into the Seventies. Eventually David said, "Let's do the whole of the Sixties." He'd taken a house south of Rome for the summer: I went down and within a week we'd laid out the story line. David worked so closely on both films with me it was unlike any experience I've had with a producer since then. Back in London, he'd call round for breakfast at 8.00 a.m. and take away the three or four pages I'd written the night before, have them copied, evaluate them, then come back in the late afternoon and discuss what the next segment should be, and I'd knock it out overnight. He had so many ideas that even if you flattened one or two, he didn't resist or try to impose himself, but simply said, "Okay, what about . . .?" Truthfully, I always felt the credits should read: "Story by Ray Connolly and David Puttnam." ' They called the movie *Sturdust* (24 October 1974). It could not have been more timely.

Everywhere one looked (or listened), in America as well as Britain, disenchantment was being squeezed out of the now soured fruits of Pop idolatry. Pop music itself was in a highly fissionable state. The social bonds among the young, which had nurtured it, were breaking up. The Beatles music on both sides of the Atlantic had forged a common language, even a sort of cathartic theatre: no longer. Things were changing too quickly for any beat to orchestrate. The generation coming of age in the United States was ostentatiously self-centred. Nineteen seventy-four was the year when people began to be noticed getting something 'off their chest' by putting the message on their T-shirts, as the fast-heat pressure press permitted the easy, cheap transfer of any slogan that the wearer willed to the cotton top that had hitherto been regarded as personal underwear, not a public billboard. 'I created this myself — it's ME,' was the attitude: an early symptom of how the kids whom Tom Wolfe called the 'Me' generation drew attention to their egocentricity. *Time* reported in the fall of 1974 that 'not since the 1950s have young people been so pragmatic in their outlook, so highly oriented towards careers and financial security'.* Increasingly, education was being prized as a means to enter the system, not subvert it: 'swinging' was out, 'connectedness' was in; and while sexuality was approached more nonchalantly and deviancy more tolerantly, and obedience was by no means the generational reflex it had been in the fifties, the predominant feeling in America reflected the demise of the counter-culture.

**Time, 16 September 1974.*

In August 1974 Pauline Kael published her now celebrated article in *The New Yorker* on the desertion of the generation that had espoused 'unproven' movies like *M*A*S*H, Easy Rider, Five Easy Pieces* and *Midnight Cowboy* and made them into counter-culture hits. This was a most perceptive and depressingly accurate forecast of where mainline American movie-making was headed. Ms Kael foresaw the pernicious impasse to which Hollywood's media-created 'events' would soon bring the industry and its audience: the 'playing for safety' that would pre-determine the kinds of films that got made ('it's safer not to risk the box-office embarrassment of seriousness') and the kinds of audiences that could be induced to patronize them (a generation in search of 'movies completely consumed in the cinemas — the "slam-bang" pictures that succeed with illiterate audiences in "underdeveloped" countries who are starved for entertainment').*

Generational change was staring one in the face in Britain, too, but it was part of a larger, more frightening pattern of displacement. Nineteen-seventy-four was the year of strikes, drought, inflation, oil shortage, financial collapse and two General Elections: the first gave Labour four more *seats* than the Tories; the second an overall Labour *majority* in the House of three. Compare *Time* magazine's famous 1967 cover labelled 'Swinging Britain', with the cover of *Newsweek* on 21 October 1974, which showed a Union Jack with cartooned figures representing all the evils in Pandora's Box about to clash head-on at the centre of the flag's red cross: 'Inflation', 'Scots Nationalism', 'Energy Crisis', 'Labor Strife', 'Ulster Terror', 'Social Unrest', 'Class Conflict', 'Common Market'. Undepicted anywhere was 'Hope' — it was even worse than the Ancient World had known!

As the three-day week established to save energy during the miners' strike pushed up the unemployment statistics, the lines of hopeful emigrants lengthened outside the offices of Commonwealth High Commissions in London, with applications for Canada up by 65 per cent over the previous year, for Australia by more than half. The 'pleasure economy' faltered, then abruptly crumpled up; gasoline prices quadrupled, then quintupled; inflation rose to 17 per cent; the balance of payments deficit topped £10 billion; unemployment hovered around 700,000; the Stock Market plummeted to its lowest point for sixteen years; bankruptcies, in one week of October 1974, averaged one every forty-five seconds in the Companies Court; and, amid reports of retired Army officers forming 'Third Forces' of private volunteers to keep the essential services running in the event of a General Strike, Professor Max Beloff, Fellow of All Souls, noted the entry into the system of 'a degree of real hatred and bitterness . . . Things which were once discussed in terms of

---

*The New Yorker, 5 August 1974.

social justice are now discussed in terms of envy, and turned into destructive attitudes.'*

Dr Mark Abrams, who had coined the word 'teenager', echoed Beloff in an important contribution to the October 1974 issue of *Encounter*. 'The value system of most people in Britain today is solidly grounded in materialism . . . A large proportion of us now place much greater emphasis on the terminal value of a comfortable life than on the instrumental value of more money.' That was comforting, in a way, since money as a unit of intrinsic worth had forfeited a great deal of the superstitious respect accorded it: its value had halved, prices had doubled, and only the credit-card companies glowed with health. But then Dr Abrams added: 'More money has become almost a terminal value: the act of spending by itself, and almost irrespective of what is bought, provides satisfaction and a reduction of tension.'

Well, not everywhere it didn't. Not among those congregations of youth who still had something to jingle in their pockets. The Windsor Pop Festival was being held on August Bank Holiday 1974, and developing what its adherents claimed was a 'celebration of libertarian democracy' when 600 policemen — no doubt unable to stand the tension of traditional values being so raucously reappraised — moved in with the morning mist. Out of 15,000 of Dr Abrams' 'teenagers', some 200 were arrested and more than 50 left injured. George Melly, performer as well as observer at the Pop scene, sang the blues in a morning-after piece published in *The Observer*. Better than most of the indignant editorials, its sad resignation served as a memorial for more than the wounded.

'The Isle of Wight, Glastonbury, these were the great manifestations of the alternative culture of love, dope, sounds, macrobiotic food, tripping, instinctive anarchism, youth, the new life-style. The last bastion of all was that free festival at Windsor last week and anyone rash enough to go there was at risk. Free food, free music, people peeing in the bushes and poking wherever and whenever they felt like it, and on Royal ground, too, *and* without permission — there'll be no more of that! The law moved in with truncheons and shut the whole thing down . . . My spirit mourned for Windsor, the pathetic and perhaps the last manifestation of peace and love.'**

Clearly, it was no longer the 'Beatles Britain'. Their success story which had matched, peak for peak, the expansionist excitement of the Sixties now beat a retreat under the blows of police sticks along with the national economy of that dreadful year. In the very same month as that Windsor 'massacre', a new play with music opened in London entitled *John, Paul, George, Ringo . . . and Bert*. It was promoted by its author, a Liverpudlian teacher called Willy Russell, as a metaphor for the general

*Newsweek, 21 October 1974.
**The Observer, 1 September 1974.

youth entropy. 'It is about the tragedy of (the Beatles) . . . they had to be taken over, made public property . . . What I'm trying to say in the show is not criticism of the Beatles, but of what we did to them . . . This is a play about the effects of money, exploitation, growing up, and it's as much about Brian Epstein and Alan Klein as about the Beatles.'*

The Fab Four had now been subsumed completely by the nostalgia industry: the back-projected, grainy black-and-white photographs at the Lyric Theatre, showing the group as they'd looked when young; the mob hysteria that erupted when they hit the top, now appeared practically archeological. Russell distanced their story by having it narrated by 'Bert', the forgotten nobody who had once played with the group and been jettisoned *en route*: his fate personified the callousness, the 'situational morality', that accompanied the high-pressure exploitation of their talents.

Now there was something almost *evil* about the phenomenon. The Beatles' screaming worshippers shut them off from hearing the music they were playing; their wealth excluded them from all but their own kind of celebrity; they were patronized by society, harried by taxmen, swaddled by sycophants, imprisoned in deals done by bigger businesses than their own. It was the earliest, and remains the most successful, attempt to demythologize the Beatles. Although John Lennon had complained that no one listened to the autobiographical truth he had enshrined in the song *Help!* when he wrote it in 1965, Willy Russell's strip-cartooned view of the bust-up ended with that song and now its *cri de coeur* was no longer a premonition of things going wrong but an obituary notice with a bite to it.

It was this national and generational mood that David Puttnam's production of *Stardust* articulated even more bleakly, if possible, when it opened in October 1974. Connolly's screen-play acted as a purgative for the Sixties: out came all the hard home-truths in dialogue as briskly paced as it was deeply scathing. There was not a jot of sympathy for any particular devil. For this reason, and against these times, it was a much more important picture than *That'll Be the Day*. The earlier film had been about innocence and temptation: this one was about manipulation and exorcism.

'While we were making it, we were quite frankly worried about the number of shows and films, here and in America, which were beginning to take a backward look at the same kind of generational experience as we were planning to do,' Connolly says. '*American Graffiti* had just come out; there was the Willy Russell play in the works, though we couldn't know about it, since it didn't open in the West End until a month or two before out film was premiered; but we *felt* the change that was apparent everywhere, in every aspect of life, and especially how people were

---

The Guardian, 11 August 1974.

looking at what seemed an impossible past — only a few years distant, but feeling as out of reach now as the last century.'

Puttnam now firmly set the future pattern of his preference, for working with talents who were new to film-making for the cinema by chosing Michael Apted, who had cut his creative teeth on television, to direct *Stardust*. 'We were basically doing a very simple thing,' Apted recalled. 'We merely put up the idea that Pop heroes are often created by other people, not themselves, and that the whole awful business is usually self-deceiving and self-destructive.'* 'Simple' maybe: but the idea would not have found much acceptance before the break-up of the Beatles as a group in 1970; and the film drew for its accuracy not only on their disputatious aftermath, but on the general disenchantment of ageing fans left behind in cold times.

Though ostensibly a sequel to the earlier film, Connolly's script could have stood on its own independent feet. The story opened in 1963, with David Essex (as the same character) personifying the directionless kind of Pop singer drifting through one-night stands with a throaty, anxious little voice that only projects his teenage dreams when it has the backing of the Stray Cats. He soon meets a guide-guru of stronger will and more devious means. It was one of the great strengths of both films to find a Pop singer willing and able to turn himself inside out in public and show the dark lining to his charisma. Ringo had performed this service for the earlier film and he had the option to appear in *Stardust*. He chose not to exercise it — Connolly thinks it may have been too near the actual Beatles experience for his comfort.

'David suggested Adam Faith. All I'd seen him in was his *Budgie* series on television, playing a sort of East End wide-boy. We all met at a recording studio off Tottenham Court Road and went out to eat. During dinner, Faith "conned" us again and again, just like the character I'd written for the film, using the same collusive kind of false crumminess and then going into his spiel. We felt we were being manipulated, but we found his act engrossing. Maybe David had given him a few tips on the quiet — I don't know — but the performance Faith put up convinced me he'd be terrific.'

And he was. As the group's 'roadie', doing deals with conspiratorial bonhomie, buying drinks and selling advantages with a 'fancy a drink?' nod and wink, Faith was a pocket Mephistopheles who takes Essex up to the high places and shows him the world. He has the passion of a pandar, the soul of a keeper. He reeks cheapness. Moving out of his seaside caravan, which he's been renting as a 'knocking-shop' for quick sex, Faith applies the same supply-and-demand business-sense of casual satisfaction to promoting the Stray Cats, getting a laundrette king to sponsor them with profits from dirty linen while a London music man

*Michael Apted, interviewed by Derek Malcolm, *The Guardian*, 19 November 1974.

(Marty Wilde as a recognizable Brian Epstein-type) hoists them up the charts.

Stardust had a clever score, with music produced and arranged by Dave Edmunds and Puttnam: it made the Stray Cats sound true to their time, so that there was never any credibility gap as one watched the group catch on with the fans, being groomed into angelic moppets in Beatles suits and sanitized for public consumption, while their off-stage life is a perpetual binge of 'pills, pot and the birds' and their in-group politics a series of conspiratorial 'fouls' that install Essex in place of the lead singer. The film moved into overdrive with the arrival of an American tycoon — played by Larry Hagman, who was to become another representative figure of villainy as the next decade's J.R. The way that the Beatles had been bought and sold in the futures market was paralleled in the exploitation of the Stray Cats. Michael Apted never permitted a caricature to be substituted for a character; and Tony Richmond's photography acted like a two-way mirror for the audience.

Looking out, one saw a world gone mad, hypnotized by these exploitative Pop idols, treating them with a reverence reserved for heads of state, rewarding them with the income of the Rockefellers. Looking inwards, one saw the cruel reality of it all, the exploited performers confined for hours in airplanes, limousines and guarded hotel suites, hostages in the hands of their manager, zeroes on the ever-escalating tax claims, growing cynical and frustrated as the more acceleration their career picks up, the less feeling they get of arriving anywhere.

Apted's television experience convincingly brought off what must be the Pop idol's ultimate trip — being beamed by Telstar to 300 million fans and performing his rock oratorio, *Dea Sancta et Gloria*, whose pompous litany is meant to be in praise of woman, though the whole set-up is an electronic celebration of one male ego whose pygmy proportions have been magnified beyond their owner's understanding, much less control. If *A Hard Day's Night* of ten years earlier had been a joyous release of Pop energy, *Stardust* was an implosion of disaffection. One had simply not been prepared for its moralizing determination: a characteristic fed into it by Puttnam and Connolly. Connolly, the newspaperman, was putting into this acidulous paraphrase of dozens of 'celebrity interviews' what legal caveats had obliged him to leave out of his published articles; Puttnam, with his nostalgia for those American movies that revealed a residual virtue in their exposés of social abuses, was seizing the chance to be a reformer without ceasing to be an entertainer. The film's tricky anti-climax was handled without compromise. Essex achieves his dream — a real solid castle in Spain — and we watch the character decline into self-extinguishing truth the way a space traveller suffers from burn-out on re-entering his own universe. 'How much does God mean to you?' a television interviewer asks in the final confrontation between the exhausted Pop idol and his global public. Comes the drug-slurred reply: 'Between two and three million dollars a year, before tax.' No one was left with stardust in their eyes.

Goodtime Enterprises was to be left with a gratifying amount of profit. *That'll be the Day* had cost £288,000 and by the mid-1980s was showing a net profit of £406,000; *Stardust* cost £555,000 and showed a net profit at the same date of £525,000. As Connolly says: 'We had done very well with films about ourselves.'

RUSSELLMANIA

Ray Connolly stayed on in California, where some *Stardust* location scenes had been shot, in order to research and write a documentary on James Dean for Goodtime's stablemate company, Visual Programmes Systems.

The project was close to Puttnam's heart. Dean had been a boyhood hero of his. He had been a loner like Dean, whose films he saw at the age of thirteen or fourteen. He had probably also been a rather lonely boy — he had one sister in the family — and Dean's 'romantic agony' had an iconic attractiveness for the generation that fed — more aggressively in America, than Britain — on its own sense of hurt, lovelessness and rebellion — soon to be brought out fighting by the rock 'n roll experience.

'A lot of Dean', according to Connolly, 'was included in *That'll Be the Day* — they'd call it an *hommage* now. Then, it was a secretive kind of bond that David and I had with a figure who'd become a myth for us. He rubbed off on the Essex character. That shot of Essex hunched up in the back of a truck was our memory-image of Dean slumping into his jacket as the train carries him home from Salinas through the valley farms to his father's place. The red of the blouson that Dean wore in *Rebel Without a Cause* was matched, as near as we could get it, by Essex's — and when Essex went into a cinema, it was one showing a James Dean film. And remember the *East of Eden* scene when Dean releases the ice blocks in an avalanche down the chute and says calmly; "I just wanted to see the ice go down the chute"? Well, Essex chucks his school-books over a bridge in *That'll Be the Day* and explains; "I just wanted to see the books go into the water." '

The film's final shot of him standing in the sea and looking plaintively at the camera, while the frame freezes, was a blatant 'steal' from Truffaut's 1959 semi-autobiographical *Les Quatre Cents Coups*. A 'freeze-frame' had become an international cliché by then: but taken with the other evidence, it shows Puttnam's generational identification with the young, the lonely, the insecure: the 'after-image' retained its sharpness for a long time.

The 80-minute film, *James Dean — The First American Teenager* (1975:

but not commercially released in Britain till 1977), cost £100,000 and by 1984 had turned a modest net profit of £49,000.

Meantime Puttnam's partner, Sandy Lieberson, had been active on the company's behalf producing (along with John Goldstone) an MGM-EMI-financed entertainment, *The Final Programme* (20 September 1973), based on a conflation of Michael Moorcock story elements and starring the SF super-hero Jerry Cornelius (Jon Finch), a teenage 007 who has crossed genes with a Nobel prize-winner, and inhabits a cosmos whose outlandishly baroque ingredients were the film's most enjoyable invention. In it we can recognize the present, recall the past, apprehend the future: time is infinitely bendable, space expandable, the only laws to be obeyed are the ones in fairy-tales. The bizarre conjunctions of the futuristic and the antiquated — the hero's ruffle-fronted shirt, frock coat and sun glasses looked as if his morning toilette had been interrupted by several different time-slips — were well served by director Robert Fuest's approach, neither playful nor pretentious, but staying just this side of surrealism.

Fuest had shown talent for graphic panache on two earlier 'period' — i.e., art deco — 'horror' parodies about the 'Abominable Dr Phibes', made for MGM's British production roster. Lieberson, too, showed his bent towards films of striking 'texture', where production design often predetermined action: later, as European production chief for Twentieth Century-Fox and then The Ladd Company, his benign influence could be felt in intricately wrought movies like *Alien* (1979) and *Outland* (1981). *The Final Programme* looked like the Beautiful People of the Sixties now 'bled off' to the very edge of fantasy experience. In fact, concern at how convention went 'over the edge' resulted in a ban being placed by London Transport on the film's poster, designed by the Pop artist Allen Jones, which showed an unmistakably androgynous silhouette: London was not yet ready for cross-dressing or 'gender bending'.

In spite of the partners' feverish work-load, Goodtimes had the perpetual problem of cash flow. It had been hoped VPS productions, serving education as well as entertainment, would provide a smaller but staple and less risky return than feature films. A TV-video series, *Romantic vs. Classical Art*, had been made with Colin Clark, son of Sir Kenneth (later Lord) Clark whose own TV series, *Civilization*, had provided viewers with such a nostalgic evocation of the interdependent harmony of things — 'such a striking contrast', as Christopher Booker later commented, 'to the bleak, divided, class-racked society' of the Seventies. In addition to the two documentaries of the Third Reich, VPS made *Brother, Can You Spare a Dime?* (director Philippe Mora: 1975), a record of the American Depression reflected through contemporary photographs and movies. In 1973 a pact was made with Ken Russell for six films on musicians which would be ready for the 'cassette explosion' that Puttnam saw happening in a couple of years time. Meanwhile they could be shown in cinemas. The designated composers were an eclectic lot: Mahler first, then Gershwin, Liszt and Vaughan Williams with two more to be announced. Only two got made: which was perhaps a mercy.

On hearing of Russell's planned attempt on Mahler's life, I had written flippantly: 'This man must be stopped: bring me an elephant gun.' Puttnam made a typically mischievous riposte, appearing in a Covent Garden restaurant, stalking up to my table and, to the alarm of other customers, laying across the expanse of white cloth a double-barrelled safari gun he had rented from the gunsmiths opposite.

But before he took the measure of Mahler, Russell made a version of Sandy Wilson's jaunty Twenties pastiche, *The Boy Friend* (3 February 1972), which reminded one that before he became notorious as the sorcerer's apprentice of the screen there had been a Russell who was a confectioner's assistant and had made *French Dressing*, which was all top dressing and nothing underneath.

The Boy Friend did have 'something' underneath: the mangled remains of the original show. It was a musical, made for MGM-EMI, which did its dancing over the body of a better one. Borrowing his effects this time from Busby Berkeley, Russell demoted the Sandy Wilson text to the status of a background event hammed up by a third-rate provincial company hoping for a Hollywood contract, and then with less reason (since he himself lately signed a Hollywood contract) proceded to fill up the foreground with his own variety of cinematic virtuosity, crying 'Bring on the fantasies' the way Berkeley was supposed to cry 'Bring on the girls'. As the principal girl was (at this date) the non-singing, non-dancing Sixties ex-photographer's model, Twiggy, the approach had its handicap. Not so ruinous, though, as trying to stage the numbers on a screen nearly three times as broad as it was high, totally unsuitable for the spectacular multiplication of leggy females whom Berkeley contrived to replicate on the perfectly rectangular screen of his day so that six dames looked like fifty. Russell's effects worked exactly the other way round.

Actually, Twiggy came out of the traffic thundering down this 42nd Street without fatal accident — though no longer a 'twig', what she had put on was 'shape', not 'weight' — and along with Tommy Tune, the skills both performers showed in Broadway partnership in the Eighties may have been tapped here. But they were not enough to salvage Sandy Wilson's original: nor did a last-minute attempt to cut its campier excesses just before the London première add anything, least of all box-office success.

Russell then turned his attention to Mahler and Liszt, both for Goodtimes, with the film of Pete Townshend's rock opera *Tommy* sandwiched in between for Robert Stigwood, the Australian impresario who was investing in British recording groups and films.

Neither of the two classical biographies shows the slightest influence

of David Puttnam. He later admitted he felt 'dominated' by the director
he had hired: he appears to have stood well back.

Russell conceived Mahler and Liszt as the 'chart toppers' of their day.
Thus both composers (personified respectively by Robert Powell, who
was put through everything including hoops of fire, and Roger Daltry, a
ringleted Pop star in concert gear with a black-and-white keyboard motif
on his eighteenth-century lapels) lead lives of continuous hyper-tension.
Perhaps the educational element in the project — which must have
grown increasingly remote as work advanced — explains why *Mahler* (4
April 1974) feels made for a class of rowdy boys who must be kept
attentive by sequences of rampant fantasy and rankest vulgarity.

For the backward members of the class, the facts of Mahler's life are
delivered by a pack of patient 'feeds', masquerading as friends,
acquaintances and even total strangers who continually interrupt the
composer in order to say things like, 'Why were you forced to leave the
Vienna opera — anti-semitism?'; or 'All your music is a hymn to
nature'; or 'What you completed perfectly in your Fourth Symphony, Dr
Mahler, is a child's view of heaven'; or 'I understand you're searching
for tranquility, Mahler'. The absolute dunces in the class would have
learnt that as the composer sweated over his manuscript paper in his
lakeside hut, his wife ran about the countryside soothing raucous Nature
into *sotto voce* compliance, unhitching the bells from the cows, muffling
the church clappers, confiscating the shepherd's pipe and buying a
round of lager for the folk dancers in order to stop them in mid-stomp.

To their continued surprise, the class might have learned that the
Mahler family were a pack of rabid Jews from London's East End,
gabbling out their money-grabbing ambitions for the boy between
gobbling up mouthfuls of hot food. That Mahler's Jewish ancestry was a
stumbling block to his career is at least arguable: but supposition
becomes grossest opportunism when translated into a fantasy showing
Mahler purging his semitic characteristics by submitting to the Aryan
disciplines of a Cosima Wagner accoutred as a 'Miss Boots-and-Whip'
and turning Wagner's *Ring* into a song-and-dance show such as might
have been staged in a classy sex-parlour under the title *The Ziegfried
Follies of 1895*. The film's anti-semitic overkill was its most often
remarked on element and must have caused its producers no little
embarrassment. It was an act even Mel Brooks could not have followed.

The dissonant clash of associative images was even more vulgarly
deployed in *Lisztomania* (13 November 1975): the composer's Dante
Symphony was performed while he fantasized himself being sucked
through the scarlet knickers of Princess Carolyn of St Petersburg into the
underworld of her vagina, where a pack of fishnet-clad furies attack him
before the director, swiftly switching tunes to Liszt's symphonic poem
Orpheus, turns the rape into a masturbatory lullaby that elongates Liszt's
penis into a ten-foot long member danced round like a maypole or
straddled by chorines before being finally guillotined by the castrating

pincers of Princess Carolyn's thighs. If misogyny is to the fore, can anti-clericalism be far behind? The Pope is played by Ringo Starr, in a cope embroidered with film-star faces, who pays a social call at the cell of the Abbé Liszt and finds him in bed with a nude nun called Olga. As musicology, the film understandably fell by the wayside. As Hollywood pastiche (Liszt as Charlie Chaplin's 'Little Fellow' with an ace of hearts on the seat of his pants) it was also somewhat wide of the mark. In all, it might have been said to Liszt to destruction from the start, with Wagner's music rearranged by Rick Wakeman presented as a Pop gig to an audience of shrieking eighteenth-century teenyboppers.

It abruptly terminated Goodtimes's ambition to cater for the musical education (and entertainment) of the masses — and cut short the company's credit. *Mahler,* a model of restraint by comparison, cost a mere £193,000, and by 1984's figures had lost only £14,000. *Lisztomania,* on the other hand, escalated to £1,200,000, and has been largely written off. Disappointment had to be borne amidst critical denunciations: there were no compensations, only false hopes. Just as *Mahler* was finishing post-production, Puttnam heard that the president of one of the Hollywood majors, a Mahler fan, wished to see it. Hoping for an American deal, Puttnam himself carried the cans of film aboard the next available flight for Los Angeles, rushed straight to the studio and into the executive screening room in time to offer the powerful man a screening for his after-dinner guests — it turned out this was all he had had in mind in the first place.

One only wishes that Ken Russell could have trusted himself and his audience's attention span more. His genuine visual flair, evident in every film he made at this period, seemed to be flawed by a deep-seated fear of losing film-goers' attention. 'I need an audience,' says Henri Gaudier-Brzeska (Scott Antony) in the film *Savage Messiah* (13 September 1972), which Russell made for MGM-British; and the director appears to echo him with, 'I must hold my audience.' The result in all his films based on artists' lives is a heightening of true incidents into absurdity for scenic shock-effect, leaving the artists stranded in a megalomaniac limbo. 'I don't care what I do, so long as it's creative,' was Gaudier-Brzeska's vow in the last few years of his life: but in this film, as in the rest, it was also Russell's credo throughout.

He is a man who is indistinguishable from the Messiah. Both men, one feels, declaim from the high places. Young Henri Gaudier is scarcely on the screen before he is scaling an Easter Island monument in the Louvre like a prisoner of bourgeois morality demonstrating on the jailhouse roof. "Ullo, 'ullo, in a bit of an artistic tizzy, aren't we?' shouts the guard, speaking for critics, too. For the Russell of this period, the life of an artist, any artist, appears to be a running, jumping and never standing still affair with the artistic gospel breathlessly enunciated between the cultural laps.

Undoubtedly his best film of the decade was *Tommy* (27 March 1975),

since a story about the raw sensate experience that Pete Townshend's
music perfectly incarnates was the best one for a self-confessed exponent of
the movie brutalism. (No wonder the film's power predetermined the
look of *Lisztomania* which followed it.) Russell seized all the opportunities
for visual wizardry: *Tommy* resembled a phantasmagoria of Dali, Bosch,
Tanguy and Yves Fuchs. A skeleton crawls with slugs, lizards and
snakes; the pin-ball machines which Elton John (in glitter specs and
gargantuan bovver boots) bids to do his will like a Pop Messiah, throb
with psychedelic razzmatazz; huge iron cannisters litter the amusement
parks like the spawn of monstrous fishes; and in one scene the consumer
society vomits back its by-products — baked beans, detergent foam,
milk chocolate — all over Ann-Margret, who rolls exultantly in the swill
the way that some far-out schools of psychotherapists of the time advised
their disciples to cavort in their own excrement. One feels inside a mind
which has blown every rational fuse: for once, one feels at home with
Ken Russell.

'My association with Ken was chiefly a learning process,' Puttnam
says philosophically. 'I learned "on the job" what I would have had no
other way of acquiring.' What exactly? one asks. 'Well, that people
making the film must never admit they lack confidence about what they
are doing. If Ken arrived in the morning uncertain of his next move,
he'd set up a complicated tracking shot and by the time the rails were
laid he'd have had it all worked out in his head. The important thing is
activity — do *anything*, but keep active.' It sounded indeed as if the
lesson had been well learnt — but Puttnam's innate conservatism could
always have been counted on to rein in this steed that was galloping off
in all directions. 'I learned that no producer can afford the luxury of
respecting a director over-much. Ken Russell was the most gifted
film-maker I ever worked with, so far as the look of the film was
concerned. When he was at the peak of technique, he was on the
Himalayas. But too often he didn't see the end to which all this had to be
applied. I am a very old-fashioned boy: I believe in the text, the script,
the blueprint. Ken took pride in the opposite extreme.' (In *Lisztomania*'s
case, the script was described as 'a slim (57-page) guide'.)

The experience had one very important consequence for Puttnam. It
confirmed his preference for working with 'first-time directors provided
they have the talent'.

'It is possible to elaborate a working relationship with a director who's
inexperienced and hence so much more dependent on me. Another
thing: no director has ever tried less hard on his first picture — that
way, one gets 110 per cent out of him.'

Out of the Russell experience, too, came Puttnam's view of
film-making as a series of confrontations: usually benign on his part, but
necessarily watchful. 'Good-tempered vigilance' describes it. But if
trouble looms, he knows his own instincts well enough to prefer a short,

sharp early row over the differences — involving even the firing of actor, writer or director — to the 'long and lingering nightmare of a film you end up wishing you had never made'. Of course, if the film (or any of its ingredients) is bigger than himself, the lesson to be drawn is just as inevitable — to withdraw oneself. This explains why one or two of his associates have spoken at one time or another of his 'walking away' when things get too tough. This is not pusillanimity, however: only a realistic appraisal of where the power lies. Moreover, the notion of a working team is as important to Puttnam as it is to Russell, though in a quite different way. Russell values the very idea of community, a sort of 'artist's collective', so long as he can be den-father. Puttnam, on the other hand, as he told Aljean Harmetz, believes 'the absolutely most important thing (about a working team) is that everyone is trying to make the same movie'.

LITTLE BIGSHOTS

Puttnam put precept into practice with his next production, *Bugsy Malone* (22 July 1976). Alan Parker was a first-time cinema director: it might be said that he had acquired reputation without power. That reputation had been earned making commercials for his own company. Puttnam and Parker had a certain common element: a love of parody, particularly parody of old movies. For Birds Eye foods, he devised a forlorn figure at a railway station seen through a cloud of steam and then trudging home accompanied by the piano theme from *Brief Encounter* to a frozen-food dinner for one; for Supermousse, it was a timorous Oliver Twist sidling up to Mr Bumble and pleading for more of 'the product'; and the benefits of drinking milk, not some other evil potion, were registered on Dr Jekyll with a brimming glassful. Commercials used children a lot and Parker was 'good' with them.

He had directed two TV films, notably *The Evacuees*, which was scripted by Jack Rosenthal, later to be Puttnam's executive editor on an important TV series called *First Love*; and the result showed his talent for 'shorthand' scene-setting, period 'flavouring', and an affinity with kids and their games of make-believe — all of which a middle-class boy like Puttnam, weaned on the very cinema 'classics' at which Parker poked affectionate fun, found much to his liking. A fellow ad-director of Parker's, Adrian Lyne, had already made a small, strange, much-praised film, *Mr Smith* (1974), about the tragi-comic afflictions accumulating around a rueful suicide in his last hours; and another colleague, Ridley Scott, was also on the look-out for feature-film material: so the impatient Parker was anxious to get started. After 600 commercials, what had he to lose . . .?

Puttnam and he were already friends — as noted, he had scripted

Melody — so David could not only be 'in charge' but 'in sympathy' with a man who assured him that, whatever else his film might look like, it would be 'distinctive'. But what else *was* it to be?

Bugsy Malone was a story Parker began writing in November 1973, and finished the following summer: a pastiche of Hollywood gangster myths that was to be performed entirely by children aged eight to fourteen. They had not only to parody an adult genre of entertainment, but in manners, dress and talk, ape adults, too. There was considerable internal logic here: many of America's best-known gangsters were 'little big-shots' who never matured emotionally — their very nicknames, 'Little Caesar' or 'Baby-Face Nelson', smacked of the nursery school, even if the owners graduated from tougher academies. They needed mother-love, rejected a father's discipline and displayed breakfast tantrums by pushing half-grapefruits into girls' faces.

Building a diverting fantasy on this theme was one thing: selling a film that resisted categorizing was another — Puttnam and Parker opposed the label 'children's film' — Puttnam spent £3,000 of his own money on vain, fund-raising trips to Hollywood; the piggy-bank only began to fill up due to a fluke meeting between Parker and Paul Williams — who was so seized by the idea that he volunteered to compose the songs and music. For Parker wanted the kids to sing and dance, too!

The budget came to just under £575,000. The National Film Finance Corporation came in for £200,000 of this provided that a major distributor guaranteed 'not less than $300,000'. ('Dollars' connoted an American distributor: only that would give such a movie credibility.) Eventually Paramount and the Rank Organization came in for all but the last £50,000 — and *that* was raised by mortgaging the homes of Mr Puttnam and Mr Parker. Thus in spite of his track record with the two Pop generation movies, Puttnam experienced the niggardly, piecemeal attitude of British financial institutions and the disproportionate amount of trouble they gave for such a relatively small risk. 'From start to finish', he said years later, '[Rank] was a nightmare. Not interfering, so much as moaning and groaning and being totally negative, and the money was always late. Thank God they've stopped production. That must have saved a lot of people a lot of pain and unhappiness.'* For Puttnam to rejoice at *any* film-maker going out of business shows the extent of anguished exhaustion he must have been reduced to: it was an early symptom of his fear of getting into 'a situation' with the paymaster-potentates. He was learning not only how to 'protect' a director: he was finding out about his own threshold of pain.

Yet *Bugsy Malone* shows nothing of this torturous financial finagling. It is a movie shaped by taste, wit, melody and infinite affection for its adult world scaled down to a child's playground. The kids who gave a joyously

---

*David Puttnam, interviewed by Minty Clinch, *Ms. London*, 21 April 1981.

spunky rendering of the 1920s sterotypes came from US Air Force bases in Britain — Parker saw some 17,000 in a nine-month tour — as well as Equity's kindergarten from which Jodie Foster was recruited as 'Miss Tallulah', a speakeasy 'chantoose' like a slinky Joan Blondell in miniature, with a hyacinthine kiss-curl dangling from a skullcap of silver-plated hair and backed by a chorus-line of cuties whose fifth-form faces were seductively contrasted with the fully-fashioned legs they kicked up in budding Busby Berkeley routines.

Everything adult was transposed into an uncondescending child's eye-view of gangsterdom without losing its underworld allure. Bullets don't fly: but that new technological miracle, the 'Splurge Gun', fires fusillades of cream-pies that immobilize casualities in the facsimile of rigor mortis. Get-away autos are pedal-driven kiddy-cars; hard liquor is soft drinks; and when rival mob-leader 'Dandy Dan', a Gatsby-ite racketeer with polo ponies on his lawn and a pubescent English butler (from the Eton Manservant Agency), breaks up Fat Sam's secret distillery, the already hard-hit bootlegger laments, 'Not the sarsaparilla racket, too!' A quartet from a junior-sized edition of *Guys and Dolls* boastfully promenade along the sidewalk asserting, 'We could have been anything that we wanted to be'; a sly little black janitor hugs a pair of tap-dancing shoes to his coveralls and yearns to be Fred Astaire in modified Blues notes (all the singing was done by adults striking a nice balance with the juvenile faces); and, best drilled of all, a gymnasium filled with black kids in boxing trunks fling notes and punches as they parody Mohammed Ali with a swaggering anthem called 'So you wanna be a boxer?'

The film-makers gave the impression they had forgotten nothing of their own childhood. Amazingly, officialdom frowned on the film: its submission as the British entry to the Cannes Film Festival in May 1976 was vetoed on the ground that it was a 'children's film' and/or 'too commercial'. It was accepted under protest; but an economy-size promotion budget compelled Puttnam and Parker to paste up their own posters (under cover of night so as not to risk encountering the display-board mafiosi on the Croisette). Being cheaply lodged in the Cannes hinterland, they had to change into *tenue de soirée* in the lavatories of the Hotel Carlton, leaving their day-wear with the concierge for collection after the screening. The film proved the festival's 'sleeper', though a non-winner: it also proved one of the best investments ever made by the NFFC. At the last accounting it had returned net profits of £1,854,000.

LEAVE OF ABSENCE

But Puttnam's education was not completed yet. A painful lesson was administered to him with the next Goodtimes project, one that had a profound influence on the solo independence he now seeks to safeguard so jealously — in as much as the financial obligations of multi-million pound budgets ever add up to 'independence'. Again it was Ray Connolly who had the idea. In 1974 he published a novel entitled *Trick or Treat?* and sold the film rights to Goodtimes — rather than Warner Bros., who were after it and who could have given 100 per cent financing. It was a Chabrol-esque story about two girls who want a baby and get involved with a married couple. It was set in Europe: the 'international' casting options were attractive and, as the plot incorporated sexual ambivalence as well as an early Women's Liberation manifesto of gender independence, it looked set to go.

It might have, too, except for two things. One was Goodtimes's financial constraints. The company simply could not afford the development costs that would have rested easy on the conscience of a Hollywood corporation. Goodtimes came down to two individuals, Puttnam and Lieberson, both with business accounts shamefully at odds with the energy, risk, initiative and success they had shown and won as independent producers. *Bugsy Malone*'s receipts hadn't begun to come in; and anyhow the arrangement with their bankers, Rothschild's, was not over-generous to them. Putting up even £30,000 (Connolly's figure) for development was a risk; the strain grew as revised drafts pushed the figure higher; one prospective partner (the NFFC) pulled out; and Hugh Hefner's Playboy film division was left to step in 'on condition' . . . The condition was that Bianca Jagger, hitherto only a seemingly bright casting notion, should be the star. She had never made a picture.

The steps along this Via Doloris have been chronicled with many a wince by Connolly in *Stardust Memories*.* It is too long, too involved and too much Connolly's story to summarize here: but the upshot was a horrendous series of interruptions to the shooting schedule in Rome, creating delays, dissensions and ultimate disaster for the film — as well as great distress to EMI which had put a portion of the money into a movie that now had to be abandoned at a cost of £400,000. Connolly concluded: '*Trick or Treat?* was an education for everyone involved. At (that price) you could say we all had a very expensive education.' A catastrophe which might have been no more than a 'blip' on the balance sheet of a Hollywood company left lasting marks on the Goodtimes partnership between Lieberson and Puttnam. It was dissolved soon afterwards, and Puttnam set up his own company, Enigma. 'There was no bust-up,' he says, 'just a simple recognition by Sandy and myself of each other's different aims and natures. But', he added, tellingly, 'I'm a bad consulter.' Never again, he resolved, would he be the moving target for everyone's aggrieved fire-power. Never again would he commit himself to a movie that was 'international' only because of budgetary obligations to the financiers.

*Ray Connolly, *Stardust Memories* (Pavilion, 1983), pp. 227–240.

'It seems to me', he said at the time, 'that if I can help anyone it's my own contemporaries. And I don't want to go like the clappers all my life. [He was then thirty-five.] So if I get a half-dozen really good directors really "motoring", in ten or fifteen years I'll be able to produce films without all the physical aggravation I have to go through now.'*

To this end he now engaged Ridley Scott, at thirty-eight a leading commercials director, to make his first feature film (and Enigma's first independent production). This was *The Duellists* (12 February 1978), on a budget of $1,300,000 provided mainly by Paramount, with NFFC participation. The American distributor probably turned the balance in favour of American stars, Harvey Keitel and Keith Carradine, to play Napoleonic hussars who are locked into a 'grudge fight' that consumes eighteen years of misspent 'honour'. Such was the stars' mastery at thinking themselves into skins, minds and manners of the combatants — as well as at handling rapiers, broadswords, jousting horses and pistols in the final stealthy stalking-match — that their customary American traits were totally subdued and they gave performances neither has since surpassed.

'Ridley's background probably pre-determined his approach,' Puttnam said in a *Marxism Today* interview, answering the query whether directors like Parker and Scott, technocrats from advertising, had the desirable political commitment. 'His father was an Army major. I think Ridley is probably the one who worried the least (about his class background). Ridley is what Ridley is. He is the one who turned up in a suit at the Royal College of Art . . . He's probably the most brilliant of any of us. Ridley's a painter who happens to use film.'** Scott had trained as a BBC TV designer, then shifted to Rediffusion TV when his efforts to turn director were thwarted. Then he got into commercials — he employed Hugh Hudson, who was to be Puttnam's third protégé from this milieu — where a prize-winning series of ads. for Hovis exhibited the painterly period texture he now transferred to *The Duellists*. He showed an eye for every historical detail, from the elaborate uniforms to the feminine fastidiousness of the men's appearance, including hair-styles worn with two braids falling beside each ear so as to cushion the sabre blows! Kubrick's *Barry Lyndon*, shown the year before, had proved an inspiration in breaking up what Scott called 'the constipation of costume drama'.

Sometime later, Puttnam revealed what a 'close-run thing' the choice of film had been. 'As regards (its) origin . . . Ridley had in fact developed (Joseph Conrad's) short story in the form of a piece presumably for television. When I came into the picture, we reworked the screen-play with Gerry Vaughan-Hughes, created the plot involving Diana Quick's camp follower and strung it out to a respectable length. This was one of

*David Puttnam, interviewed by Sue Summers, *Screen International*, 22 January 1977.
**David Puttnam, op cit., February 1982.

three pieces of material that were in development as potential directorial debuts for Ridley, but I found that having harnessed David Picker (at that time, president of Paramount) and his enthusiasm for Ridley's talent, *The Duellists* was the only one of the three projects that could be made within the parameters that were set. The point worth mentioning here is that the final decision was not a creative one, but budgetary!'

Puttnam had told Scott that he wanted the film to be a blend of not only *Barry Lyndon*, but *The Outlaw Josey Wales* — Clint Eastwood's Western. In other words, period sensibility was not enough: he wanted energy, as well. He did not get quite all he wanted. Scott's eye, though painterly, was a cold one. As confirmed in his next film, *Alien* (1979), which he was to make for Puttnam's ex-partner, Sandy Lieberson, he could break a film down brilliantly into a series of graduated 'shocks' on an audience's emotions: 'fights' in *The Duellists*, 'frights' in *Alien*. 'Whatever the feature film,' he has said, 'it's only communication after all.' In this respect, he was probably not as much in sympathy with Puttnam as Parker had been. Puttnam's temperament is a warm one: he wants to have the enormously involving experience of projecting his own longings, fears, love and sympathies on to the protagonists. This was why James Dean had hooked him: he was a boy Puttnam could understand in fact, could *be*. Ridley Scott's talents lie, as mentioned, in 'texture' and special effects: it is very unlikely *he* has ever wanted to change places with a star.

It was while Puttnam was working on *The Duellists* that he had a very unpleasant reminder: which was that he could not afford to be working this way at all. Although *The Duellists* would be a profitable investment for Paramount, its producer-distributor, and, in 1984, was nearing the break-point where Puttnam would see some return, while making it he had had to guarantee two-thirds of his own fee as 'end money' — the sum set aside, or provided by film banks, to cover crises that could unbalance the budget or even halt production. Puttnam had budgeted the film in March 1976; by the time he came to shoot it in France in a wintry October, with later locations in Scotland, Britain's balance of payments crisis had put up the prices of Technicolor and Kodak stock. Another $60,000 had to be added to the budget and Puttnam's fee would be forfeited if he went over schedule: Scott was on minimum rate and expenses. Puttnam brought the film in at the revised price: but his bank balance looked no healthier. Years of austerity had taken their toll. His producer's fee on *That'll Be the Day* had been only £8,000; £12,000 on *Stardust*; nothing at all on *Mahler*; £6,000 on *Bugsy Malone*. He had income accruing from some of these films, but taxation then took 83 per cent of earnings over £21,000 and 75 per cent of foreign earnings if they arose from work performed in Britain — as all Puttnam's had been.

In short, after seven years continuous work, making a name for himself and helping British cinema keep alive and innovative, Puttnam's financial situation was such that he could *never* hope to rid himself of indebtedness if he continued to work in Britain.

He was shooting the final night scenes of *The Duellists* in sub-zero conditions at Scotland's Aviemore Ski Centre early in 1976 when a call reached him from Hollywood. It had been placed by Peter Guber, president of Casablanca Film Works, a 'boiler house' film outfit in Los Angeles which already had the finance to stoke its creative fires but needed someone to control its head of steam. Guber offered Puttnam the job and a two-year contract. If one of those years were spent outside Britain, legally free of the crushing British tax obligations, Puttnam reckoned he would be able to make himself confidently solvent again. He recalls that he took a deep breath of very cold Scottish air and said Yes.

CHAPTER FOUR

Never Mind the Culture, Feel the Quality

*I have found that if you know how to make movies and —
more importantly — how to sell them, there is only one way
to go — right to the top. — Lord Grade*, Screen International,
17 February 1976.

It is odd that the man who was to become the most flamboyant figure on
the British film scene in the Seventies made his earliest appearance on
the cinema screen virtually unnoticed at the start of the decade. Such
was not to be Lew Grade's style at all.

But then, in 1970, he had hardly got round to thinking of himself as a
movie mogul at all. He was still a television tycoon. All he had wanted
was Shirley MacLaine for a series of half-hour TV shows to be called
Shirley's World which he intended screening on his own ATV network
and selling to ABC TV in America. 'To get the deal firmed, I agreed to
make a motion picture with her. She had this project, *Desperate
Characters*, which Frank Gilroy had written and wanted to direct.'*
The cost was $2m., and some people wondered if it could be made for
that. 'Anyone can fool me once — no one can do it twice,' Lew was
quoted as saying grimly. The figures did stand up: so did the movie — so
well that it was entered for the Berlin Film Festival in 1971 and later
shown theatrically in some countries.

Its story of two American suburbanites finding their cosy, insulated
life horrifyingly vulnerable to vandalism and worse was a typical
'festival' film, chastising all that was popularly believed (by Europeans)
to be reprehensible about the American way of life: not at all the sort of
movie Lew Grade would produce when he hit his stride. But no one saw
any omens, either, in one of the other films competing against it at

---

*Lord Grade interviewed by the author, 28 June 1984. Unless stated otherwise, all subsequent quotations from
Lord Grade come from the same source.

Berlin, though *Dulcima*, a lush tragi-comedy set in rural England and in almost every respect the opposite of *Desperate Characters*, had come out of the Elstree studios owned by EMI, where Bernard Delfont, Lew's younger brother (by about three years), was head of the films division. In many eyes, the two men seemed to have as little in common as such films; yet as the Seventies progressed, and each brother's involvement in the financing of films grew with ambition, if not sibling rivalry, their fates were linked in a way that seemed to have been expressly devised by such Fates as chuckle over the hubris that film-making breeds.

There was no question which brother, Lew or Bernie, was better known to the public in 1970. As *Time* magazine had once remarked, every Briton seemed to have three things: a dog, an umbrella and a Lew Grade story. Lew appeared to have been turned out of the same mould that had produced Sam Goldwyn Sr. He had a show-business persona of wily philistinism created by his looks and even more by his quotes. The most famous of these was: 'What's two and two make, Lew?' To which Lew's answer was, 'Are you buying or selling?' Others were added to it over the years, expressing a populist shrewdness in their generous self-mockery. Lew to producer: 'How's the Shakespeare coming along?' — Producer: ' "Shakespeare"? This is Ibsen.' — Lew: 'Well, it's all costume, isn't it?' To someone who queried whether one of Lew's productions was 'culture', his retort was: 'It must be culture: it certainly isn't entertainment.' And when one TV film which his company had produced was seen by him to be a two-hander, he was said to have exclaimed in pain: 'I've been robbed. All this money for two characters!' Such responses, by no means all of them apocryphal, were the Jewish equivalent of the Englishman-Irishman-Scotsman stories: repositories of a certain degree of ethnic truth, however crudely expressed. The style was infectious: even Lew's critics sometimes talked like Lew himself: 'The only people who like Lew's programmes', wrote one, 'are people.'

Such sayings won Lew the amused affection of the public and the gratitude of newspaper people who found colourful copy in everything about him, from the length of his cigars (seven and three-quarter inches by the tape measure that was kept to hand in the executive suite for just such verification) to the unbelievably early hour at which he arrived for work (6.45 a.m.). Then there were the superlatives that sprang so easily to his lips (a little more easily, in fact, than some of the film titles to which they are attached) when he announced his latest roster of productions costing over 50. . . but 50-what? Was it dollars Lew had said, or pounds Sterling? No matter: both were wont to appear in the same story on news pages as interpreted by bedazzled sub-editors back in London or relayed by boozed reporters who had been present at Lew's annual luncheon at the Hotel du Cap, during Cannes Film Festival fortnight, when he used to fill the hills east of Eden Roc with titles, stars, budgets and supplementary promises to the international distributors and exhibitors present that they could not possibly lose by playing his films though, of course, this year they must pay a little more for the privilege.

It was chutzpah of the most genial kind: it habitually drew applause from the well-fed guests who were only glad at that moment that they weren't being asked to pay the luncheon bill and who were always a little surprised (but nonetheless grateful) to find themselves back again next year listening to much the same speech, only the film titles having changed. The odd thing was that for quite a long time — much longer than many gave it — *it worked*. The movies did get made; they did get shown; they did make money — not all of them, but enough of them, at first, anyhow, to demonstrate that Lew kept his word. A phenomenon that bears stressing in an industry not noted for such tenaciousness.

People are often baffled when they meet men of power and expect them to behave like complex figures. Lew Grade was a complex figure who always took care to behave like a simple man. He was a man whose public stance was regularly backed by personal indebtedness; an unashamed sentimentalist who could be a hard boss; a man who mistrusted spending money on business and much preferred to give it away to charity; an 'ordinary man' who saw himself as sharing the Ordinary Man's tastes, but who behaved like a patriarch; the head of a huge conglomerate which he ran like a family business who treated the multi-million dollar products it manufactured like the manager of a delicatessen with a home-bakery in the back. The pride and pleasure he got from it was in the selling, not the cooking. That is the key to Lew Grade.

It is important to understand this man's nature, for only then will his career begin to make sense. The one shaped the other, much more than is the case with leading figures in the film industry.

The Grade family, originally named Winogradsky, came from Tokmak, in Kazakhstan, in what is now Soviet Central Asia. Lew, who was born on Christmas Day, was five when the family arrived in England in 1911. He learned much more besides English in the back-streets of London's East End, for he was soon accounted the brightest boy in the class at Rochelle Street Public Elementary School. The notion of an uneducated man who got his lessons in the hard school of experience — a notion sedulously fostered by himself as much as anyone — is belied by the fact that he was already sitting behind a desk in the school hall-way at the age of thirteen helping the headmaster run the place: that was much more the truth of things. His father, Isaac Grade, owned a cinema in the Mile End Road, but it closed during (or shortly after) the First World War and Lew and his brother Bernard, both of them nimbler on their feet than the more delicate Leslie, the third boy in the family, went 'on the halls' as speciality dancers. Bernard shone as an adagio dancer; Lew's speciality was the Charleston; and he could still perform it with brio (and enormous photogenic pay-off) as late as his 70s, when announcing good news to the show-business Press and even his stockholders. He had been briefly apprenticed to the sweat shops of the East End rag trade; but all he took away from *that* was a lifelong tendency to turn off all unnecessary office illumination, a habit of his old employers.

From January 1926 until November 1931 Lew and Bernie (who changed his name to 'Delfont' to avoid professional confusion with Lew) earned their living with a series of dance partners; and Lew's self-publicizing talents, inseparable from most things he did later on, were formed in those dancing years out of good business sense — though they must have always been a congenial part of his nature. Later, *much* later, his excessive fondness for publicity became a test-to-destruction for the independence of journalists invited to share it: if he did not kill by kindness, he certainly enfeebled the will to do ill, though he self-protectively presented himself as such an archetype of benign hucksterism that he would probably have received a good press anyhow.

His habit of reaching the office before anyone else was there, except the twenty-four-hour security guards, was also formed in these years. The story goes that his mail one morning brought a circular from the Winter Garden Theatre, Manchester, advising of an opening in the acts. Lew was on the telephone to the manager within minutes and got the business of booking all future acts there.

Ever afterwards he believed in the gifts that Jehovah bestowed on early-risers. The hour at which he reached his tycoon's office in Great Cumberland Place, off Oxford Street, figures in almost every profile of him. It exemplified more than that belief in good luck which comes from starting before the other fellow. It reminded employees (in the most exemplary fashion) who owned the key to the door. It showed the boss worked himself harder than anyone else. It testified to the touching simplicity and rectitude of his married life: for his wife Kathy, who gave up a promising singing career after an audition at Lew's offices — when she was seventeen and seeking a job — led to marriage, rose at the same early hour as her spouse to make him his cup of tea and see him into his pre-dawn limousine. It even encouraged interviewers to speculate on whether Lew toured the empty offices before his executives arrived and checked on the work in progress from the evidence they might have left on their desks. This is unlikely, though it was the prudent employee who made sure Lew was always a welcome caller when he did come visiting. To keep Lew 'in the know' was more important than keeping one's out-tray full. At least two of his right-hand men who were alleged to have tried to build empires by keeping Lew in the dark found themselves swiftly dispossessed of office. Another executive went, anonymously, on record as saying that the carpet ended when you left Lew's room —

cryptic indeed, but signifying, perhaps, the way that power lost its bonhomie when exercised behind the scenes.

Few of those writers who noted (as they were meant to do) Lew's early start to the day ever queried the cost effectiveness of being there before the mail was sorted, before essential people were at their desks, even before it was possible to start making his telephone calls to New York. Yet this begs the question: *being* there, not necessarily working there, was the selling point.

'NO. ONE SALESMAN'

Lew Grade began work as an agent in 1931 and by the late 1930s he and his brothers controlled an ever-growing section of the booking business in London and provincial variety theatres. They were property dealers, too; and their interests grew with their resources. The guiding principle behind their operation resembled the game of Monopoly: 'Someone must win because eventually he would own everything.' The war gave them extended opportunities. Their talents were in immediate demand in booking acts for the troops. Though unfit for front-line service, due to water on the knee, Lance-Bombardier Lew Grade worked a longer day than most non-combatants mustering the troops' entertainment. He is said to have carried a discharge paper in his khaki blouse duly signed, though not dated: peace wasn't going to catch him napping, either. Verbal contracts confirmed by a handshake were often the only kind there was time to make in those dark days: in any case, good faith among Lew's kith and kin meant literally good Faith. It is also true that the written word admitted fewer of those generous interpretations of the kind on which show-business thrives. Lew's style never changed in peace or war. It is related that he once found himself dining with the head of the Italian television network (RAI) who was interested in doing a co-production deal with the British tycoon for what turned out to be the life of Moses. 'I like it,' Lew said when the man first hesitantly broached the idea. The Italian continued the conversation on other topics, then deviously brought up the project again. Was a deal possible? he cautiously inquired. ' "Possible"?' said Lew. 'Haven't I just told you I like it. The deal's done.' And so, on the basis of nothing more substantial, many multi-million dollar deals were done.

Soon after he had been created a Life Peer in the 1976 Honours List, Lew received a present from his wife: a gold medal about twice the size of a silver dollar which the new Lady Grade had had inscribed at Asprey's, the Bond Street jewellers, with the all-purpose promise, 'Yes, My Lord'. At times when stars, directors and others whose services Lew wanted were proving reluctant to agree on the broad front unfettered by the details — and this, significantly, was the only time his associates were used to seeing Lew Grade out of temper — he would produce

Kathy's gift like a talisman from his pocket and say pleadingly, 'All I want you to do is read these words — "Yes, My Lord".' It often worked, too: the 'difficult' talent yielded to the quixotic nature of such a dealmaker and the belief that a hard bargain could not possibly be inspired by such a sentimental heart.

The post-war partnership of Lew and Leslie Grade really began to taste a new kind of power in 1955, when commercial television finally broke the BBC's monopoly. It introduced a whole series of corporate ploys into the big business of mass entertainment which the non-profit-making BBC had disdained to employ, or perhaps was simply ignorant of.

By that date Lew Grade had no reason to doubt his show-business instinct: after all, it had made his and Leslie's talent agency into one of the most powerful in the country. Maybe he thought that television was also just a matter of booking artists. In any case, when even supposedly shrewd financiers decided not to invest in ITV, or pulled out of it prematurely, Lew can hardly be blamed for the simplistic approach which prompted him and Leslie to put all they could afford, some £15,000 including £1,250 of Lew's personal savings, into the consortium which was bidding for the licence to supply programmes for the consumer-rich London area. The theatrical impresario Val Parnell added another £10,000. (Sums like these always look remarkably meagre in retrospect, creating the envious impression that one could have made a killing for oneself at relatively little risk: a multiple of twelve would bring the investment up to 1984 values.) The consortium was unsuccessful — 'We oversold it,' says Lew — so they merged with the one formed by Norman Collins, ex-BBC TV executive business man and author of *London Belongs to Me*, which had won the Birmingham-based Midlands franchise, soon to be named Associated TeleVision (ATV).

By April 1956 the group's money had all but run out: the station lost £600,000 inside seven months. Lew mortgaged his home, which gave him another £5,000 to invest; but it was the Mirror newspaper group's investment of £400,000 which saved the day — and confirmed Lew in his life-long instinct that being on first-name terms with 'the papers' was good for business. There was a bonus too. The Mirror group's head, Cecil King, was another autocrat whose hair-shirt brand of rectitude in private life and preference for government by decree in public affairs were similar to Lew's.

In 1962 Lew, who had been deputy managing director of ATV, displaced the powerful Val Parnell in a move that is still far from clear: but it has been said that Cecil King approved of Lew's life-style far more than he did of Parnell's. As Hunter Davies said in his tripartite biography *The Grades*: 'You might hear funny stories about Lew Grade, but you never hear scandalous ones.'*

*Hunter Davies, *The Grades: The First Family of British Entertainment* (Weidenfeld, 1981), p. 145.

Norman Collins has said that 'One of Lew's great qualities was that he could respond to things he didn't know anything about.' Things he did know about, however, he responded to instinctually, too. Programme scheduling was one such thing: his attitude to it was just the same as the attitude he was soon to show in picking the films he would make. It was simplicity itself: aim for quality, but aim conservatively. 'It was the easiest part of all,' he says. 'Everyone thought the ITV heads took hours discussing schedules. It was over and done with in ten minutes talk between us. What *did* take time were the details.' By this, Lew meant how much he was to be paid for the artists whose talents he and Leslie marketed. This was highly personal management which went in heavily for what a later generation of technocrat-executives would call 'one-on-one relationships'. Lew was in his element: it was deal-making writ in air. And highly priced air at that, as ITV quickly became what Lord Thomson of Scottish Television unguardedly but accurately referred to as 'a licence to print money'. Much of Lew Grade's programming was the watermark in the money — though, characteristically, he calls Thomson's immortal remark 'a disgraceful thing to say'.

He got his first TV series going almost as the result of doing a friend a good turn: he agreed to put up the money for *Robin Hood* when the potential producer, Hannah Weinstein, met him in the street and related the hard time she was having selling the idea: Lew then had to sell it to fellow consortium members whose capital he had impulsively pledged without consulting them: it was no hard task. He had 'tremendous success' with *Robin Hood*: not an overseas market was left unsold. At a cost of around £45,000 an episode, it returned gross sales of £5.3m. Other series were not so dazzling: *Lancelot* did 'fairly well'; *The Buccaneers* was 'nothing exceptional, it only broke even'. Comparative failure quickly bred compensating concern for quality — that magic word. Or, to put it more bluntly, for 'production values', the top dressing which enhances substance, and sometimes is a substitute for substance.

By this time the domestic gold mine of ITV was producing turnover cash that encouraged spending on quality — and this in turn helped Lew make the discovery that, as trade had followed the flag, now the deal followed the show. Quality had a 'sell and come again' element built into it: he could go back to the same address and sell another quality show, often for a bigger fee. But certain guide lines had to be observed. The appeal of the show had to be clear cut. And those who executed it — for Lew had no interest in the step-by-step creative process — had to be reliable and predictable people. Lew played safe. Sometimes he played so safe that he possibly sacrificed opportunity to predictability. In 1959 a group of writers, who included Ray Galton, Alan Simpson, Frank Muir and Denis Norden, offered Lew's consortium their exclusive services for a £20,000 annual retainer — and were turned down. The name of the game was replication, not innovation.

By that same year Lew's original £1,250 investment in ITV was worth £275,000.

He and Leslie Grade got their second big break in 1962. The United States anti-trust laws had decreed that production interests must be separated from talent representation. In the ensuing divorce, Music Corporation of America, which owned Universal Pictures as well as being one of the biggest international talent agencies, opted to remain in production. As a result, two big British-based agencies, London Management and London Artists, 'bought' the top talents of the defunct MCA office in Mayfair: both agencies were controlled by the Grade Organization, with Lew Grade as chairman and Leslie Grade as managing director. Inevitably, they often found they were doing business with themselves. In such cases they prudently denied themselves the customary 10 per cent agency fee. But there was still a considerable safety factor built into the buying and selling arrangements: they could never be knowingly undersold, nor could they unwittingly pay over the odds.

The Grade Organization also acquired an interest in Harold Davison Ltd, an agency with strong American links through entertainers like Ella Fitzgerald, Frank Sinatra and Count Basie. The brothers were not so successful, however, in dealing with Brian Epstein when they belatedly recognized that the talent he controlled, namely The Beatles, Cilla Black and Gerry and the Pacemakers, was just what the affluent youth-culture of the early 1960s wanted: it was left to the third Grade, Bernard Delfont, to attempt to secure this link through the control he exercised over the London theatres where the Beatles and the other Epstein artists performed to sell-out audiences. Epstein's early death frustrated more formal links, though Lew Grade's future conglomerate empire did finish up owning many of the original Beatles compositions. Lew meanwhile was using ATV's growing financial might to extend the company's business interests, though there doesn't seem to have been any plan in it: it was by random accumulation as much as anything.

By 1964 ATV owned studios at Elstree where many TV specials and series were shot; a puppet film company; bowling alleys; half of Pye Records, the third biggest British disc company; three-quarters of a theatrical costumier's; two TV stations in Canada; a distribution company in Australia; and control of no fewer than twenty theatres in the West End of London. In March 1965, the Grade Organization acquired Bernard Delfont Management and Enterprise Ltd, and Bernard joined the board as deputy chairman. This gave all three Grades what the *Daily Express* called 'virtual control of live entertainment in England'; while over at ATV, Lew exercised huge patronage over screen entertainment.

If there were dangers in concentrating so much power in the hands of a troika of brothers — and clearly there were — they were ignored by the politicians, whose interests are always to have a contented and none too

vigilant electorate. Critics were further diverted by Lew's increasingly
well publicized progress as 'No. One Salesman' of British-created shows
and series to the major American networks. Patriotism marched in step
with profit; and the monopolistic tendencies of the Grade empire
competed rather poorly for attention in a decade when interest was
concentrated on novelty and sensation of rather more ephemeral kinds.
ATV had established a US-based subsidiary, Independent Television
Corporation, on Madison Avenue under the presidency of Abe Mandell.
(It also had, confusingly, a London-based subsidiary, ITC
Entertainment Ltd, responsible for the production of television shows
and feature films for sales in the Eastern hemisphere.)

Lew began making regular sales trips to the USA in 1964 and by the
end of the decade he was averaging six a year and had grossed sales of
$125m. (At this time, as ATV's chief executive, he was being paid
£40,090 a year.) On one such trip at the end of 1969, Lew carried, on
typed cards that fitted neatly into his jacket pocket, details of a dozen
TV film series, dramas and musical specials as well as the names of the
American executives to whom he hoped to sell them. ABC TV was often
the most receptive buyer; and Lew frequently made sure they had first
choice — he appreciated the commercial instinct of one of the executives
there, Martin Starger. Some of the shows he sold were not even made at
the time he did the deals for them. It didn't matter: what he was selling
was the concept. He never doubted that he could then go to the artists
concerned and extract the necessary 'Yes, My Lord' from their mouths
in return for popping something nourishing down their respective
gullets.

His clients never lacked confidence in him. If they did not know
exactly what they were buying, they simply 'bought the picture' in the
assurance that it would be made as Lew promised — and look like
quality. Like Lew himself they were busy men who could run their own
empires only by leaving the creative functions to subordinates operating
within very tight guide-lines. 'All my shows are great,' Lew once said.
'Some of them are bad. But all of them are great.' Obviously, there is
more than a semantic difference here: even if a show were 'bad', its
'great-ness' was what it was sold on and its 'quality' was what permitted
the seller to call again. What counted was *the relationship*. 'They know
me,' Grade was fond of saying.

In those three monosyllables reposed much of his power as salesman.
Probity and predictability will take one a long, long way in mass
entertainment. Lew received a Queen's Award for Industry in 1967;
and, in 1969, he was knighted. Honours are especially valued by Lew:
possibly because they are intangible, certainly because they confer
approval as well as dignity. The lapel of whatever jacket he has on never
lacks his Italian and/or Papal decorations.

Each trip he took to America prepared the way for the next.

Sometimes he didn't lay eyes on a show he wanted to sell to the Americans until it was actually being screened in their New York projection rooms. Midway through one Engelbert Humperdinck special in the ABC TV screening room, he heard the network chairman grunt with approval. 'Well,' said Lew confidently at the end, 'that shows no one can touch us in a programme of this type.' His clients did not argue. He had already got an order for a series from ABC TV: now he used the 'special' to get them to advance the starting date, which would mean an extra $2.5m. to ATV. Such advance selling meant that it was 'all in the cards', and he could shuffle these as he liked, inviting the networks to pick the cards they preferred and then go back home and put the winners into production. Why did such notoriously choosy people buy so readily in advance? Because they read the reflection of what they wanted in Lew Grade's eyes. It was an instinct they recognized.

Even the very first visit Lew paid to America after the war, in 1947, had taught him something valuable. He went there on a sixteen-day trip and after fifteen unproductive days he finally booked one of his acts into a New York theatre. The important thing, besides the prestige, was that he did not rely on any New York agent who would have charged him the 20 per cent fee then customary for facilitating Lew's business; and he was able to charge his client the going rate in Britain, which was ten per cent, and thus show an immediate profit. His later dealings with the Americans were for bigger prizes: but the same principle applied — America paid for the show before Lew Grade paid to make it.

No wonder enforced leisure for such a workaholic was more hurtful than no vacation at all for ordinary folk. 'If I go away', he once said, 'I'm okay for two days. Then I'm on the phone. After five days, I can't bloody well stand it. . . .'* A colleague recalls the occasion Lew was prevailed on to take a break. He went to Paris. There, he sat in his room eating English food and making constant telephone calls to his office. He swore afterwards that it had done him good and he intended doing it again.

'HELLO, CARLO . . . HELLO, SOPHIA'

Having the never-empty cash-register of ATV behind him, and the power to dip into it as and when he wanted to, without the bureaucratic delays of less personalized corporate bodies, Lew was well placed to take advantage of the change forced on the American TV networks at the end of the 1960s by the Federal Communications Commission. The media's self-regulatory body required them to schedule a half-hour of prime-time viewing for programmes made by local stations, affiliates *or independent producers*. The networks were then pulling in some $60,000 a minute for peak-time advertising. Lew Grade stepped in as an 'independent

*Lew Grade, interviewed by John Heilpern, *The Observer* magazine, 9 December 1973.

producer', offering them programmes made with American or
mid-Atlantic artists. So close was the identity of concept, to say nothing
of other interests, that the networks had really nothing to lose by
accepting the FCC's edict and, indeed, had much to gain considering the
relative savings that a Lew Grade production could effect in the
over-priced American-based shows for network TV.

Lew was always quick — at this time, anyhow — to take advantage of
such changes in the programme requirements of the US networks, and of
their audiences' tastes. He foresaw the advent of the high-budget
mini-series by observing that the one-off specials and the half-hour
segments were failing to push up ratings. As a result, he got his two
Biblical mini-series, *Moses the Lawgiver* (directed by Gianfranco de Bosio:
c. 1975) and *Jesus of Nazareth* (directed by Franco Zeffirelli: c. 1977), into
co-production with RAI at the most propitious moment for American
sales. And, of course, such subjects were international in content and
ecumenical in emphasis: they would have a very long shelf-life. Lew's
instincts for entertainment were also nicely attuned to the more
inspirational imperatives. The writers had wanted *Moses the Lawgiver* to
open with Burt Lancaster in the wilderness, heavily meditating. Lew
would have none of that. Open on the massacre of the First Born, he
commanded: his will was done.

As the Seventies opened, Lew felt pleased indeed with the way he was
managing ATV, and he had every right to be so. The Grades had sold
their agency interests to EMI in 1967 — picking up nearly £12m. in
stock — and Lew was now concentrating all his energies on television.
ATV's profits for 1971 were its biggest ever; and though copyright on
the Beatles songs, owned by the holding company, Associated
Communications Corporation, accounted for much of this, the overseas
sales of TV programmes — from *The Tom Jones Show* to *Hamlet* (with
Richard Chamberlain), and two new series, *The Persuaders* (with Roger
Moore and Tony Curtis), and *Shirley's World* — were worth £15m., or
twice as much as the other ITV stations combined. ATV was the largest
of the fifteen regional ITV stations and was originating 25 per cent of the
commercial network's nation-wide programming.

Yet Lew was aware of two uncomfortable factors not mentioned in the
annual report. One was his feeling that there were limits to the amount
of money that even successful TV shows could earn him. A principal
reason was that they could not be shown anywhere else except on
television. Though re-runs and syndication on the smaller local stations
and mini-networks brought in useful revenue, it wasn't spectacular
enough to give Lew a sense of sitting round the big boys' table dealing
with the high rollers: it was all small change.

Now feature films were different. They were where the real tycoons
operated. For although, in reality, the Hollywood revenues were
dimmed by the huge profits of the American TV networks, the motion

picture industry still had a dazzling glamour. It was the Hollywood-made blockbuster that made the headlines. In cash terms, too, it was practically an annuity investment, playing continuously around the world, renewable with the cinema-going generations, and incorporating the succulent potential of a TV deal as well as the here-and-now satisfaction of its cinema box-office.

Then, again, Lew Grade in 1971 was within five years of mandatory retirement. Under the ITA Act, he had to surrender his executive powers as ATV's boss upon reaching the age of seventy. Although as a major stockholder and the occupant of a power-base within the company, he could still flex considerable muscle as president, to Lew's way of thinking this was by no means the same as being boss of a corporate enterprise whose accountability so often depended on his word alone. He was in the same relation to power as the British Prime Minister was to the American President: if Lew said a thing would be done, he had the power to see his executives did it, whereas the heads of the American networks with whom he dealt, despite their vaster appurtenances of office and hugely superior salaries, were often dependent on diplomatic negotiations with the system of checks and balances within their corporate structures.

The British Press were constantly dubbing him 'Mr Show-business' or 'Emperor Lew', but he knew he held his imperial fief by virtue of the financial power he possessed through ATV. Perhaps it was time to create a different sort of empire, parallel to but distinct from ATV? He also had the example of his brother Bernard Delfont to intrigue him and, possibly, make him slightly envious of 'the fun' that Bernie was having. For, by 1971, the first crop of EMI films produced by Bryan Forbes for Lew's brother had begun to appear: generally with indifferent results. But Lew may have reflected that such films failed because they were cut to a pattern that was far too British, mid-brow and middle-class to appeal to the great American mass market that he knew so well. After all, hadn't he sold 'films' that were as good, as bad or as indifferent as any of the EMI ones to his American customers on the strength of their 'quality'?

Lew Grade must have already been feeling the pull of wider horizons when he signed up Shirley MacLaine in 1970. Her half-hour series was not very successful: it came at a time when the 30-minute segment was yielding to the 50-minute series: one of Lew's few failures to keep up with electronic changes. The movie that went along with the deal, *Desperate Characters*, opened in New York at the beginning of October 1971. 'Had (Lew Grade) been here last week', said *Time*, 'he could have attended the premiere.'* As it happened, he was not in New York: but his thoughts were definitely on the movies now. 'I'm only just starting,' he

---

**Time, 4 October 1971.

told *Time* in the same report, 'I'm going to make a fortune in the film business, and I mean a fortune.' Then he added, with an uncharacteristic lapse into understatement, 'Whenever I say *I*, of course, I mean the company.'

Thus began the extraordinary production programme of movies made for the cinema and TV which occupied more and more of Lew Grade's life and his corporate finances for the next ten years. This account necessarily omits a critical estimate of most of the 100-odd works produced under his auspices. For one thing, hardly any of them dealt even remotely with things British — even the ones technically registered as 'British' by reason of their labour costs — and any attempt to reflect a changing British society through Lew's choice and treatment of stories is as foolish as it would be fruitless. Lew Grade's policy was to make specifically non-national action films: any identity they acquired came from the stars whose compliance with the 'Yes, My Lord' imperative was frequently all that the majority of these films needed to give them their pre-sale attractiveness in the world markets.

Indeed, Lew did not at first need to be global in his strategy: 'I really only did pre-sales with the United States,' he says. In other words, an American TV network's agreement, often expressed in a verbal understanding between Lew in London and his good friends in New York, was a firm enough entity for the yet unmade movie to be put down as an asset on the balance sheet. The commitment to buy it at an agreed price meant that Lew could walk into his office at that impressively early hour and, once the phone lines got busy, walk out a few hours later some millions of dollars richer — I mean, of course, *the company* would be. His early budgets were in the $2m. region, which meant that he could almost cover the cost of production before he began the film. 'Stars' were what he literally banked on: a term he later expanded to connote 'writers' (i.e., best-sellers) and 'directors' (i.e., blockbuster-makers). This concept was based on his observation, he said, that such people had not achieved their status and rewards by accident, but by performance: and they were therefore worth their pay if they agreed to repeat the performance.

This view was somewhat modified by experience: but the notion of a 'pulling agent', a pre-sold picture and lots of superlatives remained a constant to the very end. Rarely, *very* rarely, was Lew persuaded to back the unpredictable — 'unpredictable' being defined in terms of not knowing with any certainty the entertainment value he had to sell before he saw it.

When interviewers later asked about his production programme, when it was in full eruption, spewing titles, projects and stars in all directions with volcanic enthusiasm, they were frequently baffled to hear him harping on words like 'responsibility', 'standards' and, of course, 'quality'. 'It was as if the profit motive didn't really exist', John Heilpern wrote, dazedly, after an interview (which admittedly had begun at the

extra-early hour of 6.00 a.m.) *. On appropriate occasions like this Lew
would even fume about Lord Thomson's candour about the 'licence to
print money'. But it simply exposed one of the truths behind the trader.
'Never mind the profit, feel the quality,' is what he is saying to the
customer. It is the old 'buying or selling' syndrome remodelled for this
season's interviewers. Such emphatically stressed altruism serves the
seller in a much more acceptable fashion than if he were to pull out his
wallet and count the takings there and then. Likewise, Lew's constant
vaunt that he was helping to save the British film industry is hard to
understand until one accepts that the profits accruing to his company,
and the availability of studio work on some of the films that were made
in England, are the bottom line of a rather high-flown boast — in any
case, it was a boast that plenty of newspapers were all to happy to go
along with until the empire foundered.

This is a media phenomenon that deserves a book to itself: it
throws in doubt the value of not only the popular show-business profile
on the feature pages, but the soberer responsibilities of the financial
pages whose writers, in the main, showed no understanding at all of the
bizarre nature of film production and the potentially ruinous impact if
all didn't go as they had been led to believe over the executive desk-top
or from behind the lunch-time menu. In Lew's case this benign,
unquestioning reaction embraced writers in the up-market Press as well
as razzmatazz columnists in the popular tabloids. It is worth dwelling
on, for it contributed more than anything else to the oasis of 'British
endeavour' that the British media persuaded themselves existed in the
waste land of British cinema in the mid-1970s.

The Guardian, on the one hand, hailed the link that Lew Grade
established with an American financier whose backing had the collateral
of ownership of cinemas in and around Boston as 'the most important
deal [in cash terms] ever announced by a British film-producing
company . . . Sir Lew sees this as a one-man mission to revive the British
film industry.'** Nor was the *Daily Express* behindhand in recognizing
crusaders: after all, it's own masthead incorporated the image of one.
Jean Rook, a columnist more experienced in human-interest stories than
in assessing profit and loss in the film industry, linked Lew with the
national heritage, rather than anything as transient as a company
balance-sheet, when, under the sub-editor's panting headline, 'Our
Eager Knight in Golden Armour', she wrote: 'They don't make them
like Lew Grade any more. Probably because they can't get the gold
plate. He's hall-marked successful, and British-made. His unscratchable
faith in this country's solid, gleaming economic future is unique. He
says, and actually means, Churchillian things like, "Britain is not dead

*John Heilpern, op.cit.,
**Rafiq Mughal, *The Guardian*, 23 October 1975.

or backward. We've done it before, and if we all put our backs and our energy into it, we'll do it again". . . . He does NOT believe that our rot has set in. He doubts that we even have woodworm, or anything that a good soak in enthusiasm won't cure. If they put Lew Grade up at Sotheby's, he'd fetch a fortune as a rare collector's piece. . . .' And so on, for columns.*

Citing such stuff is not intended to imply insincerity on Lew Grade's part: quite the opposite. It was the passion behind his conviction that was persuasive, particularly in contrast to other film-makers' contemporary pessimism. But his enthusiasm, however dutifully reported (or exaggerated), blinded many (perhaps himself, too) to the reality of what he was doing.

John Heilpern was one of the more sceptical early callers who actually heard Lew making a deal with a 'hot shot' in New York who couldn't sleep for worry and had put an early call through to London. He probably found it difficult to get through, since the phone kept ringing with earlier calls from European-based celebrities whose identity needed nothing more than Lew's exuberant utterance of their first names — 'Hello, Carlo . . . How is Sophia?' The New York caller was soon put at ease by means that might have made for acute anxiety if he had been someone not so susceptible to the peculiar 'highs' of a business in which the 'deal' is the anti-depressant. Lew had the right prescription for this insomniac. 'He mentioned three film stars, a brief outline of the script. "Beautiful locations, a touching story. Very simple. You'll *love* it." And within five minutes, the producer in New York had promised several million dollars to the film.' Intrigued, Heilpern demanded to know 'what would happen if I phoned the same producer and offered him a script the way you did? I would say it had beautiful locations and a simple story and I would be *rich*.' Lew swiftly disabused him. 'You know what would happen? I tell you. No one would take any notice.'**

He was right, too. What he sold was not only credibility—the confidence that he could deliver the goods as specified. (How they performed was another matter, as each party recognized.) But he did so with the massive commercial reality of ATV behind him. He was using a TV-based corporation in the same way as a Hollywood studio used its production record. The potential investor was being persuaded, at one and the same moment, that he was dealing with a man whose verbal assurances were worth more than the paper they might have been written on — to correct Sam Goldwyn — and with a commercially viable organization which would be able to follow through on those promises and get the product made. It was a 'credit structure' no other film group in Britain could match; for its connections with the money-printing licence that television still represented made it

*Jean Rook, *Daily Express*, 12 December 1975.
**John Heilpern, op.cit.

independent of fickle cinema box-offices — Lew owned no cinemas at this time in Britain or elsewhere. It should be emphasized that Lew's access to finance could afford to make him independent of ATV: but it was the enormous success he had made of the latter that gave him such a good credit rating and extended it to the movies made by his separate companies, at first anyhow.

Just as Lew Grade prided himself on having 'the ordinary man's tastes', he had no blushes about sharing the ordinary man's prejudices: and this, in turn, dictated the kinds of films he backed. For instance, no 'bad language' was permitted in them in the early years. This, too, derived from his commitment to TV programmes which entered the 'sanctity of the home'. There were few exceptions. In one instance involving a programme where a broadminded mother conceded that she had tried unsuccessfully to get her child to refer straightforwardly to a 'cunt', whereas the child persisted in calling it a 'tunc', Lew had the mother's word bleeped out, but permitted her offspring's to remain on childish and thus innocent lips.

One can therefore imagine his embarrassment that ATV should have produced a documentary on Andy Warhol, shot by David Bailey, that went considerably further than mother, daughter or Lew might have thought decent or fit. (The Factual Programme Department responsible for it had been set up expressly to counter charges that Lew was interested only in light entertainment.) The film was centred on Warhol's New York 'Factory', but included clips from his films *Bike Boy* and *Trash*. It was due for networking in January 1973, under an IBA rule which forbade ITV stations to opt out of taking the documentary-slot programme, when the journalist and moralist Ross McWhirter read about it in the *Daily Express* (which, it transpired, had not actually seen it). He appealed to the IBA (which had not seen the film either) and accused it of failing in its duty to preview anything in programmes that might offend against good taste and decency. He was granted a fourteen-day Court injunction; after which time the Court of Appeal had second thoughts, editorial judgment was restored to the IBA, and Lew's programme went out. A survey later showed that of the 14 million viewers who started out watching the programme, only half stayed the course and only three per cent thought it obscene — 72 per cent found it actively boring. All of which may have reinforced Lew's belief in sharing the ordinary man's taste: but he made it plain that, where *films* were concerned, he was the first, the final and the only court of appeal.

If Lew sowed any wild oats of his own, it was probably due to his not reading the words on the seed packet properly. It was, for example, a surprise to see him associated with another of those very early films starring Shirley MacLaine, whose subject was so outlandish, so unlikely a one for him, that all he could bring himself to say about *The Possession of Joel Delaney* (1971) some thirteen years later was that it was 'before its time'. It was indeed: its time came with *The Exorcist*, two years later, a film that raided the lucrative store of public fears involving folk devils and people's possession by demons. Directed by Waris Hussein, it tapped a more specific political fear associated with Cuban hostility and maybe even Hispanic immigrants, since MacLaine's young (white) brother in the movie is possessed by the spirit of a Puerto Rican vowing vengeance on American society. In word and deed it was an extremely violent film. Lew left its distribution in Britain to a small independent company and he is not on record as having anything to do with its promotion.

His relationship with Shirley MacLaine had cooled, for reasons she sets forth adequately in one of her early series of memoirs; and in the 1972–3 period he switched his attentions to Julie Andrews, whom he wanted for a TV special and maybe a series too. In the event he got more than her services. Through Julie Andrews and her husband, Blake Edwards, Lew really got into big-time film-making.

FAIL-SAFE FILM-MAKING

Part of Lew Grade's deal with Julie Andrews involved the financing of two films starring her to be directed by Blake Edwards. The first was a love-story, *The Tamarind Seed* (27 August 1974), a romantic tangle of loyalties whose protracted unravelling enabled Julie Andrews, as the widowed (i.e., experienced), ex-mistress (i.e., desirable) of the British air attaché in Paris and currently working as a secretary at the Home Office where she is dressed by Dior (i.e., fashionable), to sleep fleetingly with Omar Sharif, as the Russian KGB man in the next chalet during her West Indies vacation. Whitehall is abuzz and the Kremlin aflame — which lover will recruit the other as a spy? 'We looked to do quite well out of it,' says Lord Grade, 'but I was not pushing Blake to make the second film: we had no suitable subject for Julie. Blake was insistent, however: I think he felt it would start people talking–about "areas of conflict", the usual thing–if he didn't do the second film. So I said, on an inspiration, "You own the Pink Panther idea, don't you? Well, why not make a sequel with Peter Sellers?" After all, the original *Pink Panther*, in 1964, was one of the big grossers and it was still taking money at the box-office. A sequel with Alan Arkin called *A Shot in the Dark* hadn't done anything like the business — it needed Peter. "You won't get Sellers," Blake said. I knew he and Peter had had their differences. "You leave that to me," I said. "If I get him, will you make the picture?" He said he would. I had Peter up to my office and a couple of hours later we had a deal. It was my hope and intention that this film would lead to a *Pink Panther* series on TV, which I thought would be *tremendous*. Then I discovered Blake owned only half the concept: United Artists owned the

Images of Britain: Lindsay Anderson, in *O Lucky Man!* in 1973 took a caustic overview of public and private corruption, with Malcolm McDowell (above, left), the hero of *If . . .*, exposed to it at every level including a brief stint at the top; in *Britannia Hospital*, 1982 (below), Anderson's savage farce about a nation having a nervous breakdown, McDowell finished up (pro tem) being 'adapted' to the demands of the brave new world. In *Chariots of Fire*, 1981 (above, right), Ben Cross and Nigel Havers in a college heat. To a world barely fit for joggers, the David Puttnam production set an inspiring example of British doggedness.

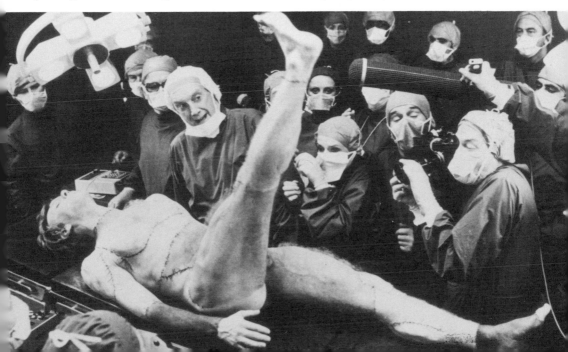

From 'left-outers' to 'no-hopers': *Bronco Bullfrog*, 1970 (above), provided one of
the earliest maps of the adolescent wasteland stretching from 'nothing to do' to
'nowhere to go' — Del Walker, Anne Gooding and Sam Shepherd share their
despondency. By *Scum*, in 1979 (below, right), the tide of youth unemployment
had risen and so had individual mutiny: Ray Winstone, bully-boy in a Borstal,
takes the measure of Mick Ford's articulate rebel fighting the rule book with
bare feet. In *Rude Boy*, 1980 (below, left), the dead-loss, dead-end face of
workless youth, represented by Ray Gange, took to the streets in anarchic
protest.

Apocalypse now: Black Britain (Brian
Bovell, David H. Haynes) was projected
as a threatening racial underclass in
Babylon, 1980 (above), banned to
everyone under 18, black or white, lest
they emerged 'confused and troubled'.
Establishment fears were also reflected in
Jubilee, 1978 (below), Derek Jarman's
masque of tribal Brits, punkish, alienated
and violent.

Rival Bonds: The longest-running
Sixties fantasy continued throughout
the Seventies and Eighties. In 1983
both Bonds appeared in separate, but
profitable, pictures: Sean Connery,
using unaccustomed horsepower, in
Never Say Never Again (above);
and Roger Moore, momentarily
indisposed, in *Octopussy* (below).

other half. I called Arthur Krim of UA and said, "Arthur, if I produce this film, will you distribute it?" Arthur was *terrifically* enthusiastic — of course they were delighted someone had brought Blake and Peter together, something they'd failed to do in ten years. We made *The Return of the Pink Panther* (8 January 1976). And it was *a hit!* An *immense* hit!'

The movie grossed $12m., of which half was Lew's. It reconciled him to the fact that the TV series would never come about: requiring the highly fissionable Sellers to commit himself to twenty-six weeks work was one reason: another was Sellers' impatience, now that Inspector Clouseau had reburnished his dulled career, to be off to America and replenish his bank balance. The follow-up to the *Return*, entitled *The Pink Panther Strikes Again*, was produced by United Artists and did so well that Lew's relatively small percentage interest netted him some more useful millions. It was a brave man who would have told him then that there was no money in movies.

His confidence was expensively displayed in a way that was soon to become ritualistic (and ultimately routine): he laid on a junket for 250 of the world's Press, invited to celebrate the *Return* in Gstaad (scene of the film, home of Blake Edwards). There were Pink Panther (pink) champagne, Pink Panther T-shirts, Pink Panther bunting in the sheets, Pink Panther hostesses, and a Pink Panther diamond worth £1,000 for the first journalist to crack the riddle to its whereabouts in the fortune cookie. 'The most famous lovers since Dante and Beatrice', Richard Burton and Elizabeth Taylor, in other words, came over from their neighbourhood chalet and dropped in: but not even they could upstage Lew.

As one of the guests wrote: 'Sucking a cigar the size of a young spruce, he delivered the message. He had, he said, given his audition as a film producer and he had passed. *The Return of the Pink Panther*, as we could all see, was a great movie. A record-breaking movie. . . At nineteen, he, Sir Lew, had been World Charleston Dancing Champion. Now he was going to be the world champion film producer. Not just major films, but major British films, and more major films than any other production company in the world was making. . . He had enough money — he, Sir Lew, personally had more money than he needed — he had enough to produce twenty major pictures a year. He would start with ten and they would have minimum budgets of five million dollars each. There would be no ceiling: the budget would ultimately be determined by the cost of the stars and the directors. Stars and directors spelled financial, artistic and critical success and that is what Sir Lew was gambling on. Yes, he was a gambler: he liked to gamble on certainties. This was what the Press had come to hear.'*

Meanwhile, he had financed — and pre-sold in America — *Farewell,*

---

*Michael McNay, *The Guardian*, 15 September 1975.

My Lovely and *Russian Roulette*. The former was a remake of the Chandler novel, directed by Dick Richards; the second an assassination thriller starring George Segal: both were produced by Elliott Kastner. The former did well; the second, poorly — though as its budget had been well contained, its pre-sale to TV ensured the loss was covered.

In April 1975 the New York chapter of the Television Academy held a 'Salute to Sir Lew Grade' at the Hilton Hotel, attended by the heads or high executives of all three American networks, as well as Lauren Bacall, Shirley MacLaine, Goldie Hawn and William Conrad. But the heart of the show, which *Variety* reported as being made possible by the guest of honour's generosity, was the Grade talent-roster: John Lennon, Peter Sellers, Dave Allen (who hosted it) and Tom Jones and Julie Andrews (who did a duet, despite Jones's voice giving out: an event not evident in the edited transmission soon afterwards). One whose voice did not fade was Earl Mountbatten of Burma who addressed the guests for fifteen minutes — again, 'remedied' in the edited version — and then introduced Lew who proved himself the hit of the night by doing — what else? — a brisk Charleston. After all, he had plenty to make him dance.

A month later, he hosted the first of his annual luncheons for international exhibitors-distributors during the Cannes Festival, sprinkling the guest-list with valued members of the American media, reserving the top table right and left of himself for producers like Elliott Kastner (*Farewell, My Lovely, Russian Roulette, Dogpound Shuffle*), Robert Fryer (*Great Expectations, The Voyage of the Damned*) and Jules Buck (*Man Friday*). He announced he was embarking on at least twelve movies, among them a Stanley and Livingstone story to be directed by John Boorman, a Frederick Forsyth screen-play and remakes of *The Scarlet Pimpernel, The Prisoner of Zenda* and *Les Misérables*. The year before, in order to increase Lew's knowledge of distribution, ATV's holding company, Associated Communications Corporation, had absorbed World Film Services, a financial services group run by John Heyman, who had been a close associate of Joseph Losey and the Burtons and had helped get some of their films set up in the Sixties. Heyman's aide, Ian Jessel, now joined Lew's ITC group. Lew 'worked' America himself, relying on Abe Mandell and Martin Starger to pump film projects at him. Jessel concentrated on markets outside America, notably in Japan and Latin America, which had been hitherto considered 'difficult' for British films: not that Lew's were much hampered by this national handicap.

But it is worth noting that the international success of *Murder on the Orient Express*, produced in 1973 by Nat Cohen for EMI, had already overcome some of the market's resistance to non-American, English-language movies round about the time Ian Jessel went to work for Lew. The welcome mat was on the doorstep. Later on, Jessel would experience considerable frustration trying to sell his boss on more 'sophisticated' entertainment in an effort to keep Lew in step with changing world tastes.

The result of this proliferating acquisition of power and projects was that Lew found himself very quickly locked into a bewildering variety of deals which would have taxed the brain of a master cracksman to keep track of the combinations. Some of his productions went straight to a major American distributor; others were sold territory by territory by Ian Jessel; still others were contracted to be shown first (and only) on American television and then sold outside America by Lew's own companies. In no circumstances, Lew announced, would he use tax-shelter money. When ATV published its 1975 balance sheet, it revealed that net bank borrowings had increased by over £9m. to £12,270,000 at 31 March 1975, mostly to finance films for theatrical release. Lew stressed that the benefit for film investment should not be impatiently awaited — not before the second year, he said. On the other hand, the 'earning lifetime both at home and abroad of a successful film is invariably long'.

Continuing, the report stated that Lew felt 'that the days of speculative film-making are over. It is on the firm basis of pre-arranged distribution that the company's production are undertaken and all monies expended now are an investment for the future.'* Few other film executives in Britain would have risked saying this about their current projects. But Lew was on top of the world, or at least of Broadway, for no fewer than three of his films were showing there: *The Return of the Pink Panther*, *Farewell, My Lovely* and *Russian Roulette*. The first two, according to *Variety*'s no-frills analysis, were 'big Broadway bangs in the gross charts'.** He was now said to be devoting 80 per cent of his time to feature film-making. Luck was certainly disproportionately on his side: usually the odds in favour of films succeeding at the box-office is one in seven — yet here was Lew Grade with one spectacular hit and another very satisfactory 'earner' in his first three features!

Such success must indeed have been heady to a man already convinced of the rightness of his instincts and the soundness of his financial strategy. Had his initial features been resounding flops, or made little immediate impact that could be exploited, he might well have pulled back. He did not: for all the signs beckoned him on into ever wider financial commitments. He was then just a year away from mandatory retirement as chairman and chief executive of ATV: but he had his film empire well established at ACC. He had had a long, successful run in television: why should he not look forward to going the distance and doing even bigger deals on the main track with the confidence that if he cleared the way in advance, there was no reason why he should stumble? Fail-safe film-making at last! Only one niggling

Financial Times, 13 August 1975.
**Variety*, 10 September 1975.

doubt had apparently insinuated itself into the middle of his excitement at the prospects ahead. 'My brother Bernard says I'm mad to make films,' he told Jean Rook; then, as if he had done his sibling duty by reporting this strain of eccentricity in the Grade family, he added, 'But it works. Anything will work, if you throw yourself into it heart and soul.'*

*Jean Rook, op.cit.

CHAPTER FIVE

Men of Property

I think the British cinema rather correctly mirrors a nation that has ceased to believe in itself, is confused and fatigued, divided and without imagination. In fact, it mirrors a nation in the middle of a nervous breakdown. . . . Our films have currently regressed to either bourgeois mannerism, nursery infantilism and rather degenerate music-hall tradition.
— Lindsay Anderson, Cinema TV Today, *19 October 1974.*

The fifty-fifth (and last) chapter of Bryan Forbes's memoirs, published in 1974 under the title of *Notes for a Life,* begins: 'I sat on the beach and watched a deformed dog urinate on yesterday's sandcastles. The dog graphically illustrated my feelings at that moment. It was Easter 1971 and I had just been relieved of all further responsibility as head of production for EMI-MGM studios at Elstree, a position I had held for two years.'* Interested parties (and their lawyers) read avidly on . . . only to be disappointed. Some day, the diaries kept by Forbes during his Elstree tenure may 'tell all', satisfying the curiosity of friends and enemies alike, for, as he said: 'I have no intention of depriving the former of necessary pleasures or the latter of summary justice.' In 1974, however, the time was 'not ripe' — at least, not prudent.

But the embittered ex-production chief's remarks were a pressure gauge of his sense of injustice. 'At first they think you can walk on water,' he said to friends soon after his resignation; 'after a few weeks they say you can't even swim.' He later added: 'I expected to walk over a battlefield when I took over Elstree, but I didn't expect Hiroshima.' After leaving his £40,000 a year job, with one year left on his contract, Forbes turned to his other considerable skills to nurse himself back to activity. He finished a novel about the film business, *The Distant Laughter*; plus his (pro tem) memoirs, and two television documentaries (on Edith

*Bryan Forbes, *Notes for a Life* (Collins, 1974), p. 373.

Evans and Elton John); then, in 1974, went to America to direct *The Stepford Wives*.

In his two-and-a-half years at Elstree, he had produced eleven films on a revolving fund of £4m., which, as he acknowledged, 'was not tiny, *if it had revolved*'.* It did not do so, and therefore, in his judgment, could not possibly start to pay off. He paid tribute to Bernard Delfont's 'act of courage' in appointing him, but allowed himself the luxury of anticipating the vintage memoirs that weren't yet ready to be decanted by observing, 'Perhaps in retrospect I wished Bernard Delfont had had the courage of my convictions more often.' To critics (inside as well as outside Elstree) who had said he enjoyed too much power, he protested that he had not had enough: he meant the fact that some of the films he produced were turned down, or left idling while bank interest totted up, by EMI's own distribution and exhibition divisions.

A true accounting of how well or badly Forbes's Elstree films did at the box-office is not available. Frequent reissues of some of them, including the two most successful, *The Railway Children* and *The Tales of Beatrix Potter*, suggest that these at least did well and are probably now in profit. Many of the rest have been written off, according to one EMI executive: therefore any monies accruing are irrelevant.

With Forbes gone, Nat Cohen, head of EMI's wholly owned subsidiary Anglo-EMI, became responsible for the group's entire film production. Cohen neither benefited from nor regretted the other film-maker's departure: it was simply 'business as usual' for this shrewd and equable-tempered man, then in his mid-sixties. 'Right from the start of Bryan Forbes joining the company, there was a sharp distinction between his films and mine,' he says, thirteen years later. 'If Bryan had a cocktail party to announce his programme, then I had a cocktail party a few weeks later for mine, too. I had all I needed to keep me at full strength.'** This 'cautious, very cautious gambler', as he described himself, who made every decision on his own, 'with no committees, no directors, no boards' to delay a quick 'Yes' or (even quicker) 'No', had generally had more success than Forbes with films that were either very safe bets indeed — like the £100,000 invested in a cinema spin-off of the BBC TV series, *Steptoe and Son*, which eventually made a profit of six times that figure; or *On the Buses*, likewise a TV spin-off, which cost £90,000 and made over a million pounds; or else, as has been mentioned, into films with box-office ingredients which Forbes, who pointedly eschewed explicit sex and violence, avoided in his own production roster. Most did well, though perhaps rather more had been expected of a comedy like *Percy*, about the world's first penis transplant: maybe it was not hard-nosed enough. Cohen was at pains to stress that *The*

**Cinema TV Today, 17 May 1975.
**Nat Cohen, interviewed by the author, 13 September 1984. Unless stated otherwise, all subsequent quotations from Cohen come from the same source.*

Go-Between, the Joseph Losey-directed film which won the Palme d'or at Cannes in 1973, had been put together by John Heyman's World Film Services and was part of *his* (Cohen's) production programme, not Forbes's. In general, he got the 'mix' right — and was soon to have a success whose size even his conservative disposition would not have dared calculate.

In March 1971 EMI-MGM productions had been formed to co-finance movies on bigger budgets than either company cared to underwrite alone: *The Boy Friend, Trilby and Svengali* and *Trader Horn* were announced, though only the first got made; the others foundered in MGM's temporary period of withdrawal from 'risk' financing at home and abroad. United States investment in British films amounted to only £17.5m. in 1970, as against £31.2m. the previous year. The down-turn became a crisis in 1971 when it fell to £8.3m.

At this time, too, EMI's profits crashed as a result of the conglomerate's huge US losses. They fell to £5,427,000 after tax for the year ending June 1971, compared with the previous year's £10,515,000. The only heartening aspect was that profits from the exhibition of films in EMI's circuit of ABC cinemas rose to £4,156,000 (compared with £3,875,000) and this in a year when admissions generally were down seven per cent. It showed that smaller audiences could produce a healthy cash flow even if the ticket prices were raised: maybe a short-lived boon, but one that the beleaguered industry grasped. EMI announced a £1.5m. cinema expansion programme at the start of 1972, multiplying the number of outlets for the films it distributed by dividing old cinemas into 'multiples' of three or even four screens. (Ultimately, this policy had the effect of cheapening the pleasures of cinema-going in ways that were unrelated to the price of the tickets: some screens seemed to produce an experience no better in colour, sound or size than the TV screens with which the film-goers were far more familiar in their own homes.)

British Lion's net profits were also falling horrendously in the 1970–1 period; the Government was announcing its intention to withdraw from the financing of films and leave it to private enterprise, if it wished, to take the risks that the State found it unacceptable to underwrite; and only the Rank Organization was making satisfactory profits, though much of these were due to its investment in Xerox copiers.

Nat Cohen therefore found himself the main source of investment hope for film-makers — a fact he deplored. 'I don't really enjoy my power — I need competition,' he said.* In fact, competition was on the way, though travelling slowly, and moving perhaps closer to Nat Cohen than he may later have found comfortable.

---

*Nat Cohen, interviewed by Tim Murari, *The Guardian*, 17 November 1973.

THE FARMER'S BOY

There can be very few photographs of Barry Spikings that don't show him with the sort of wide and pleasant grin that a country boy might wear at a Young Farmers' dance. Not surprising, really: for Spikings, born in 1939, is the son of a Lincolnshire farm manager. He remembers being taken to Westerns starring Gene Autry or Roy Rogers when he wasn't much older than two: even in those first movies, fresh air was part of his world. And the feeling that he was counting the milk yield, rather than the movie grosses, later became difficult to separate from the open-countenanced individual who, for a time, was to become one of the most influential men in the biggest of Britain's film-making corporations.

Spikings's career had provided early evidence of a wish to make things more entertaining for the largest number of people. At first these were the 5,000-odd readers of the *Seaford Standard*, a local weekly on which he had found employment after leaving school at sixteen. His talent was obvious in the deft way he later described his handling of a story which appeared as 'Percy the Perambulating Pig'. Instead of a straight reporting job, young Spikings gave this Wodehouse-like news item a whimsical twist which caught his employer's eye and led to his outdistancing the rest of the staff of two to become the paper's editor.

His ambitions stimulated, he shortly approached Fleet Street, where the term 'editor' carried more weight in those days, when there were fewer of them; but, it is said, was deflected from the very portals of the *Sunday Express* by a friend on the *Farmers Weekly*, which he subsequently joined. The paper sent him to France to report on the impact that Britain's entry into the Common Market in 1973 was having on four million French farmers. His communiques won him a Press award and he showed his nascent talent for deal-making at the prize-giving luncheon by being offered (and accepting) a TV series on farming even before the coffee stage was reached. He caught the eye of Cecil King, then chairman of the International Publishing Corporation, which owned the *Farmers Weekly*: he wondered what a junior employee was doing on TV. Suitably impressed, he transferred Spikings to a job in what was called, with enticing vagueness, the 'New Enterprises Division' of IPC. Maybe the boyhood longing to be at home on the range with Gene Autry encouraged Spikings to suggest that films, or the 'amusement business', as it was then known, would be a suitable 'new enterprise'. He rang up a friend in films to help him put together a proposal. That friend was Michael Deeley.

'I was general manager for Woodfall Films in the early Sixties', says Michael Deeley. 'After *Tom Jones*, relationships were corrupted by success that had come too quickly. After another money-making film, *The Knack*, I felt it was time to go. I left on good terms with Tony

Richardson, but I quit on the first day's shooting of *The Charge of the Light Brigade,* having fulfilled the obligation to see the film set up. I got together with Stanley Baker; we formed a company, Oakhurst, and went into film production, profiting from the Americans' "discovery" that they could make small-budget films in Europe and needn't bankrupt themselves with inflated budgets in Hollywood. We made one film (*Robbery*) for Embassy; and, eventually, five more for Paramount (*The Italian Job* was the best) before the Americans cut back. I took a year off in 1968, to think things out: it was then Barry Spikings called me and asked me to join him. Barry was busy learning. He'd been to Hollywood, which he discovered he liked very much. The funds we were to have at IPC were about £10m., quite a lot in those days. I was in the running for the post of chief executive officer and, at the interview, I made out a case for starting up a new British production programme to fill the gap left by the Americans who were then pulling out. But between the interview and the board meeting, IPC's interest suddenly cooled. Why exactly, I don't know. Perhaps Cecil King felt such a programme constituted a threat to his "money leadership" — who knows? Anyhow, the "new project" was dropped. It was the end of my prospects and of Barry's enthusiasm: neither of us saw a future with IPC.'*

Deeley left for South America to make *Murphy's War* with Peter Yates. Spikings was offered a short-term job with Constellation, an investment group with film industry connections run by Ian Gordon, a future partner of David Frost: its lustre was to be considerably dimmed by tax changes introduced by the Labour Government in the mid-1970s. Deeley confesses that at this time 'I was disenchanted with films and really wanted to find another profitable area of activity. The turn of the decade was a very depressing time for film-makers, don't forget. I wondered if the property boom didn't have the answer.'

The late Sixties-early Seventies were still the 'go-go' times for thrusting young (and not so young) entrepreneurs in the property business who had luck and financial muscle on their side. Deeley and Baker had established their offices in a new block known as Alembic House, at 93 Albert Embankment, overlooking the Thames. According to later reports, the then landlords wanted the premises and offered the two a high price to quit: instead, the tenants decided to buy the landlords out. With property values soaring, the building soon gave them a very satisfactory feeling of security that appealed particularly to Stanley Baker, a man who liked holding on to something solid. Soon, Barry Spikings became a partner. 'Stanley did not exactly warm to Barry', says Deeley, 'but said to me, "It's up to you". It struck us that the Pop music business as well as the property market was impervious to crisis, so we formed Great Western Enterprises' — another partner was

---

*Michael Deeley, interviewed by the author, 19 September 1984. Unless stated otherwise, all subsequent quotations from Deeley come from this source.

Lord Harlech, Baker's fellow Welshman, head of Harlech TV and president of the British Board of Film Censors — 'and eventually it spawned "Great Western this-and-that" for any area that seemed to have profit in it. The most active entertainment area at that time (the early 1970s) was Pop concerts: so that is what we did.'

Deeley and Spikings got on well together, though they looked opposites. Deeley was some seven years the elder. In contrast to the junior partner, he didn't look as if butter wouldn't melt in his mouth. He looked like his older associate, Stanley Baker: he looked tough, like a handsome boxer who could land a good right-and-left (and probably had taken a few in his time). When together, he and Spikings reminded people of the 'hard' and 'soft' interrogators traditionally believed to be used by espionage services to wear down a suspect traitor by respectively uttering threats or extending sympathy: a technique that film studios also liked to use on the recalcitrant.

Great Western had the distinction of staging the concert side of 'Fanfare for Europe', which marked Britain's membership of the Common Market on New Year's Day 1973. *The Observer*'s colour magazine ran a cover story in which Barry Spikings was featured prominently. It was stated that the aim of these major assemblies of youth was 'caring for ourselves in conjunction with the environment'. This laudable purpose, which went so well with the 'lovely look' observable in the eyes of so many of the young environmentalists who actually were zonked out of their skulls on marijuana, did not outlast the rapid disintegration of the Pop concert scene over the next eighteen months. 'One of the festivals we were organizing', says Deeley, 'was at Lincoln: it had thirty-eight bands. As things turned out, God agreed with the objections of the middle classes who'd had us in court before the first note sounded to promise there'd be no "aggravation". We had to have 200 police and four helicopters and it rained solidly. In spite of 42,000 kids turning up, we lost £200,000 — and that was the end of that.'

Other doors opened. 'At this time, we caught "public company fever". We could see entrepreneurs making millions daily and we asked ourself, "How on earth do they do it?" Barry had been a journalist and knew how to go round all the right people asking questions. He returned with the answers. Our building, 93 The Embankment, was the way. We were going to turn bricks and mortar into paper profits. Stanley Baker didn't like the sound of it at all: after all, he reasoned, if you had a building, you owned something. If you had paper, you might finish up only owning paper. As it turned out, of course, he was dead right. But at the time, as it was explained to us, it sounded most attractive. If you had assets like our building, the thing to do was "gear them up", see them increase in value, and go on improving them until you could realize them. But in order to go public, you had to have shares. Under the then law, you couldn't buy a building and sell it at once without attracting a punitive tax. But you could convert it into paper shares and then dispose of them. Through a friend of Barry's whom he had met at Constellation, and who was now finance director at a company called Barclay Securities, we met John Bentley.'

THE FAST TYCOON

John Bentley, then aged thirty-two, was a tall, handsome Englishman, who had left Harrow at seventeen: he had the physique of a cricket captain and, it was said, the qualifications of a 'debs' delight. At this time, in 1973, he was one of the best known exponents of a technique described as the ability to 'spot an asset situation, move in on it, case some of the assets and use the profit to bankroll the next deal . . . a mode of operation relatively new to staid British business'.* John Bentley, as in all the other things he did, was very quick at learning. After a £5-a-week job as a stockbrokers' messenger boy and a spell in Australia, where his impulsive nature sometimes ran ahead of his boss's decisions, he had returned to Britain, set up as a financial analyst and was congratulating himself on modest coups until he brought a tip to Jim Slater, oracle of the stock market and a man whose tough and sentiment-free style of capitalism was associated with the New Toryism of Edward Heath. Bentley brought Slater news about an undervalued Scottish insurance company capitalized at £3.5m., but with hidden assets near £100m. In fact, their take-over bid was frustrated and they had to content themselves with merely 100 per cent profit: but the tutelage that a grateful Slater gave Bentley enabled *him* to take over a South Coast pharmaceutical company, Barclay and Son, for £300,000 and then to absorb other companies, big and small, at a rate of one every six weeks.

In a very candid conversation with Hunter Davies at this time, Bentley put up an attractive argument for such activity. 'I make the very best use of a firm's reserves when I take it over . . . the day of sinecures is over . . . shareholders are thrilled. What I'm trying to do is get a return for every piece of plant, every pound spent, every person employed.' He claimed it was 'as simple as turning off the electric light before you go to bed'. **

It is not surprising that such a man spotted the opportunity which British Lion Films then represented. The Government had made it all the easier to see by its refusal to come to terms with the British film industry's future, particularly as this involved Shepperton Studios. As long as Shepperton had been able to break even — and it had done so in

Fortune magazine, June 1973.
**John Bentley, interviewed by Hunter Davies, *The Observer* magazine, 4 February 1973.

the boom years of the Sixties — then its owners in British Lion were prepared to accept it as a vital part of the company's film-making activities, even if an unprofitable one. The owners were Lord Goodman (chairman), Mark Chapman-Walker (managing director), John and Roy Boulting and Frank Launder and Sidney Gilliat.

But by 1969 Shepperton was incurring escalating losses, running at £12,000 a week by the start of 1972. Although the studio's turn-over for the year ending in March 1972 was £891,000, slightly up on the previous year's £847,000, an actual loss of £84,700 was sustained. British Lion's loss for the same period was £1,064,638 compared with a profit of £199,886 the previous year. There was a clear risk of the parent company's being put in jeopardy by its studio facility.

In this increasingly anxious situation, British Lion had entertained a bid from the owners of a group of cinemas and Bingo halls. In what was intended to be a reverse take-over, the Star group had offered £9.5m. Star's owners were quoted as saying (separately or in chorus it is not clear): 'In some ways . . . the cinema industry is showing a lack of responsibility.' The bid was still lying on the table, however, by April 1972: the Star group comprised about sixty companies, many of them very small, most of them in the provinces. The group itself had no film production experience and appeared to be having difficulty in giving its bid credibility. As the weeks passed, British Lion was facing in financial terms what John Boulting called 'a runaway studio situation'.

But John Bentley stepped in with a counter-bid of £5.45m., much less than Star's but, in the circumstances, more credible. It represented two Barclay Securities shares for every seven of British Lion. Bentley was quite frank about his interest: it lay not at all in film-making, but in property and advertising. His eye was on the British Lion subsidiaries, Pearl and Dean, which had an exclusive contract with EMI's chain of ABC cinemas to provide screen advertising for their movies until the year 1987, and on Mills and Allen, which owned prime-site poster hoardings. These were worth £1m. in the books: but with Bentley's expertise, and perhaps a merger with Dorlands — an advertising agency he had acquired for £2.2m. — they might be worth £5m.

Then again there were Shepperton Studios' 60 acres. If they were reduced to 20 acres — which would be sufficient to service the film-makers who, anyhow, were hardly standing in line to use the studios — it would leave 40 of the richest acres of development land in the Home Counties to be sold off, provided the local authority and the National Film Finance Corporation (which had one controlling preference share) were agreeable to the deal. Many an entrepreneur has gambled on less. For the NFFC to nod approval, it would be necessary to show that Shepperton was running 'at a material loss' and 'cannot be sustained as a commercially viable concern'. This looked increasingly the case. The buyer could also expect tax benefits from the losses which

British Lion had sustained as long ago as the 1940s and early 1950s. There was an additional £1m. of British Lion property in Central London — and a library of old films worth a conservative £3m. Indeed it did all seem 'as simple as turning off the electric light before you go to bed'.

Of course there was an immediate outcry from 'the film industry', traditionally reacting to someone who was cheeky enough to make their loss into his own profit. Allegations that 'public money' was involved quickly followed. But the British Lion directors were not sympathetic to this notion. Within twenty-four hours of Bentley's bid, they had committed 52.3 per cent of their shares to him. 'The film industry shouldn't be crying "rape" — not before John Bentley has even had time to unbutton his trousers,' said John Boulting characteristically. More helpfully, Boulting wrote a letter to *Cinema TV Today* in which he set out his personal opinion that the restrictions on the studio's sale had been proposed by the private consortium which had purchased British Lion in 1964: this being so, the financial benefits from any sale of land, referred euphemistically to as 'betterment value', should not go to either the Government or the NFFC. Neither, he wrote, could persist in 'any legitimate claim to any financial benefits which might in the future accrue to private finance which, nearly nine years ago, took over a burden from which the NFFC and the Government patently wished to be relieved.'*

This, therefore, was the situation when Deeley, Spikings and Baker showed their interest in doing a deal with Barclay Securities. John Bentley had acquired British Lion Holdings, later called Lion International, a 'shell company' for British Lion, Shepperton Studios, Pearl and Dean and Mills and Allen. 'Lion International attracted us', says Deeley, 'because it was a public company and we had a substantial asset to sell to it, namely 93 The Embankment. We swapped our building for Barclay shares. Stanley Baker did so reluctantly: but Barry was most persuasive — he had grasped the theory of "leverage". I was half-way between the two of them. We ended up owning about 23 per cent of a public company, but with more than £1m. We didn't have voting rights: but we had the money, which was more immediately to our liking. Stanley was content and even managed a smile when the cheque came in.'

Deeley and Spikings now joined the board of Lion International to build up its entertainment assets. 'We used the company equity to borrow money from the bank and acquire more shares: that's what is known by "leverage" in America, or "gearing up" in Britain. Barry's expertise was showing us how to get rich very quick. Stanley was now

*John Boulting, *Cinema TV Today*, 21 October 1972.

delighted. Being primarily an actor-producer rather than a businessman, and lacking the rigorous discipline that Barry and I had decided was necessary to run British Lion, he wasn't involved in the day-to-day decision-making.'

British Lion was now to be run on the lines that Spikings and Deeley had elaborated in the report they had originally made to IPC: the basis of it was the 'global strategy' of pre-selling films in strategic territories, principally the United States. Peter Snell, British Lion's managing director, had already bought certain projects which Spikings and Deeley felt they could see in their strategy of running 'the No. Three film company' in the industry: other projects, they couldn't use. Snell returned to independent production and Michael Deeley replaced him.

John Bentley's nominee, Beverly Ripley, now became managing director of Lion International in succession to Jeremy Arnold. Ripley, formerly the chairman of Pearl and Dean, personified the same sort of Sixties fascination with the mechanics of business wheeling and dealing; for both men, this meant a sidelines fondness for 'executive toys'. Ripley had in his office a computerized illuminated watch accurate to 1/64,000th of a second and set by the atomic clock at Houston, Texas; ten cigarette lighters; six cigar cutters (one of them made out of a Napoleonic five-franc piece); a TV with a three-inch screen (then a miniaturized novelty); a Minox camera measuring two inches (likewise a passing wonder); and a 'wave machine' that rocked its indigo-dyed water back and forth to make the gentle waves that were supposed to calm the overburdened executive mind. Such novelty items, with their emphasis upon reduction, seemed to fit the man who now tried to negotiate the 'betterment' of Shepperton Studios with the film unions. As this was being opposed by Alan Sapper's ACTT, a *douceur* was offered the 400-odd workers, namely a half-share in the retrenched 20 acres if they agreed not to oppose the re-development of the other 40.

Then just as all looked signed, sealed and ready to be kissed, John Bentley himself was the subject of a lightning take-over bid. It was so unanticipated by him that when a journalist broke the news that a financial services group J. H. Vavasseur was the bidder, all Bentley could muster was the exclamation, 'Vava-who?'

Headed by Sir Gordon Newton, a former *Financial Times* editor, Vavasseur unblushingly declared: 'We want the assets. We think we can motor them.' Stockholders were offered 87p a share in a £17m. take-over bid for Barclay Securities. By mid-February 1973, accepting a valuation of 95p a share (much less than the peak price), John Bentley agreed to sell out to Vavasseur. He promptly cashed his shares: a very wise move, as the British Stock Market debacle was just beginning.

Over at British Lion it was like being on a perpetual roller-coaster. Beverly Ripley left Lion International: Jeremy Arnold returned to the managing director's office. The plan for Shepperton appeared to have been agreed with the unions and Michael Deeley announced that his aim was to 'make British Lion the first company that producers come to'. Some 90 per cent of the sound stages at the studio had been saved, as well as what was then the largest stage in Europe for 'silent' shooting — under the Barclay Securities deal, only four sound stages would have been spared and the 'silent' stage sold. All that was now needed were some films.

FEEDING THE LION

Among the properties that Peter Snell had bought was a Daphne du Maurier short story, *Don't Look Now*. The new British Lion management got it under way quickly at the end of 1972, 'using', says Deeley, 'a mixture of the Anglo-Italian co-production treaty and German tax-shelter money'. It was shot in Venice and Hertfordshire by Nicolas Roeg in just fifty-six days. It was Roeg's third feature — following *Performance* and *Outback* — and was an immediate critical and commercial success when premiered in London on 11 October 1973. It was neither a ghost story nor an outright thriller: all that happens to the married couple in a wintry Venice happens below the surface of actual experience; but like a shiver under the skin, it sets the surface hairs stiffening.

Du Maurier's story is faithfully followed: but the compass needle Roeg follows points to the more distant latitudes of the Argentinian writer Jorge Luis Borges — his symbols of symmetry and reflection, labyrinth and water *throng* the film. Like Roeg's earlier films, it reveals its meaning only at the moment one plunges through the trap door into the abyss of madness. Its coincidences form a pattern of the uncanny: each apparently unpremeditated act precipitates one closer to an appointed destiny. Like the father and the mother (Donald Sutherland scaling himself down to fit the ambiguities of the part; Julie Christie less mannered than she had ever been) who believe against all rationality that their dead child may be 'found' in Venice, one's bearings are constantly being shaken by glimpsing the consequences of events (like the falling scaffolding in a church) before they happen.

Part of Roeg's success lies in tuning our apprehensions along the pyschic waveband that exists between the characters, so that one passes imperceptibly from one state to another depending on the strength of their interior panic. It offered one major sequence of disturbing sensuality that was to become Roeg's trademark: shots of Christie and Sutherland naked and making love were cross-cut with shots of them dressing for dinner, the union of the naked bodies bizarrely counterpointed by the formal identities they resumed with their clothes.

Don't Look Now is Roeg's best film: what the story tells and what it intimates are so well balanced.

Later, abetted by Paul Mayersberg's over-elaborated screen-plays, Roeg's films bombarded eye and mind with more sensory stimuli than either could absorb. Even so, the director's temptation to find everything expressive of something else was already present in an interview Roeg gave in which he described his obsessive satisfaction in finding a house, half-brick and half-wood, that was 'right in line with the idea that (hero and heroine) hadn't finally made up their minds about how they wanted to live . . . They were halfway all the time.'*

Don't Look Now's commercial reception in America fell well short of the expectations which had been heightened by the sex scenes in it — Roeg, rather ingenuously, hoped they wouldn't attract sensational attention. William Castle, producer of *Rosemary's Baby*, was probably right when he surmised that it was 'too arty' for American tastes.

British Lion, needing to preserve its cash flow as well as boost its production record, then released a film that John Heyman had put together for Joseph Losey to direct: an Anglo-French co-production of *A Doll's House* (5 July 1973). It starred Jane Fonda in a performance which confirmed that the cheer-leader of Women's Lib needed a step-ladder to come within reaching distance of Ibsen's liberated woman: roles of Nora's complexity were not mastered on tours behind the lines in Vietnam. Fonda's voice, face, upbringing even, were all against her: her tongue was poorly tutored for a part that required her to project a period awareness, not just a star personality. This version of the play somehow suggested that instead of a nineteenth-century Norwegian woman imprisoned by her own wifely submissiveness and society's double sex-standards, Nora was simply an American au pair girl helping out with her hosts' children and entertaining chance callers. One example of how her immersion in ideology had betrayed her sensibility occurred in the scene where Nora leaves her husband. On Losey's judicious advice in the post-production stage, Fonda toned down the vocal attack she had given the scene when shooting it: but her facial movements already on film, could not of course be re-modelled. The result is an audio-visual disjuncture at the very moment when one needed a single-minded purposiveness.

Where Losey's film scores is in its *mise-en-scène*: a Breughel snowscape where the white lie of Nora's life is reflected in every Nordic vista. By also getting adapter David Mercer to transfer the creaking exposition of Act One into an eight-minute prologue showing Nora and her friend Kristine (Delphine Seyrig) contemplating the latter's marriage, Losey creates a new plausibility for the notion of Kristine and the blackmailer (Edward Fox) falling in love. These two actually come off more memorably than the characters of the main story. Trevor Howard, as Dr Rank, goes

*Nicolas Roeg, interviewed by Tom Milne and Penelope Houston, *Sight and Sound*, Winter 1973–4.

to his grave impressively, more rueful at the prospect of surrendering the brandy glass than life itself.

But the film's limited success was rendered more painful still by the coincidence of the *other* version of *A Doll's House,* made for MGM-EMI and directed by Patrick Garland, which had opened a month or two earlier on 19 April 1973 — evidence of how quickly the finance could be found when the topicality of the Women's Movement seemed to be inherent in the subject, even if the Ibsenite manifesto was ninety-four years old. Claire Bloom was this Nora; and she did something far rarer and more subtle than banging the door at the end. She opened one — the door into Nora's self. Though the film was an adaptation of the recent stage production starring her, the camera-work of Arthur Ibbetson made Bloom's revelation all the sharper. This Nora was minutely itemized through a dozen tics of gesture and expression as a spoilt, childish, dependent wife. Toying with a fur muff, babyishly prying hubby's fingers apart as if to extract the money from between them, knowing full well his male ego is flattered by her dependence on him and his vanity boosted by his own forgiveness which makes her doubly his: Bloom consented to her kept status like the pet squirrel she mimics.

Her performance was light years away from Fonda's front-page treatment. But her greatness lay in showing us the clever woman under the fripperies: with the arrival of the blackmailer, she comes out of the wifely closet and reveals herself as a clever, ruthless, heartless woman. At the point where she destroys herself — by provoking the blackmailer's revelation — she achieves her liberation. The confrontation between husband and wife, as she contemptuously watches him panic lest her less-than-perfect past threaten his complacent present, is a memorable one. Unlike Fonda, Bloom did not make the mistake of acting as an advocate for a cause: she is simply a woman speaking her mind — a mind she has always had, but only now dares to voice. The cast was stronger, subtler, more of a whole than Losey's: Anthony Hopkins as a husband who is never so priggish that he forfeits our sympathy in adversity; Denholm Elliott as a blackmailer motivated by a gnawing unfairness rather than villainous malice; Anna Massey riding the improbabilities of Kristine by sheer good humour; Ralph Richardson's doctor actually being gnawed by the worms, whereas Trevor Howard's in the Losey film only totters on the graveside; and even Edith Evans endowing the nanny's brief role with unobtrusive character strokes.

The film had to be its own reward; for after its London opening, it was shown hardly anywhere else: the Fonda version went farther, but with less credit — and little return to British Lion.

Other films that British Lion backed, *The Internecine Project*, *Who?* and Peter Snell's production of *The Wicker Man*, about paganism and human sacrifice in the Scottish wilds, were undertaken with the hope of a profit due to pre-production tax arrangements or else simply to keep facilities ticking over while seeking to put together bigger deals that combined prestige and profit. There had to be more artifice than art in British Lion's policy. Production at Shepperton and the two other major studios had become critical: in July 1973 only six films were in production in Britain, a severe drop from the sixteen at the beginning of June 1972. Pinewood and Shepperton lay empty for a time: Elstree did little more than muffle the echoes on its sound stages with two productions. At this time, eight American-backed films were being made in Europe, but only four in Britain. 'British film-makers and companies do not know what sort of film they should be producing, for what audience,' said an editorial in *Cinema TV Today*. 'The youth market has gone, the black market exists only in America, the "now" film is yesterday's story.'

Even in Hollywood, few studio chiefs were whistling cheerfully. Though a $30,000 a week loss might be a mere drip at MGM's Culver City studios, compared with the massive haemorrhage at British studios, James Aubrey, MGM's chief executive officer, was selling off the artefacts of the golden era; and, more seriously for MGM's British partners, he announced in October 1973 the company's withdrawal from the £170,000 annual subvention it had agreed to make to EMI's Elstree facility two years earlier when MGM closed down its own British studio at Borehamwood. Elstree reacted swiftly: in November 1973, it cut its work-force of 479 by almost half. It may have been coincidence or a sign of deepening demoralization — 'crisis of confidence' was the unions' euphemism — but Shepperton's unions lifted their own resistance to 'redevelopment' of the studio land around the same time. Better half a studio than none at all: it was a lesson that *Sunday, Bloody Sunday* could have underwritten. British independent production had suffered a mini-crisis of confidence in April 1973, when Joseph Shaftel, who had announced an ambitious $20m. programme of sixteen films the previous April, suddenly went into receivership amid a flurry of anxiety at the American bank which had been his principal backer. His last British film, *Alice's Adventures in Wonderland* (cost: £700,000), seemed an aptly titled description of his policies.

To make matters even worse (if possible) the Classic cinema chain — regarded as the lifebelt for independent producers, often backed by the NFFC or British Lion, who had been rejected by the Rank-EMI duopoly — was put up for sale. Here, too, property was part and parcel of the deal. For their owner, Laurie Marsh, reportedly regarded the 190 screens as 'property', rather than 'entertainment'. He had asked EMI if it was interested in adding his cinemas to its chain: but EMI replied that it feared the deal might be referred to the Monopolies Commission — though why this should have struck fear into anyone at EMI is hard to see, since the Commission had already found the chain 'guilty' of practices contrary to the public interest but had done absolutely nothing to remedy the situation. So in August 1973 the Classic cinemas, which had been bought by Marsh for £7m. in 1971, were sold for a sum reportedly between £6.6m. and £7.2m. to Price-Freezer Ltd, a frozen-foods firm based in Shrewsbury. However, the sale was never completed — nor were the reasons ever disclosed — and Price-Freezer eventually agreed to pay the Laurie Marsh Group compensation of £250,000. It had been a near shave (or a near freeze).

It was a tribute to the 'front' of confidence that British Lion's new bosses managed to maintain that, despite all these crises, their share quotation showed a rise. It may have been significant that their backing did not come from a traditional British institution, but from a newish consortium of Italian banks operating in London. Italian banks had long experience of living with the never-ending crisis of their own country's film-makers. Besides, British Lion had the assets that John Bentley's brief association with it had dusted off. 'I was feeling quite optimistic when I went off to Barbados in the middle of December 1973 to spend Christmas there,' says Deeley. 'Then over the next three or four weeks, the British Stock Market virtually collapsed — and with it our quotation. We watched in horror: but we were powerless to do anything about it, for we had no liquid assets. Once our shares fell below 100, we were losing what assets we already had. The shares finally settled at about 35p. It was horrifying. Everything we had was wiped out: we even had to pay a small amount of money from our own resources to be quit of our responsibilities. Stanley Baker was furious and never forgave Barry and me for the whole "adventure". Every time I saw him, I could see him thinking, "Why didn't we keep our lovely safe building on the Embankment?"'

In February 1974 Lion International sold its freehold interest in 93 The Embankment: it had been owned by Lion's subsidiary, Alembic House Holdings, which was the former Great Western Investments. Its valuation the year before the recession is listed at £2.15m.; the price realized by its sale was £1.9m. — it was applied at once to the reduction of Lion's bank borrowings. In the same February, share dealings in Lion's parent company, J. H. Vavasseur, were suspended when they had crashed from 254p to a nightmare 24p following the loss of confidence in a fringe bank it owned which dealt in maximum income bonds: it was also rumoured that Vavasseur was selling its stake in Lion International.

But everywhere one looked in that terrible economic winter, finance companies were being blown out of the water by the delayed explosion which followed the collapse of the secondary banking system in Britain. The major City institutions were forever sending out lifeboats, putting together survival rafts for those companies that had gone under, and generally hugging their own far from safe harbours until the economic storm had blown itself out. Huge, rich and powerful institutions were to be picked up for nominal sums. Vavasseur got rid of its fringe bank to an insurance company, but then had to have its shares suspended again in May 1974: this time the merchant banks had to scrape together a cash facility of £18m. and Sir Gordon Newton took his leave. Deeley and Spikings were feeling like orphans of the storm. 'Fortunately, our Italian International Bank wasn't pulled into the disaster that had overtaken the fringe banks,' says Deeley, 'but its confidence was severely shaken by the collapse of respectable and solid-looking institutions. If seemingly sturdy firms could go under, what hope for a film company? I think we were spared simply because the bank couldn't see a way out and we just went on cobbling film deals together — although we were doubtful of our ability to go on very long in this fashion.'

The resilience shown was surprising indeed. It is absolutely true to say that the future of this large independent section of British film-making rested on property, not pictures; and all around the property was falling down. Yet the pictures still went on getting made!

There were some gleams of hope. The cut-back at Shepperton, which had lost £155,000 in the first six months of the financial year ending in April 1974, had at least reduced an expensive workforce from 300 to a mere 76. The studios had become a rental facility — i.e., independent film-makers rented and paid for only what they wanted, thus minimizing unnecessary and wasteful overall costs: an operation akin to cutting out the luxury frills of a grand hotel and substituting the cost-conscious routine of a motel where guests got the key and carried their own bags. Confidence in the reconstructed studio was shown when Vavasseur bought another 125,000 shares in Lion International for £75,000, taking its holding up to 51 per cent. This move, though, was judged to have been made in the expectation that Shepperton's redundant 40 acres would soon receive permission to be re-developed for housing. Shepperton's new chairman was named in 1974: he was Barry Spikings.

'We were giving desperate thought to our future, as you might guess,' says Deeley, 'and came up with one bold, indeed arrogant plan. It was to try and take over the Rank Organization cinemas. Provided the management was "reformed", this would give us access to a major cash-generating machine. But Rank wanted £39m. for them, even though the principal profits were made in the West End cinemas, then promptly lost in the inefficient provincial ones. Our counter offer was £7m. for a 99-year lease.' British Lion's consultant was Graham Dowson, formerly Rank's managing director and a man often named as heir apparent to Rank's strong-willed chairman Sir John Davis. Unfortunately, Dowson and the Rank Organization had parted on bad terms. Deeley does not know if this influenced Rank's intransigence, 'but the upshot was that John Davis gave us a dusty answer. He was not, as I remember it, going to be the person who stripped Rank of its

heritage. So the deal fell through. Had it succeeded, I believe it would
have made British Lion a viable and profitable force.'

The advantage of being locked into parlous situations is that it
paradoxically facilitates even greater risk-taking. If one is already
soaking, what do a few drops more matter? Thus, in June 1975, Deeley
and Spikings took the risk of wrenching British Lion away from the
grasp of Vavasseur's subsidiary, Lion International, whose interests
were mainly in screen advertising, poster hoardings and, of course, the
Shepperton Studios land. Deeley contended that finance would be 'easier'
to come by if one were seen to be an independent unit. It is a tribute to
his selling prowess that the bankers went along with this and a deal was
'cobbled together' to allow a five-picture programme to be announced,
including such productions as the long-delayed screen version of the
stage hit *Conduct Unbecoming*, a murder story with an unusual setting (but
few other distinctions) in the officers' mess of a crack British regiment in
India, and a film starring David Bowie entitled *The Man Who Fell to
Earth*, to be shot by Nicolas Roeg entirely in the United States but
without American financial participation. A bold venture indeed!

STARDOM EXPRESS

Although the portents were not yet apparent to outsiders, the production
policies of British Lion and EMI were starting to move in a remarkably
parallel fashion: soon they would converge. The only sign of this at that
time, though, seemed to be the surprising number of productions that
both corporations could wring out of a very tight budget. Nat Cohen had
announced seven films in May 1973: some of them were American-made
films in which EMI had a distribution interest, like Gregory Peck's
production of *The Dove* (based on the true-life adventure of a young
round-the-world yachtsman), or *The Killer Elite* (a Sam Peckinpah piece
of mayhem in slow motion). Only one of them could really be said to
arouse domestic anticipation: the first version that Agatha Christie had
ever permitted to be made of her famous mystery *Murder on the Orient
Express* (21 November 1974).

'It was my idea from the start,' says Nat Cohen. 'I just had a feeling
that, considering all the gloom and doom in the country, Agatha
Christie would go down well. The problem was to find the right man to
bring her book to the screen. She was a "difficult" woman: she had no
need of the money and she had hated all previous screen adaptations of
her novels. I asked John Brabourne to approach her.'

This was an inspired choice. Lord Brabourne, as well as being a
producer who favoured 'safe' but 'quality' pictures (*Sink the Bismarck!*,
the Zeffirelli-directed *Romeo and Juliet*, *Tales of Beatrix Potter* with the
Royal Ballet), had 'connections', as Earl Mountbatten's son-in-law,

giving him access if he cared to use it to areas in which less distinguished film people did not usually move. 'I don't know if he used the "Mountbatten connection" or not,' says Cohen, 'but he certainly gained Agatha Christie's confidence and approval. I bought the screen rights to three of her Poirot novels, including *Orient Express*. I did *not*', Cohen emphasizes, 'have any interest in the Miss Marple ones.' (His emphasis is explained, perhaps, by the woeful version of a Miss Marple mystery, *The Mirror Crack'd* (1981) in which every element, including its complement of superannuated Hollywood stars, could be said, mercifully, to have creak'd.)

Cohen admits he never anticipated *Orient Express* would become such an ambitious production. With Brabourne and the latter's production associate, Richard Goodwin, he set the budget at between $1m. and $1.5m. 'It ended up at $1.4m., but look what we got for that!' Indeed the craftsmanship, taste, ingenuity and sheer numerical talent involved was exemplary film-making and repaid the long production gestation — shooting did not get under way till March 1974. 'Finding a director was not easy. Sidney Lumet had just made *Dog Day Afternoon* and seemed a good person to try.' And was — even though the one-room drama skills Lumet displayed in his *Twelve Angry Men,* in 1959, were more relevant to solving a murder mystery in the cramped compartment of a Trans-Europe train. Lumet respected Christie the way a chameleon 'respects' its surroundings: where another director might have been tempted to give her plot a 'Hitchcock-shuddery' up-date, he preserved the 'Christie-chucklesome' period flavour. Hercule Poirot was played by Albert Finney — 'We gave him a percentage participation in the net, along with Lumet,' says Cohen. Finney played the part with a subdued wit and delicate emphasis typical of the whole production. With hair a-gleam under its oil slick like a patent-leather thinking cap, moustache a tuning fork vibrating with suspicion, and head kept continually cocked like a wise bird listening for worms under the sod, he brought Poirot to life by using finger tips, eye-balls and (one suspects) the very toes inside his boots to suggest the intelligence that lay at the extremities of his immoveable presence as he wore down the far from irresistible suspects.

Paul Dehn's screen-play remained an honest version of the book but added artistry, refurbishing Christie without importing vulgarity or sacrificing a clue. (Dehn's death a couple of years later deprived British screen-writing of its most elegant carpenter: just to see him pack Christie's red herrings into Tony Walton's exquisite 1930s train-set, like so many perfectly proportioned sardines, added a bonus to the film that subsequent Christie adaptations badly needed.)

Even so, the astonishing all-star cast was the motor that drove the film forward. 'Everyone was on a flat fee,' says Cohen, 'and, with very few exceptions, most of them got the same fee. They were only too pleased to do it. It was a case, I think, of glamour rubbing off on each other. Why, Michael Caine was very disappointed not to get a role in it!'

The dozen stars of national or international eminence generated not competition (which wouldn't have been surprising, so many of them being in front of the camera all at one time), but a contagious complicity. Which maniac among them had perforated Richard Widmark's overweening American tycoon with a dagger twelve times over? Was it Ingrid Bergman as a shy Swedish missionary behaving like a mouse already caught in the trap. Or Vanessa Redgrave as a 'debby' type who might be English rose or Venus fly-trap? Or Sean Connery's Indian Army colonel married to the regiment but not averse to an affair on the side? Or Wendy Hiller's Russian princess allying German gutturals to a complexion of perished gutta-percha? Or Michael York's fiery count with Jacqueline Bisset as his svelte countess? Or Lauren Bacall speaking Yankee home truths — but *are* they truths? — like a rattling machine-gun? Or John Gielgud as the corpse's epigrammatic butler? Or Jean-Pierre Cassel as a wagon-lits conductor fluent in as many languages as there are alibis? Or Anthony Perkins and Colin Blakeley as the deceased's jittery secretary and his dubious bodyguard? To assemble such a cast for a mere $750,000 (£370,000 then) was almost as dexterous a sleight of hand as any that Dame Agatha depended on to construct her mysteries.

'Charlie Bluhdorn' — the then head of Paramount — 'was staying at Claridge's,' says Cohen, 'and had heard good reports of the film — this was before it opened anywhere. He called me over to have breakfast. As I entered his suite, he locked the door behind me. "Nathan Cohen," he said, as if he'd arrested me, "you are not leaving this room until we have finalized a deal, and if we do not, there will be murder done. In any case, I will cut your throat . . ." We haggled over the breakfast dishes, while Charlie took calls and made some, so as to give himself time and wear me down, and he eventually agreed to put up half of the production cost and give us a percentage in the American gross. It was, for that time, a wonderful deal. But then I had luck . . . Charlie was a Christie fan, tickled pink by the film. He went down in person to the New York cinema when it opened, just to hear what people said coming out, and his executives caught it for not being present when it went on to break the cinema's house record. Paramount made about $20m., plus the TV rentals: in other territories, the film made between $10m. and $15m. In Britain, of course, it was top box-office.

'Our next Poirot mystery, *Death on the Nile* (1978), did not do quite as well in America, though the US TV networks paid three times as much for it as they had done for *Orient Express*. It did "satisfactory" business in America — and made four times as much as *Orient Express* in Japan — but overall it grossed less than the first time. *Evil Under the the Sun* (1982) did not do as well as the other two Poirot pictures. In the first place, we had only one grade A actor in it — Albert Finney — and the rest were good but regarded as Grade B at the box-office. Another thing: artists' fees had escalated beyond belief or budgeting. I could never make

Murder on the Orient Express today: I'd have to give away 150 per cent of the gross to please all those stars we took aboard in 1974!'

There was another reason, too, why the *Express* would have left the station without a lot of those stars aboard had the film been made in England a year later. They would had had to pay too dearly for the ride. For following the Labour Party's decisive victory at the second General Election of the year, in October 1974, a November Finance Bill presented by the Chancellor of the Exchequer, Denis Healey, dealt one more blow at an already groggy film industry. It proposed changes to the tax laws affecting the highest earners in Britain and thereby threatened the American movie-makers working there as well as the top-paid British artists and technicians.

Its effect was also to deter American stars from coming to work in Britain. Up to April 1974 resident Americans and other aliens paid United Kingdom taxes on only the part of their world-wide earnings that they remitted to the country. Under Healey's proposals, those resident in Britain for nine out of ten years would pay the full UK tax rates on half their world-wide earnings whether remitted or not. The real bite, however, was reserved for April 1976: after that date, tax would have to be paid on 75 per cent of world earnings, if the services generating them had been performed in Britain. The maximum British tax rate was then 83 per cent, which took effect at the low threshold of £20,000 — *very* low indeed for, say, American film-makers owning percentages in films with long box-office lives. This change created a maximum tax rate hurtfully above what they would be paying if resident in the USA, where the highest rate was 50 per cent and tax shelters were perfectly legally available.

For once, the unions and the producers sang the same song, a blues number. 'The last straw . . . all that is needed to break the industry's back,' said the ACTT's General Secretary Alan Sapper. Kip Herren, Pinewood's managing director, summed up the general reaction: 'Instead of producing revenue, the new taxes will only exclude talent.' Not only will the Americans disappear; there will be every incentive for our own home-grown talent to follow them.' John Terry, head of the NFFC, expressing the same fear, called the move 'disastrous'. The official Budget in April 1975 quickly closed a few loopholes that the already rich might have squeezed through by prudently lightening their load. It introduced capital transfer tax, making it unattractive to attempt to protect future earnings by hiving them off on to family and relatives. The maximum one could legally give away annually was £1,000. For the first time, taxpayers in Britain appreciated what it was like to be stuck with money!

The few British stars of international status swiftly reacted as predicted. Sean Connery, from the retreat he had prudently established in Spain, stated bluntly that he would not be returning to Britain to pay a fortune to a Labour Government for the 'privilege' of working there: and his next film, *Ransom* (1975), made for British Lion, was shot entirely in Norway. Michael Caine was compelled to fit any filming he did in Britain into the three unpenalized months allowable for work or private visits: this increased his cost to producers and the problems of scheduling his films. Roger Moore was likewise a reluctant expatriate: interiors for his South African melodrama, *Gold* (1975), were shot at studios in Malta instead of Pinewood — the latter lost an estimated £120,000. (Ironically, the Maltese studios were managed by the British-based Kinematograph Renters Society whose biggest British-member companies were Rank and EMI!) The upmarket British newspapers and magazines broke into a rash of property advertisements from early 1975 on offering for sale the homes in Belgravia, Hampstead or the more secluded stretches of the Home Counties which belonged to distinguished Americans-in-residence or British entertainment names who had more to lose by paying taxes than giving up their homes and leaving Britain.

One of the very earliest figures to depart was Joseph Losey. In 1974 he reluctantly left the two homes (knocked into one) which he owned in Royal Avenue, Chelsea, almost opposite the house which had provided the deceptively respectable exterior for *The Servant* in 1963. He went first to Italy, then settled in France, returning only briefly to Britain when, for example, a French film he had directed opened there. On the occasion of *M. Klein*, in 1976, he declared, 'As it stands now, there is no way I can make enough money to pay my English taxes.'* Nor did he return to London until the advent of a Socialist Government in France, with swingeing tax proposals of its own, made him hurry across the Channel again and back into the Royal Avenue residence — where he died less than a year and one British film (*Steaming*) later. Other directors who had added lustre to British films in the Sixties now worked by choice or necessity outside the country.

It was noteworthy how many British subjects could be filmed abroad with scenery deputizing for the English backgrounds: Richard Lester's *Robin and Marian* (1976) was shot entirely in Spain. Other locations selected not wholly for scenic reasons after 1974 included some in Greece, Malta, Canada, Italy, Holland, Switzerland, Ireland and even Iran. John Schlesinger was of course already well established in America, where he made *The Day of the Locust* (1975) and *Marathon Man* (1976). Now Karel Reisz shot *The Gambler* (1974) in America, followed by *Who'll Stop the Rain?* (alternatively known as *The Dog Soldiers:* 1978).

Of course with directors of such eminence, finding suitably rewarding work was also a problem: if the one solution (going to America) satisfied both concerns, they were not to be blamed. Americans who had lived in

*Joseph Losey, interviewed by Quentin Falk, *Screen International*, 27 November 1976.

Britain for some years lost no time in buying or renting new accommodation in the United States: Norman Jewison finished *Rollerball* (1975) at Pinewood and returned home.

A few film-makers broke the ten-year-spell of British residence (after which one incurred the fiscal penalties), by going abroad to make their next film: one such was Carl Foreman, who returned to the USA in 1975 after a period of residence in the country that had offered him home and work as a refugee from the McCarthy 'blacklist' twenty-three years earlier. Such retreats had to be for two years minimum duration to escape the tax axe on the exile's return: inevitably the 'temporary' turned into the more or less 'permanent' as long-established work habits were broken and attractive offers to stay on in America were received.

Other lesser-known Americans, the executives of major Hollywood companies based in Britain to supervise production or scout for projects, began returning to America, like Robert Solo (Warner Bros) and Danton Rissner (United Artists); or else they re-located themselves in Rome, Paris or Amsterdam and preferred to recommend subjects that could be made there, where *they* were, and not in inhospitable Britain.

The knock-on effect of such departures was felt by thousands of 'little people' in the British film industry: costumiers, chauffeurs, caterers, casting agents . . . Films that probably would have been shot in Britain went elsewhere simply to fit in with the fiscal arrangements of American stars who were terrified — at least, their agents were — of being caught in the British Treasury's 'bite'. Only film-makers temperamently unwilling (or unable) to uproot themselves — like Stanley Kubrick who had lived in Britain since the early 1960s, or Fred Zinnemann who pre-dated even Kubrick — showed no sign of turning globe-trotter: presumably they 'paid the price' for their preferences.

Carl Foreman in a letter written before leaving for America said: 'There is an even greater danger to the industry, I think, than the large number of people leaving, and that is the lack of money here, the almost complete drying up of finance for real *British* films — that is to say, films of purely British content — or for international co-productions. You have only to look around and see how pitifully bare the cupboard is, nothing in the studios, practically nothing outside the studios, and the only things going are the crumbs from the Hollywood table. I think that conditions are worse this year than in any of the twenty-three years I have been over here.'*

A characteristically dissenting note was sounded by Lindsay Anderson, though, if anything, it merely deepened the gloom of those hardest hit. Anderson paused long enough while directing *In Celebration* (1974), a screen version of David Storey's play destined for producer Ely Landau's American Film Theatre series, to suggest that the blame for a

*Carl Foreman, letter to author, 20 March 1975.

film industry that ignored Britain and the British should not be put wholly on the Exchequer or the vulgar moneymen. 'I think it is the *artists* who are not interested. I don't see any indication that my colleagues are bursting with ideas about Britain and not getting them financed. I think that what they do — out of some vague feeling of guilt — is use this argument about not being able to get finance, in order to justify themselves in not attempting. I think it would be better if they were honest and said, 'I find that Britain is boring and not pleasant to work in and I would prefer to work somewhere else.'* Anderson uttered these unrepentant sentiments before the full force of the tax changes became general knowledge; but there is no doubt that a small number of those who declared they had been driven 'into exile' used the tax changes to cover up for a temperamental dislike of working in Britain. It was somehow more excusable to have been 'forced' abroad than to have quit of one's own volition. Either way, though, the effect was the same: 'Britain and the British' were the losers.

INTERIM ARRANGEMENTS

The mid-Seventies coincided with the lowest point in British film-making. With the few notable exceptions mentioned, indigenously British films shot in the 1974–5 period were: (a) small-budget (£180,000–£200,000) farces and 'sexploitationers' (like the series that rang the changes on the *Confessions of a Window Cleaner/Pop Performer/Driving Instructor*); (b) pale pseudo-sequels to Sixties hits (*Alfie Darling*, *The Bawdy Adventures of Tom Jones*); (c) co-productions with American TV networks intended for the small screen there and theatrical release elsewhere (*Brief Encounter, David Copperfield, Love Among the Ruins*); (d) spin-offs from successful British TV series (*Dad's Army, On the Buses, The Likely Lads*); (e) filmed plays for the American Film Theatre (*In Celebration, The Maids, Galileo, Butley*, enlisting the talents of, respectively, Lindsay Anderson, Christopher Miles, Joseph Losey and Harold Pinter; and (f) traditional British series (Hammer Horrors and *Carry on Dick, Carry on Behind*). Big-budget movies were invariably American-backed and aimed at the international market: the Bond series, *The Odessa File, The Man Who Would Be King* (filmed entirely in Morocco partly for the fiscal convenience of Sean Connery and Michael Caine), *The Seven Per Cent Solution, Juggernaut* . . . Not one of these made the slightest claim to project British culture; most were directed by Americans; all were obligingly registered by the Department of Trade as 'legally' British films on the grounds of labour costs, thereby eligible to receive nourishment from the Eady Levy subsidy siphoned off box-office

---

*Lindsay Anderson, interviewed by Dennis Barker, *The Guardian*, 28 August 1974.

takings and meant to keep honest British flesh and bone together. These years were the lowest, the most shameful nadir of film industry fortunes. While we drove our resident talents away from creative domicile with threats of fiscal forfeiture, we welcomed the already fat and well-fed Hollywood-based transients, put them up in the best accommodation and waited on them hand and foot.

Carl Foreman ended the letter which has already been quoted with the words: 'John Woolf, John Brabourne and I are meeting about this constantly and hope to get the Prime Minister to take some action.' To many people's surprise, the Prime Minister *did*. But then Harold Wilson had always felt sentimentally protective towards the film industry ever since, as President of the Board of Trade, he had conceived the principle of the Eady Levy while walking his dogs on the beach in his favourite summer holiday resort of the Scilly Isles in 1949, or thereabouts. Historically, the Treasury dislikes and opposes the imposition of a tax which will be recycled for a specific purpose. But Wilson 'sold' the idea to Sir Wilfrid Eady of the Treasury by playing on the man's vanity. A levy named after him would be the best memorial to a Whitehall mandarin. 'He swallowed the bait,' says Wilson. 'On such little things as someone's self-esteem depends a whole industry's welfare.'*

Now, in August 1975, Wilson set up a Prime Minister's Working Party and gave it the brief of suggesting ways to re-activate the film industry. Its chairman was John Terry, managing director of the NFFC. Members included Lady Falkender (the former Marcia Williams who had been created a Life Peer the previous year: she had been Wilson's political secretary since 1956 and was his personal nominee on the working party); Carl Foreman; Lord Brabourne; Sir John Woolf; Richard Attenborough; Sir Bernard Delfont (knighted the previous year); Alan Sapper; Brian Tesler (deputy chief executive of London Weekend TV); Alasdair Milne (BBC TV director of programmes); A. W. Mallinson; Hugh Orr (representing independent exhibitors) and Lord Ryder (industrial adviser to the Government).

Before this eclectic assortment of people even had their first meeting, feathers were ruffled, intrigue was set in train and mystery created. What was the politically influential Lady Falkender doing there? it was asked. In any case, what did *she* know about films? Swift reference was made to her perceptive political memoirs, *Inside No. 10*, published three years earlier: they were illuminating, though not entirely reassuring. No mention of 'Films' in the Index between 'Filing system' and 'Flat, Prime Minister's at No. 10'. But, with 'cinema', one struck gold, or, at least, a glimmer of something, even though the entries simply referred to 'Cinema, Wilson's visits to' ('He had to be prodded into going . . . when he did go out though, he enjoyed it immensely'**). Even here, a large

*Lord Wilson to the author, November 1984.
**Marcia Williams, *Inside No 10* (Weidenfeld, 1972), p. 84.

party of film-goers is spoken of (large enough, anyhow, to include Mrs Pollard, the Downing Street housekeeper). One visit was to *Till Death Us Do Part* ('the film of the much-discussed TV series'), and a birthday treat took in *Hello, Dolly!* (no opinion recorded). It is only fair to mention at this point that Lady Falkender's shrewdness about film industry affairs (and its leading figures), whether based on independent film-going or in large Downing Street parties, was to serve the committee well. And indeed, on further thought, why not? Films *were* politics, as far as the Government was concerned: at any rate, long before they were culture or entertainment.

The working party produced its report with exemplary speed: it was ready just before Christmas 1975, and presented to Parliament in January 1976. Its contents were unsurprising: they had been accurately predicted in the evidence of the single film critic who took the trouble to make a submission to the committee. But they were welcome all the same.

Among thirty-nine recommendations ('The 39 Steps' proved irresistible to next morning's headline writers), it called for: a £5m. cash injection by the Government to NFFC funds and the right to call on sums up to the same figure annually for three more years; the swift release of the sum of £2,373,353, promised under the Films Act of 1970 which a Labour Government had passed but which had then been put on ice by the Conservative administration; a single British Film Authority to bring together the scattered and sometimes mutually competitive (when not contradictory) responsibilities shared by a variety of Government departments; and a fund to develop scripts and 'seed' new productions. The report said all the important things that needed saying (and said them with unusual force and clarity). It had the effect of getting the £2,373,353 owed the NFFC released the following March, although the Treasury immediately snatched much of it back to pay the interest on the original loan!

Whether the working party's recommendations would ever have got on to the Statute Book must remain speculative; for the man who inspired the exercise, Harold Wilson, resigned as Prime Minister in March 1976. James Callaghan, who replaced him, saw no need to adopt any of his predecessor's favourite charities, least of all one like the film industry in which there were few electoral votes. But he did set up an unfortunately named Interim Action Committee on film industry problems, which began meeting in April 1977. Its chairman was Harold (now Sir Harold) Wilson. Its impact is discussed in a later chapter.

Against this background of political procrastination and grudging assistance, the attempts of independent British film-makers to produce work of quality that was also commercial must seem positively heroic.

Michael Deeley and Barry Spikings now pushed their British Lion policy to desperate yet logical extremes. So the Americans were leaving

Britain? Then the British would go to America. A film made in the United States, financed by British money, starring British talents, but taking place in an American setting might, like the nineteenth-century immigrants, get a warmer welcome inside the 'golden door' now guarded by American distributors in lieu of any better disposed symbol of Liberty. So *The Man Who Fell To Earth* (18 March 1976) went into production in New Mexico in June 1975, financed by British Lion in partnership with the NFFC, with a conditional undertaking from Paramount to acquire it for distribution for $1.5m. Despite its location, the mood of chauvinism was so well maintained that the American technicians almost rebelled when it was proposed to continue working on 4 July: the date, said the British producers, had no significance for *them*!

The film starred David Bowie as an extra-terrestrial marooned on earth some five years before E.T. crash-landed and attempting to recharge his astral batteries, in the course of which he becomes a Howard Hughes-type industrialist recluse. By common consent Bowie was the film's unalloyed success. He had an unearthly persona both wondrous and worrisome. This Star Child had an Oxfam look: appropriately, nothing showed up when he was X-rayed. He was as unisex as the Pop fashions of that year. Without his Titian-tinted wig, which he removed to resume his alien identity, he was revealed to be without hair or eyebrows and, lower down, without nipples or navel. His love-making with Candy Clark (who wet her knickers at the shock of seeing him: a cinema 'first' of some kind, until the American version deleted it) was like watching a stick insect at work — or at play? Even entering a room, Bowie looked as if he had walked out of a De Chirico painting: he was all angular and two-dimensional. His super-frail appearance contrasted strikingly with his super-power status. Only one thing jarred: his voice. The limp English diction dropped from between his lips without weight or force: King's Road *déclassé* of the Sixties. Why, one wondered, did this heavenly body burden himself with an English accent on his visitation to America? It was typical of the Nicolas Roeg-Paul Mayersberg screen-play that it should provide a super-abundance of peripheral data without addressing itself to this kind of insistent illogically. There was an impoverishment of real interest in the film — it was much less than met the bedazzled eye.

The pathetic notion of a new prophet who, like Icarus crashlanding in the sea without causing the nearby labourer to raise his eyes from tilling the fields, is, one supposes, behind the story of Bowie's sad creature who falls by the wayside in man's meddlesome universe. By good luck the film reflected a timely renewal of interest in Howard Hughes, then riding high as a Pop ikon, partly as a result of Clifford Irving's hoax 'memoirs' which had mesmerized the nation's media five years earlier. Hughes was conceived in exactly the same unearthly terms of Bowie, flitting around like an unglimpsed potentate in the eternal night of a smoked-glass limousine, or sheltering from the daylight inside an armed fortress or the half-light of seedy motels from which he issued diktats by telephone to his minions in their well-appointed palaces of power.

The trouble was that while the film had room for two overlapping myths — the miraculous superman and the ominpotent recluse — it would not contain the non-stop stream of information that Roeg-Mayersberg fed into one's retinal nerves and frontal lobes — as if programming us for work on a puzzle that became more childish as it grew more seemingly complex. Roeg's was now one of the most mannered styles in movies. His favourite device of cross-cutting between scenes of radically different content had worked well in the love-making/dressing-up sequences in *Don't Look Now*. But the same trick now felt platitudinous. One would not have bet on Ken Russell's style ever being deemed 'compulsive lucidity' in comparison with Roeg's: but such was Jonathan Rosenbaum's judgment in the *Monthly Film Bulletin*: 'Paul Mayersberg . . . has hopefully described the result as a "circus", but with the right elbow of the trapeze artist grafted on to the left ear of the clown which is then strained through the digestive tract of the lion and shot from a cannon, a more accurate description might be an extremely photogenic mess.'*

It is an open question if the film would have done better had it arrived later, when the SF trend was established and the public was hungry for more. For, at the start of 1976, Hollywood was preparing to make no fewer than sixteen SF films. They included *Logan's Run, Space 1999, War Wizards* and — *Newsweek* reported in a story that didn't hold out much hope for this premature British-made SF effort — 'less intellectual (than *The Man Who Fell to Earth*, which had just opened in America) will be *The [sic] Star Wars*, a $9m. movie about a juvenile gang rumble against Fascist oppressors of the galaxy . . . "A shoot-em-up with ray guns", is (George Lucas's) description.'** There was also *Close Encounters of a* [sic] *Third Kind*, described by producer Julia Phillips as 'the *Jaws* of science-fiction movies'. This new trend, according to Ray Bradbury, was connected with the scepticism that young people were evincing about anything to do with progress: very soon Spielberg and Lucas would implant into those same youthful minds the strain of cinematic juvenilia associated with Saturday matinee serials — junk food for immature minds, pabulum for a childishly fixated generation that craved the reassurance of bedtime stories. What hope had an adult meditation upon the nature of aliens on earth? No one could love David Bowie the way they were soon to love E.T.

Deeley remembers showing *The Man Who Fell to Earth* to Barry Diller, then head of production at Paramount. 'At the end, he turned to me

*Jonathan Rosenbaum, *Monthly Film Bulletin*, April 1976.
**Newsweek, 22 December 1975.

reproachfully and said. "You promised me a linear narrative." It was
the first time I had heard the phase. What he meant was a start, middle,
and finish — in that order. The film hadn't got it, of course; and we
didn't get our $1.5m. conditional guarantee from Paramount. We had to
shop around quickly for another distributor and found Don Rugoff: but
he gave us only about $700,000 as an advance. What do you say to your
bankers when you come home with only half of what you said you'd been
promised?'

There was one bright spot, though ... British Lion had been
approached by Columbia to take up the foreign rights in *Nickelodeon*,
Peter Bogdanovich's comedy about movie-making in the early silent
days. 'God knows where they got the idea we had any money for that!'
says Deeley. 'Maybe my line about us being "Britain's third largest film
company" had actually impressed someone on the Coast! But we agreed
to pay Columbia $2m. and received foreign distribution rights against a
guarantee of 50 per cent of the profits. Then I went along to EMI and
persuaded them to agree to pay *us* $2m. against 25 per cent of the profits.
So we'd got our money back *and* half of the profits. That's the way we
kept afloat: that's the way it was done. Much later, when *Nickelodeon* had
turned out a flop, Bernard Delfont reproached us for giving his company
a bad deal. "Look," we told him, "we didn't sell it — you bought it." '

But EMI had been feeling very bullish at the time it did the *Nickelodeon*
deal. Its profitability had improved to £25m. before taxes for the 1973–4
year. It had been shrewdly, if cautiously, guided by Sir Joseph
Lockwood, popularly known as 'The Quiet Millionaire' because of his
unostentatious executive life-style. Sir Joseph's corporate philosophy is
interesting in view of what was to happen to EMI after his imminent
retirement: indeed he seems to have had the gift of prophecy. 'The
pioneer always pays,' he told Malcolm McDowell and screen-writer
David Sherwin in 1971, when the two were researching the background
for some of *O Lucky Man!*'s cast of drolls and had approached the EMI
chairman with the request to tell them some of 'the truths of the
business'. He obliged: 'Never make wrong decisions ... You should like
to make money, but not to spend it, unless it's going to make more
money. Don't go off at the weekend. No round the world trips with the
wife. It's not a question of morals — not morals — it's waste. Once you
allow waste it goes right down the company. You end up ruined, be you
the United States or a fish and chip shop at the Battersea Fun Fair.'*
The speech (given to Sir Ralph Richardson) never appeared in *O Lucky
Man!* It was shot but edited out. To those who recalled it later it sounded
like a scenario for several disasters that were in the making.

Sir Joseph had been succeeded as chairman in November 1974 by Sir
John Read, a man of great integrity, whose tastes ran to Elgar and organ

*Sir Joseph Lockwood, quoted in *O Lucky Man!* by Lindsay Anderson and David Sherwin (Plexus, 1973), p. 17.

music and whose background as a commander in the Royal Navy made him see the future in terms of 'stretching people' in the Dunkirk spirit of 1940, rather than going with the 'Swinging People' of the 1960s. His repugnance at the vulgar public antics of the Sex Pistols Pop group was decisive in EMI's abruptly terminating their recording contract. It is typical of him that although he did not have time to see *Murder on the Orient Express* before its première, he raced through the Christie novel so as to be able to 'talk intelligently' beforehand to Princess Anne. The film's huge success could not but make him look kindly on Bernard Delfont's film-making division.

So Nat Cohen got a quick blessing for a £6m. programme of new films he announced in July 1975. None of them was likely to do very much for 'Britain and the British', but so long as they made money . . . There was *To the Devil, a Daughter* (made in association with Hammer Films); *Seven Nights in Japan* (a romantic story about a Prince Charles-type having a transient affair with a Japanese girl while his cruiser is visiting Tokyo); *All Things Bright and Beautiful* (a country vet's story made in association with David Susskind and *Reader's Digest*); *What Ever Happened to the Likely Lads?* (a sequel to *The Likely Lads*, itself a TV spin-off); *Evil Under the Sun* (a second Poirot mystery: it was announced but not made at this time and *Death on the Nile* was substituted); and *Spanish Fly*, which cost a mere £250,000, and was made in association with a Spanish distributor and an American who had bought the rights to ninety-six books about Biggles, the First World War air ace (and could at least be classified as an Anglophile). Its plot turned on an aphrodisiac brand of sherry with lines like the master's to the manservant: 'Lay the table, not the maid.' It was all very, very cautious. To some, it looked parochial. To be fair to Nat Cohen, he knew how quickly money could be lost on films that failed — and even more so on films that failed to get completed, for the abandonment of *Trick or Treat?*, in which EMI was associated with Playboy Enterprises, had been an embarrassment. Cohen was then entering his seventies.

'Over at British Lion, we were absolutely worn out,' says Deeley, 'continually strapped for cash. After we had failed to get the $1.5m. from Paramount, our bankers wouldn't take our word on anything. I don't blame them. At one point, I heard, they'd approached a British lawyer who had worked for Paramount to take us over. Now it looked as if either history would close down British Lion — or the bank would. Yet Barry and I knew that our "philosophy" of territorial selling was the right one. We felt that if we were part of a company with good management and adequate funds, we would have the energy and resources to make our plan work. Moreover, whenever we were trying to do business in Hollywood we had experienced a curious reaction. The people we dealt with were vice-presidents of this company and that one: but they were employees, whereas *we* were British Lion — we owned our company and weren't subject, the way they were, to all the apprehensions of dismissal or demotion. Our "independence" actually elicited a resentful, sometimes bullying attitude from people with whom we were trying to do business. Now if we merged our company with a larger, richer entity, and became part of it ourselves, we would have the cash and the status without the onus. We started talking to EMI at the Cannes Film Festival in May 1975.

Who actually began talking to whom first is not quite certain. Deeley doesn't recall it precisely, but remembers Delfont talking about needing 'younger production people' — a natural 'opening' for his proposal. Spikings, on the other hand, stated two years later that the initiative to merge both companies had come from Delfont who, he claimed, had said, 'EMI . . . really wanted to have a go at cracking the international market and "we'd like you to come and do it with us".'* The success that Lew Grade seemed to be having — at that date, anyhow — in the American market with *The Return of the Pink Panther* probably wasn't lost on his younger brother at EMI. Whoever broached the take-over proposal first, it was quite obviously an idea 'whose time had come'.

'I got the impression that Bernard Delfont welcomed "young buccaneers" like Barry and myself, but had to proceed cautiously so as not to offend the "old guard" ', says Deeley. By this were meant Nat Cohen and his long-time crony Sir James Carreras, of Hammer Films, a man with great influence in the industry. Negotiations were not completed till May 1976. 'In the circumstances, we couldn't hope for a better deal than we got. Financially, for us, it had to be a disappointment.' British Lion's obligations were met; and the two partners — Deeley was the majority stockholder — finished up with just over £80,000 . . . 'not much for years of work'. They secured a promise that the name 'British Lion' would not be allowed to die: in fact, it very quickly disappeared off all EMI credits. An announcement stated that EMI saw the take-over as 'ensuring the succession to Nat Cohen,' though Cohen adds, 'I was not consulted and it was beyond my powers to influence the decision.' Deeley and Spikings had withdrawn from the board of Shepperton Studios a few months earlier and now 'EMI is essentially purchasing the production ability of the two gentlemen'. *Screen International* continued: 'The committed internationalism of Deeley and Spikings may confirm tendencies already discernible in EMI to invest their money in international projects which may not be made in Britain,' while leaving British production to 'play it safe' with low-budget projects.**

How would EMI executive responsibility be divided? Though many asked that question at the time of the take-over, it was not answered till a year later, when Deeley and Spikings made their first joint statement to

*Barry Spikings, interviewed by Sue Summers and Quentin Falk, *Screen International*, 7 June 1977.
**Screen International*, 22 May 1976.

the Press. 'If someone comes along with a project,' Deeley replied, 'a "No" from either of us is an absolute "No". A "Yes" from either of us is only subject to the other one saying "Yes", too.' And where did this leave Nat Cohen? As might have been expected, the answer was carefully couched: 'We have a clear responsibility to Lord Delfont [he had been created a Life Peer in 1976 in the same Honours List as his brother Lew Grade] and in turn to Sir John Read, who had set us financial parameters. Operating within those parameters . . . we do have a great deal of autonomy. We would not, however, at this stage, dream of acting other than in concert with Nat because, as the Press statement said, there are the three of us in partnership together.'* Naturally, Mr Cohen was asked his view. He replied that he was sitting back and waiting to see what the boys did. So were a lot of others.

*Michael Deeley, interviewed by Sue Summers and Quentin Falk, *Screen International*, 4 June 1977.

CHAPTER SIX

The Boyd Wonder

I came into this business almost totally blind and I bought experience dearly. — Don Boyd, The Times, *12 October 1981.*

In 1975, as he remembers it, Don Boyd fresh from film school, beaming enthusiastically behind his spectacles and radiating an enthusiasm that (surprisingly in view of what happened later) rarely deserted him over the next ten years, approached the heads of British Lion, Michael Deeley and Barry Spikings. He had an idea for a film which he hoped they would back. British Lion, he knew, had recently just failed to make a distribution deal for the French film that became *Emmanuelle*. Perhaps, Boyd thought later, that was why they gave him a sympathetic hearing. 'I believe they thought my film could be the British *Emmanuelle*.'* The film was going to be a study of sexual infidelity — 'That seemed to interest them.' He did not labour the point that it was also going to be about the clash between youth and middle-age — 'That was what interested me.'

However, it was not a propitious moment to come calling. British Lion was strapped for cash and already committed to film the stage hit *Conduct Unbecoming*: it was bound to be an expensive film; since its purchase several years earlier several writers, including the pricey Terence Rattigan, had come and gone on the scenario, so the pre-production costs alone were worrisomely high. Management strains were also beginning to develop between Deeley and Spikings on the one hand and Stanley Baker on the other. Boyd was given a friendly greeting and lent an attentive ear: more than that he was not given. Come back, he was told, when you've something on film: we'll look at it then. Well, it was a start . . . and Don Boyd, an unquenchable optimist, was not depressed.

*Don Boyd, interviewed by the author, 5 July 1984. Unless stated otherwise, all subsequent quotations from Boyd come from the same source.

It was in his nature to make himself agreeable. He was Scottish by birth, from Nairn, on the Moray Firth, where one didn't expect the North Sea breeze to be tempered by much mercy. But his distant origins were slightly more exotic. His family had Russian connections; Boyd himself had spent part of his childhood in East Africa and the Far East, where his father worked for an international tobacco company. Experience of British colonial rule at this impressionable age was to have direct bearing on his early career in films. After school in Edinburgh he studied drama in London, then returned to Scotland to direct some of the fringe shows at the Edinburgh Festival.

In 1968 he informed his parents that he wanted to go into films and enrolled himself in the London Film School; whereupon he was promptly disinherited. Ten years later he explained to David Lewin that his father had dearly wanted him to become an accountant and make money: the inference was that becoming a film-maker was the way to lose money.* With his allowance cut off, Boyd had to take jobs between classes and worked as a *plongeur*, otherwise known as a dishwasher, in some of the West End restaurants where he would later do his film deals. Cleaning dirty crockery at least gave him time to think, he says: it probably also acquainted him with the wastefulness that high spending, on films or food, brings out in people of otherwise moderate ambitions and modest talents.

After leaving film school in 1970, he made commercials for Shell, Chrysler, Schweppes, Coca-Cola and others and ate his heart out at the lack of opportunity to make films. The British film scene was empty and apathetic. Boyd, in common with his generation, felt personally betrayed that the high excitement of the Sixties had not lasted long enough for him to share it. He was just too late. His very youth, which would have been a bonus point ten years earlier, now told against him. Merely to be young in the Sixties was, by definition, to have talent — whereas to be young in the Seventies was simply to lack work and, if work were found, to be considered as unwelcome competition for some of those who were no longer as young as they had once felt. Boyd never forgot this sense of disjuncture. 'When I formed my own company it was because there was a new generation of frustrated young people who were not being allowed to prove themselves film-makers. The British film industry had no faith in young people then or now — I do.'

The faith was fast put to work to serve its possessor. While at school Boyd had written a scenario consisting of two parallel stories: one about a young couple with their life before them and their aspirations as yet unblemished by experience; the other about a middle-aged couple in mid-life crisis, grieving over a dead daughter and their own savourless existence. He called it *Intimate Reflections*; and it was this project, thanks to Boyd's enthusiastic presentation of the younger 'swinging' story,

Daily Mail, 23 January 1979.

which British Lion had briefly seen as 'another *Emmanuelle*'. Boyd
borrowed £35,000 from friends and his bank manager and after three
weeks' shooting he had a rough assembly and eventually enough
confidence to show the final cut to Deeley and Spikings.

But again he picked a bad moment. British Lion was now having
problems with *Nickelodeon*, the Peter Bogdanovich feature in which they
and EMI were co-investors, and which wasn't working out. They were
also trying to do a deal with Steven Spielberg for a film that became *Close
Encounters of the Third Kind*: it wasn't going well either. Boyd's little film
had to compete for Deeley's attention with telephone calls from
Hollywood. Barry Spikings, who had been unavoidably delayed, arrived
slightly late. 'But I think an hour of it convinced them that it wasn't
"another *Emmanuelle*",' says Boyd. 'The British Lion salesmen's
verdict was "very specialized fare".' They politely bowed out of it. 'I got
the feeling that although Spikings disliked it, his partner was a bit more
enthusiastic: anyhow, Deeley lent me £500 to go to the States and show
it around as my " calling card".' Boyd took the money and later paid it
back, 'which rather surprised Michael, I think'.

He carted the film around New York, Los Angeles and Milan's movie
market: the experience was 'infinitely depressing, but also of immense
value when I set up my own outfit. The men I showed it to were simply
not interested in film-making as a creative process. All they seemed to be
doing was selling films to each other. They reminded me of antique
dealers who form a "ring" to acquire an object from some sucker at the
lowest price going and later flog it among themselves for a much higher
price. In the initial stages of meeting them they tended to be welcoming,
polite, receptive . . . but they soon realized — and made it plain — that
there was nothing to their immediate advantage to be gained from a
26-year-old beginner. It was *very* sobering.'

It was also very instructive — for Boyd. He always made a point of
asking questions, 'which was a new experience for most of these men,
since very few of the people who came to sell them something were
willing to expose their own ignorance of the game the way I was. Like
most people they were flattered to have a raw beginner asking for words
of wisdom, and opened up. I'd been able to prove to my own satisfaction
that *technically* I knew how to make a film: now I was getting an
education in how to sell it *commercially*. They probably thought they were
dealing with some schizoid type who was after art one minute and
money the next. But the result got me into an early and enduring habit
of thinking of a film in terms of containable budgets and marketable
prospects, as well as in terms of workable screen-plays and potential
artistry. One thing impressed them, though: the fact that I'd put my
own money into the film. That *greatly* impressed them.'

Impatient to put his knowledge to work, Boyd again approached a
bank. 'But I knew enough now not to ask for money simply to make a

film. I got a loan to buy a building: banks like that kind of collateral *much* better. The one I bought was just round the corner from British Lion, in Berwick Street: it had a recording studio in the basement and an editing complex on the top floor. I planned to rent out these facilities, which made the bankers even more content. I was also into video cassettes, which I saw as having a great educational impact. I'd made a short, *The Four Seasons*, set to Vivaldi's music; and I planned another to feature Dustin Hoffman's ballerina wife. The cost was about £15,000 each: *most* pleasing to the bankers. I planned to spend £750,000 on five feature films, banking on one at least being successful enough internationally to cover the costs (or the losses) on the others. But then I made the first of three fatal mistakes.'

In retrospect, it seems scarcely credible that Don Boyd should not have realized that the first film in his production programme, *East of Elephant Rock* (12 January 1978), had its narrative antecedents in a vastly more renowned movie, *The Letter*, made by William Wyler in 1940. This, in turn, had been based on Somerset Maugham's story, inspired by a true incident that had become part of colonial folklore, about a white woman in the tropics who shoots her lover, protests it was a *crime passionnel* and lies her way towards an acquittal, only to be blackmailed by the man's vengeful Asian mistress.

Boyd had neither seen the Wyler film nor read the Maugham story — but he *had* heard the anecdote on which both were based. His father's work had taken young Don out to the Far East, which even in the immediate post-war period was still very much Maugham country. 'I had a deep affection for the British Empire; on an emotional level, that is, not for political ties. I'd grown up in households with many servants, in lands where a good living was to be had cheaply, among people who preserved the diehard attitudes of their forebears and an almost divine belief, not much shaken by the war, that God had set them up in authority over the inferior races and there was not even the threat of income tax to unsettle their complacency — it was the whole "white supremacy" thing.

'That was the story I wanted to tell, linking selfishness and hypocrisy with the decline of Empire and the surrender of responsibility. I felt that the story of the planter's unfaithful wife would make a good strong narrative on which to string my views on colonial rule and the sense of untouchable privilege that it bred among the rulers. When the reviews of the film came out I only then discovered, to my horror, that I was being accused of a "rip off" — that this "arrogant young fellow" was remaking a William Wyler classic without so much as a nod of acknowledgment to him or Willy Maugham.'

Another error Boyd now admits to making was employing a somewhat inexperienced writer on the screen-play's first draft — 'and then, like all young people assuming experience they don't yet possess, believing I could rework it myself and adapt it to my needs as we went along'. Acquiring such experience 'in the field' while shooting in Sri Lanka, was 'painful and expensive'. The film was budgeted at an unrealistically low £100,000, which meant that its stars, John Hurt and Judi Bowker, were on deferrals and Boyd was taking no fee at all as producer-director. Moreover, he had made it without a firm prior commitment from a British distributor, without any pre-sale to overseas territories, without even NFFC participation: no film could have been more 'independently' produced, nor more vulnerable.

Good reviews were essential if the movie was to have any chance of recovering its cost, never mind seeing a profit. And here Boyd made the third 'fatal mistake'. 'I appealed to the better nature of the film critics,' hs says. 'In my naive enthusiasm, I let slip a few indiscreet comments which were intended to "hype" *East of Elephant Rock* as a bold new venture by a young film-maker: except that the actual impression they conveyed was of an arrogant young fellow out to change the face of the British film industry.' Still wincing at the painful memory five years later, he said: 'I presented myself as a young guy new to the business, which was true, and asked (the critics) to be nice to me. They weren't.'*

They could scarcely be blamed. Seldom has a film been so maladroitly presented to the waiting critics, an impatient bunch at the best of times, not given to responding to soul-stirring speeches worthy of a wartime Prime Minister in which it was stressed that the entertainment they were about to see was truly *British*, made with *British* money, embellished by *British* talent. The film merely proved that patriotism is all right up to a point, but by itself it is not enough.

The old-fashioned title, *East of Elephant Rock*, redolent of the labels one expects to see affixed to extinct species in a natural history museum, seemed just right for the subject, which was the injustices of colonial policy. Unfortunately, the screen-play's rickety construction, not content with making capital out of the sins of Empire, attempted to add compound interest to the total by depicting the carnal sins of some of the servants of Empire, and eventually abandoned politics for the passions. Boyd gave evidence of knowing how to involve one in a real sense of people and place: the small-timers of a backwoods administration, living it up in feudal style, clustering ever more tightly together at the cocktail parties as colonial unrest reaches flashpoint intensity. The scenic glories of Sri Lanka gave a perspiring sense of social authenticity to the re-creation of the recent past. His production showed plenty of resourcefulness — an amazing amount, considering his budget — but the ambitions he demonstrated would have looked uncomfortably crowded inside *three* films.

One colossal piece of miscasting apart, his characters are solidly

---

*Don Boyd, interviewed by John Higgins, *The Times*, 12 October 1981.

convincing. John Hurt plays a minor Colonial Office official with a left-wing bias, who wades in among the tea planters talking like a *New Statesman* editorial rather than an uncapitalized human being, and proving a threat to their profits along with even less stable institutions such as their marriages. Like many of his kind he slams the system while taking the pick of its comforts, which include a compliant native beauty, never acknowledging that this droit de seigneur may be just as reprehensible as the political kind of overlordship.

But the film's most rounded character is not Hurt: it is Jeremy Kemp, as the plantation foreman, who takes the film's limp scenes between his teeth and shakes life into them. He puts all the man's weaknesses together to form a terrifying picture of the boss class. With his gammy leg, Digger's hat, park-warden's stick, dottle-and-spit approach to conversation and his randy, racist, gin-soaked approach to the people who give him his living, he is a desperate, flawed, pitiful, truthful person, clinging to the system even while ridiculing its formalities, the sort of man for whom putting on a dinner jacket is 'dressing up as the head waiter', yet totally dependent on colonial status to give him his only sense of 'belonging'. Kemp's acting is one of the most vivid pieces of character-drawing in Seventies cinema: it has been undeservedly forgotten amid the general ridicule that the film attracted. Part of this is regrettably due to the miscasting of Judi Bowker, a more piquant, less scared-looking Sarah Miles, but just too small an instrument in every way to play the murderous range of passions that jealousy suddenly thrusts on her.

Clancy Sigal, in *The Spectator*, called Boyd 'a real hustler, the kind of go-getter the British film industry probably deserves at the moment,' though he conceded, 'I'd rather have seen *East of Elephant Rock* than the two infinitely more polished French pictures this week.'* What generated most critical vehemence was the unacknowledged — because innocent — resemblance between the film and *The Letter*. Apart from his lack of wisdom in incorporating it into the film in the first place, Boyd showed his inexperience in introducing this particular twist far too late in the story. A film that began with political pretentions suddenly veered off course into a second-rate Bette Davis melodrama — without Bette Davis, alas!

With very few exceptions, the critics were scathing. Philip French, deputizing for *The Times*'s man, showed least mercy (in Boyd's opinion, anyhow). 'The writer-director Don Boyd', French wrote, 'has of course embellished his tale with some political background, mostly attached to John Hurt as a liberal (and briefly naked) civil servant. If possible, this aspect is handled even more ineptly than the love story, with not the remotest understanding of colonial politics in the post-war world.

*Clancy Sigal, *The Spectator*, 21 January 1978.

Elephant Rock is badly lit, badly edited and badly acted. Typically in the course of a love scene on a railway platform, the station clock moves back half an hour.'*

However, the same paper, a week later, threw up an unexpected ally. 'At a time when the British film industry desperately needs sympathetic encouragement, it is sad that such a worthy endeavour by a young director . . . should be greeted with such a distorted — and to those who know — unfair reception.'** So wrote Bryan Forbes, who later said, not entirely jocularly, that the letter had cost him good reviews for his own films ever since *The Times* published it. Ironically, if Forbes had not taken to his typewriter in defence of Boyd through a letter which served as a note of confidence in his potential as well as a bond of sympathy-in-suffering, it is probable that a large section of the British film industry would not have collapsed quite so brutally as it was to do five years later. That tale will be told in due course.

NIGHTHAWKS AND OTHER BIRDS

Boyd licked his wounds, sadder, wiser and poorer. Getting *East of Elephant Rock* shown in the cinemas, unhelped by good reviews, brought him a cash-flow problem. 'At this time I was approached by Roy Tucker, an accountant specializing in tax law, and today one of my best friends.' Tucker had let his own enthusiasm for show business create problems for *him*. To promote the idea of a replica of an Elizabethan theatre, he had made a video film of a period production of *Romeo and Juliet*: now he came to Boyd for advice on how to sell it.

The tax accountant and the impatient young film-maker formed an alliance. Tucker, according to Boyd, acquired 49 per cent of the latter's company — capital which Boyd immediately put back into the business, taking a fairly modest salary of £15,000 to meet his own and his family's needs. Roy Tucker undertook to invest in film production, maintaining an arm's-length distance from the creative decisions, and to assist Boyd in financing, promoting and marketing his films. According to Boyd, his partner was occasionally consulted by the tax authorities; for at this date, *circa* 1979, the creation of film finance by imaginative and perfectly legal use of the tax loopholes was still a relatively new game in the City.

It was the clever arrangements devised by Tucker within his Rossminster group of companies which served as a 'sort of blueprint' — Boyd's words — for the financial scheme that was hesitantly approved and tolerated by Treasury officials until its abuse by sections of the film industry led to its 'surprise' abolition in 1984. Whether or not this link

*Philip French, *The Times*, 13 January 1978.
**Bryan Forbes, *The Times*, 20 January 1978.

can be established quite so clearly, there is no doubt that with Roy Tucker's assurance that the bills for the films could be met Don Boyd was enabled to do the deals to make them much more easily than some of his contemporaries: the 'Boyd Wonder', as he got to be called, was on his way.

One film that Boyd financed — along with West German TV money and a list of individuals and institutions as long as one's arm — was *Nighthawks* (8 March 1979). For a number of years it was the only serious 'above ground' film about the problems of living and working as a homosexual in London without also being part of an alienated community.

Nighthawks is a film about individual loneliness, not sexual exploitation. It is low-key and factual, anxious not to be accused of displaying the range of its wares so as to 'sell' its product: it retains a reticence that serves it all the better for inviting the inspection and understanding of the 'straight' world. Many of the people in it were real-life London gays. What *Nighthawks* got very right indeed was how the promiscuous male pick-up was always ending and beginning again, never continuing: its characters made contacts, rather than formed relationships. Its chief character was a young geography teacher in a London comprehensive school — one could hardly get more normal than that! By day, he teaches; by night, he cruises. Eyes restless, endlessly sipping his lager, he quietly, modestly even, sorts out the talent in the gay discos — and the night's company falls into his embrace, sometimes . . . and then again, sometimes not. 'I've put two sugars in . . . Sorry, I've forgotten your name.' One would probably laugh if this were a comedy of heterosexual strangers waking up together for breakfast. But it's the flash of lonely revelation in such dialogue that time and again cuts one directly into the gay world of one-night stands. 'Morning comes early in a stranger's bed. . .' That keynote line from Richard Baskin's *Welcome to L.A.* suite of songs could be this film's, too.

The sketchy story follows the boy, played by Ken Robertson, to his meeting with a fellow-teacher (Rachel Nicholas James), who draws him out without — thankfully — 'reforming' him: rather the opposite. The aftermath of the school dance is a burst of courageous frankness about his gayness in front of his class. The scene slightly misfires: it uses real London schoolchildren (which adds to its authentic interest), who either spoke the crude taunts written for them or else improvised insults of their own as they quiz their teacher about his gay life. It is supposed to be his baptismal 'coming out'. But the accent of interest is not on the teacher's candour and courage, but on the terrifying generation of pubescent bigots the schools are rearing: little faces of childhood already set in the plaster of adult prejudice. So much for education in the ethics of tolerance, never mind the facts of sex!

Nighthawks, written and directed by Ron Peck and Paul Hallam, could almost be used as a tracer element to uncover the stealthy advance of just such prejudices into the areas of sexual tolerance which it was thought in the Sixties had been cleared of decades of legal constraints and cleansed of layers of social stigma. Not so. The film was screened around the world, in some countries quite freely, in others (such as Greece) with censorship and legal harassment: but in Britain of the mid-1980s, it had all but gone underground again as prejudice and apprehension once again caused the gay community to lose momentum, if not heart. On 30 December 1982, the tabloid newspaper, *The Star*, actually singled out *Nighthawks* as a ground to attack Channel 4 TV for its policy of buying controversial films: 'It must not be shown on TV.' Derek Jarman, whose own film *Sebastiane* was also adjudged a threat to something or other by the same news-sheet, commented drily in his diary entry for the last day of 1982: 'Today the *Telegraph* printed a statement from Channel 4 denying that they intended to show either *Sebastiane* or *Nighthawks*. They explained that they had been bought as part of a "package". Times change. Last week they completed the show print for transmission.'*

Thanks to Roy Tucker's skill at finding finance, Boyd was able to announce in October 1978 that he was moving away from films with miniscule budgets like *East of Elephant Rock* and *Nighthawks* into the riskier area of movies budgeted at around £1m. One of these was to be a horror film with a modern metropolitan setting, *An American Werewolf in London*, to be directed by John Landis, a young American who had scored a spectacularly unexpected success with *Animal House*, the movie that made slobbish humour into a staple screen genre and propelled John Belushi into what proved to be self-incinerating stardom. Landis, a much more sophisticated joker than his American movie suggested, had discovered he and Boyd shared an excitement for the sheer mad fun of the film business, where one could finish up with a mess on one's face *à la Animal House*, or an equally gross fortune sticking to one's hands.

'Great! we must make it,' Boyd exclaimed after a single reading of the *Werewolf* script; and, to do it cheaply, they resolved to shoot it on location in England and as soon as possible. Landis talked with Universal's then production chief Ned Tanen: he committed to it at once. 'The budget was $3m.,' says Boyd, 'generous by our standards up to then, cheap by theirs.' Landis's partnership with his fellow American George Folsey would have disqualified Boyd from producing the film; but it is likely he would have been executive producer, and taken an appropriate percentage of the profits, had he not made what he now acknowledges to have been a 'bad misjudgment' in announcing the project in an advertisement mock-up as one of 'his' films. 'I think John didn't like being included in a Don Boyd line-up. Goodbye to *Werewolf*! I

*Derek Jarman, *Dancing Ledge* (Quartet, 1984), p. 10.

didn't even rate a participating interest in it — I was still too much of a beginner to dictate terms like that. I wish I had. It made millions — just when I needed some of them.'

He comforted himself with getting the first of his bigger-budget movies into production for his regrouped organization, now known as The Boyd Co. *Sweet William*, which began filming entirely on locations in North London between September and October 1978, was based on Beryl Bainbridge's novel about a priapic Scot who cuts a chauvinist swathe through the bed-sitter set and, of course, destroys the thing he claims to love. Directed by Claude Whatham, who confirmed his *That'll Be the Day* skilfulness in comprehending the inarticulate tensions of the generations, *Sweet William* is that rare kind of British film in which the women for once outnumber the men. It was a risky film, too, for 'liberated' times; it said that it's a woman's lot to take it lying down — and a man's pleasure to give it.

Yet it is not itself a chauvinist polemic, despite Sam Waterston's seductive ability, like the eponymous herbaceous plant, to hop from one bed to another: he's hardly in through the door of the new flatlet than he's asking 'Now, where do you lie down?' The girls are not treated as sex objects: they are well-acted, highly individualized young people of the 1980s. One hesitates to say that Boyd's production encourages one to view William from their vantage point, since so many of them are literally underneath him, in taxi-cabs, bed-sitters and even in a maternity ward. But precious few previous movies — and none of them British — have suggested so well how the two sexes look to separate satisfactions. The man needs sex for physical self-esteem, but can't find any emotional maturity in it; the girls goes for it out of the sort of desperation engendered by shared digs and semi-lonely life, but can't turn a hit-and-run serial of philandering into a steady relationship, never mind marriage.

The film is filled with the desperate promiscuous tensions of the last years of the Seventies, ravelled subtly and unravelled sadly, anchored in puritanism as well as permissivenes.. If one were looking for individual faces to fit the opportunism that grasps at William as the left-over life of the Sixties, one could not collect a better gallery of representative Seventies girls than Jenny Agutter, Geraldine James and the rest . . . while Waterston resembles the romantic manifestation of available manhood which the Sixties advertisements told one appeared to girls who immersed themselves in a Badedas bubble-bath as a tall, wind-blown, gypsy-looking youth, springing out of nowhere with a far from obscure object of desire in his eyes.

Two eras meet in *Sweet William* and several generations, too, since it knows so well where its characters fit into family and society. Thus Daphne Oxenford is instantly recognizable by every girl from out-of-town as the Mum she left behind, fitting her hat primly over her

provincial perm while still in her petticoat, and freezing her own mate —
played by Arthur Lowe in one of his all too rare 'serious' roles — into
numb obedience in whose every silent glance is an exercise in piteous
autobiography. Yet mother and daughter can snuggle down under the
same eiderdown and giggle together at William battering on the window
like a Finsbury Park Heathcliff.

Boyd's catholicity of taste, or, perhaps, business restlessness, also led
him to produce (along with Jeremy Thomas) *The Great Rock 'n' Roll
Swindle* (15 May 1980).

Distributed by Virgin Films, an offshoot of the records company
whose rise and rise as an eclectic conglomerate under Richard Branson
was still a few years off, much of it had been shot between 1976 and late
1978, some by Russ Meyer before Malcolm McLaren, begetter of the
Sex Pistols, had him fired. Looking back at the film from the
mid-Eighties, it has immediate interest as a forerunner of all those
video-clips promoting Pop groups which have become a mainstay of
MTV in America, and have been a raucous incubator of baby talents
like *Swindle*'s young director Julien Temple who took the chance to
transfer their 'sixty cuts a minute' style to feature films.

But it is also a valuable chronicle of the souring of the Pop scene in the
late Seventies. Police harassment at a Jubilee concert on the Thames,
attacks on the Sex Pistols in the streets, the group's misbehaviour at
airports (which caused an image-conscious EMI to settle their contract)
give the film a lively sense of self-commentary. McLaren's gospel of
'Terrorize, Threaten and Insult Your Own Useless Generation' is linked
directly to the group's own history and the media's instant complicity.

The totally unself-critical nature of television exposure has seldom
been as ruthlessly demonstrated, along with the shamelessness of the
records industry whose own members took parts in the film to re-create
their roles in the signing and sacking of the Sex Pistols. The fact that the
three principals, Mary Millington, Nancy Spungen and Sid Vicious,
were all dead, by suicide or murder, when the film was released
validated its nihilism better than any attempt made in it to push bad art
to the extremes of shock and profitability. It is the kind of film whose
overt opportunism actually gains in lustre with time: this is indeed how
it was as the revolution turned into reactionary money-grabbing.

FINANCIAL STRATEGIES

Don Boyd was riding high as an independent producer by late 1978.
David Puttnam's absence from the British scene — as recounted earlier,
he had gone to work in Hollywood to restore his financial fortunes —
seemed to ensure Boyd's succession to the status of a 'one-man film
industry', at least as far as the media were concerned. To be fair to him,

however, he never exploited his position by any snide jibe at Puttnam. Quite the contrary. 'David helped me at every stage with what one could call "political" advice about who mattered in the film industry,' he says. 'Though he never creatively involved himself in my work, he introduced me to the Hollywood executives, agents, etc., to whom he had access. I see David as a different animal from myself. We're both determined to "fly the flag", work with directors who are "new boys" but committed to the idea of cinema in the sense that they know the different set of responses to a movie that define it as one for cinemas or TV. Above all, we want to make films about British life and culture that will appeal to our generation. David's more of a politician, skilful at figuring out where the power lies and how to alter the balance in one's favour. But we both share the same satisfaction in that we've been able to make the films we've wanted to because we *liked* them.'

All the same, Boyd's next production was one which Puttnam would probably have shied away from making. To make *Scum* (20 September 1979), Puttnam might have decided, would run the risk of glamorizing the very violence it condemned as endemic in the British system of Borstal training for young offenders. There would have been more than a little truth in this. Boyd found the film ready-made, so to speak. It had started life as a £120,000 production for BBC TV based on a script by Roy Minton and directed by Alan Clarke. All had seemed set for transmission when the BBC took fright over its contents. Unremitting brutality, gang sodomy and a final suicide were hardly the things to be showing at a delicate juncture in the corporation's negotiations with the Home Office — the department also responsible for Borstal management — to get its annual TV licence fee raised. Boyd acquired the rights and Clarke remade the movie for the big screen with commendable economy. It was shot inside six weeks, between 10 January and 17 February 1979, at Elstree Studios and in a disused South London home for old people which required next to no refurbishment to convert it into a penal institution. The budget was a thrifty £250,000. It was then rushed to the Cannes Film Festival in May, where it opened to good 'territory' sales in the market place within a few days of Boyd's *Sweet William* being premiered in London. While *Sweet William* turned out a financially successful picture in the longer run, its marketing was weak, whereas *Scum* quickly and fully realized all the hopes and money invested in it.

Its opponents predictably — but justly — charged it with sensationalizing the 'facts' of Borstal life, observing that such facts were possible, but their accumulation to the extent they did in one place was improbable: it left out the humane and successful side of treating young offenders. To which the only reply was a brazen acknowledgment that it did. The film dramatized the negative forces of a system where the warders, to a man, look the other way and allow the boys to impose their rule by fear, fist and the boot. A lot of it looked like *Midnight Express* British-style, down to the multiple sodomy committed on a defenceless boy. Its acts of grossness were self-referring: its authority figures, like the governor's religious martinet or the matron's uncomprehending rule-book stickler, were ineluctably trapped in the system as surely as the boys — more so, even, since life set no release for them except retirement.

But there is a humane connection with *The Loneliness of the Long Distance Runner* some seventeen years earlier. The voice of reason and rebellion is admittedly not class-based, as it was in Courtenay's case: but it used the system in the same way to defeat the system. Not by an act of open rebellion, but by a constant and cynical erosion of the system's oppressive certitudes. The undermining of Borstal authority was entrusted to a worthy Courtenay successor, Mick Ford, as a sardonic internee, a thinking and articulate rebel, who plays by the rules — pretending to be vegetarian, refusing to wear leather boots on religious grounds — in order to subvert the rule-makers. It is Ford whose Machiavellian tongue gives the film its moral *tone* — though it is an inadequate substitute for the moral *perspective* that the whole film should have possessed.

Scum was Boyd's biggest hit to date: and it is worth examining the financial strategy that made it and other Boyd Co. films attractive investments. Tax deferrals were the basis of it. This is treacherous ground to explore; and it is largely due to a sure-footed journalist with an economics background, Lorna Sullivan, that interesting facts about Boyd's operation came to light in an article she wrote for *The Sunday Telegraph* on 3 February 1980.

Her inquiries, based in part on Roy Tucker's information, illustrate the fiendishly inventive machinations that were forced on British film-makers — though some, admittedly, found the financial game attractive as well as lucrative — by Britain's failure to provide any sustained support for production other than the inadequate and constantly vulnerable NFFC. According to Ms Sullivan, 20 per cent of the finance for *Sweet William*, *Scum* and Derek Jarman's *The Tempest* came from limited partnerships which the investors could legitimately set against tax. Records showed that twenty-six individuals paid £369,750 into three such partnerships in 1979 in order to obtain tax losses of over £1.5m. after allowing for the 'gearing up' of investments — which was customary in such transactions. 'The paper loss is about four times what the taxpayer contributes. A few weeks — or even days — later he leaves the partnership taking the loss with him, along with an ever so slight hope that some day, after everyone else has taken a cut of any eventual profits, he might also get something. This small hope technically transforms tax avoidance into tax deferral.'

Ms Sullivan also reported on a very complex network of holding companies, some based in Guernsey and the Isle of Man, areas hospitable to such investments because of their different legal systems and independence of British fiscal laws. 'Before the film shows a profit, the British directors of the general partners — Boyd and his colleagues — resign. They are replaced by two Bermudans and a secretary in Guernsey. The result is that when profits start to flow in there are no UK directors or shareholders to catch the taxman's eye. And the high-rate taxpayers, who bought their paper losses, will be protected from unwanted profits by their partnership agreements which have left them the tiniest slice, if any, of the pie.' Scrutiny of the records at Companies House, Cardiff, showed that Roy Tucker and his Rossminster group of financial services companies had begun their association with Don Boyd's film-making in 1976 — as Boyd has confirmed — when a former Rossminster bank lent Boyd's company, Kendon Films, £30,000; the next year Tucker went on the board of a newly formed holding company for all the Boyd film interests; and, at the same time, this company lent Kendon £134,000; not long afterwards an Isle of Man-registered company took a debenture over the holding company and its assets. In September 1980 Tucker became a Kendon director, though apparently content to leave to Boyd the decision where to invest the funds that such dexterity had made available.

There have been few more detailed accounts of an independent film-maker's operations at a time when government disincentives to investment were the order of the day. In July 1979, however, the Inland Revenue began to look more critically at schemes like these; and there was the feeling that such inventiveness as they demonstrated ought to be more strictly defined — and, if their inventors' ingenuity still outran the inspector's powers of restraint, then some declarative legislation would have to be introduced. All this contributed to the steady build-up of sentiment among Whitehall's permanent fiscal advisers that if the film industry was so good at self-help of this nature, it could do without Government assistance. The 'privatizing' policy of abolishing film subsidies and telling the industry to rely on self-generated investment was evolved by the Treasury's higher civil servants, frugal — indeed self-denying — men and women who didn't usually lunch or dine at The White Elephant or Les A. or the Variety Club's top table, in response to what they had observed of the 'tax avoidance industry' that grew up in film production over these years even if it was perfectly legal.

Boyd put two new films into production in February and March 1979. One was *Hussy* (1980), directed by Matthew Chapman and made under Roy Tucker's tax-deferral schemes. A sentimental melodrama set in British clubland about an escort — i.e., prostitute — attempting to leave her past behind her in a freeze-frame happy-ever-afterness, its best feature was Helen Mirren. The other film, a documentary entitled *Blue Suede Shoes*, celebrated the rock 'n roll sub-culture from Bill Haley's legendary tour of Britain in 1957 to his triumphant comeback twenty-two years later.

ROAD TO DISASTER

Boyd spent much of 1979 in America working on the most ambitous film he had yet undertaken — one whose disastrous outcome was still reflected in the ambivalent view he took, five years after the event, that only in a business where money and myth seemed to share the same unreality could a nightmare of this scale come to pass. 'The most notorious and largest, the biggest failure in financial terms (I have ever made),' he recalled in 1983, proving that even as *Honky Tonk Freeway* receded into film history, the enormity of what it stood for was more glaringly imposed on his mind.*

As mentioned earlier, it might never have got made at all but for Bryan Forbes's loyalty to a badly mauled fellow film-maker. With tender feelings for the savaging which Boyd had been given over *East of Elephant Rock* — after all, Forbes knew what it was like to be set on by the running dogs of the media — he asked the younger man to go to America as a second-unit director on the film that Forbes was to make for MGM at Pinewood Studios: an updated sequel to *National Velvet* with a background of the upcoming 1980 Olympics entitled *International Velvet*. Perhaps Forbes hoped that going back to work 'in the field' would re-establish Boyd's badly shaken confidence in his abilities as a director. He asked him to shoot material on the pre-Olympics horse trials to be held at Ledyard, Massachusetts: this was round about October 1977. 'So every day,' Boyd recalls, 'when the film unit was moving from our Boston hotel to the show-jumping grounds, a 40-minute journey by freeway, I seemed to see America, the *real* America for the very first time. I'd made previous visits by air. Now I was fascinated by the inter-dependence of motor-car and highway and the urban hinterland we glimpsed, with its cafes, pull-ups, filling stations, supermarkets, movie houses, even brothels: there seemed a world, a whole eccentric universe, surrounding the freeway. I decided there and then that this must be the subject of my first American film. The best films come from one's instincts; mine told me this was the one to make.'

They also (sometimes) come from good writers: Boyd set about finding one to share his excitement, at not too high a price, though. 'The system in America with the large agencies is that the major writers have a price which they never reduce.' So, with endearing candour, he went to William Morris, one of the two or three top talent agencies, and asked, 'Don't you have some eager youth sitting around whom you think may

*Don Boyd, in a talk to students at the University of Guildford, 23 November 1983. Quotations from Boyd's talk are combined in the following account with the author's interview with Boyd.

be rather talented and who could be interested in this crazy idea of mine?' He was given a bundle of scripts to read and 'out of them I selected Ed Clinton, told him the idea, commissioned him to do a treatment. I wanted a film that would be episodic, not a normal narrative, with a bunch of characters, several separate sets of them, and everything in the movie was to be connected to the freeway — and I wanted it to be a comedy. The film was to be written very specifically for a budget between two and three million dollars. I saw it as a small-budget, but stylish "road" movie, the sort of thing I could shoot wherever we stopped out of the back of a truck.' Clinton came back with a treatment that was all episodes, but no story. 'That worried us both.' Then the writer telephoned one evening to say he'd found the narrative link — 'This small Preston Sturges-like town by-passed by the freeway and upset about the snub to its dignity and the threat to its trade. It does everything in its power to see that the freeway is connected to the town.'

Boyd now departed from the usual approach to a writer, which is to say: 'Be off, we'll look at your draft and call you.' 'In this case, I was determined to soak up America and all its eccentricities along with the writer and work the ideas we picked up *en route* into the script.' The odyssey threw up much new material: but Boyd acknowledged later, 'What I wasn't doing was thinking that (all these ideas) could be terribly costly. There wasn't some nasty character such as I am now, a *producer* saying "You can't possibly have ten or eleven different locations, 103 speaking parts, your own freeway specially constructed and an elephant on water skis as well." I was saying, "Great! Let's have it all!"' In June 1978 Clinton turned in the first draft of the script. 'It was one of the funniest I've ever read. I was so excited! I was sure we'd hit gold!' After a second draft (replacing narrative exposition with visuals) he was 'still sure we could shoot it with a bunch of friends for three to four million dollars'. (Already the budget was starting to escalate.)

Barry Spikings, who was now head of EMI's production, had been one of those who liked *East of Elephant Rock*: 'One day you're going to do something big,' Boyd recalls being told by him. As a gesture of respect to this perceptive friend, Boyd sent Spikings the second draft to read while he went off to Florida to do some budgeting there and explore with the producer of the second-unit footage of *International Velvet* whether he would produce *Honky Tonk Freeway*. (Boyd intended directing it, but felt he needed a producer familiar with the American set-up.) Sometime in August 1978 a call came from Spikings and, after some desultory talk on other matters, Boyd asked politely, 'What did you think of *Honky Tonk Freeway* script? To my great surprise, he said he thought it was the funniest script he and his wife Dot had ever read. He said, "We want to make it." I said I saw it as a small film. He said he didn't think his board would go along with that: EMI policy was then to make big films with established names in order to compete in the American movie market.

How big was "big" I asked. I got the impression that "big" was around
$10m.'

So a small 'cottage-industry' type of approach to a little comedy was
changed into a self-consciously 'big' picture with a major budget — and
Boyd now had to grab hold of his project in order to stop it running away
from him completely. He himself was not an 'acceptable' name as
director on a major feature, even though he had got Peter Bogdanovich's
positive reaction to the idea of producing it. At William Morris's annual
Thanksgiving Day party in London he met Spikings. 'Barry said he had
shown the script to Joe Janni, who wanted to produce. I went berserk! "I
thought I was still going to produce!" I screamed. Barry laughed it off,
then said we must offer the script to Janni's former partner and friend,
John Schlesinger. If he committed to it, then EMI would back it. I met
John: we took to each other at once. We met with Barry, worked out a
deal with the lawyers. Bernard Delfont, who was then chairman of EMI
Film and Theatre Corporation, was brought in at the end, shook hands
on the deal and we knew we were set to make this massive film. Nobody
at that time had made firm budgeting plans: there was an "atmosphere"
about what it would cost — the parameters of the budget we had in
mind were now ten to fifteen million dollars. Schlesinger stipulated that
he wanted Howard Koch Jr., whom he had worked with on his
American films, as producer: so we had in effect *two* producers, with me
ending up doing much of the "line" work at the actual shooting.'

As a director has the major impact on how a film turns out — and a
director as tough-minded as Schlesinger had become after his
Hollywood experiences did not hesitate to flex his muscle — the script
was now torn completely apart. 'Nowadays', says Boyd, 'I would put my
foot down and say "No". At that time I allowed it to go on and agonized
about the changes my idea was undergoing.' These involved 'endless
research' into the multiplicity of characters, since Schlesinger liked to
acquaint himself with their backgrounds, even though nothing of this
might be directly relevant to what appeared on the screen. Most of 1979
was spent in this way. Shooting was set to begin in January 1980.

One thing (amongst others) Boyd found he had underestimated was
Schlesinger's perfectionist nature, backed by his hard-won right to the
'final cut'. 'Every decision John made was rational, some were inspired:
but even minor changes were bound to make a large impact on the
budgeting, scheduling and final shooting.' By the end of 1979 Boyd had
set up production offices for this British-financed film at the Goldwyn
Studios, Hollywood, and planned to begin shooting in Utah during the
snowy season, move over to New York (which would also 'double' for
Chicago), then down to Florida to use the section of specially
constructed freeway before the summer rains brought their paralysing
humidity, and finally back to the Hollywood studio where the brilliant
Italian designer, Scarfiotti, who had worked with Visconti and

Bertolucci, and whose perfectionist nature equalled Schlesinger's, was creating the sort of sets that would give the film a feeling of size in keeping with its budgetary ambitions.

Boyd was now feeling rather overwhelmed by what he had started. 'I was having to oversee the freeway construction, negotiate with the Governor of Florida, persuade a small community to hand themselves and their town over to us for the location shooting, and deal with very difficult local unions. In short, I was having to handle not only the creative side but very complicated administration. I was dealing with a thousand or so employees and feeling like the managing director of a factory where I really only knew the board of directors and a few of the floor managers.' It was all very different from 'the sort of thing I could shoot with my friends out of the back of a truck wherever we stopped'.

The risk element was now huge. Even so, the crew never bargained for the catastrophe that occurred once filming moved to New York after a successful shoot in the snows of Utah with a temperamental elephant which had to be accustomed to the idea of water-skis by the time its star turn came to be filmed in Florida. News arrived that the rains had preceded them to Florida. Mount Dora (the principal location) was looking waterlogged and construction on the special two-mile highway had closed down. It was resolved to go straight from New York/Chicago back to Hollywood and shoot on the studio sets which the designer and crew were now ordered to work on round the clock in order to have them ready.

The budget had now risen to nearly $18m: the new emergency rescheduling pushed it up to $21m. Though Schlesinger profited from the total control that studio conditions allowed him, everyone had to contend with the instant exhaustion that set in when the unit got to Florida in a 90-degree temperature to shoot expensive night-time scenes 'on two miles of tarmac in the middle of nowhere with no home links at all'. When it was all finally over, Boyd recalls, the aftermath was miles and miles of unedited film, a sense of abandonment as the key people left for other films, and severe psychological depression among those left.

In this mood they took an important creative decision. 'We moved back to England and set up our production office at Twickenham. We decided we were British film-makers working on a massive canvas of America and we were going to come up with a film to knock the world down with — as Europeans.'

In retrospect, the irony of this is brutal. Here was the biggest film that EMI had backed as part of its policy to meet the Americans on their own scale, with subjects that were indigenously American (and, it was hoped, had international appeal, too) and made in the identifiable heartland of America — yet it was being put together in a modest little London studio, thousands of miles from the prime audience it had to please, in order to get back a budget that was now in excess of $22m.

The English working ambience accentuated the British overview of the American characters up to their quirky tricks. 'I now feel it was slightly patronizing,' says Boyd. 'We imagined that our approach was as valid as an American's. Consequently, the editing period was almost one of arrogance. We thought satire was at the root of the comedy. We were quite happy to be satirical, and a little cynical, in our approach.' Later he was to blame himself for this loss of objectivity. 'David Puttnam is the master of that kind of objectivity and has often expressed his frustration to me at the post-production period when he has to try to convey to a director that he's being a little too subjective about the film he's just shot.'

Maybe, Boyd mused, they ought to have involved Barry Spikings at this stage: after all, he was reminding them who was paying the bill — which now stood at over $23m. But Spikings did not see the final assembly till it was ready for him and the other EMI executives. 'Barry thought it was the funniest thing he'd ever seen. The five or six other people there thought the same. They were all English.' Feeling they were on to 'an absolute winner', they then tidied up the film and a 'married' — or final — print was made. At this stage it hadn't been seen by any section of the mass American audience for which it was intended; and any alteration to a print that combined the sound track and the visuals would be much more expensive. But to have their labours tidily packed into a stack of cans gave Boyd and company 'a false sense of security . . . and we celebrated New Year 1981 in terrific form'.

Then, like the traditional hangover, came an unpleasant and increasing sense of doubt. This was due to the dreaded previews system used by American studios to 'check out' a picture before release with a 'representative audience', so that it can be altered if necessary before money is spent on prints and promotion. The print was delivered to Universal, which previewed it to 'a quite sophisticated audience' in Seattle.

'We executives all showed up in our limousines accompanied by perceptible paranoia. But the audience that had come was the kind that might be expected to enjoy the film; and laugh they did. Quite a lot. But not as much as John and I hoped. And not nearly as much as Universal hoped. They were given cards to fill in — how they reacted to the characters, events, etc., and back at the hotel we analysed them. Very, *very* gloomy! They made us suddenly start to re-assess everything. We previewed it four more times: we changed sequences and narrative; we experimented with voice-over and music. In short, we diluted our original instinct, not because of some objective opinion we could argue with, but because of those damn computerized preview cards! The Americans are used to handling them: sometimes they can be useful. But they weren't useful to the film at that stage in its life.

'Worse followed when we got round to discussing how it would be screened and marketed. By now Universal had "inherited" all EMI productions following the debacle of the company's plan, in association with Lew Grade, to set up its own distribution outfit in America, and now we had a completely different set of publicity people to "educate". They insisted on even more previews and expressed great concern. So we entered into battle with Universal. . . A bad mistake. We British arrogantly assumed we could tell them how to do their job, which caused all kinds of different advertisements to be produced, different commercials, different trailers. And the budget kept on rising. There was confusion, indecision and hard feelings all round.'

By this time, too, Hollywood had been hit by the commercial disaster of Michael Cimino's *Heaven's Gate*, a $40m.-plus debacle which released a collective backlash against the extravagantly budgeted picture that couldn't be sold. From being a 'difficult' film, *Honky Tonk Freeway* suddenly became a 'very bad news one'. The media began paying it attention: but not the flattering or useful attention that Boyd and the others felt it needed. The British involvement in the making of it merely seemed to embitter the comments: who *were* these people who'd made a movie 'put-on' about Americans? Boyd believes this feedback proved fatal. 'It predisposed the public to dislike the film before even a single ticket-buyer had set eyes on it. It is vital to protect a film's media image. Even if the public have heard absolutely nothing about it while it's being made, it is immensely important that the first thing they do hear should trigger a feeling that at least it's worth considering a visit to the cinema when it gets there. The advance word about *Honky Tonk Freeway* created exactly the opposite feeling.'

By ironic coincidence, at the very moment his film was causing such nervousness and loathing, Boyd was conscious of Universal's unmixed support for another film it was promoting, this time with far greater expectation of success. The film, which opened the very same week as *Honky Tonk Freeway*, was John Landis's *An American Werewolf in London* — which had briefly formed part of Boyd's own production plans a couple of years earlier! *Werewolf* was a tremendous success: though *Honky Tonk Freeway* was now being accepted as a disappointment, no one anticipated the overwhelming and instantaneous calamity it turned into on opening in America. 'When we opened in New York,' says Boyd, 'John Schlesinger was in Canada promoting the film in Toronto. Our reviews were, well, mixed: but there were a couple of raves that raised our hopes. They were false hopes. *Variety* called us "*Nashville* on wheels", which made the heart leap, then the review crucified us.' This influential paper said: 'The overriding question about EMI's *Honky Tonk Freeway* is why anyone should want to spend over $25m. on a film as devoid of any basic humorous appeal. . . [Its] long-term commercial appeal appears to be almost nil.'*

*Variety, 19 August 1981.

Up to the day this review appeared, Boyd had been regarded by 'my peers in the Hollywood community as the producer of what was then the biggest film being made in America. I had my office at Paramount, a suite in the Beverly Wilshire; I was fawned on by stars, agents and directors. After *Variety*'s verdict, only one acquaintance called: and the week we opened I really felt I had caught some contagious infection. And of course I had — its name was "failure". In my heart of hearts, I knew the film hadn't worked. What neither I nor anyone else bargained for was a disaster on such a scale . . . of such consequence.'

The film was quickly withdrawn from cinemas where it had opened: exhibitors were either compensated or had their programme replaced by reissues of proven successes. 'For months afterwards, it kept being brought up in article after article, in interview after interview, as a Terrible Example. We were universally reviled as incompetent spendthrifts, ego-trippers willing to bankrupt the honest exhibitors of America. One felt *hunted*! *Variety* had delivered an initial one-line pronouncement of doom positioned directly under *Honky Tonk Freeway*'s title: 'Won't pay toll'. Its invaluable sequence of capsule comments on the state of business in the nation's cinemas was no more lenient: 'Stalled' 'Out of gas', 'Dead-End', 'Crashed'. The news flashes on a highway disaster. Boyd felt himself the chief victim. In his dazed condition he vainly speculated whether Americans resented the movie's send-up of American life-styles because *British* money had financed it. But would All-American backing have made the film-going electorate of the Reagan years any more sympathetic to a film that satirized the very grass-roots of Republican power? Who knew? And, in any case, those who paid the piper with American money would probably have had him play a different kind of tune.

Honky Tonk Freeway's impact on the fortunes of EMI was decisive: as a later chapter indicates, it helped seal the fate of the last concerted effort — to date, anyhow — to 'beat the Americans' at their own game of blockbuster film-making by employing them to play the game for the British.

Don Boyd returned to London, reckoning (correctly) that work was the best medicine. 'During all the time I was in Hollywood I had kept my London company going, at considerable cost. We had lost about £600,000 over the two years I had been, in effect, an absentee film-maker. So I had to put my *Honky Tonk Freeway* producer's fee into The Boyd Company in order to staunch the financial bleeding.'

Fortunately, having kept on his personnel, he was able to get two films into production quickly. Both showed he had lost nothing of his eclectic touch. *An Unsuitable Job for a Woman* (13 May 1982), produced by Boyd for Goldcrest Films in association with the NFFC, was based on P. D. James's detective story and directed by Christopher Petit who may have hoped to break out of the arthouse constraints of *Radio On*, his first feature film, financed in 1979 for £80,000 from German sources and the British Film Institute Production Board, and reach a wider audience in a more familiar genre. As things turned out, however, the mystery elements simply seemed a pretext for an excursion into Petit's barren and derivative landscape of non-relationships. Budgeted at what Boyd calls a 'rather high' £800,000, it pleased neither Petit's admirers who saw him as 'an English Wim Wenders' nor gained a new audience for a 'plot' which was reduced to a series of ponderous implausibilities by the 'alienating' approach.

The other Boyd film, produced by him for HandMade Films, the company set up by Denis O'Brien, an investment consultant, and ex-Beatle George Harrison, was *Scrubbers* (11 November 1982), a title which suggested it had been conceived as the distaff side of *Scum*. Directed by Mai Zetterling, it soon abandoned its pretentions to be a serious study of shortcomings in a Borstal detention centre for girls and turned into a series of comic or vicious 'turns', a floor-show behind bars in which the unlovable inmates were incited to do 'their own thing' and most of them allowed to overdo it wildly. If it proved anything, it was nothing to do with the absurdities or inhumanities of a system in which convicts and keepers were cut out of the same length of material which society had rejected: while the advantage that was claimed for letting a woman direct a story about her own sex's confinement under lock and key conferred no more merit on the cast than if they had been at the beck and call of a raging male chauvinist. But, with a very modest £550,000 budget, *Scrubbers* was a box-office success at a time when Boyd badly needed a reward in cash or kind. 'I had the satisfaction of knowing that, whatever their success or failure, these films, like all the others, had been made because I personally liked them. I suppose the total cost of all the movies I made in Britain up to 1982 was £1.5m., which is comparable to the annual overhead of a major British production company.

'I think that my example encouraged others who have probably been slightly more prudent than I have and have got greater rewards for smaller risks. We got indigenous British films under way again at a time when production and the creative will were very, very low. Our example was passed on to other independent companies with larger funds available — like Virgin and Palace Films, offshoots of the records, rock and video industries, which are part of the renewed vigour of the British scene in the early 1980s. One of my assets has been the personal relationships I've enjoyed, especially with directors. I'm longing to work with theatre talents like Trevor Nunn and Bill Bryden, theatre people whom one can enthuse with an idea and not just pass a property to. I rely on instinct: I'm a man who asks, "How about a film about. . .?" or "What would happen if. . . ?" This way, one has a sense of a film growing organically out of the cultural or social climate which prompted the idea in the first place.'

Boyd smiles and adds: 'I can tell you the serial number of the film stock I want. I'm familiar with the range of lenses that a picture may need. I know what percentages a distributor in Sweden might demand. I am aware of the collateral I need to offer a bank before it will give me the money I want. Keeping all this in one's mind *and* negotiating contracts with creative people *and* retaining a sense of the audience for which it's all intended — it's something that's taken me a long time to acquire. I may not succeed every time: but I do manage to keep in work. You could describe me most accurately, I guess, as rather more than a film producer, as, say' — the beamish gleam back in place — 'a director-orientated audience-conscious film-marketing editor.'

CHAPTER SEVEN

The Return of the Native

The British are coming. — Colin Welland, at the Oscar
awards ceremony, 1982.

The main reason for David Puttnam's leaving England in 1977, on a two-year, half-million dollar contract with Casablanca Film Works of Hollywood, was financial: as he says, if he didn't earn more money and pay fewer taxes, 'I would have been in debt till my dying day.' But another reason why far-off American seemed attractive at that moment had to do with *Agatha*.

Puttnam had worked for months to set this film up in England — they were months of increasing frustration. Based on Kathleen Tynan's original screen-play, it was an odd genre of film, a mix of fact and fiction, a 'speculative mystery' inspired by Agatha Christie's unhappy first marriage and her disappearance from home in December 1926, when she had been discovered in a Harrogate grand hotel living under an assumed name resembling that of her husband's mistress. Tynan surmised that it was Col. Christie's infidelity which caused his wife to go to Harrogate and plan her own suicide in a way that suggested his mistress was to blame. The film wasn't conceived as a 'whodunit', but as a 'what's a-do'. It invited one to put two and two together and come up with the answer to why Agatha was prowling about the chilly medicinal baths in midwinter, noting down details of the hydropathic equipment, including apparatus resembling an electric chair, and come up with a suicide-as-murder plot as ingenious as *The Murder of Roger Ackroyd*. But as things turned out, the mystery element was almost superfluous. Michael Apted's film was at its best when probing the anguish of English middle-class respectability sheltering from public headlines. It was a morality play, rather than a mystery.

The Rank Organization at first backed the film as part of its re-activated production programme; then it abruptly withdrew its finance when a couple of long-serving board members recalled that Col.

Christie had been a Rank company director after his marriage to Agatha was dissolved. Wouldn't it have been a 'bit off', they argued, to present him as a cad in a Rank-financed film?

Puttnam was forced to act quickly: for he had already signed Vanessa Redgrave as Agatha, the Australian actress Helen Morse as one of the 'New Women' of the Twenties who stiffens the shy Agatha's resolve, Timothy Dalton as Archie Christie, Vittorio Storare as photographer and Apted as director. He rushed the project to the financier Jarvis Astaire, who had recently become Dustin Hoffman's British representative. Hoffman eagerly said 'Yes' to the picture. One reason had to do with his own difficult marital situation at that time and the attractiveness of working outside America. Another was his desire to acquit himself of his obligations to First Artists, the recently formed stars' co-operative that was already falling short of expectations since the films its members made for other companies were frequently more successful than those they made for their own. Hoffman owed it a film: *Agatha* would be that film. But once he had agreed to *Agatha*, it became a 'Dustin Hoffman picture'. The script had to be radically re-worked to promote his character — an American investigative reporter who 'happens' to be in England at the time of the disappearance — from fourth in the cast-list to above the title and, at least, to co-star billing with Vanessa Redgrave.

Puttnam thus found himself in the grip of an obsessive superstar: he did not relish the experience. It was too much like the *Trick or Treat?* nightmare. His enthusiasm and energy encountered an ego and obstinacy much greater than his own. Hoffman's role swelled: Helen Morse's shrank to a fragment. Puttnam had to recognize the star's presence was restructuring the picture *his* way; and there was little he himself could do about it. 'Up to then', Alan Parker said later, 'David hadn't had a smash-hit . . . no breakthrough picture in Hollywood terms.' On the other hand, Hoffman had: so it was on him that the money was riding. Apted called it all 'a horrifying experience'. It contributed to the film's going 25 per cent over budget.

How Puttnam then reacted illuminates the limits to which he is prepared to go to retain — or salvage — his independence. Sometimes it is better to abdicate than resist. 'When you work with David,' Ray Connolly was to write, 'he seduces you. You think he's your best friend. When things go wrong, he withdraws and gets involved in something else.'* Which is precisely what he now did.

In a letter to Jarvis Astaire dated 29 October 1977, from the Excelsior Hotel in Valetta on the island of Malta, Puttnam bowed out of *Agatha*.** He called the communication 'a sincere and emotional message' — and it was all of that. A multiplicity of captains, he said, now ruled the ship

*Ray Connolly, BBC TV's *Omnibus*, quoted in *Daily Express*, 18 December 1982.
**David Puttnam Collection, British Film Institute.

where he had been used to full control: he apologized if this way of putting it sounded grandiose, but stressed it had been the basis of any success he had so far achieved. He believed the production to be 'already out of control': he predicted 'it will become more so during the next several weeks'. With *Trick or Treat?* behind him he had resolved never to get into that kind of fix again. He acknowledged that, as a general rule, 'elements in the production' lost confidence in the script being shot (or about to be) and attempted to improve it to death. 'The script is always the target for attack because it can't argue its own case.' He did not welcome random 'inspiration-orientated' changes (by whom, he didn't say). He foresaw the projected overage to be in the region of £500,000, which would inevitably bring the completion guarantors into the act; and arriving at an accommodation with them, he warned Astaire, would cost *you* money. In the circumstances, he bade as graceful a farewell as he could — and 'got involved in something else'.

This time, that 'something else' was the film Puttnam had been preparing in harness with *Agatha* — *Midnight Express*. (It began shooting on 17 September 1977; *Agatha* began on 5 November 1977.) In many ways *Midnight Express* was the ideal film for a producer who wanted to become a temporary expatriate. It was going to be shot in Malta, which was doubling for Turkey. Puttnam was therefore able to leave Britain in the early spring and win immediate relief from the tax man; yet he could easily fly back to Britain for the permitted three months to attend to his other film business. There was an additionally attractive factor in taking the escape route to Malta. It was a refuge from *Agatha*. 'I went through the agonizing and cajoling,' he said much later, presumably referring to the difficulties caused by Hoffman's addition to the cast, 'and I found myself asking if I really wanted to be (in England) with this worrisome American pest when I could have been having a great time in Malta. I have no doubt that I made the right decision, but I sometimes think that if I had not had both films on the go I might have had the tolerance to stay with (*Agatha*) and deal with it.'*

Malta was a part of the world that 'no one in Los Angeles had ever heard of, so they couldn't find us if they wanted to!'** The title *Midnight Express* was said to be prison argot for taking an escape route. The story was derived from experiences of Turkish prison life related (and possibly embellished) by a young American who had been caught smuggling drugs at Ankara Airport during a hijack alarm. Billy Hayes was incarcerated in the 'insane' wing of the prison after assaulting a witness who had perjured himself: he escaped by one of those semi-divine interventions which, in a Bresson film, are the physical collateral of the hero's spiritual faith. Hayes was presented throughout the film as 'victim' — that and only that. Being young, American and abroad, the

*David Puttnam, interviewed by Michael Owen, London *Standard*, 14 May 1982.
**David Puttnam, interviewed by Minty Clinch, *Ms. London*, 21 April 1981.

character fitted into the self-pitying neo-romanticism of the largest film-going age-group in America — and, it must be noted, into Puttnam's own romantic identification with the James Dean ikon-figure of his own teenage years.

Alan Parker, who had directed *Bugsy Malone*, was thirsting for serious attention as the maker of a 'significant' picture: his hand in *Midnight Express* was calculatedly brutal, forceful and explicit. Its story was a catalogue of horror, an injury list of grievous bodily harm. Giorgio Moroder's score was designed to arouse audiences to anger: it 'cued' the feelings one was meant to have and, in retrospect anyhow, reminded one of the importance that Puttnam attaches to hitting an audience's emotions with the music track a fraction of time in advance of its mind.

But in this case the anger was channeled into xenophobia as much as catharsis. Immediately it was shown, *Midnight Express* evoked powerful protests from Turkey's military government: well, that was only to be expected (hoped for, maybe). But then complaints came, in increasing volume from people concerned by the blanket condemnation of the whole Turkish race, or so it was alleged, for all the sufferings heaped on Billy Hayes, including being sodomized.

Puttnam now bitterly regrets the film was conceived in a way that made such charges plausible. Had it been an overtly political film, he thinks its brutality might have been more satisfactorily interpreted as an attack on the country's correspondingly brutal military rulers. But the truth was it seemed to have more in common with an American genre movie in which relentless suffering generates commercial excitement. If properly handled and hyped this can earn a lot of money and steer the star towards an Oscar for the highly visible degree of his screen 'suffering'. 'I discovered too late that Billy had — shall we say — a much more "complex" background than I'd been led to believe,' says Puttnam. 'It was supposed to be the story of a basically good boy who behaved stupidly and brought inordinate punishment on himself. Looking back, I think we film-makers were "conned" over that one.'

In *Marxism Today* he was more explicit about pinning part of the blame on his capitalist partners. 'I went into shock after I'd done *Midnight Express*. I thought it was a really good, well-made picture until I saw it with an audience, and then I suddenly realized that, as much as anything else, we'd been ripped off. We thought we'd made one film, but in the end we'd made exactly the film Columbia Pictures (the distributors of the Casablanca Film Works production) wanted us to make: a very commerical film where the audience is actually on its feet saying "Go on!" during the scene [where Billy Hayes bites off his Turkish tormentor's tongue]. We thought they'd be under the seats: they were cheering. That's the kind of misjudgment I realized I was capable of.'*

*David Puttnam, interviewed by Roy Lockett, *Marxism Today*, February 1982.

As well as compromising his integrity, the film reminded Puttnam how easy it was to slip up artistically. He had failed to evaluate it thoroughly before shooting. 'I felt I had approached it from north, south and west,' he says, 'but had forgotten to approach it from the east. . .The character of Rifki [the informer whose tongue is torn out] was *Iranian*, not Turkish: but I let this be edited out of the finished film. It might have diffused the racial odium, to some extent. Then again, we deliberately didn't sub-title the Turkish prosecutor's speech; we hoped we'd make film-goers identify all the more with Billy, who's standing there desperately trying to guess from the strange sounds of a foreign language what his fate is going to be. The speech contained a clear, reasoned argument for punishing drug traffickers: but as no one (except the Turks) could understand it, their viewpoint wasn't appreciated in most of the world's cinemas and went unnoticed in all the reviews.' The film's commercial fortunes weren't hurt by these omissions: quite the contrary. On a gross cost of £2,654,000, [negative cost: £2,228,426] it had returned net profits of £8,400,000 by the end of 1984: it was Puttnam's 'breakthrough' film, his first real international success.

He quickly discovered that success of this order does not create opportunities so much as confuse them. The phenomenal success of George Lucas's *Star Wars* was reviving interest in the medieval film genre, romances with a heavy content of chivalry, faith and special effects. For his next film Puttnam wanted Ridley Scott to make the Tristan and Isolde legend. The trouble was, Puttnam conceived it as a romance; Scott, as a strongly textured epic re-creating (as in *The Duellists*) a precise period feeling in physical furnishings and romantic conduct. This would have required a large budget: not in itself insuperable, as *Midnight Express*'s box-office success was assured. But for Puttnam the problem was how to spend the money on the hardware without diluting the humanity — or the passion. With a conviction based on his boyhood screen heroes he believed that emotionally strong and moving (and commercial)films came about when people identified with the feelings of the characters in them. At $15m. to $20m., he figured, this wasn't a realistic expectation unless one was a David Lean — a film-maker who shared Puttnam's belief in basic human emotions. Even Lean might have had trouble showing feelings inside the suits of mail that Ridley Scott would have taken to like an armourer's apprentice. So Tristan and Isolde languished . . . and Puttnam immersed himself in Hollywood.

SWEET CHARIOTS

Yet before 1978 was over David Puttnam returned to England and set about completing the balance of his Casablanca contract in the cutting rooms of London. Due to a peculiarity of the fiscal systems of Britain and America, he did not have to spend a total of two years out of Britain in order to gain the full tax advantages. The American liability runs from January to December; the British year from April to the end of the following March. Provided one does not spend more than six months in the USA one was not liable for tax; provided one does not spend more than sixty-two days in Britain one was not liable, either. Juggling his dates and utilizing his 'permitted days', Puttnam spent in all twenty months actually away from Britain — with great and legitimate gain to his bank balance. That he returned to Britain at all, never mind so early, surprised many people. 'He was the most American of all of us in his work habits and his attitudes,' said Michael Apted, 'yet he took to America the least well.'*

Apted surmised that maybe Puttnam had run into a lot of hustlers in Hollywood and feared that if he stayed too long among them he might take on their less than lovable traits. There is something in that: but Puttnam's Hollywood period signifies the existence of deeper uncertainties about himself than he would admit to nowadays. There he was, well established in the world's film-making capital, and he found it eerily unwelcoming and emotionally enervating. The practical problems of Hollywood film-making made him *more* aware of his strengths as a *British* producer and convinced him of his shortcomings under the American system. He had begun work on a film that would be eventually entitled *Foxes*: it starred Sally Kellerman, Jodie Foster and various American teenage hopefuls, and was to be directed by yet another of Puttnam's recruits from the commerical advertising world, Adrian Lyne. (Lyne was the director who, in 1974, had himself financed a 38-minute tragi-comedy entitled *Mr Smith*, a wittily observant odyssey of a Feiffer-like Englishman [Peter Barkworth] through all the frustrations of what turns out to be his last day on earth.)

Foxes was not congenial material for two Englishmen: it got to be even less to their liking when studio executives began hinting that the family tribulations of the Beverly Hills rich, as portrayed in the screen-play, were too close to home; couldn't they be moved down a social class or two and re-located in 'the Valley'? This faced the Britons with delicate decisions of class, accent, clothes and all the peer group rites of Valley girls which they considered themselves incompetent to make; they were also temperamentally disinclined to listen to other people's guidance. Puttnam found he couldn't any longer trust his instincts: for a producer, this was like being a dog without a sense of smell. 'If I was casting a similar part to [Sally Kellerman's] in England,' he explained a little later, 'I'd know instinctively if someone was physically right for it, whether the associations were right, and exactly how she'd look — all

---

*Michael Apted, interviewed by Joan Goodman and Mike Bygrave, *The Observer* magazine, 16 August 1981.

Saints and sinners: Two controversial films from a pair of the most individual British talents. The Monty Python team poked fun at a parallel tale of the life of Christ in *The Life of Brian*, 1979 (above). Derek Jarman's Latin-tongued *Sebastiane*, 1976 (below), was a tale of homophilia on the far-flung frontier of Rome.

Style and appearance: In hard times
and boom times, the production
design of British films spanned all
styles and budgets with distinction:
Dirty Dan's gang with dreaded
splurge guns operated their racket in
a gangland made for *Bugsy Malone's*
little bigshots in 1976 (opposite,
below). Julie Christie, golden girl of
the Sixties, recycled into a post-
holocaust scavenger in *Memoirs of a
Survivor*, 1981 (right, above). Anthony
Higgins played the recorder, perhaps
the instigator of murder in the period
puzzle *The Draughtsman's Contract*,
1982 (opposite, above). Big sister
(Georgia Stowe) was caught up in her
little sister's dream-world of
threatening nursery toys and fairy-
tales of disturbing sexuality in *The
Company of Wolves*, 1984 (right, below).

In a national cinema virtually devoid of overtly political films, *The Ploughman's Lunch*, 1983 (above), was outstanding. Against the fast-breaking story of the Falklands War, anti-hero Jonathan Pryce (having a publisher's power-lunch with David De Keyser) manipulated events and fabricated history to his own advantage.

the way down to what earrings she'd wear. I'd have a basis of knowledge to draw on going back to when I was born.'* In Hollywood, he realized, he didn't even know which newspaper such a woman would read. Then there were all sorts of subtle and not-so-subtle 'interferences'. Not exactly demands, more 'suggestions'. Had the story *got* to climax in a teenage suicide? Yes, Puttnam would say at first, because that's what the picture is about. But couldn't it be just an accidental death? Well, maybe. . . . Then, why not spice it up a bit sexually? Then, why not put in more music? The kids love music. Let's have a real big score. Adam Faith traipsed in and out of the film as a rock impresario awkwardly supervising the kid-size neuroses of the American characters, and perhaps holding Puttnam's hand for old time's sake and *Stardust* memories.

Puttnam was back home and re-established in Britain for two years before this Hollywood product of his misspent months arrived on the London screen to embarrass him briefly. (It was a sign of how little rush there was to show the film that Jodie Foster's self-styled 'lover', John Hinckley, jun., had to make his attempt on President Reagan's life before *Foxes*, and Ms Foster got to many screens.)

What Hollywood taught Puttnam was that he didn't function in a studio environment ruled by insecurity and devoid of what he calls 'the commonsense that's the basic tenet of movie-making'. There was really no mystery why he 'came home' — he'd made the pilgrimage to Rome and discovered he preferred to worship his own domestic gods at altars which didn't demand human sacrifices. If privation of the flesh was preached in austerity England, at least it was not the starvation of the spirit. But he brought back with him what turned out to be the true treasure he had found in Hollywood — or, rather in the unlikely location of the Malibu beach colony. He had rented a house there and, during a depressing bout of influenza, found himself reading a book from the owners' eclectic collection: a history of the Olympic Games. 'I'll tell you I've always known what I could do,' he once said to an interviewer, 'it's quite a weird talent. Let's say I've read five disparate things during the course of a year. I find I can take a passage from one, a photograph from another, and a quote from a third, and make them into a whole. . .'**

Broadly, this is how *Chariots of Fire* came into being. The Olympics book was the first element of working collage. Puttnam's attention was fully hooked when he reached the 1924 games, held in Paris, in which the elements of conscience rather than the politics of sport played an influential role. What often goes unremarked about *Chariots of Fire* is that it is not the story of a rivalry: its two heroes, Harold Abrahams and Eric Lidell, don't run *against* each other: they run *for* their ideals. It is the strength of their separate faiths that permeates the film and provides its

*David Puttnam, interviewed by Simon Perry, *Variety*, 11 June 1980.
**David Puttnam, quoted by Goodman and Bygrave, op.cit.

moral energy — for, as far as action is concerned, it is a rather flaccid film. For Puttnam it represented an important breakthrough into the area of moral issues. Of course *Midnight Express* had had its humanitarian message — where it could be distinguished from its commerical exploitation. But *Chariots of Fire* at last made the issues flesh.

Hitherto, Puttnam had been hesitant about venturing too deeply into the area of morality lest he find himself caught in a vacuum without human attachments. But Hollywood had taught him he needed to be sustained by ideas as well as scripts. 'To spend a year of your life and then look at the result and not feel any sense of identity with it leaves me feeling very empty. Inevitably, you start thinking about how much money you might make. You've got nothing else. You haven't got any emotional investment in it.'* On returning to England in 1978 Puttnam had fallen into discussion with a Jesuit priest of his acquaintance: this led to counselling of an *ad hoc* kind and, in effect, he was told to ease up on himself and accept success. None of this cured his restlessness, but it could be that his need to turn his conscience over and ask himself *why* he was striving to excel, *whom* he was attempting to please and *what* it would profit him to gain an Oscar (as *Midnight Express* had done) but lose the world of personal endeavour — it could be that all this soul-searching prepared a very fertile ground for the seeds of *Chariots of Fire* and the conscience-racked achievers in it.

Britain actually won *three* gold medals at the 1924 Olympics and it was originally the intention to focus the film on *four* characters: the three winners and the loser, Aubrey Montague, whose daily letters to his mother proved invaluable source material about the games. But the other surviving winner wanted some up-front participation in the film and Puttnam, in any case, was finding Abrahams and Lidell summing up so much of what he wanted to say that 'the third man' was dropped. So, too, was the losing athlete. The remaining two fought the good fight (or, rather, ran the good race) for God and against prejudice.

Serving God was one thing: putting Mammon to work for him was another. '*Midnight Express*', says Puttnam, 'was the only film I'd made up to then where I didn't have to worry about money.' It took him nearly two years to get financing for *Chariots of Fire*. The story was at first regarded as 'too English'. Puttnam protested — by that argument, wasn't *Midnight Express* too Turkish? No, he was told, *it* was about a nice *American* boy having unspeakable things done to him. *Chariots of Fire* was all about the British behaving honourably to each other. Where was the drama? Where was the confrontation? 'Good God,' Puttnam says, 'in the present state of the world, I often thought, do they want confrontation written into *every* movie?' Considering the aura of 'British achievement' in which *Chariots of Fire* basked once it had swept the 1982 Oscar awards,

---

*David Puttnam, *Film and Television Technician*, November 1979.

it cannot be too heavily emphasized that British financiers were so lacking in commercial acumen, never mind patriotic spirit or sporting instinct, that the eventual $5,891,000 gross cost [£4,032,859 negative cost] was put up by Twentieth Century-Fox on the one hand and, on the other, by Allied Stars, the film-making offshoot of an Egyptian shipping line run by a movie buff called Dodi Fayed. Except for the initial 'seed money' essential to developing the Colin Welland screen-play on which the production finance could be raised, there wasn't much British cash in the movie. The development money and a small final investment came from Goldcrest Films, which jibbed at participating in the high production budget, though it retained a 7.5 per cent interest in the box-office net and, according to Puttnam, had made some £750,000 by 1984. Thus Goldcrest did nicely out of it — and deserved to do so — but not as nicely as it would have done had it been a major backer. To be fair to Goldcrest, the project was presented to it at the moment it was evolving from a financing and investment company into a major production force. In view of the crucial contribution Goldcrest was making to the British film industry by the mid-Eighties, its origins deserved to be looked at in more detail: they are typical of the ways in which so much of the initiative in British film-making 'just growed'.

THE EARLY BIRD

Goldcrest had been conceived by Jake Eberts, a Canadian banker who dabbled in films, and spread its wings in 1977 when Pearson Longman Enterprises and Electra Finance Co. Ltd announced they were joining forces to create a source of pre-production film finance. The new group, Goldcrest Films, was part of the financial empire controlled by Lord Cowdray, reputedly the second richest man in Britain. Through S. Pearson and Son it had interests in engineering, oil, mining, merchant banking, land and information technology and already owned *The Financial Times* newspaper, Penguin Books (and Penguin's American affiliate, Viking), the Longman publishing house and the Westminster Press group of provincial newspapers. Initially, Goldcrest had a revolving fund of £250,000. These resources were first put behind part-financing the film versions of books published by Penguin (or related companies), apparently with the mutually advantageous idea of helping the film sell the book, and vice versa. Hence its earliest investment, *Black Jack* (1980), a picaresque period tale based on a book in Penguin's Puffin series for children and financed by Goldcrest in association with the NFFC. To many people's surprise, Ken Loach and Tony Garnett were respectively director and producer; it was their first costume picture. They were plainly unhappy outside the contemporary scene: the film's historical realism resisted dramatic condensation and its story was ill adapted to their preferred method of improvising 'the truth' that players were supposed to mine (and often did) from present-day traumas near to their own experience. The tale of an apprentice boy in 1750 did not fit comfortably or credibly into these film-makers' familiar dialectic of showing a hardy individual escaping from the restrictive social conditioning of his day. It proved not to be *Kes*-in-costume: but something far more shapeless and patchy.

Another Goldcrest venture paid off handsomely, however. *Watership Down* had been first published in November 1972 by Rex Collings; it then appeared as a children's Puffin book in 1973 and in 1974 as a Penguin: at which point Richard Adams's allegory took off into the stratosphere of best-sellerdom and contemporary classics, with nowhere else left to go for profitable exploitation except the screen. Its tale of the long march of Everyrabbit was a cosy idealization of England's past: it anticipated the retrospective longings of 'Thatcher's England', with its hankering after 'Victorian values', where everyone had their place in the warren of society and kept to it, women were thought to be satisfactorily defined by their role as home-makers; and the Welfare State had not turned hardy individual initiative into marrowbone jelly. In short, a High Tory myth articulated through the politics of the rabbit warren and the redoubt's external enemies.

The film of *Watership Down* (10 October 1978) was necessarily a much simpler affair — a hop-skip-and-a-jump through the book, though it seldom deviated into Disney-ish whimsey or denatured its rabbit cast by coy anthropomorphism. It was directed by an American, Martin Rosen, working with a team of animators installed in a purpose-built 'factory' in London's appositely named Warren Street. 'Nothing cute, nothing cuddly — more Wordsworth than Walt Disney' had been the aspiration: it was not quite that, but a Conservative Party conference would have cheered the case it made out for elitism and free enterprise. Apart from a Balkan seagull, myopically accident-prone and full of squawking bombast (who was 'voiced' by Zero Mostel in his last film role), the movie kept much of the book's Anglo-Saxon tone intact — if tactful. Such qualities of polite fidelity were characteristic of some of the projects that Goldcrest backed or (later) produced. Martin Rosen had produced Ken Russell's *Women in Love*. When seeking a production budget for *Watership Down* he had approached Jake Eberts, who was then working in London. Eberts had gone to Pearson Longman and Electra House investments who saw the advantage of having a Midas touch to work more wonders for it and conscripted Eberts: whereupon the company became much more active and ambitious. Eberts and his friend and former Harvard Business School classmate, James Lee, who headed Pearson Longman and had made the initial investment in Goldcrest, brought to the company some highly sophisticated means of financing films and at the same time benefiting investors — Eberts had been among the first to see the usefulness of tax-shelter deals.

Before very long Goldcrest had to decide whether or not it wanted to grow beyond its prudent dreams. It had to make up its mind either to be a genuine film production company initiating and backing its own projects or else remain a broker discounting other people's projects for the sake of profitable interest repayments and a 'piece of the action'. There was not much argument which was the better move. If one is a financial 'fixer', one is usually well down the line when (or if) the hand-out comes along. On the other hand, if one wants to share in the first pound or dollar earned, one must make a bigger financial investment — and take a correspondingly bigger risk. Under Eberts, Goldcrest evolved in the latter direction.

As well as *Chariots of Fire*, Goldcrest provided the development cash (not the production budget) for *Gandhi*; and it was the latter's global success, in which Goldcrest participated, although not to the same extent as the major American backer, Columbia Pictures, which emboldened it to take the leap and become a fully-fledged production company. It had opened for business in a small office over the Oppenheimer merchant bank and stockbroking house with the modest means already noted: by 1983 it had made a trading profit of £900,000; owned a portfolio of shares valued at £24.6m. in some seventy film properties; had £12m. in the bank; and could call on credit to the value of another £10m. It began offering limited partnerships in film projects to City investors in 1980 and 1982, coming away with £8m. and £9.4m. respectively. The new partners were institutional, mainly the pension funds of private and State-owned industries and insurance companies: individuals could not share in the Government-regulated tax advantages. Goldcrest avoided Arab money: it also kept away from direct American investment, saying this was to protect its creative independence, although strong beliefs were expressed that Goldcrest-initiated projects were discreetly 'auditioned' for likely American buyers or distributors before investment decisions were taken. James Lee, Goldcrest's chairman, also spoke of investing heavily — £10m. was mentioned — in the new cable programming revolution that seemed about to begin in Britain in 1982–3, perhaps seeing cable as a means of releasing major feature films after the American pattern of Home Box Office which financed movies for cable and theatrical release. The little bird was growing into a big one in these ebullient months. It was a foregone conclusion that David Puttnam would soon join the board. After the success of *Chariots of Fire* it was a certainty.

Puttnam, to be fair, protested that he was always given 'too much credit' for the film. But, once again, in choosing a director he had shown nerve and discrimination. Hugh Hudson was then forty and had not yet made a full-length feature. The head-start he had on other film craftsmen was approximately of 30 seconds' duration, though this was quite enough to show his brilliance as a maker of TV commercials. He was one of the most prize-laden directors in this area. Even in his Eton schooldays, Hudson had a sharp eye for film and made 8mm. shorts.

After school, advertising beckoned more welcomingly than the film studios: ITV was just starting when Hudson was mustered out of his Army service, and commissions to make commercials were abundant. In ten years he reckons he got through 1,500 commercials, winning praise for having a 'natural' eye for composition — a virtue seen in the opening moments of the sea-shore runners in *Chariots of Fire*, recorded in the impressionistically 'hazy' perspective of long-ago but backed (Puttnam's choice, this) by Vangelis's 'cue' music which throbbed with endeavour. Puttnam later remarked that, once a movie was shot and cut, the composer's was the most important contribution, a comment that showed the importance he attached to guiding audiences to be in emotional empathy with the visuals. Vangelis's score struck an artful note of selfless striving after excellence, and this was how the film ultimately 'sold' itself to audiences at a time when 'inspirational' movies were in short supply; one that was honest as well as good was even rarer.

Hudson had good business judgment as well as sensibility on his side. He had given proof of this when making a TV commercial for a brand of lager and had set it in an English pub *circa* 1930 — not *too* far ahead of the *Chariots* era — and then, at enormous expense, persuaded Robert Krasker, Carol Reed's cameraman on *The Third Man* in 1949, to come out of retirement and light the set for the then virtually redundant black-and-white photography he wanted to use. As almost all other TV commercials were in colour, this exception projected its product with strikingly nostalgic individuality. In another series of cinema and TV commercials for an Italian aperitif, Hudson 'storyboarded' details from Renoir's paintings, then scoured the Paris flea markets for an antique lens to shoot a series of Impressionist tableaux on French locations with which Renoir would have had at least a nodding familiarity. Another of his ideas involved shooting a two-minute commercial — unheard of at the time — for an Italian-made car which showed it being assembled by robots to the 'Figaro' music from Rossini's *Barber of Seville*.

'Making commercials gave me discipline, taught me to create atmosphere and tell a story crisply,' Hudson says. It also taught him independence. He gave his loyalty to British agencies because he had found that American clients drained him of ideas, then sometimes re-cut his film to please their State-side clients.

At the time of *Chariots of Fire* Hudson had been suffering from a 'touch of the forties' and a nagging feeling of being overshadowed by the more public glory of some of Puttnam's earlier advertising-industry 'discoveries' who had made good in feature films. Ridley Scott had been his employer; Alan Parker had been his co-worker: both had made names in 'the big movies'. (It was Hudson, in fact, who had gone to Turkey to shoot documentary material on the sly for *Midnight Express*.) Hudson had made a 1972 documentary on the racing driver Juan Fangio: 'Like Fangio,' he said, 'I believe in knowing my limits.' Puttnam, too, believed this was a virtue. Yes, of course, one's reach should exceed one's grasp, or what's a Heaven for? — as Browning asked — but not so impetuously as to dislocate anything. After turning down screen-plays like *The Omen: Part 3* ('a nonsense story requiring only fancy decoration'), Hudson jumped at *Chariots of Fire*. It was individual: it was positive.

REVENGE IS SWEET

Puttnam and Hudson put in a very long time casting the film — fourteen weeks. This was largely because Hudson insisted that if *exactly* the right people were cast, one's work was well ahead by the time filming started. A lesson learnt from commercials. The theme appealed powerfully to a man who is, temperamentally, in the 'grand romantic' tradition that came to its finest (occasionally overblown) flowering in the David Lean films of the Sixties onwards. The lure of the film to Hudson's eye lay in its intangible aspirations — it wasn't about winning, but striving.

Its release in America coincided fortuitously with another grand romantic gesture from the bygone past when nations could afford such luxuries as going to war for what they believed to be a just cause — namely, the Falklands War. There was a definite pro-British feeling in most of America at the time — the Brits were not going to be pushed around, the way the Americans had been in Vietnam. The untarnished glory of Britain's air and sea armada rubbed off on everything British — even to the revival of the long baggy running shorts worn by Ian Charleson and Ben Cross who were cast as Liddell and Abrahams.

Unashamedly, the movie put one in touch with sentiments that had so long lain publicly unexpressed one had begun to wonder if they ever existed: love of country, fear of God, loyalty to the team, unselfish excellence in the pursuit of honour, becoming modesty in the moment of victory. Puttnam was able at long last to find a set of Anglo-Saxon attitudes that could be decently set beside the American ideals he had seen in the films of the Forties and Fifties. Like many Hollywood films in those eras, *Chariots of Fire* was about achievers, not celebrities: people who did things because, well, because they *must*, without fuss, show, subsidy, commercial gain or narcissistic public preenings on a hundred chat shows.

The film went through American cinemas like a cleansing breeze dispelling — for a time, anyhow — the fug generated by the high-pressure commercialism that went by the name of 'sport'. The jogging boom was peaking and the film pulled this cross-generational activity's devotees into the cinemas in their tens of thousands to give them the tangible experience of the moral goodness that can go with physical fitness. Even the minor theme of the Cambridge University Establishment's anti-semitism aligned the film's sentiments with those of a substantial section of Jewish America; while Liddell's Sabatarian principles fitted into the professed (if not often practised) Christianity of the rest of America. Even the end titles, telling one that Abrahams became a VIP in the world of sport and media and Liddell died a Christian missionary in a Japanese prison camp, connected with the fashion that *American Graffiti* had started for following the fates of fictitious (or, in this case, factual) characters beyond the story: the truth raised a lump in the throat, at least of those who stayed for the credits, and harnessed the chariots even more powerfully to nostalgic emotions.

Granada TV's mini-series based on Evelyn Waugh's *Brideshead Revisited* had not been seen in America when *Chariots of Fire* opened — in any case, as it was not networked, it would have had minimal effect — but its impact on British audiences set the capstone on the emotions which *Chariots of Fire* built up: the young aristocrat (Nigel Havers) who was in the habit of having his butler place brimming glasses of champagne on the hurdles he leaped in practice heats, might have strayed (or sprinted) in from *Brideshead*'s ranks of minor eccentrics.

Of course there were heretics . . . 'I think it would be a howl to double-bill (*Chariots of Fire*) with *The Loneliness of the Long Distance Runner*, which I did not like in its time, either,' said Pauline Kael. 'It's quite funny when you think about these two films as expressions of two different eras, because Tom Courtenay in *The Loneliness* threw away the race rather than win it for those bastards he hated.'* And one of Puttnam's compatriots, Don Boyd, expressed much the same view when, according to Puttnam, he said that 'it's a jingoistic picture . . . [Don] honestly believes it's a film about the State's domination of the individual.' Boyd's view does indeed sound like the gnashing of teeth by an impassioned 'liberal' film-maker against the 'Falklands Factor'. Pauline Kael's view, though more flippantly expressed, has an astute appositeness, seeing the film as a throw-back, rather than a sell-out, to an un-reconstructed England of effortless class superiority.

However, the two runners don't share the values of the ruling class: and their athletic prowess sets them over and above any conscious need to rebel. They are already — to use a phrase that was about to come into vogue — 'the right stuff'. This consensus feeling is a big part of the film's persuasiveness: we follow the fortunes of individuals, striving for a

---

*Pauline Kael, interviewed by Wendy Allen, *Stills*, Vol. One, No. Five.

personal best, not as egoistic stars and certainly not as class enemies out to throw the race and spite the Prince of Wales. Interestingly, when Puttnam was asked by a not wholly sympathetic interviewer whether this preference for directors trained in commercial advertising had robbed his film of political thrust, he chose to answer in class-orientated terms, even though he saw the virtues of his 'protégés' as more diverse and idiosyncratic than any shared background they had. 'Hugh [Hudson] has the kind of upper-class guilt which is a very heavy burden . . . [he] has never been able to justify to himself the advantage he started life with. Alan [Parker] works off a kind of working-class anger. Ridley [Scott's] background probably predetermined his approach. His father was an Army major . . . [Ridley] was the one who turned up in a suit at the Royal College of Art. They all thought he was very strange. Ridley's a painter who happens to use film. Alan is the most complex character and certainly hasn't defined himself yet. He is somebody who works off conscience.'*

At the Academy Awards ceremony in Los Angeles, on 23 March 1982, *Chariots of Fire* won four 'Oscars', including that for the 'Best Picture'. As Nick Roddick remarked, it was 'the first British film to do so since *Oliver!* (in 1968) and the first British film ever to do so in twentieth-century clothes'.** Colin Welland, accepting the 'Oscar' for the 'Best Screen-play', uttered the phrase that had headline writers sighing in contentment at someone else's doing their encapsulating work for them — 'The British are coming!' That old 'Redcoat' alert may not have caused many of the Hollywood studios' chief executive officers to tremble: they could always reach for their cheque-books, not their muskets (and, after all, the film was 50-per cent American backed). 'All the same,' Roddick continued, 'national euphoria reigned for all of forty-eight hours: David Puttnam became a super-star, the Vangelis theme music entered the Top Twenty, and *News at 5.45* played itself out to shots of young men in baggy white shorts splashing along the beach at Broadstairs.'

What were David Puttnam's private thoughts at that moment? When asked at the time, he said the expected thing . . . the generous thing. But a couple of years later, the question recurred during a particularly wet Cannes Film Festival — a mood that encourages a sort of suicidal frankness. What did he *really* feel looking out over the sea of faces on 'Oscar Night '82', some of them famous, many powerful, all now turned towards the man whom a few of them had backed and many, many more had turned down when he had come to them bearing projects? 'I was thinking how sweet it was to have my revenge,' Puttnam confessed. He added, 'Isn't that what Oscar-winners always think?'***

*David Puttnam, *Marxism Today*, op.cit.
**Nick Roddick, *Sight and Sound*, Summer 1982.
***David Puttnam to author, 24 May 1984.

GLASGOW BELONGS TO HIM

Three days after the Oscar ceremony Puttnam stood in a mucky field in Scotland making a deal with a farmer for the use of his cows in a film to be called *Local Hero*. Some were surprised that he and Hudson were not paired once more on the multi-million dollar *Greystoke: The Legend of Tarzan, Lord of the Apes* (12 April 1984). But *Local Hero* (which cost £3,080,000, nearly half the figure of *Chariots of Fire*) gave Puttnam what he needed. 'The film is all of a piece. There's nothing artificial jammed into it. It's the opposite of a "manufactured" film' — which *Greystoke*, by its nature, *had* to be.* But although the film was evidence of Puttnam's sincerity in seeking the project with which he could feel 'comfortable', irrespective of self-important scale or prevailing fashion, this omits a few hard truths he was still discovering about the nature of the film industry. Puttnam did in fact agree to produce *Greystoke* for Warner Bros., who had acquired the screen-play from the writer-director Robert Towne. Towne's own Olympics-inspired film, *Personal Best*, had hit expensive production troubles, which forced him to put up the *Greystoke* scenario as collateral. According to Towne, Warners did not wait for him to complete *Personal Best* and so become available to develop *Greystoke*. An understanding was swiftly made with Puttnam, and he (again according to the understandably aggrieved Towne, who had nursed the project for fourteen years) asked Hugh Hudson to direct it. *Greystoke*'s script, Hudson has said, was 'brilliant', but only half complete — the jungle section. Towne's outline for Tarzan's return to civilized life, as heir to a Scottish earldom and ur-activist for Animal Rights, looked to Hudson to be rather too satirical. Extensive revision was needed. Puttnam could also foresee a lengthy pre-production period fraught with unpredictable elements and incalculable costs as human players were located and tested for their convincing simulation of simian behaviour when made up as apes. It would indeed be a 'manufactured' film, made in England, yet under the daily scrutiny of a major Hollywood distributor and within their reach and influence by telephone or human 'trouble-shooter'. Not an atmosphere Puttnam ever found congenial.

He soon sensed other signs of potential dissension. These had to do with the fundamental differences between a producer and a director in this situation. 'They may seem petty,' he says, 'but they precipitated the break between Hugh and me. Hugh was being wooed by studios that, a year or so before *Chariots of Fire*, had snubbed him as an untried talent. A major film company always prefers to have a "relationship" (a sense of mutual advantage) with a director or a writer rather than with an independent producer. The reason is simple. The producer is always thinking of his *next* production, in which the company may or may not

---

*David Puttnam, interviewed by Todd McCarthy, *Variety*, 23 March 1983.

participate. On the other hand, the company very likely has a project of its own with which it would like the director or the writer to be involved. The contacts with Warners over *Greystoke* ought to have been routed through me: it wasn't working out like that. Warners were going straight to Hugh. Some people, it appeared to me, were unable or reluctant to impose a proper discipline on themselves. We were already involved in a very tortuous film. I saw early on that the budget would be insufficient. And I know that *I* would then be the recipient of those "two o'clock in the morning" calls from the Coast telling me to "sort things out" — "things" that are much better dealt with at four o'clock in the afternoon, British-time. So I said goodbye to the project: with regret, of course. But it freed me to make *Local Hero* and begin pre-production on the film that became *The Killing Fields*. Hugh was tied up for two years on *Greystoke* alone.'

Thus another clean break, leaving as few raw edges as possible round the relationship, proved a profitable as well as a prudent course of action for Puttnam. That Warners apparently did not bear him rancour is suggested in a later interview he gave in Los Angeles. 'Based in London,' said the writer, 'Puttnam can develop as many film scripts as he wishes, with Warners picking up his overhead and development costs in exchange for the first shot at any projects he develops.'* Such an arrangement seemingly dated back to *Midnight Express* in 1978 — 'an unusual length of time, given the inevitable executive suite turnover at most (Hollywood) movie companies.' Puttnam said, 'All I know is that it works. It's good for them and good for me. My job is to deliver comparative bargains at a very keen price. I try to make the studio's decisions as easy as possible. Warners trusts me to an amazing degree, they really back me.'** Almost certainly, no other British-born and British-based film-maker was enjoying such support: only Stanley Kubrick, a long-time resident in England, was reported to have a similar arrangement with Warners. It contributed to Puttnam's confidence in the post-*Chariots* period. Although he said that the Oscars didn't bring him immediate offers of production finance, he acknowledged that they facilitated access to money — he could have had this relationship with Warners in mind.

Warners, though, did not choose to go along with *Local Hero*, a story that had begun (like Puttnam's last three British movies) with an eye-catching news item in the papers — this time about a simple-living, but stubborn-minded Scottish crofter doing a deal with a huge American oil company. 'It struck me as an entertaining idea for a gentle, amusing "culture clash" — how American oil money mixed (or didn't) with Scottish savvy. A film that could combine something of Ealing's drily whimsical *Whisky Galore* [US title, *High and Dry*] with those warmly

*Dale Pollock, *Los Angeles Times*, 12 July 1984.
**David Puttnam, interviewed by Pollock, ibid.

optimistic human comedies of Frank Capra or Preston Sturges I remembered seeing.'

Once again he went for 'new blood' in picking a director — new to *him*, anyhow, for Bill Forsyth had already made two eclectic comedies. Puttnam had seen *That Sinking Feeling* at the Edinburgh Film Festival and liked it: *Gregory's Girl* he had had the opportunity to produce, and had turned it down. 'I felt I'd already paid my dues to "rites of passage" films like *That'll Be the Day* and *Stardust*.' He can be forgiven: for Forsyth is a director who resists being poured into already labelled bottles. His comedy — especially the empathy it establishes with young people — has a pure malt poetry all of its own distillation.

He is arguably the rarest British film-maker of the Eighties: his observation is directly taken from life, then conceptually refracted through the prism of his own quirky Scottish nature. He has a natural knack of putting an edge on everyday innocence. 'Have you had breakfast yet?' he was once asked politely at 9.00 a.m. in a BBC radio studio in London where, after an overnight flight from New York, he was about to launch into a two-way link with a Glasgow interviewer. Forsyth said he was in the middle of breakfast — then added, 'I made sure to ask for the soggy kind of toast, so as not to crunch on mike.' A line delivered dead seriously, whose mockery was heard by the speaker's inward ear. It was typical of the double-takes, aural and visual, that Forsyth requires one to make in appreciation of the characters through whom he works to construct his view of life. The 'serious' problem of what kind of toast to consume while broadcasting shows a quirky ability to disregard the rest of life while concentrating on the next mouthful.

Forsyth's films have this same eccentricity. They originate deep in the man himself: a shrewd Scot with a deceptively quiet side to him that makes his comparative youth — just thirty-six in 1984 — appear to outsiders like collective wisdom. He sees more than he says: what he says is more frequently than not two-edged. Asked why he made his first two feature films with youngsters (in one case unemployed Glasgow kids; in the other, comprehensive-school children) he says with a serious face: 'I told them I was a film-maker. I was going to exploit them. I thought kids would be easier to dominate.'

Youthfulness brings out the best in Forsyth — his own youthfulness certainly did in *That Sinking Feeling*, whose jobless characters devise a plan to burgle a plumber's warehouse and make off with ninety stainless steel sinks. (When one greedy lad wants to add a toilet bowl to the loot, he's soberly warned: 'Leave that — those things are too easily traced.') *Gregory's Girl* placed Forsyth's talents in the steadier production hands of Clive Parsons and Davina Belling and the sturdier financing of the NFFC — though the budget was well under £500,000.

'We felt', said the NFFC's managing director Mamoun Hassan, 'that Bill Forsyth is one of those rare writer-directors who are able to treat serious subjects with great warmth.'* He compared him with Renoir and Milos Forman, adding that such humanist qualities were expected from *them*, but not quite so often from British film-makers. But the point is, Forsyth is *Scottish* even (and well) before he is British: the Northern lights illuminate his characters, giving them a 'foreign-ness' distinguishable from those people down South called the British. He has even more in common with Truffaut and Rohmer, to judge from his two films about adolescence; and he can slyly insinuate a bit of behavioural comedy, *à la* Tati, into a fleeting observation, like the two boys seen from a distance apparently having a fist-fight, then revealed as actually beating off a swarm of wasps. Forsyth's sympathy with young people's oddities — and later, not-so-young people — helps him expose the incongruities inherent in the ordinary. He builds up to a sense of cosmic comedy by showing the universal perplexities that can be created out of humdrum life if the bent in nature exists. His sheer abundance of jokes, verbal, visual, physical, absurdist and simply latent, is extraordinary. Like the breakfast toast, they are fitted into the transient moment, perfectly rational and straight-faced, yet provoking laughter by their disparity or incongruity.

Forsyth 'got into' films by answering a newspaper advertisement for a school-leaver and found himself a factotem in a small industrial film company which was greatly aided by the boom years for the Scottish building trade. He was among the first intake at the National Film School in 1971, but stuck formal training for only about six months, fearing, perhaps, that too much training would inhibit an imagination which is stimulated by his perception of the accidental. (He was nevertheless given his NFS diploma in 1983: a drop-out who had decidedly made good.)

Gregory's Girl (11 June 1983) is about a gawky sixteen-year-old schooboy whose persistence in failing to score goals on the soccer pitch causes the coach to advertise for new talent. Along comes a girl with the ball at her feet: which, pretty soon, is where Gregory is, too, unembittered and totally enamoured of her, but not a whit wiser about soccer or, for that matter, the wiles of girls who dribble him along like the football at *their* feet until he finishes up not with the girl of his fancy, but with the one who fancied him all the time.

There was scarcely a minute in the film that lacked freshness. Set in a New Town on Glasgow's outskirts, its modern, slightly Tati-esque architecture was attractively played off against the soft-focused day-dreams which had all the characters in thrall, of whatever age and wisdom they might be. The facts of life, like the job prospects or the dole queues, are not absent from the film, but simply haven't begun to intrude on the kids' consciousness. They have a little more time still for

*Mamoun Hassan, *Sight and Sound*, Autumn 1981.

dreaming, like sleepyheads exploiting the last few moments between the alarm clock sounding and missing breakfast.

Forsyth's characters are always positioned at an angle to the more serious business of living. They are dreamers, forever reversing our expectations of their reactions. While the girls slave away at the science benches, it's the boys in the cookery class who whisk cake mixes and crack eggs with role-reversal devotion. The headmaster looks a monster, but turns out a moonstruck romantic stroking a Joplin-esque rag out on the school piano during his mid-morning break. It is interesting that Forsyth's reply to a question about his own childhood was akin to David Puttnam's: it was, he said, 'remarkable only for its unremarkableness'. Films, in both men's cases, provided the escape into dreams: in Forsyth's schooldays, a master used to screen a 16mm. print of *M. Hulot's Holiday* on the classroom projector.

Forsyth has not only a talent for mime: his characters express themselves as much as anything, by *movement*. But he has a talent with words that often derives from some familiar phrase of grave import being positioned in the scene so that it gives way like thin ice and precipitates us into the depths of absurdity. The lavatory-bowl joke in *That Sinking Feeling* has already been noted: in *Gregory's Girl*, the great problem of creating a unisex football team is pinpointed by the headmaster with the solemnity of a Foreign Secretary squinting at the day's agenda of threatening world crises: 'The showers . . .' Then to the games master: 'Think you can handle it?' Sex rears only its funny head: but it's enough: Gregory (while still in his shorts) chastely covering up his nipples when a girl butts into the locker room ; a schoolgirl slipping into a phone booth to turn herself into an after-class sexpot by the judicious removal or reversal of her school uniform; the English mistress halting a reading of Shakespeare so as to flirt with the young window-cleaner who used to be a boy in her class and is now wooing the housewives on the new estate — for old times' sake, he gives teacher's specs a shine, too. The Scottish accent is also a great help to Forsyth. It gives a precocious worldliness to the utterances of children who, in the softer South of England, would still be waiting on the 'Lollipop Man' to escort them safely across the road. In the tougher latitudes of Glasgow, everyone is a proficient performer in the adventure playground of adolescence.

Forsyth's films have roots precisely because their maker's own roots are still where he was planted. In 1984, with four acclaimed films behind him, he was living alone in a tiny Glasgow flat, looking across business premises and domestic rooftops, an urban perspective he calls 'an entire social history of the city'. For inspiration he rides about on a ten-speed Elswick Stag racing-bike, the proudest among his few possessions. If John Betjeman, the late Poet Laureate, had been a Scot, he might have resembled Forsyth. Like Betjeman, Forsyth has a great sense of community — of being part of a tight-knit group. Betjeman's power-base was, of course, the middle-classes: Forsyth's vision transcends class and, like Scotland, is essentially classless in the English sense of the word 'class'. It is significant that Forsyth never went 'into television', like so many film-makers forced to keep body and (perhaps) soul together between features. In television one has often to sacrifice 'vision' for 'production', the poetic eye for the manufactured object.

Local Hero, produced by Puttnam's Enigma company for Goldcrest Films, showed Forsyth's vision was capable of crossing international latitudes intact. Burt Lancaster's Texas tycoon may have oil beneath his feet, but his eyes are those of an impassioned astronomer and fixed on the stars; his acolyte McIntyre sent to deal with the Scots on the basis of his name is, in fact, Hungarian in origin and easily seduced by the engaging escapism of the Hebridean 'Brigadoon'; even the Russian trawler captain who puts into port is a speculator in the dreamland of the capitalist Stock Market; and the only characters with a degree of detachment are two local temptresses and the local Mr Fixit who switches hats (hotelier, lawyer, accountant) like a quick-change artist (if anything in the place can be said to suggest celerity).

Again Forsyth knows how and when to play off his unsentimental pragmatism against our romantic expectations. His films are never solely conceived as comedies. He admits to being frightened still of 'being serious'. He tends to hide behind events and characters. It is his elliptical approach that lends them such an engaging air of detachment. He considers himself still very much the adolescent. 'No one grows up,' is one of his most frequent — but nonetheless sincere — assertions in interviews. 'I found myself thirty years old and still an adolescent. I started to look at people all round me and found out they were all like me.'* Thus the young people in his films are often put into adult situations — a daring gang heist, a Don Juan in love — and, conversely, his adults often do childish things the way that unobserved grown-ups do. Forsyth named Alexander Mackendrick, American-born but also Glasgow-educated, as the film-maker with whom he feels most affinity — and thereby distanced himself from Ealing Studios' sense of consensus English chumminess and put an approving tick beside the sterner material of the Scots-American.

What Forsyth seldom mentions is the dolefulness to which Scottish humour is prone. His films tend to disguise this as irony of the kind that's practised on English tourists, generally going over their heads but vastly pleasing to the locals. But he knows his own countrymen are not exempt from putting a good man down for no reason than his Scottishness. He is fond of telling a story about the Scot who climbed Everest: an achievement greeted with general acclaim except by the man's compatriot who says, 'That's all very well, but he's still got to

*Bill Forsyth, interviewed by Lawrence van Gelder, *The New York Times*, 11 May 1982.

come down again.' Forsyth's films allow him to sublimate a melancholy that doesn't often come out and stand inspection, but is there to be guessed at.

He feels a need to live alone: the reason for his success, he has drily noted, 'is not being married and adopting a good simple life-style'. The hero of the film *Comfort and Joy*, which he made after *Local Hero* (both titles are ironic), is a disc jockey, an isolate who is also a communicator — a man, one feels, with much of Forsyth in his make-up. The bachelor mood assisted by long bicycle rides in which he mulls over his ideas — reassured by familiar boyhood streets, though missing landmarks like the house where he was born — fosters the creation of a community mood which conceals the alone-ness of its maker. *Local Hero* had a touch of Shakespeare's cosmogony, a glow of *The Tempest*, re-located in northern latitudes, with a Prospero in the shape of Burt Lancaster and even a black Caliban in the beachcombing figure of the local priest from the Caribbean, as well as two heroines named Marina and Stella for their all-encompassing knowingness towards their mortal pursuers. The place is only tenuously connected to contemporary time: at one point the hero's watch is marooned in a rock pool while its owner diverts himself with the webb-footed Marina. The landscape (which Forsyth reconnoitred carefully from a helicopter) acts like a superior force, imposing its own patterns on the Locals and Aliens (which would have been a better title, perhaps, than *Local Hero*).

The American film-maker Robert Altman also has this captivation with the community, and it is no wonder that Forsyth feels himself in sympathy with him. But the Scot works on a different scale from Nashville, to music of time rather than the concert stage. He reminds one of his compatriot J. M. Barrie, another self-confessed arrested adolescent, who filled *his* Never-Never Land with private fancies and sly winks. But Forsyth is harder, crueller. . . . There is a prime example in *Local Hero* where a pet rabbit has finished up in the casserole, and has its leg spooned up out of the stew by the cook, like an anatomy lesson, to demonstrate to the two sentimentalists that it was broken and wouldn't have mended anyhow. The solemn obliviousness of the characters to *anything* but their own centre of gravity is what gives a Forsyth film its air of detachment — we are not buttonholed, sucked up to or invited to identify with anyone. Conversely, it is when Forsyth, in his rare moments, becomes self-conscious and draws a caricatural line round a character (like Lancaster's manic psycho-analyst) or indulges in pure fantasy (like the marine biologist-cum-mermaid) that we feel the dreamer has awoken. He walks best who walks by himself — and on his own territory.

LOVE AND MONEY

Local Hero was well received critically and commercially: at the last audit (1984), it was showing a net profit of $109,000, with appreciably more to come from re-releases, television sales and cable syndication.

By the middle of 1982 Puttnam had significantly expanded his film enterprises to create, in association with Goldcrest and Channel 4 Television, a series called *First Love*, a blanket-and-coverlet title permitting a wide range of plot, period and character, the only constant factor being the passion aroused by the narrative. The flip label of 'Gymslip Drama' was glibly applied to the stories which were usually set in adolescence by an unsympathetic TV executive; but Puttman saw the series as a nursery for new talent, much of it now emerging from the National Film and Television School. 'It's been a wonderful proving ground,' he says, 'I would seldom have taken a chance in feature films with the young people who are talented but have little experience until they had the chance to prove themselves in the *First Love* slot.' The average budget of the first six was £490,000, with Channel 4 and Goldcrest each putting up roughly half. Shooting time was between eighteen and twenty days. 'They revealed the young crew's capacity to organize a production as well as being artistically imaginative.'

P'tang Yang Kipperbang (a schoolboy's world of home and school in 1946 with all the adolescent rites of the period and the middle-class background) was written by Jack Rosenthal and directed by Michael Apted and was almost a re-run of Puttnam's own background, a little more up-market and mythologized. *Experience Preferred But Not Essential* (an evocation, in Philip Larkin's words, of the period 'between the end of the Chatterley ban and the Beatles' first LP', was set in a Welsh hotel where an enthusiastic but innocent girl takes a vacation job) was directed by Peter Duffell. The third, *Secrets,* directed by Gavin Millar, was about the confidence instilled in a girl by her discovery of contraception; and *Those Glory Glory Days*, directed by Philip Savile, was about a trio of schoolgirls and their crush on a Sixties soccer hero.

All these films depended heavily on adolescent nostalgia, chummy male- or female-bonding, secret slang and other rituals, and a generalized but usually accurate re-creation of what it felt like to be middle-class. Much of this common character was probably imparted by Rosenthal's general editorship: he had written the first TV film, *The Evacuees*, to bring Alan Parker to attention. But the films were well received by viewers — and, even more gratifyingly, paid their way at first. The American cable companies, then engaged in fierce competition for product which the networks would not (or could not) show, found such films a visibly original product to offer subscribers. They had the right aura — and the right price. *Experience Preferred But Not Essential* even had the distinction of achieving theatrical release by that discriminating distributor Sam Goldwyn, jun., and it played for satisfying returns in selected situations in America.

But production costs were continually escalating. By 1984 Goldcrest's chairman, James Lee, referred to the worrying situation in which the average shooting cost of a *First Love* film had risen to £600,000. Yet Channel 4 was reluctant to increase its previous £200,000-odd commitment, leaving Goldcrest to find the difference 'from somewhere'. By that date, too, the US cable networks were in trouble; some had gone out of business; the market competitiveness for fare like *First Love* had vanished. This, as much as anything, accounted for the decision to turn some films that were thought of as *First Love* candidates into fully-fledged feature films. One that transcended its origins was *Cal* (1984), whose story of a guilty love between two Ulster Catholics involved in terrorism, one as accessory and the other as victim, was enlarged successfully to cinema dimensions by writer Bernard MacLaverty, director Pat O'Connor and Puttnam himself so as to chart the loyalty and suffering of the wider Ulster community. Distribution prospects for such 'enhanced' films were much brighter than the one-off exposure they could get on television. But Puttnam's attempt to put a couple of the early *First Love* series into theatrical release in Britain, 'and see if there really is life after TV', was poorly received, and probably proved definitely that there *wasn't*. The result was doubly unfortunate. Not only did the double-bill not make money; but it failed to help Puttnam in his plan to push Channel 4 into a firmer commitment to exploiting theatrically a series which he felt had made him some enemies among the network's more radical executives because of its 'cosy complacency and middle-class virtues'.

In late 1984 Goldcrest revealed some surprisingly candid figures suggesting the obstacles confronting any attempt to use a TV series like this as a launching pad for film talents and production finance. Production costs had risen from £395,000 for *P'tang Yang Kipperbang* to £616,000 for the most recent film, *Winter Flight*. Against total costs for the series (to date) of £4.1m., the biggest slice of revenue was £1.8m. from Channel 4; other income was 'variable'. Only three of the films were selected for release inside America by Twentieth Century-Fox (worth £143,000 each) and consequent rest-of-the-world video distribution by Thorn-EMI (£90,000 each). The biggest disappointment had been the 'collapse' of US cable revenue. The first three films had netted about £264,000 each: the remaining five had picked up only £200,000 between them! It was also claimed that their stories made them unattractive to the American market. It was all extremely disappointing.

Goldcrest's mini-series, *The Far Pavilions*, had been poorly received in Britain (and fared no better in America), being compared unfavourably to the much superior ITV production of *The Jewel in the Crown*; and although Puttnam had nothing to do with the production, Goldcrest's backing for films like *Cal* would obviously be influenced by the company's view of the market's resilience and its own place in it. Jake Eberts left Goldcrest in November 1983 with one of Goldcrest's major productions, *Another Country*, on the brink of release, and went to head the European production programme of Embassy, the American corporation headed by Jerry Perenchio and Norman Lear, whose interests in American cable and TV production had made them good front-runners in the 'cabling up' of British homes — seen as the new 'licence to print money' of the Eighties. This view was ruthlessly dashed when the Government actually published the rigorous financial rules applying to the game this time round. Eberts took with him to Embassy the new John Boorman film, *Emerald Forest*. In February 1984 another Goldcrest board member, Sir Richard Attenborough, was announced to direct the film version of the longest-running Broadway musical, *A Chorus Line* — for Embassy Pictures. Embassy had acquired the cable TV rights to Attenborough's *Gandhi* for a reported $20m. and had announced a $71m. production fund.

Before Eberts arrived Embassy produced one British film, *Champions* (1984), about a real-life jockey who conquered cancer and won the Grand National. The movie was unplaced. Perhaps discouraged by this and the dim British cable outlook, Embassy's London activities languished. Eberts left in 1985 without putting one project into production. In mid-1985 Embassy's parent company in America was acquired by the Coca Cola Company.

For a short time the usual rumours that follow such executive moves threw Goldcrest's future plans out of focus. But James Lee moved quickly. The company ceased to be a subsidiary of S. Pearson in May 1984, and became an independent entity; around the same time it made a successful trip to the City and raised £22m. for film and television production. Lee looked forward to a future public quote. Eberts's place was not left vacant long. It was filled by Sandy Lieberson, who had represented The Ladd Company's production interests in London after a short and abortive spell as president of Twentieth Century-Fox. Lieberson had been unable to push ambitious projects of his own on to the Ladd Company's roster and had been forced to watch the parent company suffer huge losses on such space epics as *The Right Stuff*, which effectively ended its influence as a production force in the United States.

And so, midway through 1984, those two old partners, David Puttnam and Sandy Lieberson, found themselves on the same Goldcrest board of directors and also as separate heads of two financially viable and artistically successful production companies explicitly committed to making 'British films' or films that reflected 'a British view of the world'. For Puttnam, the test would come soon — with a film that was American in story, theme and principal casting and financing: *The Killing Fields*. The story of coincidences and ironies in the never-ending crisis of British cinema was far from depleted!

CHAPTER EIGHT

Swim and Sink Together

You must accept that they all don't come out right. — Barry Spikings, Variety, *20 May 1981.*

'My brother Bernie says I'm mad to make films. But it works. Anything will work, if you throw yourself into it heart and soul.'* Thus Sir Lew Grade as he approached his sixty-ninth birthday, which fell on Christmas Day 1975. Perhaps because he knew he had to retire as chief executive of his television empire at seventy, he was feeling less than seasonally mellow. 'All these damned jingle bells,' he continued. 'People know it's Christmas. They don't want someone jumping out of a paper hat shouting "Merry Christmas!" every ten minutes.' This was a common occurrence on television, of course; even the power of programming what people would see had lost its savour for Grade now that he was 'into films'. He yearned for some 'good dramas and thrillers' on the box to supplement the 'damned bells'. And though he didn't specify which film company should be the supplier of alternatives to the paper-hat greeters, his own production outfit now had twenty features in the making and was quite capable of supplying that 'ordinary family' which Lew had in mind and bidding them, as the carol put it, 'with heart and soul, rejoice . . . rejoice'.

He was able, none the less, to shrug off the ungracious if not exactly unseasonable criticism levelled at him that Christmas by no less a person than his old Italian partner, RAI Television, because he had taken commission for placing their mini-series *Jesus of Nazareth* in the twin stables of NBC TV and its sponsor General Motors. 'Absolutely normal,' he snorted, bidding RAI remember how much employment he had brought to Italy. Not just *Jesus*, but that other co-production, *The Origins of the Mafia*.

Rome was at the centre of his thoughts that year. He had been created

---

*Sir Lew Grade, *Daily Express*, 12 December 1975.

a Knight Commander of the Order of Merit of the Knights of Malta at a ceremony in the Eternal City: there, too, he had a 'continuing relationship' with Carlo Ponti, which had begun while the Italian producer was between planes at Nice Airport and Grade had been staying at nearby Eden Roc. 'We started talking at 5.36p.m. We finished at 5.37p.m., and we had a deal. *That's* the way to do it.'* *The Cassandra Crossing (1976)* was conceived in that wink of an understanding: it starred Ponti's wife, Sophia Loren, and was just one of a multi-picture programme which Grade announced in May 1976 at his Eden Roc luncheon during the Cannes Film Festival. He was going to spend £50m., he said from the top table, adding, 'In this business, you have to reach for the sky. So we will spend most of my money on eight monster films . . . Not eight films about monsters,' he corrected himself, lest the sleepyheads nodding over the food and wine served to the 200-odd exhibitors, distributors and media people might get it wrong. 'Films which are big in size and big in stars and which people around the world are going to want to see. I will also make another four films at about £1m. to £2m. each. That's what I call small.' The listeners thanked God (and Grade) that the difference between 'big' and 'small' was not something they had to spell out on long-distance calls to their news desks that hot afternoon.

Lew had invited his brother, Sir Bernard Delfont, to be among his guests, even though he headed the film-making division of the rival corporation EMI. He didn't occupy the top table, of course, but was seated below the salt and among the generality of the guests, perhaps to show that if there was a healthy sibling rivalry, there was certainly no sibling collusion. Later on, Sir Bernard tended not to be part of the proceedings. But then he had his own 'film show' to get on the road, or, rather, across the Altantic, now that Michael Deeley and Barry Spikings had been recruited to bring new production energy into EMI and supplement — some said supplant — that elderly statesman Nat Cohen.

Lew's high-profile approach to show-business protected him from criticism — at least when the good times were rolling — in a way that his brother's lower-keyed attitude did not. Both brothers were vulnerable to the charge that they were pouring money into films that could not remotely be thought of as 'British' either in character or content. Lew could claim, of course, that their 'international' character made location filming essential, which generally ruled out the use of British film studios. In some cases, like *The Eagle Has Landed* (1976), the plot was essentially British — a fictionalized wartime assassination attempt on Churchill's life — to give credibility to his protestation that he was assisting the native film industry. In any case Lew had been so 'Transatlanticized', even before he switched emphasis from television to

---

*Sir Lew Grade, interviewed by David Lewin, *Daily Mail*, 21 May 1976.

films, that the accusation of 'not being British enough' simply did not stick to him the way it did to his brother's production roster at EMI. Delfont had not personalized his company in the same way. EMI was British: it owned British studios at Elstree; it owned a circuit of British cinemas. And yet the truth was that it had embarked on a programme of investment in American-made films — films made in America, by Americans, with Americans as stars — which was vastly more ambitious than any domestic British production programme in recent memory.

'When Barry and I joined EMI, directly responsible to Bernie, the company had very limited experience in selling the films it made to the rest of the world,' says Michael Deeley.* The movies it produced, with a few exceptions like *Murder on the Orient Express*, were far too limited in appeal. The biggest slice of the world market was the United States. If you sold your film there, you were in clover. Our idea was to see if that part of the market would buy the idea for a film of ours and then, if it did, go and make the film there. We always asked ourselves in advance, would the American market put up 50 per cent of the budget? Had the Americans that degree of confidence in the product? If they had, we went ahead. If they hadn't, we didn't. It was that simple at first. No film, we resolved, would be made without the vital American deal being consummated first. Maybe if the Japanese, or the Italians, liked the idea we would consider other means: but the American sale was the fail-safe basis for our deal.

'To start with we had a revolving fund of $8m. to begin pre-production and make the package attractive to the American distributors; then, when they came in with an advance against American distribution, we had their money to begin producing the picture. We were so successful at first that we had a production roster worth $36m. funded by this slender means, although you can imagine the tap-dancing that had to go on! We used the pre- and post-production stages of the film to sell it to the "foreign" markets, that's to say the ones outside America. Thus we were always re-financing ourselves; and the fact that we had the Americans backing the production was a great source of confidence, and not only to us — it also brought prestige to the non-American buyers of the film. No one could tell the difference: to them and their audiences, it looked to be a wholly American movie.'

Thus three important deals were clinched at the very outset of the Deeley-Spikings programme: *The Deer Hunter* was set up with Universal and budgeted at $9m.; *Convoy* with United Artists, at $8m.; and *The Driver* with Twentieth Century-Fox, at £4.5m. (The deal on *The Driver* was so successful in relation to its low cost and foreign sales that it was into profit even before it was made.) They also made a spectacle-adventure *Warlords of Atlantis*, at Pinewood Studios and on

---

*Michael Deeley, re-interviewed by the author, 21 November 1984. Unless stated otherwise, all subsequent quotations from Deeley come from this source.

Malta, for $2m. — that was the British film. The other films, to all intents and purposes, were American, employing American directors and stars: Michael Cimino for *The Deer Hunter*, with Robert De Niro, Christopher Walken, John Savage and Meryl Streep; Sam Peckinpah for *Convoy*, with Kris Kristofferson and Ali MacGraw; Walter Hill for *The Driver*, with Ryan O'Neal, Bruce Dern and Isabelle Adjani imported from France. This policy was, in short, a calculated reversal of the Sixties trend which saw major Hollywood companies rushing to 'trendy' Britain to make films there that would look British, even if the money that paid for them was wholly American.

When questioned at the time on the ethics of putting such a policy into effect when the native British film industry was lying flat on the ring and being counted out, Deeley was pugilistically unrepentant. 'First, it shows the Americans we really mean business when we take the action to them. We are now more heavily committed to making movies in America than some of the traditional powers of Hollywood like MGM or Warners are just now. Our show of strength will increase the willingness of Americans to come in on films we shall soon be making in Britain.'*
He mentioned *Death on the Nile*, then continued. 'EMI is a vast supranational group' — it owned the third largest records company in America, a sizeable film library, and had chunks of money invested in such genuinely American films as *Close Encounters of the Third Kind*. 'And it has huge electronic successes in the field of medicine — its body-scanning machine is a world-wide winner. It was time to establish ourselves as a film-making force to match our strength and leadership elsewhere.'

Sir John Read, EMI's chairman, put it less robustly when he told New York investment analysts that one had to proceed extremely prudently about getting into expensive international pictures: it was very different from making little British pictures for the seaside trade — a remark that all too accurately described the British production scene in mid-1977. But Sir John loyally backed the Deeley-Spikings vision and it was assumed that much of his economic confidence had to do with the reassuring forecast of the 'miracle' body-scanner which EMI was then marketing in the USA. It was all rather like the Rank Organization which could rely on its 'miracle' Xerox copying interests making up the losses it incurred on films.

Actually, Deeley was far less confident than he sounded at that time, as regards EMI's fortunes. Some seven years later, he recalled, 'When we made the British Lion-EMI deal in 1976, we were regarded as the "experts" on America, and, boosted in my own self-esteem, I warned that EMI was rash to count on its body-scanner being given *carte blanche* in America. The Americans, I said, were not going to stand aside and let

*Michael Deeley, interviewed by the author, *Evening Standard*, 9 June 1977.

this admittedly wonderful British medical invention take over their market. But my fears were pooh-poohed — "EMI was not going to have any truck with American companies, etc., etc. It was big enough to look after itself." The fact was, EMI was *not* big enough, and when the American interests got their Government to act and scale down Federal-funded spending on the EMI body-scanner, our profits were bound to go down. But we didn't reckon on seeing them crash, from £70m. to £17m.! That was the end for EMI. But since much of that residual £17m. came, ironically, from Delfont's film-making division, why Bernie was the blue-eyed boy.' This apocalypse, though not exactly 'now', was looming not far ahead.

Meantime, Deeley and Spikings brushed aside criticism when it appeared in the British Press — very few indigenous voices, in any case, were raised to question or condemn the classical 'mercenary' practice of paying others to look after one's own interests and do one's work. 'Really, such criticism was irrelevant to what we were doing,' Deeley says. 'We were letting the Americans judge their own market, instead of taking the lofty attitude that it was clever of us foreigners to make a picture there: we were giving them the judgmental role.' Deeley went to America to oversee the pictures, leaving his joint-managing director, Barry Spikings, at home to 'look after the store'. He recognized later that this was a bad tactic: 'I should have been at home, covering my back, for I always had the feeling that the Old Guard was chipping away at my authority, trying to drive a wedge between so-called young buccaneers like Barry and me.'

The disadvantage of being at a distance was brought home to him abruptly one day by an angry telephone call from Delfont. The latter had just finished reading a screen-play submitted by the Monty Python comedy team; it was a parody of Biblical events based on a youthful innocent's accidental acquisition of divinity entitled *The Life of Brian*. 'To this day', says Deeley, 'I don't know who leaked the screen-play I'd found so funny to Bernard Delfont: but he castigated me for presuming to make a film that was "blasphemous" — "EMI wasn't going to incur the odium of such a film, etc., etc." "Bernie," I said, *"The Life of Brian* is not blasphemous. I can assure you of that as a Christian." I must admit this was pitching it a bit strong: but he wouldn't have any of it — "I'm not going to be accused of making fun of Jesus Christ." So Terry Jones and the Monty Python people took their screen-play to HandMade Films, got the backing of Denis O'Brien and his partner, the ex-Beatle George Harrison, and shot it in Tunisia, which can't have posed many "Christian" difficulties. It made a very great deal of money.' As it was shown in EMI cinemas, the company eventually got some of the profit — and, of course, incurred none of the odium.

THE FIRST CRACKS

The two Grade brothers — both of them created Peers of the Realm in 1976 — stepped up the tempo of their American-angled production plans. Lord Delfont ducked the occasional, the *very* occasional pro-British brickbat lobbed his way, generally by one film critic who had bought a single share in EMI stock so as to be able to ask embarrassing questions at the annual general meeting of stockholders. Lord Grade behaved with the jubilant guiltlessness of a child totally ignorant of the error of its ways. Looking at Lord Delfont watching Lord Grade do a few Charleston dance steps to wind up an industry luncheon, one wondered if he, too, yearned to be the 'heart and soul' of the party. Probably not.

Having embarked on a film programme he hoped would appeal to the American market, Lord Grade's next step was to secure an American partner with whom he could share the box-office there, instead of having to surrender at least 30 per cent of the gross to a distributor who wasn't part of 'the family'. he found one in a Boston-based exhibitor, General Cinema Corporation. Their partnership, Associated General Films by name, had funding from the First National Bank of Boston. Not that Lord Grade was strapped for cash: on the contrary, ATV's profits were soaring: they rose by a colossal 81 per cent in 1976–7, from £6,151,000 to £11,161,000 despite the industrial recession that was biting deeply into British manufacturing industry.

There never seemed a better time to Lew Grade to try and secure a foothold in the American market — 'crack it', as the phrase was. Associated General Films financed five films; to Lord Grade's bitter disappointment, none was a blockbuster on the scale of his early *Pink Panther* hit. 'The first one, *The Cassandra Crossing* (1976), cost just over $3m., and we got that amount back out of Japan alone. *The Eagle Has Landed* made quite a lot of money; *The Domino Principle* (1976) broke even. *March or Die* (1976), about the Foreign Legion, went well over budget when Gene Hackman suffered an accident and lost money. *Voyage of the Damned* (1976), well, it should have done better.' Some of these films performed well in specific foreign territories, where they were indistinguishable — to the general public — from Hollywood-made movies. But from General Cinema Corporation's point of view, the trouble was they they did not do well enough in America, where the company stood to share in the receipts: disenchantment soon set in. Lord Grade discounts reports current at the time, that his partner wanted more creative involvement, especially in the choice of stars. 'It was never GCC's business to make the films,' he says bluntly; 'that was my responsibility. If I wanted to make a film, that was it: we made it.'

This has the ring of truth all right; but it was an unfortunate truth for a partner to have to recognize. Lord Grade's regal habits, shaped by his reign at ATV, unfettered by boards of directors (much less 'partners'), were bound to make for differences. He did take advice, but generally only when he could see the clear link with profits: thus he surprisingly backed an Ingmar Bergman production, *From the Life of the Marionettes* (1980), when it was a matter of reasserting his corporate leverage over some European distributors. Otherwise, he trusted to his own instinct. He stressed his respect for Dick Smith, GCC's chief, when their partnership came to an end within two years. Yet it was this 'respect' that involved Lew Grade in the most fateful decision of his career, one that eventually contributed to the loss of the very empire he had spent his life building.

'One day Dick sent me a package by express airmail. A set of galley proofs. I recognized the title of the book, *Raise the Titanic*. It was one I'd really been offered by the author's agent and had rejected because it didn't appeal to me. I'd said No to the agent right away: I didn't even read the manuscript when I heard what the story was about.' But now perhaps because he saw a manuscript being made flesh, so to speak, turned into a book, becoming *a property*, about to be published in the market-place, perhaps even sold to someone else . . . he started reading the galleys. 'I sat up all night and in the morning I called Dick Smith and said, "I must make this".' Then he found Stanley Kramer, the film producer, had already beaten him to the film rights: so a deal was done. According to Lord Grade, the rights in *Raise the Titanic* were transferred to him for $400,000 and it was understood that Kramer would direct any movie based on the book. Obviously it was going to be an expensive movie: how expensive, Lord Grade did not yet know. After an agonizing production schedule he would have spent an unrecoverable fortune on *Raise the Titanic* — and coined the most rueful of all the self-deprecating wisecracks attributed to him: 'It would have cost less to lower the Atlantic.'*

By the end of November 1977 *Screen International* — not a trade paper that usually stuck its neck out — was boldly suggesting that 'the next twelve months could prove make-or-break time for Lord Grade'.** The basis for this forecast was the distribution gap that had been left in the American market by the withdrawal of GCC and the growing resistance it was claimed non-US exhibitors were putting up to Lord Grade's demand for higher advances. Yet in the offing was a production roster representing a $97m. investment. Among the pictures on it: *The Big Sleep, The Boys from Brazil, The Medusa Touch, Love and Bullets, Charlie* and *Double Feature* (which became *Movie Movie*). Grade could say with some truth: 'Mine is the biggest film production company in the world.'*** But had he learnt anything from the slight slackening

---

*Needless to say, it has been impossible to trace this to source.
**Screen International*, 26 November 1977.
***Lord Grade, interviewed by James Bartholomew, *The Financial Times*, 21 August 1978.

in the outflow of figures? Well, he replied, the important thing to get right now were 'the words, the producer and the director'. Stars no longer seemed quite so important. A *Financial Times* reporter did a quick computation of the possible state of the Grade empire. 'Borrowed money for film production (in 1977) rose from £10m. to 22m., say an average of £16m. The profit was £2.3m., or £3.9m. if the interest charge is added on. The gross profit of £3.9m. on capital employment of £16m. is a return of 24 per cent. Not a spectacular return, but good.' Then switching to the appropriate currency for blockbusters, the same perceptive commentator noted that one of them 'can make $50m. to $100m. at a stroke. This is the bull's eye Lord Grade is aiming for. The low-risk strategy is designed to enable him to have as many throws as possible while letting the law of averages do the rest.' But he warned — even more shrewdly in view of what was to come — 'The main danger is a series of flops . . . the vital credibility which enables Lord Grade to pre-sell the films would be damaged.'

Over at EMI all was not going smoothly for Michael Deeley, either. By October 1977 he was beginning to feel the strain of commuting between London and Los Angeles to supervise the films that EMI was making in partnership with its three American majors: *Convoy, The Driver* and *The Deer Hunter*. Sam Peckinpah's increasingly erratic behaviour was pushing up the budget on the first. It was also likely that *The Deer Hunter* would go over budget. It had been initially brought to Deeley when he was at British Lion in the shape of an original scenario by Louis Garfinkle and Quinn K. Redeker entitled *The Man Who Came to Play*, a reference to the 'torture' game of Russian roulette which was later severely criticized as a fictional importation into the already palpable and authentic horrors of Vietnam. Deeley bought the script for $19,000 and brought it with him when he went to EMI. 'If anyone at EMI had actually read it,' he says, 'it's fate would have been the same as *Monty Python's Life of Brian*: I'm convinced of that. They would have hated it, not understood it and turned it down.'

Towards the end of 1977 Deeley was told that it would ease the strain on him if he were to locate himself permanently in Los Angeles. 'I was never quite sure about the solicitude behind this suggestion. It certainly split Barry Spikings from myself; we were the most efficient production set-up around at that time. I didn't fancy being based in America: it meant selling my home in London, paying double taxes, etc. I believed my function was to establish EMI as a major force in the film world; then we could exploit our position, and I was anxious to integrate with an American production outlet. I had established close relationships with at least four of the Hollywood majors, but I didn't see that living next-door to them would move this plan along. Sir John Read had to be asked to tell me to go to America. It was planned that I'd be there for three years.'

Things turned unexpectedly tough in the first six months of 1978.
'EMI were unable to get Orion Pictures to put up the 50 per cent
guarantee we always sought for a film called *The Last Gun*: we paid off the
production rather than go ahead with it on those conditions. It was to
have cost $5m.; all Orion would advance was $2m. We then got rid of
Peckinpah, who was uncontrollable, edited *Convoy* in five weeks and
released it. We had received the first cut of *The Deer Hunter*, but we were
having trouble pre-selling it in foreign territories. We had opened
discussions with Lew Grade and Ian Jessel at ITC about selling jointly
overseas, but the response we got was not encouraging. "We're well
fixed in the foreign markets — what do we need you for?" was how I
interpreted it.'

All this time rumours had been reaching the elegant EMI office over
the Van Cleef and Arpel jewellery store in Beverly Hills — a site, it was
later insisted, when accusations of extravagance were flying around, that
had been obtained at a most moderate rent — to the effect that all was
far from well with the parent company back in London. 'We kept
hearing EMI was getting into deeper financial trouble,' says Deeley,
'but we tried to ignore it by working all the harder.' 'Trouble' proved an
understatement. What was happening was a debacle. The reaction of
American interests threatened by EMI's bodyscanner had been fiercer
even than Deeley anticipated. The company had also run into severe
maintenance problems. Worse, the funds that American medical
institutions relied on to purchase the machine were subject to Federal
Government alteration. And home-based American companies were
speedily developing their own 'miracle' machine and waging a successful
'trade war' for contracts. The value of EMI's stock fell disastrously.

'Half-way through 1978 Bernie Delfont came over to Los Angeles and
met Barry and me. What he had to tell us was shattering. We couldn't
make any more pictures, was what it came down to. EMI hadn't the
money! Well, we suggested, why not borrow some? After all, we have
three major films as collateral. Won't our films be useful in replenishing
EMI's profits? But Bernie was adamant. The game was up. Barry and I
walked home after the meeting in a total daze: we didn't even have the
satisfaction of being told the full reasons for the ultimatum — the
attitude was simply, "It's not working out." Barry said to me, "Have
you thought how you're going to handle this?" "Barry," I replied, "I
think we've just been fired."'

'We discussed setting up shop in Hollywood and "doing it there". But
the collapse of all we'd worked for could not have come at a worse time.
For Barry, anyhow. I had an iron-clad contract — five years at
American rates, three years still to run, a half-million dollar settlement
coming to me. But Barry was simply on a few weeks' notice — at £20,000
a year I suppose, plus expenses. A dire plight. At least we were still good
friends: that was something. But I felt very embittered: quite brutally, I

wanted to get out. It had all become very ugly. I decided to work on my own for a bit: but I had a dispiriting hunt. I went to China in September 1978, and by the time I got back it was a whole different scene. Barry had made the best of an impossible situation — he was still at EMI as chief executive of EMI films directly responsible to Lord Delfont.'

THE TWO TITANICS

While all this was happening in his brother's company, Lord Grade was busying himself with plans to plug the distribution gap left by GCC's withdrawal. First National Bank of Boston was approached: it was made plain that a partner would be desirable. EMI was an obvious candidate; indeed, with Lord Delfont in control of the film projects there, it was a fraternally attractive one. Therefore, in November 1978, it was announced that ITC and EMI would be forming a new US-Canada distribution company for their own films, and other companies' productions which they decided to pick up, capitalized at $38.5 m. and, according to the two brothers, handling $175m.-$200m. worth of productions in an 'initial surge' of twenty-two pictures. Lord Grade was named chairman: Lord Delfont, vice-chairman; Martin Starger, currently president of Grade's US-based Marble Arch productions, became president; and board members included Jack Gill, deputy chairman and deputy chief executive of ITC's parent company ACC, and Barry Spikings, now chief executive of EMI Films (as already noted) and head of EMI world production. The new company was called Associated Film Distributors. Both ITC and EMI guaranteed to make a minimum of twelve pictures a year for at least four years. Though fifteen of the first twenty-two films had been previously announced under one title or another, Martin Starger said confidently that the agreement made AFD the 'eighth biggest distribution company in the world'. The tendency to talk in superlatives had not been moderated.

Deeley says that had he still been with EMI at the time this merger was proposed he would have screamed murder. 'We'd have been speculating in a market we didn't know. Instead of getting the Americans to put their money where the distribution set-up was, we would have been gambling on our own chutzpah, over-confidently assuming we could do the job as well as they. I think I know what happened. Lew's company probably ran a computer print-out on the pictures we had co-financed with the Hollywood majors to find out how they would have done had we distributed them in America ourselves — and came up with hugely gratifying results. Well, that was fine — on paper. But when the Hollywood people heard of Associated Film Distributors being formed, all the majors with whom we had had a "relationship" during my time at EMI got angry. The Oscars had come through by then for *The Deer Hunter*. It took five Academy Awards, including the ones for "Best Picture" and "Best Director". EMI was "hot". Yet instead of entering into partnership with a Hollywood company, it set up AFD and entered into competition with the Americans for a share of their own market. It was the very opposite of the policy that Barry and I had spent years bringing to the point of profit.'

If Lords Grade and Delfont had any fears, they did not let them show. By now the latter had become EMI's deputy chairman. After all, his film empire was the division with the healthiest glow as EMI's profits crashed in the bodyscanner disaster and the group's financial prospects worsened until there was a serious prospect of insolvency. Spikings had stepped into Delfont's job, and an enthusiastic and talented producer, Peter Beale, was brought in as Spikings's number two. Among the Grade and Delfont productions announced at this time for distribution by AFD were: a Franco Zeffirelli biopic on Maria Callas; the Ingmar Bergman film (*From the Lives of the Marionettes*); a Lina Wertmuller Italian-language production (*Vengeance*); two projects (*Cafe Society* and *Can't Stop the Music*), both to be produced by Allan Carr (whose successful promotion of *The Deer Hunter* inside the Hollywood Establishment had made friends for it in Universal and, some said, tilted the preferences of Academy members towards it in the Oscar voting); a John Schlesinger-Joseph Janni production entitled *The Wife; Saturn III*, a SF story that teamed Kirk Douglas with Farrah Fawcett Major; a remake of *The Jazz Singer*, with Neil Diamond in the Al Jolson role and Lord Olivier as his cantor father; a Stanley Donen thriller called *The French Villa; The Chinese Bandit*, which Deeley had taken with him as part of his severance settlement from EMI; and two thrillers based on novels by Alastair MacLean and Robert Ludlum. Also named was *Raise the Titanic*, though now without Stanley Kramer: he had been replaced as director by one Jerry Jameson, whose experience in raising the sunken aircraft in *Airport Two* seemed to qualify him for further marine operations.

It was pre-eminently the kind of roll-call dear to Lew Grade's heart. Even though the majority of the pictures announced would not get made, for one reason or another, merely to announce them was an earnest of AFD's intention to be in there with the Hollywood majors, elbowing them aside for a share of their home market. Lord Grade's confidence, besides being endlessly self-generated, was solidly based on a peculiar arrangement of Associated Communications Corporation's share capital. Although a publicly listed company, a mere 156,000 shares out of a total of 54,300,000 were of any value when it came to formulating company policy: the rest carried no voting rights. The Grade family held 24 per cent of the voting shares and, at this time, could rely on another 15 per cent of the enfranchised shares which were held by long-time show-business associates or high-level ACC executives. He was therefore immune to any unfriendly take-over bid: not that any raider was visible on the financial horizon at this stage. And he could afford to ignore the nay-sayers among the powerful City institutions holding non-voting shares in ACC: not that any discordant voices were being raised, there, either. So long as ACC showed a profit, all was contentment; and it had never failed to do so.

All this had enabled Lord Grade to carry out his immense production programme with a confidence enjoyed by no other film-maker outside the Hollywood Establishment. Though owning a *minority* of shares in his company, he in fact possessed a *majority* voice in any decisive say-so. Even if they had wanted to, shareholders were debarred from effective protest; not that they wanted to. What was becoming apparent to humble film critics, seated below the top table at the lord and master's annual Eden Roc luncheon but cocking an ear to the neighbourly disenchantment of some of ACC's European distributors eating and drinking their way through the promotional spiel, was disregarded (if indeed they were aware of it) by the financiers back in the City of London. Most of these supposedly well-informed people had no inkling of the enormities that film-making in such circumstances could lead to. (Hence, perhaps, their rage when they finally got the bill.)

Looking back, *Raise the Titanic* can be seen as an awesome omen of what was soon to ensue with escalating speed and highly damaging publicity. Had any other film, had any other *title*, been the one to engulf Lord Grade in deep financial waters, it is possible he might even then have escaped the worst of the retribution that the very media which had so often feted him would shortly inflict upon him. But that word 'Titanic', with all its connotations of historic disaster, was the deadliest of curses: it found its way into virtually every headline written during the crisis period. It soon detached itself from the box-office fate of one specific film and became a general metaphor for the fate of Lord Grade's huge communications empire.

The making of that film was fraught with troubles from the start. 'We had a first draft script that was obviously unsatisfactory,' Grade says, 'and while we were revising it, we decided to build the boat to save time. Well, we built it too big. The principal Titanic model was 55-feet long and there wasn't a studio tank in the world big enough to sink it in and then raise it up from. So we had to build the tank. Using the sea, or a lake, as some people suggested, simply wouldn't have worked, for it was essential to film the scenes in clear, clean water.' Bernie Kingham, Grade's right-hand production chief in Britain, obtained a site in Malta and the tank was built there, 300-feet long, 250-feet wide, 35-feet deep. 'Unfortunately, it leaked. No sooner had we filled it up with water, then it ran out. We had to keep a large stand-by staff on full pay while we were plugging the holes. Meanwhile, various other models were being constructed in California and they alone were costing us $6m. — the sort of budget I'd been used to spending on *a whole picture*! At this time *Raise the Titanic* was budgeted at $20m. But we started production in the Malta tank six months late. And no sooner had we put the models in the water than we had to take them out and reconstruct them — their relation to each other was on the wrong scale. Then we sank them, and they kept bursting — the water-pressure was too much for them. It was endless! It was expensive!' The film ended up costing $34m.

An unexpected and infuriating complication during these months was the simultaneous production of a film with the title *SOS Titanic*. Its producer was Lord Grade's brother, Lord Delfont! The wits made the obvious joke: that Bernie would have sunk his Titanic before Lew had raised *his*. But to Lord Grade, it was no joke. According to David Lewin, he expostulated to his brother, 'What are you trying to do to me Bernie? We had the idea first. How would you like it if I had made *Assassination on the Orient Express* when you were filming *Murder on the Orient Express*?'* Lord Grade put on a good face in public, however, quipping that the models in his films would cost more than his brother's whole production; in private he seethed with annoyance. '*SOS Titanic* was being made for TV in America,' he says, 'but I knew it would have theatrical exposure in some foreign territories where my film would also play in the cinemas. *Raise the Titanic* was a completely different kind of film, but the association would harm it. People don't look too closely at these things, and when *Raise the Titanic* arrived on their neighbourhood screen they might even believe they'd already seen it!' This may indeed have been the case. Japan was the only territory where, according to Grade, the local distributor bought up *SOS Titanic* and put it on the shelf: In Japan, *Raise the Titanic* did excellent business.' He spoke severely to his brother, 'but Bernie said he had a commitment to his US backers and couldn't afford to shelve his *Titanic* "just because we were brothers". Well, I understood that: for although we were brothers, we'd always gone through life in friendly rivalry. All the same, it was just what I could have done without at that time — *another Titanic*!'

OUT-RANKED

Both the Grade empire and EMI were running deeply into trouble in 1979; but Lord Grade's remarkable personal power, his friendly relations with journalists and the ebullient attitude he still adopted in public enabled him to act with the single-minded boldness of the apparently unassailable autocrat. In February 1979 ACC paid £12.9m. for the major sectors of Laurie Marsh's Inter-european Property Group,

*Lord Grade, interviewed by David Lewin, *Daily Mail*, 12 March 1979.

which had last been in the news when Pricefreezer Ltd made its abortive bid to buy it. No slip-up this time. The 130 screens in the Classic circuit now passed into Grade's hands — to provide him with a British distribution outlet for his seemingly unstoppable flow of films — as well as a Los Angeles hotel and the so-called 'Eros site' in Piccadilly Circus on which it was proposed to build a theatre. Such expansionism seemed to signify how well things were going. Across the Atlantic Martin Starger was also bullish, announcing a $145m. film investment programme, fifteen films in all, including a Western, *Barbarosa*, a version of Tom Stoppard's play, *Night and Day* — and *The Muppets Movie*. This last film was to prove the only film distributed by AFD that could be called a substantial money-maker — though even the money it made would be inadequate to cover the immense loss that was in the making and, ironically, this 'lucky strike' at the American box-office was like a whiff of oxygen to a man who was by then groggy with punishment. It put Lord Grade back on his feet — only to have him walk into the final knock-out.

For ACC this terminal shock began to arrive in a series of mounting business reverses. First, its profits for 1979 80 were badly cut, from £16.31m. to £14.1m. before tax, though this was due in part to an eleven-week strike on ITV in the autumn of 1979 which deprived the company of advertising revenue. A far worse threat loomed over the very ownership of the lucrative TV franchise which Lord Grade had inherited when ATV became the principal ITV contractor in the Midlands. The Independent Broadcasting Authority, reacting to criticism of the network's allegedly mediocre programming, now looked like insisting that ATV should lose, or, at any rate, share, its Birmingham-based TV fiefdom. Even though ACC's film and TV production and distribution division actually showed a small rise in pre-tax profits, from £2.25m. to £3.93m., the colossal cost of *Raise the Titanic* was mounting all the time. In 1981 the *Titanic* bill was presented: and ACC made the first loss in company history, some £7m.

In fairness, not all of it was due to one wretched film. The company had upped its borrowings to March 1980 by some £46m. to a total of £80m., used in part to finance the purchase of the Classic cinemas, a deal that now had to be justified by the box-office success of Lord Grade's and other producers' films. But the films were not fulfilling the hopes (and cash) invested in them. Eight films released in the USA by AFD in 1979–80 grossed only $42m., all but $4m. of this sum coming from *The Muppets Movie*. In addition to meeting its own marketing costs, AFD had to contribute to the production budget of EMI and Grade projects. It had put $10m. into one of EMI's most enthusiastically backed productions, *Can't Stop the Music,* starring the Village People, who were at the top of the Pop charts when the film was conceived as a vehicle for them. By the time it came to be shown, they had been eclipsed by other

groups. 'Two hours too long and two years too late' was the most cutting
of the critical dismissals levelled at the film. It was estimated to be a
$17m. flop. Barry Spikings took it especially hard. 'It was against my
values, but I thought it would make a lot of money,' he was quoted as
saying a year or so later. 'It was the only film I ever made just to make
money,' he added, penitently, 'and that is the wrong way. You have to
make something because you believe in it.'*

Time, however, softened even these harsh strictures, slightly. *'(Can't
Stop the Music)* has done well in Australia and the video sales are holding
up,' Spikings said later; and, as if good intentions had been thwarted
rather than more commercial values, he reflected that, 'It was planned
at a time when the world looked black: the news was all of violence,
kidnapping and hostages. We were looking for a product which, with its
very exuberance and even mindlessness, would be right for the escapist
mood in America.'** Other projects submitted to EMI, but turned down,
included *Chariots of Fire* and *Gandhi*: presumably, their unattractiveness
did not lie in any lack of 'mindlessness'.

Spikings had considerably more success with *The Elephant Man* (1981),
director David Lynch's study of the pathetic Victorian 'monstrosity'
incarnated with touching reticence by John Hurt. It recovered its
modest production cost inside Britain alone: but since the production
company was that of the American comic Mel Brooks, it could not swell
the AFD revenues in America. *The Jazz Singer* proved a disappointment,
critically and commercially, though Neil Diamond's record sales would
see it into profit.

But if things were getting tough for Lord Grade in 1979, they were
now traumatic for EMI. Desperate for ready cash, the company tried
selling its prestigious music division to Paramount for £70m. The deal
fell through. Profits crashed to the floor, from £65m. in 1977 to a pathetic
£11m. in 1978–9. The future looked to be in short supply until a saviour
arrived in the shape of Thorn Electrical Industries which offered £157m.
for the ailing company in October 1979, upped it to £169m. in
November on a part-cash, part-share basis, and had its bid thankfully
accepted in December. That same month *Honky Tonk Freeway* went into
production; and Thorn-EMI, as the merged companies were henceforth
known, thus inherited one of the biggest losses made by a single film
when, as related in an earlier chapter, the $26m. flop opened and rapidly
closed in America not many months later. For the succeeding years the
film commitments entered into by EMI were like time bombs in the
Thorn-EMI boardroom until Peter Laister, on taking over as chief
executive, was able to impose a programme of vastly reduced
ambitiousness. But by that time everything else had changed, too.

And what, it may be asked, was Nat Cohen doing all this time? What

*Barry Spikings, interviewed by David Lewin, *Daily Mail*, 20 May 1981.
**Barry Spikings, interviewed by John Higgins, *The Times*, 18 June 1981.

did he think of the disaster he sensed in the making? It's doubtful that his urbanity ever deserted him: if so, he had certainly recovered it when he came to reflect on the period some time later. 'I was going through, well, an awkward stage at EMI, not quite sure where I was supposed to be; not in charge, yet not excluded from policy-making; not often consulted and rarely finding people available when I wanted to consult them. A delicate situation. . . . I suppose you could sum it up this way: I was very fortunate that as these costly deals were being made I seemed to be losing control of picture-making in the company.'

Unlike Cohen, others did not sit it out: Peter Beale quit his job under Barry Spikings with a year still to go on his contract. On taking over as managing director of EMI Films, he had called it 'the best job in the world'. Now he returned thankfully to independent production, and with characteristic good manners left his reasons to be guessed at. Clearly it was an uncomfortable position to be riding on the tailboard of a juggernaut which had too many drivers at the wheel.

EMI and ACC were not the only stricken entertainment giants as the next decade opened. Mortal sickness assailed the film side of the Rank Organization which, in June 1980, abruptly wound up one of the most extraordinary erratic production programmes that any British company had put together. In the five years up to 1976 Rank's investment in film production had been nugatory — a mere £1.5m. a year.

But, in 1977, it brashly announced it was back in the game. Anthony Williams was appointed to head its production side. Williams had joined Rank's ten years earlier as a graduate trainee; he had experience in theatre management (State, Kilburn: Odeon, Richmond) and the exhibition-distribution business (at Rank's Tuchinski cinema-chain in the Netherlands). His enthusiasm was boundless: his knowledge of boardroom politics and organization rivalries was narrower. Like Bryan Forbes at Elstree, he now found his own company's distribution outfit was not always the most eager taker for many of the pictures he put into production.

They were in truth an odd lot: the overriding formula seemed to be 'something for everyone' — the predictable end result was 'nothing for anyone'. *Wombling Free,* a spin-off of a children's TV series about the anthropomorphized Wombles of Wimbledon Common who set junior citizens examples in tidiness, arrived too late on the big screen to fill any box-office with cash, never mind the litter bins with trash: it was quietly disposed of to television. *Eagle's Wing,* a Western, stylishly directed by Anthony Harvey, was deemed 'too arty' for the shoot-em-up crowd and had trouble getting wide bookings in Rank's own circuit cinemas. *The Lady Vanishes* and *The 39 Steps* were ill-advised remakes of Hitchcock classics, rendered even more pallid by comparison with the earlier films. *The Riddle of the Sands* was not intended to be a children's film, but an adult version of Erskine Childers' classic tale of spying and small boats set on the eve of the First World War; but that's how it ended up looking — though no children's film could hope to succeed at a cost of a million pounds. Another classic adaptation, *Tarka the Otter*, had at least the virtue of never dating — otters can be annuities for film-makers. *Silver Dream Racer* was a cleaned-up biker drama with David Essex which failed to get the Pop fans revved up.

A fatal sense of unadventurous orthodoxy characterized every one of these films except the last to appear: Nicolas Roeg's *Bad Timing*, with Art Garfunkel testing his so-called male chauvinist 'dignity' by indulging in sex with a female character who was half dead. The title was truer than intended. Some Rank board members felt that necrophiliac copulation didn't fit the company image: better a blue chip than a blue movie, or, as one unidentified executive stigmatized it: 'A sick film made by sick people for sick audiences.'

Apart from *Bad Timing*, all these Rank films were determinedly 'clean-faced', not one of them sporting the teenage acne of hard rock, punk violence or petty bourgeois criminality that characterized independently made films like *Scum*, *Rude Boy* or *Quadrophenia*. Yet this was where the big money lay, like it or not. Rank never succeeded in selling these films to any major US distributor — they were viewed there as 'dated'. 'They had no emotional spark,' said one American buyer. Rank's losses on its films were actually absurdly 'modest' as these things go — only £1.3m. by the end of October 1979, for a total investment estimated to be about £10m. But a company founded by a Methodist flour miller, J. Arthur Rank, in order to bring Christian values into popular entertainment, was ill disposed to gamble on bolder projects. It cut its loss and left the table to other players before the stakes got raised by inflation and the cries of pain from the boardroom grew shriller. As Ed Chilton, Rank's managing director, put it rather stand-offishly, 'We felt there were better things we could do with our money based on shareholders' interests.'*

Anthony Williams, who left Rank and became an independent producer, later spoke with the bluntness of a bitter memory. Rank, he intimated, had never got behind its own product. The 'less than co-operative' attitude taken by the distribution division affected international confidence in the films — for why should foreign buyers be interested in movies that couldn't command the loyalty of those who made them? He gave the impression that the considerable exhibition outlets Rank owned through its British cinema chain might, in some way, have been used as leverage to get the American majors to book the films in their own country. 'A sort of blackmail then, by any other name?' his interviewer asked.** In the polite British way of doing business, the word seemed startlingly raffish: in America, it wouldn't have

---

*Ed Chilton, *Screen International*, 14–20 June 1980.
**Quentin Falk, interviewing Anthony Williams, *Screen International*, 26 December 1981.

caused a raised eyebrow. Ed Chilton, Williams's immediate boss at Rank, kept a huge black stuffed grizzly bear in his office at Pinewood Studios: but nothing like its hug was ever applied to American visitors. A sedate little luncheon was given for the small American company that eventually filled the gaps in its own exhibition outlets with some of the Rank pictures: and that was that. When Wardour Street heard that the biggest British company was pulling out of film production, the reaction tended to be, 'Were they ever in it?'

The Economist (remembering Rank's lucrative stake in Xerox and the way the tail wagged the dog) put it more acidulously in headlining its report: 'Copier Company Quits Films'. Given the company's timidity, the journal said, Rank's decision to pull out was not so surprising as its 1977 decision to go back in. At least it did not need to send for the Man with the Gong, Rank's famous living trade mark who once heralded the sonorous arrival of each of the company's new productions on the world screen, in order to know for whom it sounded. This time, in tones of funereal finality, it sounded for Rank.

THE MUPPETS MORTGAGED

The £7m. loss that ACC announced in 1981 brought one trouble positively tripping on the heels of the next. The institutional shareholders had now been alerted, and were alarmed: but they could do little without voting power. Asset after asset was suddenly placed on the auction block in an attempt to placate them and restore confidence to the ailing management and liquidity to its coffers. The Classic cinema circuit, acquired less than three years earlier, was put up for sale; so was the hotel in Los Angeles; so was the theatre site in Piccadilly — in a bizarre re-run of the *Titanic* mistakes, it had been found *too small* for the theatre planned to be built on it! Beset on every side by adversity, Lord Grade mortgaged two of his dearest possessions. First National of Boston and other banks advanced a useful $46m. against future profits from *The Muppets* television shows and the *Jesus of Nazareth* mini-series. Even so, it wasn't enough to cover the massive £26.4m. loss incurred on film production and distribution as well as net borrowings which stood at £74.5m. And although the profits of ATV rose from £3.9m. to £4.8m., ACC had finally received its orders from the IBA to cut its holding in the ATV television network by 51 per cent, seriously weakening Lord Grade's old power base for international wheeling and dealing.

The amazing thing was that, even amidst such savage retrenchment, programmes of future film production kept on being announced to feed the voracious appetite of AFD, to keep its staff occupied, to pay their salaries and the rent on their offices and to sustain the rapidly waining confidence of exhibitors. What had been proudly planned as a means of conquering the American market from within, had now made hostages of ACC and EMI. Its insatiable demands had to be supplied: it was as brutally simple as that. A muted Lord Grade conceded, 'We certainly won't be making eight or nine films a year any more. We'll only go in with partners and only when we have covered 90 per cent' — hitherto it had been 50 per cent — 'of the costs through selling TV and cable rights.'* He started production on several films: *The Legend of the Lone Ranger, On Golden Pond* and a life of John Paul II entitled *Man from a Far Country*, and bought the William Styron best seller, *Sophie's Choice*, for filming. He pinned his hopes to *The Great Muppet Caper* opening across America in mid-June 1981. But all too soon it showed it wasn't going to repeat the success of the first Muppets film and ACC's only blockbuster.

But of all the films being blamed for the deepening crisis, *Raise the Titanic* was the one to which continual reference was made, in cartoons as well as text, in headlines that were disaster metaphors for more than an ocean liner. 'Grade Clears Decks After Titanic Loss' (*The Sunday Times*, 28 June 1981); 'Titanic Loss, Other Anguish, Hits Lord Grade' (*Variety*, 30 June 1981); 'Iceberg That Wrecked an Empire' (*Daily Mirror*, 27 June 1981).

ACC took the unusual step — for a British company — of writing off all its film losses in one year. As long as Lord Grade held on to his controlling interest, his board went along with this: but an 'Inner Cabinet' was set up whose terms of reference, though vague, were interpreted by the media as a discreet constraint on his one-man rule. As a face-saver, it was unwelcome; as a curb, it was unsuccessful.

On 1 September 1981 Jack Gill, ACC's deputy chairman and the man often (too often, perhaps, for Lord Grade's liking) named as the heir apparent, suddenly left the company amidst speculation of a *coup d'état* that had failed. With him, he took a compensatory 'golden handshake'. Accustomed perhaps to Lord Grade's own fondness for hyperbole, the media didn't underestimate the size of this parting present: a figure of between £500,000 and £800,000 was plumped for. Well, why not? It beggared the more precisely calculated pension of £72,833 a year that the fallen executive would enjoy: but, compared with a film budget, it was a mere *pourboire*.

Lord Grade might yet have ridden out the turbulence created by Gill's departure, but the alleged size of this six-figure compensation hastily voted by the ACC board united the media in vociferous indignation and this, in turn, roused the anger and apprehension of City investors. 'Some reporters were chasing a drama that seemed bigger and better than anything ACC had ever managed to put on the international television screen,' wrote one observer. 'And this time Grade himself was cast as the villain.'** This was the opportunity that the Australian business tycoon

*Lord Grade, interviewed by Nick Gilbert, *The Sunday Times*, 25 March 1982.
**Patience Wheatcroft, *The Sunday Times*, 25 March 1982.

Robert Holmes à Court had been waiting for. Up to then, this secretive man had been lying quietly under these troubled waters. Now he rose from them like 'Jaws'.

Holmes à Court was one of the richest men in Australia. He owned several homes, a stud farm, a stable of 100 racehorses, a quartet of Rolls-Royces and the Bell corporation, a textile firm he had acquired in 1973 and from which he had expanded into television stations, newspapers and (appropriately) earth-moving equipment. He was said to be worth $US 85m.

He had appeared to be sympathetic to Lord Grade and had even sided with him in his differences with boardroom members. In return, he had been treated in the immediate post-Gill period as an ally rather than a contender. All the time he had been quietly buying ACC shares and, at the time of Gill's departure, owned about five per cent of the non-voting stock: not enough to give him power, but enough to get him attention. By December 1981 he had increased his holding to half the non-voting stock. Yet he still seemed content to keep quiet, let Lord Grade do the talking and lend such aid and comfort to him as one multi-millionaire might be expected to give to another in the duress that even very rich men occasionally have to undergo. His reward was to be invited to join the ACC board. In January 1982 Lord Grade arrived at the Manila International Film Festival in search of the rest and refreshment that an event like this offered a man who was missing the flattering limelight he had once enjoyed, and not at all relishing the critical scrutiny to which the British media were now subjecting him and his company. To at least one of the British film critics present in Manila he hinted that Holmes à Court's ascension was part and parcel of his own doing: on 6 January 1982 he had pledged his 26.8 per cent of the voting shares to the Australian, possibly in the expectation that the latter's financial assets and self-assurance would help steady ACC in the investors' eyes.

What then ensued within ACC's walls is still a matter of contentious accounts. One financial commentator later speculated that Holmes à Court presented such an alarming picture of potential bankruptcy to a panicky boardroom that its members put their salvation completely in his hands. Whatever the truth (or, rather, the ranging interpretations of events), the upshot was mortal for Lord Grade. On 24 March 1982, Robert Holmes à Court was voted into office as chairman and chief executive of ACC. Lord Grade resigned from the posts in which he had reigned supreme for so many years, retaining only the job of chief executive of ACC's film-making division, ITC, where the empty offices and bare desks were a painful reminder of the boast he used to make about the 'paperless office' where everything was kept in the boss's head.

If Lord Grade was out of business, so was the grand strategy devised by ACC and EMI to market their films in America via an 'own label' distributor. Faced with huge losses on current films and continuing administration costs, AFD shut shop at the beginning of 1981. Sir Richard Cave, Thorn-EMI's chairman, commented in the annual stockholders' report: 'Our attempt to gain a stronger foothold in US theatrical distribution through AFD proved to be a real disappointment.'

This is a wondrous example of the way that terminology may be used in such documents to reduce the impact of bad news. If AFD's failure was a 'disappointment', what would it have taken to precipitate a 'disaster'? The AFD loss was estimated to be $62m. It was split 60–40 to Thorn-EMI's advantage after subtracting from it a guarantee given by Universal, the Hollywood studio, to pay $5m. a year for the next five years in return for the rights to distribute in America the films that AFD would have handled. Without this contribution by one of the very studios which AFD was supposed to have cut out of the game, the loss would have been scarcely of the order of a 'disappointment'. Yet the remnants of the British film industry raised hardly a protest: not surprising, perhaps, since ACC and Thorn-EMI constituted two-thirds of that industry and the Rank Organization, the other third, had recently voted itself out of the business of film-making.

It was left to a 'voice from the past' to speak what many thought, but few expressed. 'Today the curtains should be drawn over the industry from Wardour Street to Elstree and Pinewood,' said John Boulting. 'We should all be in mourning. . . . If (EMI and Lord Grade) had studied the history of our industry and if they had more knowledge of the film industry as distinct from the TV industry, then I do not think they would have made what appears to be a most calamitous mistake.'[*]

Barry Spikings tried to put the best face on it. The Universal link-up could even improve the prospects for British production, he was reported as saying. 'Universal have a lot of marketing clout to get the best possible share of the American market.'[**] In a sense, this was true: in the context of the AFD aspirations, it was wildly irrelevant. And, as time went by, the link-up with Universal became a source of frustration to the new order at Thorn-EMI who were aware that, under its terms, Universal had first call on any Thorn-EMI film up to the end of 1985, being able to select those that might be thought capable of generating substantial box-office (from which Universal would recoup a handsome distribution fee) or reject those which did not seem to fit the company's policy or view of future profit. It was clear where the advantage lay: the attempt to produce films independently of Hollywood had ended up giving Hollywood the 'take it or leave it' decision on current and future product.

Lord Delfont must have been as saddened as his brother by this turn of events: but he had relinquished his responsibilities as head of

[*] John Boulting, reported by Dennis Barker, *The Guardian*, 3 March 1981.
[**] Barry Spikings, ibid.

Thorn-EMI Entertainment and Leisure in November 1980, some months before it happened. 'I shall be remaining close to the film side,' he was reported saying, though it was clear that he did not wish there to be any confusion on this score for he added, 'but I emphasize that Barry Spikings is in sole control, and my capacity will be purely to offer advice to him should he feel that he wants or needs it.'*

Spikings again showed himself nothing if not optimistic. Despite one of the most expensive reverses in film industry history, he shouldered his responsibilities without undue gloom and, according to *Variety*, declared that the venture had been 'worth trying, but that the timing was off'.** His confidence in the future ('My Five Year Plan' was how *Screen International* headed an interview with him at the end of the year) found striking support from at least one Thorn-EMI executive, though in the immediate wake of the *Honky Tonk Freeway* disaster it is not surprising if corporate bullishness was tempered by personal reticence. 'Look,' the unnamed man was quoted as saying, 'that's behind us now: let's get on with the business.'***

Spikings proved loyal to another much-troubled film-maker, Michael Cimino, whose *Heaven's Gate* fiasco was even then threatening the commercial viability of United Artists (which was ultimately taken over by MGM) and declared his wish to work on 'a more modest project' with Cimino. He then showed that the faith reposed by British producers in American film-makers to do their work for them was undiminished (except in the 'more modest' regions of investment) by announcing at the Cannes Film Festival in 1981 a $23m. six-film programme. It included (at $4.6m.) *Frances* and (budgeted at $8–10m.) *Tender Mercies*, both subsequentially critical hits; but also two films which indicated a somewhat more than token desire to mollify British critics of this overseas investment policy; David Gladwell was to make *Memoirs of a Survivor* (budgeted at $1m.) in Britain, with Julie Christie; and Lindsay Anderson would direct *Britannia Hospital* (at $2.5m.), both projects co-financed with the NFFC. The announced budgets of these two British films amounted to scarcely a fifth of the single most expensive Hollywood-based movie, *Weeds*, (budgeted at $15m.), the story of a San Quentin lifer who gets into show-business, included in the package (but not made). Still, it was a beginning. . . .

The remainder of Barry Spikings's tenure as Thorn-EMI's chief executive for film and TV programming was bedevilled by bad luck and worse news. The choice of Brian North, who had gained his commercial experience with Burton's, the men's outfitters, to be managing director of EMI Films under Spikings struck many as placing too great a faith in the garment industry's historical capacity to throw up film moguls of the

---

*Lord Delfont, quoted in *Screen International*, 8–15 November 1980.
**Variety*, 20 May 1981.
***Screen International*, 5–12 December 1981.

calibre of Zukor and Goldwyn: but since North suffered a heart attack almost immediately and hardly got down to work, this remained an open question. More of a set-back was the £10m. loss sustained by the film division of Thorn-EMI in 1982. A 'slimming down' operation was begun: 'Everyone has been overreaching,' said Lord Delfont.* In January 1983, with a year of his contract remaining, Barry Spikings and EMI severed their relationship by mutual agreement. 'Being a studio head is a very precarious business,' reflected Lord Delfont, by that time a non-executive director with the company. 'I think Barry probably had too much on his plate.'**

His brother might have said 'Amen' to that. Lord Grade's final months of tenure at ACC were not happy ones, either. By cruel irony, some among the last batch of films he had put into production were the very ones that won critical plaudits, prizes even, as well as making a respectable amount of money at the world box-office. But the kudos (and a great deal of the cash) now went to Universal, the AFD inheritors of *On Golden Pond* (which took a clutch of Academy Awards in 1981) and *Sophie's Choice*. Lord Grade was justly proud of both films, though his enjoyment of 'Oscar Night' may have been tempered by the obligation that didn't sit easily on his independent shoulders — of reportedly having to turn in his expenses to the new boss, Robert Holmes à Court. It was just the kind of annoyance that confirmed him in his antipathy to those chores relating to the management of public companies, so much more onerous than the show-business handshake between partners or the old simple promise of 'Yes, My Lord'.

Other irritations multiplied like Biblical plagues. The very media which had sycophantically danced attendance on him, even at the unearthly hour he got to the office in the morning, now turned on Lord Grade with as spectacular a display of *schadenfreude* as anyone could remember. His ebullience was characterized as overweening folly, his intuitive taste as obsolescent obduracy, his well-earned appurtenances of office — the several Rolls-Royces, the 124-foot yacht, the Cessna aircraft (even though apparently ordered for Jack Gill's use) — as gross extravagances. It was, perhaps not fortuitously, disclosed that he was entitled to five per cent of the gross of *Jesus of Nazareth* (up to a ceiling of $1.6m.) — as if that were a sin! Against this had to be set the fact that he had made no provision for ACC to pay him a pension: perhaps he had taken seriously his own frequent and jocular claim that he would be in the job till A.D. 2001 — when he would be 94, an age at which a pension is as necessary as a third leg.

Lord Grade stayed with ACC for some further three months: the unhappiest aspect of them, according to him, was seeing old associates

---

*Lord Delfont, quoted in *Daily Express*, 17 September 1982.
**Lord Delfont, quoted in *Daily Mail*, 4 January 1983.

and employees down to the humblest office staff take their enforced departure against what he insisted had been his own wishes and expectations. He had already lost Ian Jessel, the globe-trotting sales chief at ITC and one of his main links with the all-important distributors and exhibitors outside North America. Jessel left to work in the United States for the theatrical film division set up by the CBS TV network. He had privately expressed disenchantment with the way things were going at ITC well before the *Titanic* disaster. Later he went on public record, saying, 'Long before I went there, ITC had the reputation of doing good deals. Well, the calibre of the product since then hasn't always matched the calibre of the deals.'* Guarded words: but they said it all.

Lord Grade's eventual decision to take his own leave 'was really due to the fact that I didn't want to have anything to do with a public company, preparing reports, turning in expenses, etc. Lew and Leslie Grade Ltd and The Grade Organization were not public companies: they were privately owned and controlled firms. I preferred the personal way of doing business: I didn't want to be involved in committee decisions.'

On 6 March 1982 Lord Grade severed all links with the organization he had helped found and which he had run for twenty-seven years. But he did not drop out of sight for long. On 23 March 1982, over a strawberries-and-cream tea, and champagne dispensed with Hollywood extravagance at the Inn on the Park, Park Lane, he announced that he had that day become chairman and chief executive of Embassy Communications International, a West Coast entertainments empire founded in January 1982 by two American TV and film entrepreneurs, Norman Lear and Jerry Perenchio. He would be reporting directly to these gentlemen, he said, thus reverting to his preferred practice of dispensing with tedious boardroom memoranda and the red tape of formal approval. 'People like Jerry and Norman respect me for keeping my word,' he said. His salary would be more than he got at ACC: a figure of £250,000 a year was mentioned and not denied. And he had lots of film production plans. . . .

To accommodate the photographers, he executed a few of his old Charleston steps with acceptable nimbleness on the marble floor of the lobby. 'All my life', he said to a bystander, 'I've liked to work. Why do I do it? Not the power: who needs it? Not the money: how do you spend it? I ask you, is it fair to ask a man who is having so much fun to stop?' Someone was ungenerous enough to mention the ill-fated film that had been the start of his downfall. 'Look,' said Lord Grade, 'I said I'd raise the Titanic. I did. The trouble was, I didn't raise it high enough.'

---

*Ian Jessel, *Screen International*, 13 October 1980.

CHAPTER NINE

Bad Days in Babylon

*Appetite grows by what it feeds on: American films create the
audience for other American films, but there are so few
British films dealing with British life and manners that they
are a largely unknown quantity to British audiences. Every
British film has to create its own audience unaided.*
— *NFFC Report, 1979.*

The absolute beginners were the truly poor of the Seventies: the
film-makers possessing more aspirations than years of experience and
next to no 'credits'. Their hopes of finding finance were piteously small.
The National Film School which opened its doors in late 1970 (with
twenty-five students) had neither the ambition nor means to launch its
graduates into production. Their term-time film exercises would help
make the school's reputation as a talent-incubator, one on which the
industry by the Eighties was keeping a close self-interested eye. The
school, which by then incorporated TV training, was having to schedule
multiple screenings of the 'diploma works' as there wasn't space for all
the potential employers at the one-night screenings it had been used to
holding. But the school was not the answer to an impatient young man
with a film script in the Seventies. Nor was there then any Channel 4 to
act as 'publisher' of the works of independent film-makers and give them
exposure in the cinemas before transmitting them on the box. None of
the major TV networks financed theatrical films to any extent in the
Seventies. The reason was brutally simple: such investment was not
regarded by the Inland Revenue as 'relevant expenditure' chargeable
against tax. It would have been a self-indulgence. Moreover, the film
unions would not have taken very kindly to agreements being made
between the big networks and independent film-makers whose budgets
couldn't have stretched to the high-scale remuneration, never mind the
'perks' of the job, that the ACTT and other craft unions had won from

the networks by the ultimate threat of being able to 'pull the plug' and stop both programmes and advertising revenue.

For the National Film Finance Corporation, the Seventies were the harshest, leanest years since it was set up as a State bank for independents in 1949. It spent the decade being financially harassed by a series of contradictory Government policies: one minute they seemed to assure its future, the next they indicated that film funding had no right to State subsidy at all. The way in which the NFFC was seriously paralysed and steadily impoverished throughout the decade stands as a lasting rebuke to both of the political parties and to Britain's professed faith in a film culture.

As related in *Hollywood, England*, the decade had begun with the new Films Act's promise to increase the NFFC's borrowing powers to £5m. (provided the Treasury agreed), supplement its power to contract non-secured loans up to £2m. from private banks and relieve it of the obligation to pay interest on past debts now deemed largely unrecoverable. Promises, promises. . .!

By June 1970 all the NFFC had actually received was £1m., just enough to discharge its current overdraft. At the start of 1971–2 it squeezed another £500,000 out of the Treasury, just enough to fund *another* overdraft. The new Tory Government which had imposed this regime indicated its desire to withdraw completely from film financing by offering only a further £1m., and that on condition the NFFC raised £3m. from the private sector. All the NFFC succeeded in attracting was £750,000 — from ten institutions, including its own bankers. In this turn-of-the-decade period the NFFC was reduced to financing a bare two per cent of British-made films. Although it had received 200 projects when the Films Act seemed about to make it relatively flush with cash, few of these were worth five minutes' consideration. The commercially attractive scripts of quality went first to the American majors based in Britain, even though they, too, were cutting down production drastically while their parent corporations in Hollywood feverishly tried to reduce their overstocked inventories.

No wonder the NFFC incurred severe losses every year throughout the Seventies. In its 1972 report it noted plaintively that over its twenty-three year history to date it had funded 731 features and 173 shorts for an aggregate loan of £28,642,684. This melted no Whitehall hearts. On the contrary, the actual loss of £750,817 recorded in 1971–2, more than the previous two years' losses put together, sharpened Government hostility. The 1973 report told the pathetic tale. . . . The principal film bank in Britain had been forced to invest in commercially safe (well, 'safer') but culturally negligible movies like *Ooh. . .You Are Awful!* (a Dick Emery drag farce); *The Cobblers of Umbridge* (a spoof of the radio programme *The Archers of Ambridge*); and *Steptoe and Son Ride Again*.

During 1973–4 *Stardust* was the only film approved for a loan. It alone among the 134 projects submitted that year seemed to have a chance of commercial success — what sweepings the other 133 must have been!

Things had improved slightly in 1975, due to profits flowing in from *Stardust* and Frankie Howerd's farce *Up Pompeii* which had been co-produced with Columbia's British-based company. Losses were reduced to £286,164 and nine projects were now backed (among them a six-part children's TV series) although there proved to be only one money-spinner among them, *Bugsy Malone*. However, the NFFC at least showed signs of being able to resume taking calculated risks: it had investments in *The Man Who Fell to Earth*, *The Romantic Englishwoman*, *The James Dean Story*, *Lisztomania* and a Peter Hall co-operative venture *Akenfield*, which will be examined shortly.

However, such films illustrated the dilemma in which the NFFC was historically trapped. Although they were the kind of films that a country needs if 'culture' is to have any meaning, they were all high-risk investments for a corporation charged by Parliament with functioning on commercial lines. John Terry (who was knighted in Harold Wilson's 'Resignation Honours' in May 1976) might well have asked himself what on earth the nation wanted for its money! What the NFFC wanted was clear — more money. Things seemed suddenly to improve in February 1976, with the publication of the 'Terry Report' by the working party set up by Harold Wilson the previous year: Wilson himself announced in March that the Government was going to make another £2,370,000 immediately available out of the £5m. promised by the Films Act of six years earlier.

But 'immediately' is a long time in politics: Wilson had resigned in April before the money was paid over. Nonetheless, Sir John Terry claimed to perceive 'a mood of optimism' sweeping the film industry. A 'mood of opportunism' would have expressed it better as the same old dog-eared scripts flooded into the NFFC's offices in Soho Square and the Association of Independent Producers — a ginger group of young-ish talents which first met in February 1976 with the aim of 'broadening the base of finance and exhibition' — called for all £2.37m. to be spent on 'realistically budgeted' movies foreseeing maybe fifteen blooming each year where the frozen earth had been used to supporting only single figures.

Alas, it was the money that melted away. . . . In a move typical of the total unreality of the accounting methods used by British Governments in dealing with such an eccentric business as film-making, £703,000 of this £2.37m. was instantly clawed back by the Department of Trade to cover the interest that the NFFC owed on loans made over the previous two years. Lenders, in short, were also takers. The NFFC itself got a mere £200,000 to put into the National Film Development Fund to finance script development — for films there was not the money to make. And, of the £1.5m. balance, the Department of Trade advanced only

£620,000 — a thin amount of butter to spread over five films (*The Sailor's Return* and *The Disappearance*, both of which suffered lengthy delays in their theatrical release, *The Shout*, *Black Jack* and *Tarka the Otter*). The NFFC was icily informed that the remaining £800,000 would not be made available until 1978 — and would probably be depleted by interest payments. For good measure, Sir John Terry's salary was also frozen. 'At present,' said this stoic, 'we are not in a position to consider any films which may apply to us before April of 1978.'

These were the economics of *Alice in Wonderland*. The Government lent with one hand and took back with the other: new money was furnished simply to provide the means to repay the interest on the old. It had everything to do with keeping the books straight at the Treasury: it had absolutely nothing to do with maintaining a viable, never mind prospering, British film industry. By 1978 the NFFC had only £300,000 left in its kitty. Asking for 'More' now meant begging the Department of Trade to return the interest it had confiscated the previous year. But Sir John noted that if such interest repayments and operating costs were excluded from the calculation, the cost of the NFFC to the taxpayer would have been only £70,000 annually. Put another way, the sum of £9,745,583 which was the total loss to date since 1949 was roughly the same as the budget that EMI Films were starting to invest in what would turn out to be one of the biggest loss-makers of the decade, *Honky Tonk Freeway*. Though only a third of the films in which the NFFC had invested money went into profit, it had helped to make 750 films possible: the *Honky Tonk Freeway* money paid for one film only — and that one a resounding financial failure.

In 1978 Sir John Terry reached the mandatory retirement age of sixty-five and left the NFFC to continue an active industry career with a firm of solicitors which had long-established film connections: he also remained a shrewd second-in-command to Sir Harold Wilson, who now chaired the Interim Action Committee he had helped set up as Prime Minister. Terry's successor, appointed in January 1978, was Mamoun Hassan, a forty-year-old Saudi-Arabian who had come to England at the age of ten and who had been the only active film-maker to sit on the NFFC board. Prior to that, from 1970 to 1974, he had been head of the BFI's Production Board, then head of direction at the National Film School. The next NFFC report reflected a new tone: acerbic, sceptical and not at all in awe of Treasury mandarins or Trade Department diktats. As the NFFC's 'life' had been guaranteed by the 1970 Films Act only until the end of 1980, its report in March that year had a sort of 'qu'est-ce qu'on risque?' tone!

'There are those who wish the corporation to retain its "commercial" mandate and others who want it to support the production of "art" films. It is a common misconception that "commercial" films make money — most of them do not. So the term "commercial" defines an attitude rather than a realistic expectation of returns. As for "art" films, there are too many which are so defined only by the makers of the films themselves'.*

These were cutting words to find in a Government agency's report. No doubt they were noted with pursed lips by the Civil Servants with responsibility for advising their political head, at that time the Trade Minister, Michael Meacher. To some, it seemed as if the Government was being read a lesson by a remarkably strong-minded young man and told that it simply did not know about such things as films. As things turned out, the Government (be it Labour or Tory) was quite prepared to demonstrate over the next few years that what it did not know about, it did not care about, either. That, though, was to come. . . . The tragedy was that throughout the decade just ending, the independent film-makers who *did* care — and care deeply — were the very ones who laboured and suffered and only sometimes succeeded.

ONE-OFFS AND WRITE-OFFS

Somehow or other, interesting films managed to get made in the Seventies by relative newcomers or the occasional professional working on a 'non-commercial' subject. But they were made against the odds: some were 'one-offs' — and some were 'write-offs'. The lack of continuity was part of the heartbreak: it reduced a promising career to a start-stop series of tenuous hopes and hurtful rebuffs. It led to the attrition of ambition. It depleted creative zeal and allowed the batteries of self-confidence to run down. One had to adapt to the precarious state of life it entailed and some did so better than others.

Barney Platts-Mills owed his feature-film debut to the enlightened patronage of the old British Lion — the Boulting Brothers and Launder and Gilliat — which distributed *Bronco Bullfrog* (15 October 1970), a film he had shot for £17,000 over six weeks in London's East End using locals and young professionals. It is a film by which we can precisely date the onset of youthful disenchantment in the cinema once it was seen that the affluence of the Sixties wasn't going to stay around and let Bronco's generation share in it. From this film on, whenever the young are featured in British films it is with growing resentment against society and deepening individual despondency. The 'drop-outs' still commandeered the newspaper headlines in 1969: *Bronco Bullfrog* switched attention and compassion to the 'left-outs'.

The world that the film showed was geographically located in Stratford East, but it occupied a far vaster tract of adolescent awareness stretching from 'nothing to do' to 'nowhere to go'. Its human blight was

*NFFC Report for the year ending 31 March 1979.

urban boredom. Its hero was Del, an apprentice welder in a dead-end job, whose father lives with a girl-friend but resents his son's own interest in sex. Yet the aggressive puritanism manifested by the middle-aged against the young is almost a welcome sign of energy, for Del's mates are drained of any vitality that could knock the sharp corners off this unfriendly environment.

One of the most striking features of the film in retrospect is its lack of any generalized violence — that, of course, was on the way. But, at this date, an anti-social nature was simply an anti-tedium response. The kids break into a cafe, but only for sparse change and stale cakes; their occasional punch-up has only a half-hearted punch behind it. The direction won a considerable battle against some amateurish acting and unintelligible accents to show the feelings under the skinhead — this razed-scalp style had first appeared among young working-class Londoners in 1969. Permissiveness still seemed as far off as the moon. 'Wanna come wiv us termorrer night?' — 'Arright' — 'Come up for yer?' — 'Ta-ta'. Boy-meets-girl boiled down to such shifty, suspicious exchanges. The countryside is imagined to be the hospitable place of refuge: but the hope of finding work there is dashed. Back in London, the police are waiting. . . . The showdown comes at the pad of the eponymous Bronco, a beefy Borstal escapee whose room bulges with loot from hijack jobs that he hasn't a notion how to convert into ready cash. His type was to reappear later in films like *Scum* as the articulate rebel who believes the best way of breaking the system is to out-suffer the worst it can inflict on one.

The haphazard events, picaresque street life (carried over from Platts-Mills earlier short, *Everybody's an Actor*) and low-key realism all helped create a good feeling about this director's future. In his second feature, *Private Road* (30 September 1971), a girl from Esher runs off with a layabout writer and both find Nature dampening their enthusiasm for the drop-out life in the wild. It offered amusing insights into family life — this time a notch or two up the social scale — but, alas, lacked the immediacy of *Bronco Bullfrog*. Thereafter, Platts-Mills himself became something of a 'drop-out' from the film scene, surfacing in the 1980s with a film, *Hero*, made *in Gaelic* for Channel 4 and none too successfully recapitulating an old Highland myth.

From the British Film Institute Production Board under Mamoun Hassan came one of the earliest — perhaps the first — of the films dedicated to the plight of Britain's displaced Asians. *A Private Enterprise* (20 November 1974) was directed by Peter K. Smith and co-authored by him and Dilip Hiro. Smith had been a member of the Australian Diplomatic Corps, but had exchanged status and security for sympathy and experience and gone to observe the Asian immigrants in the English Midlands whose daily life was a maze of small, desperate decisions. In no way was the film a polemic on race relations. 'My purpose is to speculate, not to impose my own view, which is where again I differ from someone working in Ken Loach's area,' he said.* Smith had already made films on groups of people who were social or ethnic outcasts: aged East-Enders, Salvation Army dependants, and those Ukrainian Russians who had fought on the German side in the Second World War but had fortunately escaped forced repatriation after the war and were living on in the South of England where they had been brought to work as (highly expendable) bomb-disposal crews.

He consulted no community groups when he came to shoot *A Private Enterprise* — hence the film's refreshing freedom from any sense of victimization: the Indians in it saw themselves as movie stars, not representative casualties of a reluctantly multi-racial Britain. His young hero, played by Salman Peer, wants to fit into the English social scene, but lacks capital and confidence to set up in business for himself; while Birmingham middle-class life regards him as exotic a misfit as the red plastic elephants he hopefully peddles in the street to tittering passers-by. Humanity rather than dialectic marked the film: a rarity in its BFI context. Like *Bronco Bullfrog*, it was a crossroads film, showing the British Asians at a transition point in their economic fortunes. The feckless hero was in this respect rather an exception among an immigrant race that was adapting to — and profiting from — the middle-class tolerance of the British much better than the expatriates from the Caribbean with more aggressive identities and less malleable skills.

Absent from the film was any hint of the racist backlash suffered a few years later by these Asian entrepreneurs whose industriousness made them resented by shiftless Brits. On the other hand, Smith's film is already remarkably critical of the Asian *nouveaux riches* whose dream of nirvana is endless shopping trips to Harrods. Ironically, when the film was shown on TV in 1982, a *Guardian* writer condemned it for the very quality of 'non-involvement' that Smith had emphasized was its virtue when he made it. It was described, with grotesque inaccuracy, as 'an immigrant's version of *Room at the Top*'. *Billy Liar* with ethnic undertones might have been a kindlier approximation. Unfortunately, for obscure reasons, Smith did not follow up his success: his talent was not to reappear in the cinema until the mid-1980s, though the way these things have of coming about brought him and Mamoun Hassan together again and the tragi-comedy of ethnic conflict was now explored in *No Surrender, No Surrender*, a tale of Catholics and Protestants whose antagonism is only moderated by the fact that all of them are pensioners.

Mamoun Hassan also played godfather-producer to another BFI-sponsored movie, *Winstanley* (17 November 1975), which, although it was set over 300 years ago, had strong contemporary parallels that put

---

*Peter K. Smith, interviewed by Derek Malcolm, *The Guardian*, 14 January 1975.

a cutting edge on its historical perspective. It was the story of a determined eccentric, Gerald Winstanley, a seventeenth-century burgher who had lost everything in the English Civil War. He took to living on the land with a commune of like souls who dug themselves so tenaciously into the Surrey hillside that they were called 'The Diggers'. The parallel was with the organizers of some of the 'Free' Pop festivals of the Seventies, especially the riotous one staged in Windsor Great Park in August 1974, whose 'drop-out' organizer Sid Rawle was actually conscripted by the film-makers, Kevin Brownlow and Andrew Mollo, to bring along his ragged retinue and play 'The Ranters', a raucous sect of layabouts hired by the villagers to attack Winstanley and his radicals by cacophonous brute force. 'When the Ranters walked into the commune (built for the film) there was no doubt what kind of people they were,' Brownlow later wrote. 'The actors playing the Diggers, who had not met them before, reacted exactly as they were supposed to. They froze and then recoiled in suspicion and alarm. During the lunch break the atmosphere was icy, and it took most of the day before Sid Rawle had melted the hostility.'* Apprehension and resentment of just this sort and degree would be expressed throughout the Seventies by the outwardly respectable against the increasingly wild and tribalized appearance of the young.

Winstanley is a film to listen to as well as look at: the strong and beautiful clarity of the scriptures infused the language of Winstanley, played by Miles Halliwell, and even his grammar was like an additional turn of a dagger finding its chink in the enemy's bigotry. As they had done in *It Happened Here*, their speculative film about a German occupation of England which showed their skill in inventing a possible 'future', Brownlow and Mollo demonstrated a kindred talent for re-creating an authentic past. Instead of being so much dead weight, the historical veracity exemplified by animal husbandry, confined to strains of cattle and pigs extant in the seventeenth-century and bird-song minutely edited by an ornithologist to incorporate only birds indigenous to Surrey, actually inspired the players in incarnating their historical forebears. Unfortunately, this film, too, had no issue. Brownlow and Mollo did not find Hassan's successors at the BFI Production Board as sympathetic to their ideas and ways of working and they went their separate ways: Mollo as historical adviser on various films and Brownlow as devoted and triumphant restorer of Abel Gance's great epic, *Napoleon*. There was no continuity that could keep such inspired people together and at work.

Winstanley was well timed: it coincided with the social unrest that the gathering economic crisis was producing in the mid-Seventies and it suggested a continuum with the more recent past reflected in the

*Kevin Brownlow, *Monthly Film Bulletin*, April 1976.

multi-part production on ITV, *Days of Hope*, mounted by Ken Loach and Tony Garnett along with the writer Jim Allen. This deeply 'committed' account of social conflicts between the conscription fever at the outbreak of the First World War and the collapse of the General Strike in 1926 had been begun when Edward Heath's Government was in power: when it reached the TV screen in September-October 1975, the struggles of long-ago with their resonating accusations of betrayal and sell-out were viewed against the background of the Labour Party's annual conference, Harold Wilson's attempt to grapple with 26-per cent inflation wage claims running in some instances at 35 per cent, and a tenuous agreement, called the 'Social Contract', intended to mollify the fiercer unions. *Winstanley*'s vision of England in disarray was historically apposite.

Between 1972 and 1984, Mike Leigh made only one independent cinema film. 'Not making more has been one of the major disasters of my existence — and of the British film industry,' he said in 1984.* But this needs immediate qualification: in the twelve intervening years, Leigh 'created' ten full-length films for BBC TV as well as eight plays for the stage and one for radio. His 'crime', as far as cinema-film financiers were concerned, was his preferred method of 'devising' a film through a series of mutual inquiries into character between the players and himself, improvising dialogue, distilling observations, rehearsing the 'likelihoods' and varying the 'eventualities' emerging in performance until a highly sophisticated state of awareness was created — at which point it was filmed and 'fixed'.

Such heightened realism is what separates him from the documentary manner of 'social cinema'. It also does away with one of the few tangible things that bankers rely on in financing a film — the advance script. Leigh's films are filled with epiphanies, moments of self-revelation emerging from (a) the player's own ingenuity in improvising, and (b) the strict secrecy he enforces in respect of individual roles. That's to say, two 'characters' meeting each other know no more than two identical people would know if they met in similar circumstances. 'The premise is . . . that the social situation is appalling and negative (though) there is no question of showing people as helpless or being on the receiving end as far as their dignity goes.'** The 'plot' evolves out of what he and the players 'bounce off' each other. Given different players, a different plot might evolve. Normal acting methods, he believes, force players to prostitute themselves — they are denied the chance to transcend their abilities by having a text fixed for them. On one occasion two of his players (representing a repressed wife and her bureaucratic husband) took a fourteen-mile walk, playing the characters all the time; on another, an actor turned quarry labourer for three weeks in order to 'get

---

*Mike Leigh, interviewed by Paul Jackson, *Western Mail*, 10 March 1984.
**Mike Leigh, ibid.

into' such a role. Such a 'method' obviously works better with some characters than others — notably sociopaths, obsessives and disconnected teenagers. Leigh's choice in the matter is thereby narrowed: but it gives his 'creations' a density unusual on stage or screen, and therefore all the rarer.

His film *Bleak Moments* (25 May 1972) was based on his stage 'creation' performed in 1970 at the Open Space Theatre: it cost a mere £18,500, mostly put up by Albert Finney's Memorial Company with a token sum from the BFI to give it 'experimental' status and permit union rules (and pay scales) to be relaxed. It was about society's marginals: in this case, a girl from bed-sitterland and her sister who's 'a bit dopey'. Into their lives come people as repressed as themselves: a teacher of extreme gentility and frigid responses; a hippy who inhabits a garage and resembles an urban Hobbit; and a professional jolly girl-friend whose own domestic misery is exposed in a funny-pathetic scene when the genteelly collects her mother's false teeth from the bedside using two saucers the way that waiters exchange dirty ashtrays for clean ones in chic restaurants. These people's conversation is slow, painful, held down to a confessional hush. One felt sorely tempted to shake them and tell them how life was passing them by.

But the film's power was precisely this: by its protracted, almost immobilized scenes, it pierced one with the emotional truth of everyday repression in the corners of life one would have ignored if left to oneself. The sheer loneliness of life in suburban London was better recorded in this film than in any other of the Seventies. Had the film industry been willing to adapt itself to Leigh's methods by offering him modest financing and not asking questions in advance, he might have used the cinema to record the increasing desperation and 'disconnection' of people in the Seventies. As it was, television fell heir to a rich chronicle of social impoverishment that it was contractually prevented from showing to cinema audiences at that time. Later on, when Leigh's *oeuvre* for TV was given a very limited exposure in specialized cinemas, there was an immediate and touching connection made with the younger generation whose own 'bleak moments' had stretched into the long-term damage of unemployment in the Eighties.

The position of Peter Hall in the Seventies cinema was different. He seemed to be 'the man who had everything', except the willingness of critics to grant that he made *films* and didn't simply film *theatre*. An unfair charge: but one persistently made in an Anglo-Saxon society mistrustful of people who seem 'too clever by half' and exercise their talents from a position of apparent privilege. There was a deep underlying envy at work here. Hall did seem to have achieved too much success too quickly for some people's liking: He had status, power and appeared to have the money, too, though his published diaries later showed him prey to the financial worries that are the lot of most people

and their accountants. But the impression created by his ubiquitousness
in theatre, on television and in his earlier sorties into cinema, was of
someone who had got off paying his full dues. He was part of the
Establishment, his critics charged, even before he had embraced the
Revolution.

Kenneth Tynan became just such an Establishment man after his
appointment as dramaturge at the National Theatre: but Tynan
managed to preserve a reputation as an iconoclast, even though
effectively muzzled as a theatre critic, by helping create the sexually
'outrageous' show *Oh, Calcutta!* But even he found the going harder as
the anti-permissive backlash of the Seventies gathered force. Tynan had
been the first man to say 'fuck' on live television — something one could
never have imagined Peter Hall doing. But the very medium of
broadcasting, which he had advantageously turned to his own notoriety,
took an extremely sophisticated revenge on him in 1975 when his
proposal to give a five-minute talk on Radio 3 about 'The Language of
Love' containing no four-letter words but only invented words vaguely
suggestive of deviant practices, was countered by the BBC's edict that he
must make it a twenty-minute talk — or nothing. Tynan withdrew,
rather than face the daunting prospect — even to someone of his fertile
imagination — of having to invent the hundreds of examples necessary
to fill twenty-minutes, instead of five.

In the same months as this incident occurred, the colour supplements
of the principal Sunday newspapers were filled with an advertisement
featuring Peter Hall smoking a cheroot and sitting at a piano in
conspicuously tasteful surroundings. The caption almost instantly
became one of the decade's catch-phrases, frequently employed as a
crushing put-down. 'Very Peter Hall, Very Sanderson', it read.
Sanderson's was the middle-class's favourite wallpaper firm and the
endorsement of its surface product — a small matter in itself — cast a
wide and baleful ambiguity on Hall's other achievements, including his
forthcoming appointment as director of the National Theatre which was
due to open in stages from March 1976. It was interpreted as damning
evidence of bourgeois conformity at a time in a man's career when
adventurousness was required. The imprecation of 'Money!' which Hall
later called down on his own head as he wrote up his diary wasn't lost on
columnists and critics.* 'Hateful,' he noted later. '(The ad) was a
mistake.' But by that time, it was too late. In October 1975 he began
appearing regularly on ITV as presenter of *Aquarius*, a programme
which seldom strayed from a middle-of-the-road view of contemporary
arts. This further damned him in the eyes of those who saw him as a
midbrow achiever satisfied to set consensus standards.

The British film he directed in 1974 simply could not prevail over the

*Peter Hall's Diaries, edited by John Godwin (Hamish Hamilton, 1983). Entry for 12 June 1975.

expectation that it would reflect Hall's 'comfortable' view of a contemporary classic which said raw, uncomfortable things about rural England and the people whose lives and natures had been formed by it. This was *Akenfield* (12 January 1975).

Hall was a Suffolk man born and bred and he seemed to see his own rural forebears as kith and kin to the farming folk in Ronald Blythe's book: and so, in a sense, they were. Filming the book was therefore for him what tracing one's ancestors would be for foreigners — a return to one's roots. With a cast of 150, not a professional actor among them, and a script that was no more than a twenty-five page *aide-mémoire* secreted away from the cast, he set about improvising the look, dialogue and experience of life in Blythe's composite village of Akenfield using as his frame one day in the life of a present-day farmhand whose grandfather is being buried. The same actor played father and grandfather, as well as the farmhand. The theme derived from the one visit that the grandfather had made to Newmarket, a forty-mile walk, to look in vain for a stable-lad's job: his only excursion into the outside world. 'Where you start, you stay,' in other words — a message belied by Hall's own career, but nonetheless pathetically appealing.

The inhabitants of two Suffolk villages responded 'like a revelation' when asked to improvise the lives they knew. 'The closeness of village life was sometimes oppressive to them: which warded off the danger of the film's temptation to be too rustic and "Olde English". It really was a co-operative at work. I hadn't felt so moved and involved since I directed my first play (twenty-one years earlier). We were doing something only cinema could do, for the camera had to be there and "at the ready" to catch "life" when it was invented: it couldn't be pinned down in advance or rehearsed as our cast were entirely unused to speaking lines written for them.'*

The way the film ended ensured that no one would mistake it for a piece of Arcadia. Along a wintry lane leading to the outside world walks a man in the bundle of rags that was the uniform of the rural unemployed in the Twenties. He is heading out of the village where 'tied' houses make for tied lives . . . the village that imprisons more of its sons than it nourishes. But Akenfield refuses to release him — and on his return journey he turns, by means of a touching time-slip, to look into a motor-car from the 1970s and glimpses his grown-up grandson en route to London and a freedom he will never know.

Hall planned the film for five years, refusing finance if it involved unacceptable changes. Could it be relocated in the American Midwest? asked someone. Could it be built around Jon Voight if he assumed a Suffolk accent? Finally, London Weekend TV put up £60,000 for the right to two screenings; the NFFC invested £20,000; and Hall and

---

*Peter Hall, interviewed by the author, 18 July 1974.

producer Rex Pyke deferred their fees: the total budget thus raised was £120,000. The film was shot in Techniscope, a 'letter-box' shape suited to Suffolk's wide, low horizons and — more practically — allowing two 'frames' to occupy the space of one: a useful economy which also meant that the TV version would convey a different spatial impression. In all, Hall was paid about £800 for what represented a full year's work spread over five years.

The gamble was increased by *Akenfield*'s unique exhibition schedule: it was seen first in one of London's specialized cinemas and almost simultaneously on television. Hall had hoped that even if 5–6 million people saw it on their home screen, another million or so might take in the cinema experience. In fact, the television screening was seen by 14–15 million. Cyril Bennett, LWT's controller was 'over the moon', Hall recorded in his diary — 'and so am I'. But a few weeks later he was writing: 'A depressing meeting on *Akenfield*. We have eleven cinema bookings in the regions, but no money to finance publicity. And the film is coming off (at its London cinema) on 15 March where the business has dropped completely. Is it because everyone saw it on television?'*
He also noted that *Akenfield* got 'wonderful' notices in America, but could not find a theatrical distributor: it was judged uncommercial. The production company, Angle Films, attempted to distribute it in Britain; but revenues amounted to only £1,200 against accumulated debts of £20,000. London Weekend made an offer of £10,000 which would allow Angle Films to pay creditors 50 pence in the pound on the understanding that this would free the film from legal constraints and allow it to be distributed theatrically overseas. In addition, LWT was willing to exchange 50 per cent of its overseas TV rights for 50 per cent of the world theatrical rights. It was hoped this would help the creditors.

Thus ended the work of years in setting up an independent film and testing whether there was life after television. Within six months of its première, *Akenfield* had turned into a salvage operation. A profoundly discouraged Peter Hall has not to date directed another British film.

YOUNG PROSPERO

Of all the young independent film-makers of the Seventies, Derek Jarman was the most prodigiously gifted. He proved it possible to make highly original, low-budget British movies that bear the stamp of the times even though cut to the visionary bias of their maker. He did what Fassbinder and Herzog proved in Germany, though, this being Britain, he had to rattle the begging bowl in ways they never did. Jarman accepts the chore: after all, to be both beggar and chooser at his level is the sort

*Peter Hall, op.cit., 25 February 1975.

of independence that only the most successful film-makers have won at *their* level. He insists his films have mostly been begun as ways to amuse himself or his friends in the gay underground and have only later surfaced to rapturous or controversial critical reaction. One or two of them have made a surprisingly large profit, though Jarman claims to have seen very little of it. 'I can't keep track of money. I haven't even an accountant. I prefer not to think where it goes or to whom. I don't want the feeling of "bad blood" in my relationships.'*

Jarman's ambitious are tremendous, his needs few. Most people at one time or another have yearned to pull their own small world into one room and shut the door on the bigger universe outside. Jarman has done it. Anyone calling on him in the late Seventies would have had to press a door-bell, one that actually squawked like a bank-robbery alarm, in a barrack-type apartment block off Charing Cross Road. Up in an industrial-type elevator, across an open-air ramp like a prison cat-walk, then into — well, a single room with a kitchen alcove. This is Prospero's cell. Its occupant, though, looks more like a monk than a magician. His close-cropped hair at that date — a sort of 'high skinhead' — seems made for a cowl. Droopy shirt, baggy pants: but on one foot an orange sock, on the other a green one, the multi-coloured evidence of a man who works fantastically in many media, in films, painting, ballet, opera, but lives basically in one room with a pallet bed on the floor, a perpendicular settee like a church pew — 'and this'. He gestures at a solid pillar of books, about four feet square but reaching to the ceiling, that stands in the middle of the floor — an atomic pile of literary energy that fuels his imagination. Jung's works leap out at one as well as Shakespeare's, Blake's and other mystics'.

In the days he was called 'the English Andy Warhol', Jarman used to live and work in a riverside warehouse at Tower Bridge. It burned down: these books are the salvaged kernel of his library. One feels sure that Prospero likewise treasured the magic lore saved from his shipwreck. *The Tempest*, which Jarman turned into a weird and wonderful film, is the key to his mind and world. 'The masque, that's what I love, and the magic.' He opens an album of hand-made Japanese paper to show sketches for a stage production of the play that was to have starred himself as Prospero, but never got produced. 'Prospero was to have played *all* the characters.' Adhering to every page, like a dazzling postage-stamp, is a tiny square shard of mirror glass. '*The Tempest* is a mirror. People see whatever feature of themselves they want to — and can re-interpret it forever.' Intended for the Round House theatre at Chalk Farm, the play would have been a startling production. 'It turned the centre of that auditorium into an island made of huge

*Derek Jarman, interviewed by the author, 16 July 1982. Unless otherwise stated, all subsequent quotations from Jarman come from the same source.

polystyrene rocks painted silver. All the surrounding space was to be flooded with water. People would have walked on to the "island" over bridges and sat among the "rocks". The play would have been performed in the rigging of the sunken ship — this was well before Peter Brook's version of *A Midsummer Night's Dream* which suspended the cast from trapezes:' No wonder David Bowie once called Jarman 'a black magician'. Not so, he protests: 'The *film* is the magic, the dark art, not its maker.'

The son of an Air Commodore and a mother who was one of Norman Hartnell's assistants in the *haute couture* business, Jarman was a secretive, sensory-fixated child reared in the immediate post-war years in a requisitioned apartment in Rome where his father had been posted — 'a *novecento* flat, furnished in Fascist style, which had belonged to a relative of Count Ciano, Mussolini's son-in-law, and had a Titian on the wall and a junk room filled with ostrich fans, silvered Christmas-trees and ball-gowns from the Thirties. It was my favourite play-place: I was five then. It must have been the seedbed of later things.' His playmates were also exotic, the children of a refugee Jugoslav family with real or acquired patrician airs — 'they lived it up in art-deco grandeur . . . suits of armour, tiger skins on the parquet. It was like a Ken Russell movie.'

An ungainly, 'difficult' child in his later minor-league preparatory school in England, he excelled in the art class, once polishing off all the poster-paint that the school was allocated in that period of austerity by drip-feeding it on to fifteen huge imitations of Jackson Pollock, all done in one day, too. He was also good at gardening, another form of pattern-making. King's College, London (English and art history) and the Slade School of Art followed — 'not as exciting as I'd hoped: little liberty, a lot of discipline'.

At this era he was more *Hair* than hair-shirt in the image he presented to the world. He preferred solitary film-going to painting in communal studios. His gestatory gamut of 'influential' films now looks singularly orthodox, but in those days had the impact of novelty on a generation which, as *Hollywood, England* has indicated, worshipped newness above all else: *Hiroshima mon amour*: *L'Année derrière à Marienbad* ('which I adored'); all the current Fellinis and the first 'underground' showing of Kenneth Anger's *Scorpio Rising*, heady with homo-eroticism and macho-fetishism. Jarman had been brought up Low Church ('and hated it'): he became fascinated by High Church ritual, liturgy, all the 'play-acting' at the altar, the odour of incense and sanctity. His early movie preferences suggested ways to him in which he could liberate his predilections out of the sacristy and into the film studio in works that mixed masques, revelry and fancy-dress pageantry.

If he admits to taking the idea of a warehouse workshop from Andy Warhol's New York 'film factory', he is quick to deny any master-disciple relationship — 'Warhol's movie-making lost its promise for me when it got to be like his art, repetitious and monotonous. All those boring Polaroids!' Another essential difference between the two of them: if Warhol was 'the hole in the record', as his aide Paul Morrissey once called him, round which all else turns, then Jarman is the needle that plays the music.

As Hockney had done three years earlier, he made a pilgrimage through America in 1964 by the Beat Poets' road, met the *Easy Rider* set, scraped an acquaintance with Bob Dylan and Joan Baez . . . 'I wore a Beatles-style cap — their cult had just hit America then — so everyone who knew them also knew I was English and trendy, and it helped. To be English and on the Coast was quite rare then'.

Unlike Hockney, though, he didn't allow himself to get pulled into the American bloodstream. He preferred the masque's formalities to the freaky life of hippies. He already knew he would be happier back in the court-circle of Elizabeth I (perhaps helping John Dee, the resident astrologer, set the Coronation date) than in the sloppy anarchy of the rural commune. Where he resembled Hockney was in bringing colour back into opera and ballet when, some years later, he designed *Don Giovanni* and Ashton's *Jazz Calendar* ('we made costumes out of *pink* blankets'). After a cursory glance at his sketches in 1969, Ken Russell impulsively invited Jarman to design *The Devils*. Jarman concluded that Russell had been captivated by his personal life-style and saw him as a mad romantic artist who wrote his own rules — a seductive and recurring motif of Russell's films. As he had up to then seen none of his future patron's films, Jarman rushed out to catch *Women in Love*. He said Yes immediately and was munificently rewarded with a £200-a-week contract — 'a fortune then'.

His architectural studies ('with a bias to Piranesi') stood him in good stead, though a childhood infatuation with *The Wizard of Oz* was evident, too, in the use he made of bricks to endow the Loudon convent architecture with a stylized other-worldliness — *white* bricks, though, not the yellow ones of Oz-land. His brilliant use of *cramped* space, which caused the characters to bend themselves into strange postures as if already feeling the tortures to come, was much commented on and derived from his appreciation of Eisenstein — 'the only film-maker to use architectural grandeur to analyse the people in it.' (A somewhat overblown statement: but one knows what he means.) Budgetary economies sabotaged his concept of a non-naturalistic court in *The Devils*: it was built, but never used — 'the Royals simply adjourned to Pinewood's back lawns'. But similar economies were brilliantly overcome when he came to design Russell's *Savage Messiah*; and when he made his own first feature, he had the experience of conjuring a lot of effects out of very little means.

Sebastiane (28 October 1976), co-directed by a BBC TV film-maker, Paul Humfress, was shot in England and Sardinia in under five weeks and cost only £15,000 — 'about £8,000 of that raised from sales of my abstract landscape paintings, the rest from friends like James Whaley and friends' friends'. Its title — which is the Latin vocative ('O Sebastian') — refers to the Roman centurion who was martyred by arrows and later granted sainthood, though few Roman Catholic pieties were celebrated in Jarman's vision of St Sebastian's brief, earthly and sensuously homosexual exposure to profane love and agonizing death at the rough outpost of empire where Diocletian had banished him in a dispute over his Christianity in AD 304. Sebastian sets himself far apart from his comrades and a commanding officer who attempts to close the gap with physical favours is repulsed and takes the revenge that lost the Roman Empire a soldier, but gained Renaissance painters their favourite sado-masochistic subject.

In a brilliantly evocative book, *Dancing Ledge*, that reads as if it had been constructed by a jewelled magpie of more than usually eclectic tastes, intensely personal, infuriatingly discursive and rivetingly voyeuristic, Jarman later gave a hugely entertaining view of filming *Sebastiane*. For him, its attractiveness lay in the historical opportunity that artists had seized over the centuries to use a sacred subject as an occasion for studies of the male nude. Of course, the film, by suiting the action to the 'stills', provided its own more relaxed age with other seductive features. Its undraped centurions ('anway we couldn't have afforded armour'), passing their time between sentry-go in homo-erotic wrestling bouts, caught the tail-wind of Gay Lib in Britain and elsewhere. The film was swiftly carried by it into profit, though its world-wide critical response was varied. In America it was classified as a porno film and refused advertising space in newspapers; the French disliked it; but in Roman Catholic strongholds like Spain and Italy it was a runaway success. 'In Rome', Jarman wrote in a characteristically camp footnote in his book, 'Alberto Moravia came to the first Press show and praised (it) in the foyer saying it was a film that Pier Paolo would have loved.'* Its use of dialogue, couched throughout in Dog Latin, was a titillating piece of scholarship and in its best moments it conveyed the life as well as the limbs of its characters. In Italy, it is said to have grossed £250,000 — 'but I didn't go out of my way to grab any of it. I just made the film I thought my friends would want to go and see.'

PUNK AND CIRCUMSTANCE

If friendships dictate films, then Jarman's friends were responsible for a film that caught the dark side of the Seventies and the early Eighties as ominously as *Performance* had done in its decade. *Jubilee* (23 February

---

*Derek Jarman, *Dancing Ledge*, edited by Shaun Allen (Quartet, 1984), p. 165.

1978) was Jarman's next work and a major film of the era under review. It was the first full-length film to draw its looks and threats from the phenomenon of British punks. It was a violent collage of everything Punk that was then around; and it came to be a glossary of many even more violent phenomena that were on the way as British society changed its nature and things got harder and more hopeless for the unwaged.

As usual, the Pop music industry was the main communications channel for the bad news. 'The Sixties were clutter: the Seventies are empty,' said Andy Warhol. To be young and British in the mid-Seventies was to know the truth of that. The Pop stars of the time were separated by their own success from the great mass of young people now coming of age in a different society. Some of them had become Pop super-stars and moved abroad to avoid British taxes — much as some of Britain's brightest film talents had done — and when they returned it was for *hommage* and shows that George Melly stigmatized for being of 'increasingly elaborate theatricality'. 'What was basically changed for everybody,' he added, 'is that the expectation, the belief that everything is getting better, has given way to the knowledge that everything is getting worse.'*

And not just for the young, but for the middle-class people who were no longer quite so young and found the economic options rapidly diminishing and so distancing them from a sympathetic (or even participatory) interest in their children's freakish diversions. 'The Discreet Plight of the Bourgeoisie' was how *The Guardian* labelled a series on middle-class 'hardship' in November 1976; while that same month *Newsweek* featured a cover story on 'Britain's Battered Middle Class', squeezed by high double-figure inflation and a devalued pound sterling now worth $1.65 as against $2.32 two years earlier.

There were other signs of battening down the hatches. Fast-food outlets multiplied in this period, their cheap and handy 'junk' fare thus establishing itself as the nutritional mainstay of many penny-pinching people. A feeling was rife of authority mustering its forces to control what people had in their minds, never mind their stomachs, by repressing the barely won liberties of earlier years; it helped polarize opinion and divide the generations. Some of those performers, producers and, yes, journalists in the media, who had been prominent trend-setters in the Sixties now began their return journeys to profitable and prudent conformity. Youth was helped define its outcast identity quite as much by these defections as by its own angrier manifestation of change. There was a feeling of growing persecution, which, of course, fed on itself when no other fare was at hand.

In July 1977 the editor of *Gay News* was prosecuted for publishing Professor James Kirkup's allegedly blasphemous poem about a Roman

*George Melly, *Evening Standard*, 18 October 1976.

centurion engaging in acts of necrophilia with the crucified Christ. The charge had been launched by Mary Whitehouse and was then taken up by the Director of Public Prosecutions. No literary or theological evidence was called for the defence: none was needed, according to Judge King-Hamilton, as it was necessary only to show that blasphemy tends to cause a breach of the peace. *Gay News* was convicted and its editor received a suspended prison sentence later quashed on appeal. The confidence of the gay world, and the paper's circulation, were both severely shaken.

In August 1977 Pasolini's *120 Days of Sodom* was hastily removed from a Soho cinema under threat of Common Law action by the police for 'keeping a disorderly house'. This was in spite of the management's protest that 'the audience was not the normal mackintosh brigade. These people were Pasolini followers, ladies in evening dresses and gentlemen in evening suits.' It's doubtful if Pasolini would have recognized such disciples: but perhaps if they had been 'the normal mackintosh brigade' no action would have ensued. That same summer saw one of the fiercest attacks against paedophiles published in *The Sunday Telegraph* under T. E. Utley's name. There was even harsher evidence of a divided society: in the first six months of 1967 there had been 71,060 unemployed youngsters under the age of twenty; in 1977 there were 252,328 — no wonder the prevailing style of Pop was dubbed 'Dole Queue Rock'.

At that date there were at least thirty 'fanzines' being published in Britain, amateurishly edited but greedily read periodicals devoted to this new politicized sound that thrived on the boredom and reflected nihilism. Actually, Punk rock had entered the national consciousness at the end of 1976 when the Sex Pistols, who had been signed to a £40,000 a year contract that October, uttered profanities on a live TV show and behaved with such scant regard for other decencies that EMI abruptly terminated the relationship. Poorer but unabashed, the group were then heard in 'full filthy cry', as Robin Denselow called it, at an Amsterdam concert in January 1977, looking 'more like effective stage villains than revolutionaries'. But a number they created specially for the twenty-fifth anniversary of the Queen's accession created a furore. 'God save the Queen,' went the words, 'God save the fascist regime/She's not a human being/There is no future.'* 'We don't care' and 'So what' went the refrain. Predictably, the main retail outlets, Boots, Woolworth and W. H. Smith, refused to stock it and the BBC to play it: but it became the best-selling record in Britain during the official Jubilee Week in June 1977.

By this time Punk had become a form of 'street theatre' in London, with fights erupting on Saturday afternoons in Chelsea's King's Road

*Glitterbest Ltd.

between third-generation Teddy Boys in Edwardian finery and Punks in all the poly-coloured glory of cockatoo make-up and Huron-style haircuts. Sixty-one arrests were made over the four weeks of high summer. 'Once again the kids are galvanizing their energy behind the popular heroes and media of their own,' wrote Mark Williams, 'but this time they're not holding flowers and loosening up their psyches on hash and LSD. Instead, they're stamping their boots and taking the only drug they can afford, when they can get it, which is speed — amphetamine sulphate.'* But inner consciousness, stimulated or otherwise, was outwardly very visible, not least in what Williams called 'unfathomable hair-dos, safety-pin jewellery and waste-bin fashion and the quaint Punk habit of spitting on each other'. All of these were surely signs of the degraded image that many young people had of themselves, their alienation from the rest of society, and their sullen expectation of a worsening lot as the rejects of an increasingly uncaring world. 'Punk' was defined in the dictionaries as not only 'rubbish, waste matter', but also, more ominously, as 'combustible stuff'.

From just such times and tribal rites, Derek Jarman drew both his friends and the fantasies he channelled into his film *Jubilee*. It was he who encountered a girl who was to be one of Punk's very first madonnas. Named simply Jordan, she stood outside Victoria Station wearing a very short white plastic mini-skirt with a see-through front panel, extremely high heels and hair like a Bunsen burner at full flame. He impulsively took her to Paris to see the Mona Lisa, thereby upstaging Da Vinci's lady for perhaps the first time in the history of the Louvre. Both of them were thrown out of the museum for 'disturbance of the environment'.

Sensing the violent edge on the wind of change, Jarman scraped together £50,000 — a proportion of it from Middle East gays — and made *Jubilee*, a film 'by, with and for my friends'. There was absolutely nothing in it for one's comfort, but much to raise one's apprehensions about the dangerously alienated youth of the 1970s. It was a collective nightmare, a phantasmagoria assembled from dole-queue despair, a mirage of anarchy in the youth waste-land, a whirligig of disturbed teenagers from some contemporary Bedlam.

Compared to films like *A Hard Day's Night* or *Help!* it was a shock to see how wilfully the youngsters in it had mutated away from normal shapes and become a new genus rather than a new generation. Like one of its most shattering images, *Jubilee* resembled a Molotov cocktail in a champagne bottle hurled in the public's face with a despairing battle-cry — 'No future!' Jarman's skills blended characters, design, music and action into a 'horrorshow', pitched midway between Punk opera and blank verse. T. S. Eliot's *Waste Land* resonated in its bleak language; Andy Warhol's freaks assumed domestic but far from docile shapes.

*Mark Williams, *The Observer*, 10 July 1977.

It opened not in the second Elizabethan Age, but in the first, in 1578, with the Virgin Queen (Jenny Runacre) ensconsed in courtly splendour at the country home of her magician, Dr John Dee (Richard O'Brien) and allowing the good doctor to transport her to her namesake's realms 400 years later. Deptford, where once she welcomed her explorers home from the New World, is now a waste-tip; costume has been metamorphosed from court finery into the uniform of bondage whose zips, straps and safety-pins signify the constraints clamped on the social rejects who sport it. Girls with cherubic or butch faces, cheeks rouged and painted like cracked tiles, dressed in Dayglo rags or vinyl tatters, hair in spikes or cropped to the very scalp; boys who look like famished maggots; rooms cluttered with prize loot; slogans of 'HATE' and 'WAR' reversing the Flower Children's creed of 'LOVE' and 'PEACE'; omnipresent TV sets flickering with narcissistic Punk rock concerts: Punk London rises like a savage Phoenix out of the ashes of Swinging London.

The media are not the only recognized 'reality'. Pornography is 'better' than sex. Old England has been put to new uses: Westminster Cathedral is the scene of an orgy; Buckingham Palace (bought from the liquidators) is a recording studio. Through the film swarm Jarman's friends and acquaintances playing characters whose names are as outlandish as the performers themselves; Amyl Nitrate (Jordan) a Fascist Pop singer goose-stepping a version of *Rule Britannia* to victory in a Eurosong-type contest; a pyromaniac called Mad (Toyah Wilcox); a French *au pair* (Hermione Demoriane) who bears her name, Chaos, stencilled on her cheekbone; a nympho by the name of Crabs (Little Nell); and a sexy tiddler (Adam Ant) netted out of the Rock pool who is 'snuffed' to death in a pink polythene bag like a potato crisp and flung into the Thames as neatly trussed as one of Boris Christo's notorious 'wrappings', whereupon he comes back to life and serenades his murderers with an unresentful ballad like the charmed corpse in a medieval tale.

Jarman's ear proved a radar cup to catch all the noises that currently filled the British Isles. Brian Eno had done the *Sebastiane* score; now *Jubilee* was fixed up with ghoulish groups with names like death wishes: The Electric Chairs, Maneaters, Siouxie and the Banshees, Amilcar, Susi Prinns, Chelsea and Brian Eno again. Every note in the film expounded the Punk manifesto: 'If the music's loud enough, we won't hear the world fall apart.' It was. But there was despair as well as din in it. Jarman veered from black humour, like an Olde English maypole wreathed in barbed wire instead of ribbons; to realistic horror, like the ritualistic murder of a rich Pop star called Lounge Lizard and the castration of a police officer — events that gratified the Punk hatred of authority and what Johnny Rotten had called 'the millionaire groups singing about love and their own hang-ups. . . . You don't sing of love to people on the dole.'

Dee Hepburn, happily invading the male stronghold of the changing room in *Gregory's Girl*, 1981 (above), a comedy that launched Bill Forsyth as one of the new decade's most original talents.

New faces for the Eighties: Julie Walters (with Michael Caine) in *Educating Rita*, 1983 (above), inherited the comic, provincial naïvety of Sixties star Rita Tushingham. Phyllis Logan, in *Another Time, Another Place*, 1983 (opposite, above, right), brought the freshness, vigour and conviction of a younger Vanessa Redgrave to a love-story of a Scottish farmer's wife freeing herself from her oppressive community through a man who is a prisoner of war not prejudice. Jeremy Irons, an actor of powerful quietude, refracted the tragedy of his compatriots back home by playing a Pole stranded in London in *Moonlighting*, 1982 (below, left). Rupert Everett (with Cary Elwes) stepped impressively into Malcolm McDowell's shoes in *Another Country*, 1984 (opposite, above, left), tracing the genealogy of treason to the public-school system. Miranda Richardson (with Ian Holm) portrayed Ruth Ellis, Britain's last woman to be hanged, in *Dance with a Stranger*, 1985 (opposite, below, left), a pessimistic backward look at 1955 Britain showing the double standards still being applied thirty years later. Stephen Rea, in *Angel*, 1982 (opposite, below, right), an audacious vision of Ulster terrorism in terms of an American *film noir*, exemplified how the ordinary guy can become an avenging machine.

The British kept coming — and winning the Oscars. David Puttnam (above, right), with a victory handful for *Chariots of Fire* at the 1982 Oscar ceremonies: all the time he was thinking how sweet revenge was. Sir Richard Attenborough (above, left), with an armful of Oscars for *Gandhi* at the 1983 ceremonies.

Two scenes in particular encapsulated grim chapters of social history. One was a bitterly funny monologue by an ex-mercenary (Neil Kennedy) whose garden flower-beds are filled with plastic blooms purloined from graves in public cemeteries; the other was a Hamlet-like soliloquy by the kind of boys whose spiritual horizon has been blocked by council-built towers and whose only window on the world is the moron-making telly. With awesome accuracy and in cheated tones, they recapitulate the 'hope to be dead by twenty-five' feeling of the Blank Generation. One of them was played by Ian Charleson who emerged out of *Jubilee*'s chrysalis some three years later as the clean-limned front-runner and defender of all things English and Christian in *Chariots of Fire*. He was Derek Jarman's first super-star! Ironically, all mention of his Punk past was expunged from his filmography issued by publicists at the time of *Chariots of Fire*. It had taken only a very few years to realize the prediction that Geoff Mungham made in his monograph *Working Class Culture*: 'Punk will become commercialized, the lyrics of the songs will be cleaned up and the Punk will become accepted.'

Contrary to the fears of censors and other keepers of the status quo, *Jubilee* did not win large and riotous audiences when it was premiered. Film-goers took sides over it. 'For an audience who expected a Punk music film, full of "anarchy" and laughs at the end of the King's Road, it was difficult to swallow. They wanted action, not analysis.'* But at the date of its release it seemed the ultimate merger of cultural fantasy and social reality. 'Whereas in *Sebastiane* we lived in a world outside the film, in *Jubilee* our world became the film.'** It was prophecy as well as allegory: the riots staged by the have-nots of London's Brixton and Liverpool's Toxteth in the early 1980s were biding their time in *Jubilee*. One final irony: the London cinema which premiered the first authentic Punk picture of the time was owned by EMI — which had dropped the Sex Pistol's contract so hurriedly a year or so before.

Jarman's next film, a version of *The Tempest* (1 May 1980) which cost £150,000, most of it put up by Don Boyd in what its director later called 'a mad moment of commitment', confirmed his fluency as a masque-maker who magicked the play into contemporary idiom without losing its timelessness. He dressed Ariel in a pink boiler-suit, gave Miranda ethnic dreadlocks, pressed Caliban into service in a butler's uniform, cloaked Prospero in stage magician's robes and had a realistically shipwrecked Ferdinand walk full-frontally nude out of the North Sea. He fashioned the play as a dream: the sound-track sighed and heaved with electronic noise, as if a sleeper were breathing in and out while pictures chase through his brain. The Punk-ishness didn't desecrate Shakespeare: it re-decorated the text. It permitted new interpretations to be plucked out of performances that judge, in the nick of time, where the Bard ends and the King's Road begins. The climax

*Derek Jarman, op.cit., p. 172.
**Ibid., p. 176.

was flamboyantly camp with lines of sailor-suited Mods dancing a hornpipe as Elizabeth Welch, a Goddess in clouds of saffron, sang *Stormy Weather* and Ariel donned a white tuxedo and crooned his bee-sucking lyric like someone whose tipple has been the cocktails which were then coming back into fashion at 'Happy Hours' in bars all over London, rather than old-fashioned nectar.

The film did very well in Britain and on the Continent: but Vincent Canby's unsympathetic review in *The New York Times* effectively killed it: 'Very nearly unbearable . . . a fingernail scratched along a blackboard, sand in spinach. . . . There are no poetry, no ideas, no characterizations, no narrative, no fun.' The poor American box-office cost Jarman finance for his next project, which was to have been a study of Caravaggio, the seventeenth-century Italian painter, called the first of the moderns by Roger Fry for his way of inserting secular, indeed sexual life into nominally sacred subjects. Jarman saw him as a schizoid personality ('no half-shades in that chiaroscuro technique') and, it goes without saying, as a homosexual. These unorthodox views made Italian financiers leery of putting up the money. So he joined the queue for finance from Channel 4's film-making division which had at first seemed the answer to the prayers of the 'alternative' film-makers. He was speedily disillusioned. 'Channel 4, in spite of a much vaunted alternative image, was to turn out all Beaujolais Nouveau and scrubbed Scandinavia, pot plants in place. It wasn't *our* alternative: independent cinema was to remain independent, disenfranchised by a Channel for the slightly adventurous commuter.'*

The early years of the Eighties didn't bring any reward to Jarman for his spartan if jubilant sense of independence. Teachers' organizations warned schools off his version of *The Tempest*; Channel 4 was attacked by the tabloid Press, reacting to the anti-gay backlash, when it bought *Sebastiane* (and *Nighthawks*) for screening and, at the time of writing, has shown neither; and the selection of films drawn up to represent 'The Revival Years' by the principal of the National Film and Television School and his associates in the run-up to British Film Year 1985–6, succeeded in excluding every film Jarman had made. Somehow he found the hardiness to survive and subsequently made some boldly eccentric short films. But then he belongs to the tradition of Wilde and Beardsley and Cecil Beaton, aesthetes with a hard core. Like them, he knows (and enjoys) the value of confounding conventional expectations. Like Jean Cocteau, too, he has forged links between a generation and his own personal mythology. The hardened Punks of the 1980s eventually responded to *Jubilee* the way that the existentialist proto-Beatniks of 1950 did to *Orphée*. Jarman can pose in public as adroitly as Cocteau and, similarly, impose his vision *on* the public. The self-denying ordinance of

*Derek Jarman, op.cit., p. 207.

his life-style should not deceive us: it reinforces his feeling that, as he puts it, 'all is within reach of me'. He has a huge appetite for the world outside his cell.

RUDE BOYS, BLACK BOYS

It was hardly surprising that British mainstream cinema returned to the theme of youth at the end of the Seventies. Movies follow — and sometimes, as in the ferment of the Sixties, propel — mass shifts of behaviour, especially when the other media obligingly 'put it all together' for them in print and pictures. New sources of finance became available from the mini-boom in the new recording companies with discs to promote and images to brand on the young consciousness. But Franc Roddam's *Quadrophenia* (15 August 1979) felt as if it had been made not in a time-slip, but a ghetto. For why go back fifteen years to the time when teenage life is starting to swing if one is going to look no further than the nose on one's face? Inspired by the disc of the same name made by The Who, it pandered to contemporary youth's romanticizing self-pity by showing what it supposed life to have been like for a Mod hero of the Sixties. Played by Phil Daniels, he plunges to his death over the cliffs of the South Coast, taking with him lots of stridently orchestrated 'sympathy' but no insight into how his times they were a-changing. Nor did the movie-makers give much sign that their vision of the future wasn't obscured by the dead-end life of the pre-Honda generation. The film was devoid of the feeling of kids being part of a larger society than their own back street, something that even the meanest American movie seemed to manage effortlessly.

Much superior was *Rude Boy* (25 February 1980), financed by the impresario Michael White and produced by Clive Parsons and Davina Belling. It was made by the team of Jack Hazan and David Mingay, who had explored the world of David Hockney in *A Bigger Splash*. Although The Clash were the nominal stars, the real theme was a Britain that was falling apart. It opened with a white boy spitting at a Royal limousine and closed with a black boy in a prison cell being forced to sign a 'confession'. Whereupon the camera cut to a smiling Mrs Thatcher being dropped at Downing Street after consenting to the Queen's invitation to become Britain's first woman Prime Minister. In between abrasive start and cynical finish lay a frightening and squalid vision of the 'Two Englands'. One was a land where the Prime Minister talks about creating prosperity hand in hand with bigger police forces; the other, a place where dead-end, dead-loss kids with the looks of mindless zombies mix in race riots, support neo-Fascists, collapse insensibly at Punk concerts and degenerate into youngsters with the eyes of old men that see 'No Future' scrawled in the graffiti of their daily existence. The movie used concert footage of The Clash in action and followed the fans on the morning after up to the door of the magistrate's court to be dealt with.

The hero wasn't a professional actor, but a shambling, sleepy-eyed twenty-year-old son of a Brixton taxi-driver who well personified the 'rude-ness' of the title as defined in its eighteenth-century meaning of 'simple, unsophisticated, uneducated, uncivilized'. Interestingly, the film was premiered three nights after the Royal Film Performance of 1980. That year it was *Kramer Vs. Kramer*, a much less alarming film for the Queen to see, as it was only about a marriage falling apart and not Her Majesty's own realm.

Perhaps to balance the Fascistic views expressed by many white kids in the film, it felt obliged to show the harsh lot of young blacks. The use of hidden cameras to monitor black delinquents dipping into purses and pockets in shopping precincts, followed by re-enacted dawn raids by the faceless upholders of Law and Order in a massive series of 'overkill' arrests in a black neighbourhood, was unlikely to mollify anyone. But it had the effect of bringing home to many whites the impact of the bitterly resented 'sus' (for 'suspect') laws giving police the powers to 'stop and search' — usually young blacks.

The growing tensions between the races began seeping into national cinema through the work of independent film-makers. Not one major company devoted a film to the subject in the Seventies. Always latent in the community and growing more and more visible in the harassment of 'coloureds' and blacks by gangs of neo-Fascist whites, racial fears became dramatically sharp-focused in the autumn of 1975, when three black criminals, interrupted in an armed raid on a Knightsbridge pasta restaurant, took hostages and defied the police for several days. Blacks with guns: this was the alarming aspect of the Spaghetti House siege, though many of Brixton's ghetto residents could have predicted things would come to that from the way that urban violence involving blacks in America was becoming part of British folklore, too. Martyrs were needed.

The Spaghetti House siege, according to how one viewed it, would show blacks in a bad light and thus worsen relations with the police, or it would make blacks more sympathetic to police problems. (On the whole, sentiment inclined to the former view.) There was fear that the police would start raiding East End homes in a search for arms; or that the siege would be read for its 'political' message and be misrepresented as a black 'uprising' against white authority. 'We find it very difficult to get the average Englishman to believe that the police can ever be brutal,' one black community leader was quoted as saying at the time. The outcome was happy in the sense of lives saved by the police tactics of patience and the phenomenon of 'transference', or the sympathetic bonds forged between captors and captives, of which this was then an early manifestation.

Otherwise, things were not so clear cut. Though the Law managed to prevent a political twist being given to a criminal act, the exhaustive investigation of black culture in Britain which took place as a result, as if the entrails were being read for pernicious omens, ensured that black consciousness in Britain was effectively heightened. It is likely this would have happened anyhow, as black militancy fed off the rising unemployment statistics among young blacks. In largely black Brixton at the end of 1975, there were only twenty jobs available for every 100 applicants. An influential paperback entitled *White Media and Black Britain*, published in October that same year, chided the Anglo-Saxons for recognizing blacks in Britain only when they were in conflict with 'the natives'. For the first time, the word 'Babylon', referring to the Caribbean blacks' none too affectionate description of Britain, gained wide currency when the then police commissioner for the metropolis objected to its appearing in a schoolgirl's poem that had been entered in some official competition. (At this time only twenty-three of London's 20,000 police officers were black or 'coloured'.)

In 1976 the Race Relations Act had to be revised to quieten the apprehension roused by National Front demonstrations: despite which (or, perhaps, because of it), social tensions increased, and in February 1976 two Sunday colour supplements were itemizing the armoury of weapons now being issued to British police forces. Although IRA terrorism in mainland Britain was the official reason for stepping up such defences, rising black militancy was the unspoken (or, at any rate, unwritten) additional worry. An attempt to defuse the situation through a situation-comedy about a black family, launched by London Weekend Television in April 1976, failed to cement the races in self-deprecating good-humour and was denounced by black leaders as an insulting example of racial stereotyping!

Perhaps the earliest film to reflect the dangerous identity crisis of British-born blacks was Horace Ové's *Pressure* (1975), scripted by him and the Trinidad-born novelist Samuel Selvon, and filmed among black communities in Notting Hill on a minute budget from the British Film Institute's Production Board. It was about a well-educated black boy who fails to find a job and, disillusioned further by what he sees as the abject subservience of his parents to white values, drifts into militant politics. At the end, though, he is undecided whether his plight is a specific black one or a symptom of general economic decay in Britain. As David Wilson wrote: 'It is the measure of *Pressure*'s originality that, for all its rough edges, it foreshadows what has actually happened.'* This

Monthly Film Bulletin, April 1978.

referred to black leaders' welcome rejection of organized militancy in Britain during 1977. In spite of its urgency (and moderation), *Pressure* had to wait over two years to get a commercial showing: it is not being unduly cynical to suggest that the Notting Hill race riots on August Bank Holiday 1978 helped it 'surface'.

The first 'race' film to get fairly wide circulation was another independent production, *Black Joy* (2 November 1977), produced by Elliott Kastner and based on Jamal Ali's play about an innocent young immigrant, *Dark Days and Dark Nights.* Director Anthony Simmons transposed it into seething Notting Hill and provided it with the energy and salty dialogue of a Joan Littlewood production at Stratford East in the 1950s. A flashy, swaggering fly-boy (Norman Beaton, star of the sitcom TV series criticized by some blacks) and his brassy tongued 'woman' and Artful Dodger of a son who cannons into all the film's other shady characters like a black billiard ball (with an eye on their 'pocket' too) — such people were without the social realism that their sombre circumstances would have thrust on them in life. Their resilience betrayed the makers' anxiety that lively qualities of entertainment should compensate for the more downbeat truth. The characters were as Dickens might have drawn them, had he lived to see the New Commonwealth carrying its cardboard suitcases to Old London. Race relations didn't come into the picture — much. For one thing, it was not about black and white, but black and black: not at all as inflammatory as the news stories. Its virtues were its ethnic relish: repartee came rat-tat-tat, with a candour that white players couldn't have handled without sounding vulgar. Racial tensions were played down in favour of showing how many ethnic elements were being stirred in the cracked old mixing-bowl of working-class (once white) London. *Black Joy* settled for saying that it takes all kinds to make a world.

It cost under £300,000 — with the NFFC coming in for about half of that — but it failed to find an audience. Its attempt to mediate between the communities was not reflected in a Gallup Poll taken in February 1978, which indicated that 49 per cent of those Britons questioned thought that non-whites should be offered financial 'aid' to return home. (The fact that 'home' for many of them was *Britain* seemed irrelevant in the inquiry.)

The presentiment that a racial underclass was in the making had to wait a couple more years before finding its more frightening form in a film. But in *Babylon* (6 November 1980) no compromises were allowed to tone down the hue of black or the cry of despairing anger among a gang of Deptford youngsters who sometimes lapsed into such thick Jamaican patois that sub-titles were used to interpret what they said. This integrity is all the more commendable (and surprising) since the film was technically the work of whites — directors Franco Rosso and Martin Stellman, producer Gavrik Losey and photographer Chris

Menges, with finance from the NFFC and a records company interested in exploiting the reggae soundtrack. Against a wall of deafeningly amplified reggae music, a young black with dreadlocks flopping like octopus tentacles 'toasts' the bleak lot of himself and his brothers with sorrow and defiance. The smoky haze of *ganga* weed quivers like Caribbean heat as dozens of black kids take up the refrain: 'Four hundred years/Pain and misery/All that Babylon is giving/I can't take no more of that/No, I can't take no more of that.'*

Little actual violence erupts among the boys of Rasta faith and English birth, but their thoughts, words and life-style have the premonitory explosiveness of rolling thunder. This was not a mediation movie, but a red alert. The whites in it were either threats or were themselves victims. For once, a film made no bones about how difficult it was for whites to enter this world: the white misfit caught in the undertow of the black gang's exoticism draws the recoil of anti-white prejudice on himself. One saw for the first time in a major film the fractured nature of what was officially — and hopefully — known as 'the black community'. Orthodox engagement ceremonies among the blacks, awash with as much gentility as any similar rites among the *petit bourgeois* whites, are contrasted with the Rasta priest in his embroidered gown who evokes a messianic message with his prophet's wand and offers communicants a puff from a pipe of 'herbs' to 'calm the mind'. But always one returns to the music, vibrant and threatening as the Law's sledgehammer blows which rain on the door of the reggae club in the last few seconds and collide with the beat of the black band within.

That the film could frighten the Establishment soon became evident. It was given an 'X' Certificate by the British Board of Film Censors, thus barring it to great numbers of the black community under the age of eighteen. What emerged from the ensuing protest seemed to be the old, shameful story of censors claiming to possess paternalistic wisdom and exercising a condescending 'duty' to protect those they think are immature or stupid enough to misread such a film's 'message'. 'Confused and troubled' was how the BBFC imagined young British blacks might emerge from *Babylon*, thinking that attacking whites was the only protest open to them. One had to suppose that the BBFC believed they would no longer think that way once they reached the enlightening age of eighteen.

Another worry was some of the obscenities spoken in the film by the blacks. The distributors tried to appease the censorship board by leaving these untranslated by sub-titles — thus ensuring that they would protect the sensitivities of white ear-drums. Lest it be thought that white English censorship was thus depriving the very people of Brixton from seeing their life-style on the screen, seven members of the Commission for

---

* © Diversity Music Ltd.

Racial Equality (six of them black) were consulted. It is of interest that five of them reportedly favoured letting the film be seen by age-groups as young as the over-fourteens until they entered the censor's sanctum and listened to his anxieties. They then voted to confirm his 'X' Certificate by five to two. Thus the Commission for Racial Equality allowed itself to act as 'a priori' film censors, encroaching on individual freedoms which had nothing at all to do with 'equality', racial or otherwise.

The impression left was that the film had been banned to younger age-groups not because street-wise black youngsters might be 'confused and troubled' by it, but because it didn't reflect the 'benign' thinking of the authorities who made racial policy. In a letter to the British distributors, the BBFC secretary, Mr James Ferman, said: 'We all believe that it will become a classic of its type and be around for many years, so that those black youngsters who cannot see it today will have their chance before very long.'* Unfortunately, souls don't stay on ice — much though censors and others wish they did.

TERMINAL CASES

Memoirs of a Survivor (24 September 1981) and *Britannia Hospital* (27 May 1982) can be said to mark the passive and active tenses of a nation's ceasing to believe in itself. Both films appeared in the period of Thorn-EMI's recoil from financing big American money-losers. Both, it must be conceded, were small British money-losers. But they had compensating satisfactions to offer. They wore the mark of the times in which they were made. They also showed the distance that two of the brightest talents of the Sixties had travelled along the road to the Eighties.

By lending her presence to *Memoirs of a Survivor*, Julie Christie certainly ensured its financing. For although the burnish had worn off her 'Darling' persona in the years when she had espoused some of the more portentous campaigns of politics, human rights and the environment, Christie brought a compensating collateral of personal 'commitment' to Doris Lessing's post-Apocalyptic vision. She played a survivor of some unspecified holocaust preoccupied with the waste-land of the metropolis, or the part of it seen from her upstairs window, and periodically vanishing through the wallpaper into the stifling unemancipated life of a middle-class Victorian family whose affluence conceals an analagous spiritual desolation.

The Michael Medwin-Penny Clark production, directed by David Gladwell, was surer in delineating the topography of post-nuclear nightmare than in dissipating the heroine's trauma in any revitalizing

---

*James Ferman, letter quoted in *Evening Standard*, 6 November 1980.

way. The giant egg that mysteriously appeared at the end as a totem object of the New Future shed a surrealistic radiance: but by then it wasn't strong enough to disperse the lugubriousness overshadowing the body of the picture. There were some who regretted Christie's progress from the bright centre of her generation's cinema to its penumbra. Her off-screen reclusiveness (except when one of her 'causes' was at issue) recalled Glenda Jackson's almost fetishistic disowning of her own fame. She willingly lent herself as a sort of currency for what other talents might wish to purchase and appeared in Sally Potter's *The Gold-Diggers*, produced in 1984 by the BFI, in a role that almost wilfully marked a wider withdrawal from 'popular' cinema into emblematic polemic for women's rights.

Britannia Hospital was judged by some people as showing Lindsay Anderson coming full circle: the left-wing revolutionary who trounced the Establishment in *If . . .* in 1969, now transforming himself into a right-wing reactionary using the unions as whipping boys. Such a view was simplistic. Anderson's was the anger of a moral reformer, a traditionalist whose ire is kindled by the state of chaos into which the realm has fallen — and who uses anarchy of a more formalized kind to reflect it and purge it. *Britannia Hospital* turned out to be his most powerful piece of invective against the mess that Britain was in. Its very title was a metaphor for a sick country in the throes of a nervous breakdown.

One might call it Anderson's *Devils* since it, too, is set in a hospice where the people are possessed by all kinds of contemporary demons. Health Service workers let the lame languish and the stricken perish as they go on strike to defend their tea break; kitchen staff stoke up the class war by refusing service to the patients in the private wing, who include a black African dictator occupying a luxury suite along with wives, concubines and chickens; a Royal visitor resembling Queen Elizabeth the Queen Mother arrives at the very moment coloured immigrants clash with riot police and has to be smuggled past the pickets as a casualty in mummifying bandages; Buckingham Palace's spokesman is a bossy, scowling midget; and a Royal lady-in-waiting is played by a blue-chinned drag artist. Through it all stalks a 'progressive' surgeon — the same 'Frankenstein' who believes that man is the sum of his vivisected parts. Think of a human vice — cowardice, cupidity, stupidity, duplicity, Royal pomp and circumstance or proletarian bloody-mindedness — and Anderson's misanthropy had a place for it in a film that ran the gamut from satire and slapstick through black comedy to outright Grand Guignol in which a headless *and naked* corpse runs amok in the operating theatre.

Anderson and his screen-writer, David Sherwin, were primed by the NFFC with £400,000: then Thorn-EMI came in with producers Clive Parsons and Davina Belling for another £1m. (though the budget escalated to twice these sums). Caught by the patriotic fervour of the Falklands War which boded ill for the fortunes of a film lambasting Britain, Thorn-EMI tried to delay its release: but it was already locked into the 1982 film festival at Cannes, where figures of Falklands casualties were flashing in light bulbs across the facade of the Hotel Carlton just below the skysign for the musical *Annie* and just above the cut-out cartoon advertising two new Pink Panther films. It was a macabre juxtaposition that Anderson himself might have devised. The film was given a 'blanket release' in Britain, playing simultaneously in many cinemas, whereas it might have been better to have nursed it along in a few and build on the basis of discriminating business. But compared with losses which its backers had incurred on other, far more extravagantly financed films, the commercial damage was small and the artistic consolidation great. Just as *If. . .* defined the revolutionary Sixties and *O Lucky Man!* the self-serving Seventies, *Britannia Hospital* became its maker's final communique (to date, anyhow) on the terminal malaise of the Eighties and a world that could not wait to extinguish itself.

CHAPTER TEN

All Fall Down

The last two years have made me realize that what you need to survive in the film industry isn't talent or confidence, just sheer bloody-mindedness. — *Mamoun Hassan,* The Sunday Times, *10 June 1984.*

'Depend upon it, Sir, when a man knows he is to be hanged in a fortnight,' Dr Johnson wrote to Boswell, 'it concentrates his mind wonderfully.' Depend upon it, too, when a man has just resigned from office rather than wait to be hanged at someone else's convenience, it loosens his tongue marvellously.

Such a man was Mamoun Hassan on 14 June 1984. That day he had handed in his resignation as managing director of the National Film Finance Corporation. He had held the job for just five-and-a-half years. To have to quit was hard and disappointing. But it caused him no embarrassment, none at all, to convey the news to Kenneth Baker, the Minister for Information Technology, whose remit at the Department of Trade included responsibility for films. The two men had met only once since Baker has succeeded Iain Sproat, one of the few Tories *not* to get returned to Parliament at the 1983 General Election. 'You don't get to know people you're intending to execute,'* was Hassan's dry comment. The sentence of death on the NFFC had been seen coming as long ago as two years. The way it was delivered was entirely consonant with the Government's — *any* British Government's — deeply rooted philistinism where culture in general, but *film* culture in particular, was concerned.

It had seemed almost too good to be true when the NFFC was restructured in 1981 — which it *had* to be under the 1970 Films Act that extended its lifetime to that date only. The old form of Government funding was to be ended, Hassan was told. Since the 'old form' had been

---

*Mamoun Hassan interviewed by the author, 14 June 1984. Unless otherwise stated, all subsequent quotations from Hassan come from this source.

half-hearted and tenuous at best, stony-faced and illusory at worst, Hassan was glad to be put on a new footing that seemed to promise an income calculable in advance. The NFFC had its debts written off: it was to be given a 'once and for all' grant of £1m.; and, more important, it was to get, for the next five years, a grant of £1.5m. from the Eady Levy tax on box-office takings (or 20 per cent of the Eady Levy: whichever was the greater). It could also borrow up to £5m. (previously £2m.) — provided it could find lenders. This offered continuity — though not safety, since cinema attendances were continuing to drop at an alarming rate. (They were a mere 64 million in 1982, compared with 1.6 billion in 1946.) The levy would also have to help support the National Film and Television School (£500,000) and the BFI Production Board (£125,000).

The more the NFFC and these institutions had from the levy, of course, the less there would be to go round other British film-makers. Not that one need grieve too much about that; by this time, the levy was already of minor importance. Its prime defect in rewarding the already profitable British films (which thus didn't need it) at the expense of those that had done poorly (and thus didn't get it) has already been commented on. The offence was compounded by the fact that, usually, the former films were the ones produced in Britain by major Hollywood companies. Some abuse of the levy was already glaringly evident. It had become a practice for one or two of these companies to buy up a British-made short film which was then put into distribution with a high-earning American film. The latter pulled in the crowds: the former benefited, because the Eady Levy paid out *twice* as much for shorts as for features. In one notorious case, the 'short' distributed with a very popular feature made over £200,000 in Britain — money put into the Americans' pockets that had been intended to help genuine British movie-makers. Not that the latter were guiltless. Sometimes the only way of getting one's British film distributed on the two major cinema circuits was to make over one's levy subsidy *in advance* to the distributors, who were under no obligation to re-invest it in one's next project.

So flagrant had these abuses become that the government actually listened when the Wilson Interim Action Committee recommended limiting the sum of money that any one film could take out of the Eady Levy to £500,000 and abolishing the 'more-favoured status' for shorts. This was done: but with the *total* Eady Levy shrinking, it was like patching the hole in a boat's gunwhales after the deck is under water.

If the NFFC's income was now coming regularly from this source, its ultimate fate also depended on the source not drying up: for the Government was now plainly signalling its desire to withdraw from the public funding of film-makers and leave the job to the market forces of the Eady Levy and the appetite of private investors.

'There is no film industry in Europe which stands on its own two feet without some kind of support, whatever its country's political complexion,' says Hassan. 'Britain, its Government had decided, was to be the exception. There is no deep belief that we in Britain have a tradition of film-making like the American or the European scene. There is constant denigration of our achievements, continuous belittling of our hopes. There is always the feeling in the film industry that we don't know where we have come from and don't care where we are going to. When I took over at the NFFC, I soon discovered the huge ambiguity we represented in this sort of situation.' That 'ambiguity' found pungent expression in the NFFC's 1983 report: '. . . the industry has always expected more from the Corporation (than its support for films which stood a reasonable chance of commercial return). In the mythology of the industry the Corporation was, and is, relied upon to encourage and introduce new talent and new ideas to nourish mainstream cinema.'

As Hassan expresses it less formally: 'We are *required* to have a commercial set-up, yet are *expected* to have a cultural policy. On the one hand there's a great fear about giving us "too much" money lest we start behaving in an arrogant way: on the other, we are seen by many British film-makers as having almost a duty to *lose* money by assisting them. If Thorn-EMI gave such people the "turn-down", it was not taken to be arrogance, simply a business decision: when the NFFC turned them down, the attitude was "What do you mean! Aren't you there to finance us?" During my tenure, hardly a week went by without our getting letters from rejected petitioners which more usually than not began "I'm surprised and puzzled . . ." "Surprised and Puzzled" became the generic name for people who spelled out their attitude in more or less polite language. Either way, it came down to: "You people can afford to lose money because you're given it by the State and should feed the worthy whenever they open their mouths."

'We were regarded all too often as "the last hope" — a friend who will lend when they are in need. When we said No, it usually spelled the end for some long-nurtured project and the NFFC suffered the backlash of their resentment and even panic. It was the schizoid split between "art" and "business" which is built into the NFFC's thirty-six-year history.'

Hassan had been less than happy with the broadening of the NFFC's membership board. Instead of the traditional bankers, accountants and lawyers, its appointees from 1980 on were drawn from the catchment areas of the Press and TV journalism, film production and exhibition and film schools. These new 'creative' representatives certainly brought a liveliness to their duties, judging the commercial/artistic worth of projects submitted for financial backing. But the zeal which was sometimes brought to the job wasn't always the 'cool hard look' that Hassan required. He came to hanker for the moneymen's quick and ready adjudication: it appeared that certain submissions engaged the passions of some board members too directly — or too narrowly. One battle was waged over the issue of British films being made by foreign directors. Was the NFFC in business to back Jerzy Skolimowski's *Moonlighting* (1982), in which Solidarity's resistance to oppression was brilliantly refracted through the agonized dilemma of a Pole stranded in London? Should it assist Nagisa Oshima's Anglo-Japanese co-production *Merry Christmas, Mr Lawrence* (1983), which had a British producer in Jeremy Thomas and a British star in David Bowie, but was shot entirely in the Pacific area by a Japanese? Should it put money into *Heat and Dust* (1982), whose creative troika (James Ivory, Ismael Merchant, Ruth Prawer Jhabvala) were not British — did their film sufficiently illuminate British life and manners in India in the 1920s to compensate for this deficiency? Mere 'moneymen', Hassan felt, listening to the boardroom battles, might not have wrung their hands so anxiously over such nice distinctions as his 'creative' associates did. It came as a relief, greeted by him rather cynically by this time, when two of these films proved notable successes — after they had been backed from non-NFFC sources. After that, he found, the opposition grew rather more muted. More wryly, he greeted a letter from Andrzej Wajda, the Polish director, congratulating him on backing *Britannia Hospital* — *not* a notable financial success — and hailing Lindsay Anderson's satire on the British malaise as 'one of the best Polish films made in the last ten years'.

But then what *did* constitute a 'British' film? The only officially recognized definition was so contemptible as a guide to life and manners in Britain as to be of no assistance to the NFFC's decision-makers. This was the one derived from the Film Acts 1960 to 1980 which gauged a film's fitness for registration as 'British' at the Department of Trade by the sole criterion of 75 per cent of its labour costs being rendered by British (or EEC and Commonwealth) citizens. Provided this was observed, then it didn't matter a damn if 'foreign interests' (i.e., Hollywood) contributed the cash or controlled the production company. Thus Barbra Streisand's *Yentl* (1984), shot on location in Czechoslovakia and in a British studio and set in a closed Jewish community in Poland, was an officially registered 'British' film by virtue of its labour costs – and, up to October 1984, had taken £67,721 from the Eady Levy. If one were a cynic like Wajda, one might have called it 'one of the worst Polish films made in the last ten years'.

THE MINI-MAJORS

What made Mamoun Hassan's disenchantment more painful was knowing that although the NFFC was willing to invest in more than half the budget of a project it liked, it could not afford to go the whole way. As its 1980 report had conceded, 'the Corporation's commitments have not acted as a sufficient incentive and producers have found it difficult to obtain the balance'.

But where else could producers look for finance in the early Eighties? Rank had pulled out of production in a sulk. Thorn-EMI, under their newly appointed films and TV chief, Gary Dartnall, were thankfully withdrawing from the 'blockbuster mentality' brought on by some of EMI's costliest ventures in High Hollywood. But setting up a British production programme took time — the more cautious one was (and Thorn-EMI were now very cautious) the more time it took. Verity Lambert, who was brought over from Euston Films, a subsidiary of Thames TV which had won laurels with TV series like *The Sweeney* and *Minder*, about police methods and small-time criminals in well-observed social settings, would find a dismaying number of people at Thorn-EMI who had a cautionary hand on the brake.

Then there was Goldcrest, whose policies have already been examined. But Goldcrest was becoming enamoured of the so-called 'international film'. The cost of this almost always required one to get into bed with an American partner. The most fruitful example of such a coupling was Sir Richard Attenborough's *Gandhi* (1982), a twenty-year project which its producer-director had cherished, in and out of several beds, with a messianic zeal and a political skill that was very nearly a match for its eponymous hero-saint's. It had won eight 'Oscars', including the 'Best Picture' award and that for 'Best Actor' which enabled Ben Kingsley to pole-vault to stardom as spectacularly as Peter O'Toole had done with another martyred prophet twenty-two years earlier in *Lawrence of Arabia*. But those who believed, as Mamoun Hassan did, that 'British films are social, or they are nothing,' had to be content with the illumination that 'retro-epics' like *Gandhi* shed on contemporary British attitudes. Like the mini-series *The Jewel in the Crown*, in 1984, the settings might be historical, but the feelings related to today.

HandMade Films was a curious outfit to find in this context, since the feelings *it* put its money behind related to the distinctly eccentric side of British life and manners. The operation itself was, like some of the early films it backed, small and idiosyncratic. It was based in part on the Beatles fortune of George Harrison and run by him and his American manager, Denis O'Brien, a hyphenate personality, lawyer-accountant-banker, whose enthusiasm for the Goonish side of the British had survived (but only just) a traumatic spell as Peter Sellers's manager in the early Seventies. HandMade was formed early in 1978 to rescue Monty Python's *Life of Brian* from Lord Delfont who, as remarked, was anxious to banish it from his company's production roster on grounds of possible blasphemy. O'Brien and Harrison financed the film for $2m., sold it country by country with no up-front money, and thus made some keen deals that enriched the company as well as O'Brien's appreciation of oddball British humour. At first, HandMade looked dangerously close to a second-hand operation: for it also rescued another film that had been virtually disowned by its maker, this time Lord Grade, who thought that *The Long Good Friday* (26 February 1981) was too violent to show on ATV (for which one of his subsidiary companies had made it) and wanted to censor it into bland respectability. For £700,000, the film was acquired by O'Brien — who first made sure it didn't offend George Harrison's non-violent outlook — and was released theatrically to solid success everywhere except, oddly, in America where the politics of gangsterdom might have been expected to prove appealing.

The Long Good Friday is an important 'social' movie of the times: its violence is only the bloodied wrapping paper on a hunk of fresh-cut life. It had the distinction of being almost the only film at that date to have a Tory as a hero-figure, though this must immediately be qualified by stating the Bob Hoskins's character is an example of Toryism gone to the bad and patriotism gone even further that way. Hoskins, who was established by it, like Ben Kingsley, as a supporting player of great power who could be a star in the right role, portrayed the East End criminal as capitalist — a more successful example of the Kray-type gang boss whom Richard Burton had incarnated so vividly in *Villain* ten years earlier.

A property speculator who has fought and frightened his way up from Dockland; an implacable defender of private enterprise and the profit motive; even a good disciple of the EEC engaged in launching a crooked re-development scheme with aid from the Common Market: Hoskins is a monster because his hankering for the Conservative virtues is so wildly at variance with his practice of the terrorist ones. On the day of the launching with a party aboard his Thames-side yacht, his brother is blown up in the Rolls-Royce, his best buddy murdered in the swimming baths and a bomb planted in his West End casino. As he wallows in affronted incredulity that such liberties are being taken with his 'turf', he discovers that the IRA are behind it as part of their extortion racket to raise funds for their murder campaign in Ulster.

The heavy mob preyed on by a heavier mob: *The Long Good Friday*, written by Barrie Keefe, produced by John Hanson and directed by John Mackenzie, was one of those films that converted the bloodmark of their violent genre into a watermark for their times. It was a deeply subversive political vision, implanting cynical truths in the social scene so as to turn it into a minefield that explodes in one's face. Helen Mirren, for example, is cast as a girl who once went to Benenden school with Princess Anne and now goes to bed with a public enemy, thus personifying the sexual slumming that matched the up-market trading of the turn of the decade.

HandMade had financial stakes in several other now-indigenous movies also characterized by violence of a perverse kind, *Venom*, *Tattoo*,

The Burning among them, but the Python-style comedy became the company's artistic logo and much of its profit. It backed *Time Bandits* (16 July 1981), directed by Terry Gilliam and written by him and Michael Palin, a series of absurdist glosses on nothing less than the Creation of the world, which involved a flying squad of Time-tripping dwarfs employed by a sadly fallible Supreme Being to stitch up the holes that He had had to leave in the universe.

In style a pop-up chronicle, with Gilliam's cartoonist energy as its driving force, it could have been read as a commentary on the abrasive synergism of the Pythons themselves, Messrs Gilliam, Palin, Jones, Chapman, Cleese and Idle ... 'a rambunctious, competitive assortment', as George Perry put it (though he was describing the dwarfs), 'constantly jockeying for power and each imbued with unique idiosyncracies.'* Adopting a 'slow play-off' release pattern for the US, in contrast to the 'blanket' release to which some attributed the failure of *The Long Good Friday*, but taking care to spend a reported $6m. to $8m. on promotion, HandMade grossed some $45m. with *Time Bandits* in the States alone.

But, thereafter, the Pythons lined up with a Hollywood studio, Universal, to make *The Meaning of Life* (1983) in return for a pledge of complete working freedom. One explanation offered was that HandMade's ambitious plans for them had unsettled the Pythons' 'group identity'. Thus the comedy team with the biggest money-making capacity since the Beatles disbanded passed into the American orbit. Gilliam's latest film, *Brazil* (1984), was also made for a Hollywood major, Twentieth Century-Fox.

Individual Pythons continued to make films for HandMade with funding that was independent of both the tax-shelter arrangements used by Don Boyd and the merchant-bank connections of Goldcrest. O'Brien's Euro-atlantic organization was a £5,000 company with 4,999 shares owned by a Luxembourg-based holding company, presumably primed by George Harrison's cash flow from his Beatles royalties.

O'Brien probably welcomed the respite from working with all six Pythons at once. Yet neither Michael Blakemore's *Privates on Parade* (1983), with John Cleese, nor Richard Loncraine's *The Missionary* (1983), written by and starring Michael Palin, performed as well as HandMade's investment in them warranted, although the latter, a satire on the way in which a Good Samaritan gives in to his weakening will-power in the Edwardian era and ends up a better brothel-keeper, showed not only wit, but a period design not equalled in a comedy of its type since *Kind Hearts and Coronets*. HandMade's ventures into other comedy genres, such as *Bullshot* (1984) and *Water* (1985) failed to find

*George Perry, *Life of Python* (Pavilion, 1983), p. 174.

successors to the Pythons in the comedy team of Dick Clement and Ian La Frenais.

But HandMade returned to form with *A Private Function* (29 November 1984), a brilliant comedy set in 1947 in which a black-market pig represents not only pork in an austerity Britain where everyone is emotionally as well as nutritionally undernourished, but power as well to the social climbers (Michael Palin and Maggie Smith) who hijack it. Written (as his first cinema script) by Alan Bennett, directed by Malcolm Mowbray and produced by Mark Shivas, this biliously funny film (more French gall than Ealing comedy) pitilessly itemized the purgatory of the petit-bourgeoisie historically trapped between the heaven of the gentry and the threatening inferno of the working class. The triumph of this and other of its productions confirm that, in spite of its American muscles, HandMade has a feel for the class complexities of the English social scene that no other single company has come near to emulating with such sureness and consistency.

The record companies began diversifying their film investments at the end of the Seventies. Up to then, a 'film' had meant to them simply 'concert footage'. The aim was simple and self-serving. Showing it was a way of 'compensating' fans who had been below the minimum age that local authorities set for admission to the concert before issuing a licence for it. But then Charisma Records produced the eccentric *Sir Henry at Rawlinson End* (1980) with a strawberry-nosed Trevor Howard starring in Vivian Stanshall's parody of in-bred aristocracy, and the music of the Bonzo Doo-Dah Dog Band made up the sound-track; and Virgin Films distributed *The Great Rock 'n Roll Swindle* (in which they had a £150,000 investment) and helped promote the Sex Pistols. Record companies were supposed to have a sharper awareness of where the youth audience was 'at'. After all, the same kids who bought discs went to movies: and more of them now bought discs. . . . Like most of the logic of show-business, this was sadly fallible. *Babylon* neither won a youth audience, nor promoted Awsad's reggae discs because, as Martyn Auty has surmised, reggae was already selling well in the shops and needed no 'hype' from the cinemas.* A. & M. Records invested in *Party, Party* (1983), a 'youth-pic' which Terry Winsor had 'enlarged' from his National Film and Television School apprentice film, with no fewer than 38 numbers packed into 98 minutes, though some of the tracks had to contend with the noise of the party held while the parents were out — and lost.

But the best-known music-based group to turn large-scale film producer in the Eighties has been Virgin Records. It has a high public profile due to the publicity given its owner and his most prized asset: in other words, Richard Branson, Virgin's quirky chairman, and Boy George the 'gender-bent' lead singer of Culture Club. These two hold

*Marty Auty, *Stills*, July–August 1983.

the media's attention, though it must be admitted much in the way that people do who stand on high window ledges and are urged to 'Jump!' by the crowd in the street. Branson has diversied with startling rapidity from his mail-order records business founded in 1971 into publishing, board games, video, London night-spots and a transatlantic airline. His enthusiasm knows no bounds; but whether this signifies business acumen or a peculiarly brief attention-span is debatable. Almost every published picture of him suggests a beamish persona occupying the mid-ground between the Cheshire Cat and Walter Mitty. This is, of course, no bad alloy for strength in the movie business which thrives on the hyper-active personality.

His real power base in his project is Virgin's huge revenues: it was Britain's biggest independent record company in 1984 with 10 per cent of the market. This enabled it to move swiftly into film financing and decide to put up a percentage or even the whole of the budget. No other British mini-major enjoys such freedom or, at any rate, cares to deploy it. Under Al Clark and Robert Devereux (who is Branson's brother-in-law), Virgin pumped cash into Zelda Barron's *Secret Places* (1984), an attractive if rather 'soft' offering, given the brash Branson outlook, based on the rites of passage of a girls' school in wartime England; and then into *Loose Connections* (1984), a 'road' movie of the boy-meets-girl type directed by Richard Eyre, which blunted the feminist edge of Maggie Brooks's script by misjudging the considerable charm that Stephen Rea's greater experience than his female co-star brought to what had been intended as a fairly piggish chauvinist role. Neither film did particularly well; but Virgin's investment was partially protected by having the NFFC as a partner. No more immediately successful was its venture into an Anglo-American mood with *Electric Dreams* (1984), a love story set in San Francisco with a user-unfriendly computer as the boy's rival for his girl's affections. It was expected to produce a success comparable to the reputation its director Steven Barron had established as a leading exponent of the video-clips used to promote Rock stars on the Music TV channel. A wealth of three-minute experiences, however, did not yet add up to a feature film. What gained Virgin its credible coloration as a serious contributor to the British film industry was the film of George Orwell's *1984* (11 October 1984).

THE FILM OF THE YEAR

The first shock that *1984* conveyed was that of seeing a film that did not look at all like the year of the title. That shock past, the rightness of it all had to be recognized: the date Orwell used was simply a numerical metaphor. He saw the future through 1948's bleak outlook on the Cold War: a world without plenty, people still subject to the orders of bureaucrats, a make-do-and-mend Britain where some were already more equal than others. He extrapolated the future out of the present — and saw that the future did not work. Michael Radford, who directed *1984* and wrote the screen-play, and Simon Perry who produced it, captured this basic 'datedness' in the best sense: they made a 'period' film where everyone was expecting a 'futuristic' one. Even the omnipresent TV screens, those two-way windows through which orders are barked at the ideologically slipshod, which act as watchdogs of the workers and as voyeurs spying on the sinners, are not the slick monitors of contemporary mass media but follow the curvature of old-style TV cabinets. The message on them also came from a Yesterdayworld of global wars re-fought with obsolescent weaponry over blitzscapes that recalled the look of much of Orwell's still uncleared bomb rubble: they were re-runs of the pre-missile era patriotism that Radford and Perry imagined Orwell had had dunned into him in the Second World War, as if the British Broadcasting Corporation and the Central Office of Information were united in sinister and authoritarian collusion.

The whole film was like a vast time-slip, superimposing one era on another, leaving no room to breathe for the proles caught in between.

John Hurt, the martyr-figure of the British cinema, played Winston Smith, looking like a Giacometti sculpture whose flesh has been austerely eroded down to snapping point to reveal the essence of a minimal existence. The colour of the film might have been applied by Francis Bacon: it drained people, places, life itself of their humanity in one utility palette of the shades of putrescence. When Winston and his girl were caught in flagrant nakedness by the Thought Police, their bare bodies had the pallor of the lime pits, not the glow of the love nest.

Richard Burton died not long before the film's release: but, as O'Brien the inquisitor, he looked visibly touched by his own coming mortality and additionally transfigured by an accident of dialogue that referred to it. The famous Burton voice that in its time had over-orchestrated many a dud score was now reduced to a solo instrument to pick out the dark notes of punishment and the complex syntax of 'doublethink'. The movie was dedicated to Burton: one could take it as a gesture of forgiveness to a British talent that had been prodigally wasteful of its own promise.

Not the least startling thing about the movie was the condensed production schedule it had been forced to observe in order to appear on the screen in the year to which it referred: or so its literal-minded backers insisted. Permission to make it at all was wrung from Orwell's widow (and copyright holder) only a short time before her death by an American lawyer and Orwell admirer, Marvin J. Rosenblum. The original budget had to bear the consequence of the hasty preparation, and Virgin, perhaps as a nervous reaction to its prospects of recovering its cost, dubbed portions of a score composed by one of its groups, The

Eurythmics, on to the film after its release, in the hope that, maybe, the record sales would compensate for any box-office short-fall. This was legally permissible, though it remained unacceptable to Perry and Radford. Both had to agree, though, that Virgin had been impeccably staunch during the months when the film's cost, originally 'guestimated' at £2.6m., then budgeted at £3.7m., had escalated to a final £5.5m. Despite lukewarm, or, rather, frigid reactions from the members of the American Academy who saw it at 'Oscar' nominating sessions — to the consternation of Al Clark, who was present, there were mass walk-outs and reproaches of the 'depressing' vision it offered — the film was expected to have recouped its cost at home and overseas by the end of 1985.

Radford and Perry were part of the so-called post-Puttnam wave: both had an instinct to see Britain and British film-making as part of European culture — rather than Britain as an English-speaking country not far from America. Perry, who physically resembles Puttnam on the days when his beard has not been brushed, had been a film director, a London-based reporter for *Variety*, as well as head of the National Film Development Fund — a subsidiary of the NFFC set up in 1976 to make loans for script development. It can be assumed, therefore, he had few illusions left about the film business. But he has preserved his *passion*: Radford, too, who adds slightly defensively; 'By passion, I don't mean sentiment.'*

The two had teamed up earlier than *1984* when Radford, then a television director dismayed by the impermanence of his work, asked Perry to leave the NFDF and produce his first cinema feature, *Another Time, Another Place* (7 July 1983), about a wartime romance between a Scottish farmer's wife and an Italian prisoner of war assigned to work on the land. It was a movie that had the wind of change in British films blowing freshly through it, as naturalistically as any of its outdoor scenes. It was as much about what happens when two people of different latitudes come together as about a love affair between an attractive but repressed woman in a tight-knit community and a man whose status is also that of a prisoner.

The skilfully articulated story, scripted by Radford from a novel by Jessie Kesson (who had furnished the material for his earlier prize-winning TV film *The White Bird Passes*), told how the sensual Neapolitan man helps the woman achieve her own liberation, though at great cost to his own liberty. Radford showed a capacity to elicit performances that could work emotionally on audiences; and the decision to use un-subtitled Neapolitan dialect created a closeness between film-goers and the heroine as they empathized with her attempts, at first displaying halting curiosity then wary affection, to

---

*Michael Radford quoted by Nick Roddick, *Stills*, July–August 1983.

come to terms with the stranger hungry for news of home and seeking compensation in this alien territory and people when none arrives.

For once, one felt, British cinema was on a continental latitude without the need of a co-production treaty. Phyllis Logan as the wife added a completeness as well as a conviction to her playing that no other actress in the Eighties has so far approached: she changed outwardly as well as inwardly, her face and her performance seeming to bend life her way and take possession of it. Measured against the young Vanessa Redgrave, she was more than equal — and she has maybe more to offer if British cinema will give her the chance, and the parts.

CHANNEL 4

By far and away the most stimulating addition to the sources of independent finance for film-makers in the early Eighties was the new television network, Channel 4. As noted earlier, it differed from the other networks in one relevant aspect: it was a 'publisher', not a 'producer', and thus benefited from the tax advantages of investing in the programmes, including films, that other people made for it. Its intention was to release certain suitable films in cinemas, establish them as theatrical films and use the exposure gained (and, one hoped, the favourable reviews) to commend them to TV viewers at a later date. These last two words were, of course, to cause much contention among film-makers: for how much 'later' would the TV screening be? If it were too close to the theatrical release, there would be a reduced pay-off for the makers: not just in box-office terms, but in the more sensitive, intangible and probably more jealously desired area of 'reputation'. For reputations were still made on cinema screens: whatever the audience shrinkage, the publicity achieved by a cinema film was flatteringly wide; its credentials (and those of its maker) were established in a bigger league than the home runs scored on the 'box in the corner'; and the film's exposure ensured the ripples of attention did not die away in a night and the morning after, as was the case of the 'one-off' TV film. Exposure of this nature was called a 'window'.

After the initial enthusiasm of finding a patron like Channel 4 had subsided, argument inevitably ensued about how long the window should be kept open. Within Channel 4 itself there was a difference of opinion. Jeremy Isaacs, its chief executive, was said to be more sympathetic than some of his subordinates, particularly among the commissioning editors, to the understandable desire of film-makers to have a generous amount of big-screen time before the window is shut: against that was the view that Channel 4 was not in business to keep Britain's cinemas in business. It was a dilemma that is still unresolved, though its unfairness will be mitigated, according to Isaacs, when

Channel 4 has sufficient number of films to feed the greedy schedules with re-runs, thus giving new productions more exposure in the cinemas, if they justify it. That, of course, depends on the business they do; and the truth is that film-goers from very early on in the Channel 4 policy of patronage got wise to the fact that a film so billed would appear on TV soon enough to save them buying box-office tickets.

The two main cinema circuits remain far from well disposed to the idea of playing such movies. For one thing, exhibitors had a loose 'understanding' not to book movies backed in whole or part by television: a hangover, no doubt, from the days when certain producers were threatened with the black list if they sold their cinema-financed films to television. Once at least, Channel 4's own impatience frustrated a more realistic attitude on the part of some exhibitors. One Channel 4 film which had done very well in the few independent cinemas where it had opened was about to be tried out at some thirty Rank-owned cinemas of the better class: in addition, some 3,000 video cassettes of it had been ordered. Within days of a Channel 4 announcement that it would be screened on television in the coming months, the Rank cinemas lost their enthusiasm for it and the cassette order fell to under 300.

Nevertheless, British cinema's 'revival' (as it had begun to be called by 1983) owed much of its reality to this channel; and certain film-makers owe their established reputations to it, too.

In 1981, its first year before transmissions began, Channel 4 commissioned twenty films from independents on a co-production basis, though these included movies (like David Puttnam's *First Love* series made in association with Goldcrest) which at that time were intended for TV exposure only. The films began reaching cinema screens — and foreign film festivals: where the best of them started the 'word of mouth' that alerts the world grapevine very quickly to the fact that something is stirring. Colin Gregg's *Remembrance* (1982), a highly naturalistic sailors' 'odyssey' set in the rowdy purlieus of Plymouth in the hours before the Fleet sailed on Nato manoeuvres, won the top prize at the Taormina Film Festival; and its good reception in Britain wasn't hindered by what would be called the 'Falklands Factor' which persuaded Buckingham Palace to send for it, presumably to help Her Majesty feel closer in spirit to her son, Prince Andrew, then on battle duty in the South Atlantic. The Queen's reaction to this rowdy picaresque movie went unrecorded: but the gesture helped Channel 4, if not the Fleet.

Skolimowski's *Moonlighting* found godfathers in Channel 4 and Michael White after being turned down by the NFFC (it and *Remembrance* both acknowledged a pre-production lifeline thrown by the National Film Development Fund). *Moonlighting* shared the 'Director's Prize' (with Herzog's *Fitzcarraldo*) at Cannes in 1982. Karl Francis's *Giro City* (1982: in association with Rediffusion Films) was set in Ulster and

Wales and explored the opportunism of politics in national and local government (and, to its credit, in television news coverage). Barney Platts-Mills's Gaelic folk-tale, *Hero,* was generally judged an indulgent aberration on the part of someone in Channel 4. Then the Channel, as film-makers say, 'got lucky' — spectacularly lucky. Two films it backed showed that virtue was not to be its only child: it would foster virtuosity, too. In order of their commercial release in Britain, they were Neil Jordan's *Angel* (5 November 1982: in association with the Irish Film Board) and Peter Greenaway's *The Draughtsman's Contract* (11 November 1982: in association with the BFI Production Board.)

Jordan, a young Irish novelist, had John Boorman's benevolent guidance as executive producer for his compelling re-working of the Ulster tragedy in terms of a *film noir* that never once mentioned politics but found in that province's heart of darkness a thematic parallel with Boorman's first Hollywood film *Point Blank.* It pushed its young sax player (Stephen Rea), who has witnessed a terrorist killing at a local country 'hop' in South Armagh, into a cross-country crusade of vengeance that sucks him, like a Chandleresque Private Eye, into the nihilism of meaningless violence and almost destroys him. It was one of those rare creations in British cinema, a truly conceptual film on which nothing is imposed but out of which everything can be read; it placed Jordan at the top of the newcomers' league. Like Kubrick, he has a strong literary element in his film-making — the language is non-naturalistic, but in a way that enhances naturalism not disrupts it — and, like Kubrick again, his camera-eye for images of disturbance yet beauty is potent.

His second film, *The Company of Wolves* (20 November 1984), also recalled Kubrick in the way Jordan deliberately turned his back on critics' expectations of what he would do next — what he did do was as original as *Angel,* if totally different. His movie situated the fantasy world of fairy-tales, in particular Perrault's *Little Red Riding Hood,* at the point where their cautionary lessons overlap and are in conflict with the inhibited desires analysed by Freud and the archetypal myths categorized by Jung. His script collaborator, Angela Carter, offered her own compressed fables for Jordan's imaginative expansion the way Nabokov had offered his *Lolita* for Kubrick's witty transposition of obsessive lust into frustrated desire. *The Company of Wolves* confirmed Neil Jordan as the most imaginative film-maker of the Eighties with the most to offer British cinema — provided he stays a part of it. It was financed, at a reported £2.25m., from two main sources. One was Palace Pictures, a vigorous new multi-media company headed by Nik Powell, a former partner of Richard Branson at Virgin. The other was ITC Entertainment, the subsidiary of Lord Grade's ACC empire which had been so brusquely taken over by Robert Holmes à Court, and which thus made its return to mainstream movie-making with more critical (but also more unobtrusive) success than any of the films it had produced under its former lord and master.

If Jordan took Raymond Chandler as the inspiration for his moral structure, Peter Greenaway, in *The Draughtsman's Contract*, took Agatha Christie as the model for his engaging seventeenth-century tale of murder and detection in the manor house. What raises it far above Christie, of course, is its deliberate 'unfairness': it is not a mystery meant to be solved — for one thing, many of the clues are simply not present — but a lesson in how to look at so-called reality and yet miss the all-essential part of it. Antonioni and *Blow Up* spring to mind: for the twentieth-century fashion photographer's random snapping of what could have been a murder in a London park is replicated, *mutatis mutandis*, in the seventeenth-century landscape artist's sketching of the random elements in the scene that could add up to the crime. What neither he nor Antonioni's hero see, because of their 'blind' eye, is their own come-uppance. Both record everything and understand nothing.

The metaphysics that Greenaway thus handled so fluently were translated into a visual elegance seldom equalled in the ordinarily prosaic British cinema. Scenes became visual essays on the various interpretations of 'reality' without losing their topographical exactness to time and place — even the baffling figure of the male nude 'living statue' which appears from time to time and, at one point, pees from its plinth in lieu of a fountain for the entertainment of the alfresco diners, is based on the fashion of penny-pinching seventeenth-century land-owners to press their servants into impersonating the classical nudes of Greece, rather than spend money in freighting the real thing over to their ancestral acres. It was also a very English film in the sense that the 'outsider' is made the victim of society — 'manners makyth murderers' is the legend one half expected to see graven on its end titles. It would have pleased the radicals in Channel 4.

Originally, the film had a 'final basic' budget of £305,000: it escalated to some £320,000, which compared favourably with the £410,000 for Jordan's film, but was considerably over the original calculations. Such sums, though, were heady ones for the Production Board to be handling, even at a time when its head, Peter Sainsbury, admitted that 'the "experimental cinema" which we supported in the mid-Seventies hadn't even been finding minority audiences'.[*] The decision had therefore been made by the Board to concentrate on low-budget feature films suitable for theatrical release in which recognizable people spoke to others of like appearance, occasionally making successful contact. The BFI has continued this policy, sometimes with Channel 4 participation — as in Christopher Petit's *Flight to Berlin* (1984: also in association with West German TV); and sometimes not — as in Edward Bennett's

---

[*]Peter Sainsbury interviewed by John Hopewell, *AIP & Co.*, March 1984.

Ascendancy (1984), an imperfect conjunction of a *Return of the Soldier*-type plot and a fashionable and historically inexact attempt to pin the blame for Ulster's 'Troubles' on the Protestant 'ascendancy', which nevertheless took first prize at the 1983 Berlin Festival.

For one dangerous moment 'BFI' seemed to stand for 'British Film Industry'. Alan Parker saw the danger of this in the encouragement it might give the Government to close down the NFFC and substantially increase the BFI's subvention to supply the 'British' element in the nation's film industry. 'What irritates me', he said, 'is that people forever on the periphery of the creative process seem to have had the loudest voice of late.'* To Parker, it appeared as if Anthony Smith, the BFI's director, had already begun speaking for the NFFC! Smith was probably more aware of the danger the BFI ran if it seemed to be so successful — at least in the eyes of Lord Gowrie, the Minister for the Arts, whose department supplied the BFI budget. Questions might be asked about whether the BFI was serving art or commerce. Such was the prevailing Tory orthodoxy that the BFI's funds might in fact be *reduced* if commerce seemed to be coming out top. Indeed the amount of the BFI's grant from public money was in bizzarre contrast with the nugatory Government pocket-money doled out to the NFFC and, if it proved anything, it confirmed that bureaucratic structures founded principally to look after the past (like the BFI) are more-favoured children of the State than small businesses struggling to finance the future (like the NFFC). In 1970–1 the BFI's grant was £524,004; in 1974–5 it had risen to £1,537,000; in 1980–1 to £5,829,000; and in 1982–3 to £8,469,000. In 1983–4, which was to be effectively the NFFC's last year of active existence, the NFFC's principal source of income, from its share of the Eady Levy, was a beggarly £1,500,000.

Perhaps it was consciousness of this shameful disparity that accounted for the hasty withdrawal of the BFI from seeming to invite people to view it as an 'alternative NFFC', for Peter Sainsbury felt himself compelled to state: 'The BFI's production division is not and will not ever be in the business of attracting and building up commercial investment in the British film industry. It is in the business of providing . . . arts subsidy.'** In other words, the film unions who might also have been raising their demands for wage-scales in keeping with a commercially minded BFI were told to back off; and the Minister for the Arts was reassured that the BFI production facilities were not going to put themselves on a Big Business footing and have to forfeit public subsidy. Small may be beautiful: it is also safer.

---

*Alan Parker interviewed by Nick Roddick, *Stills*, July–August 1983.
**Peter Sainsbury, letter in *AIP & Co.*, April 1984.

THE GREAT BRITISH CARVE-UP

In mid-1983, a movie appeared that recorded the temper of the times in Britain with unusual precision and an historical truth that will be even more valued as history takes one further away from the time of the Falklands War against which the events in it unfolded. It was *The Ploughman's Lunch* (26 May 1983: backed by Channel 4, Goldcrest and Michael White). To have the war itself as a background mood on which to project the up-front deceit in society was the sort of marvellous luck that sometimes attends bold enterprises like this, begun with an idea of topical relevance but pushed unexpectedly by events into contemporary significance. For Ian McEwan and Richard Eyre, writer and director respectively, it meant constantly revising the screen-play during shooting so as to take advantage of a quickly-breaking political event in real life like the Falklands War that cynically illuminated the very thesis of their film — how so-called 'history' is constantly in a state of 're-writing' according to how the Establishment wishes to interpret the past so as to justify the present. The texture of the film was London in the Eighties: its pattern was composed of political cynicism and human opportunism. No wonder it was not altogether loved, particularly by people of the Left who felt an injurious (and, they felt, unjust) bias at work in the way it exposed the self-centredness of a working-class boy whose skills lie in the manipulation of people and events to his own advantage. In an engrossing way, it recalled *Room at the Top* updated to the Eighties.

The personable but badly flawed young man on the make was this time played by Jonathan Pryce. Far more self-assured and socially mobile than Laurence Harvey's town-hall clerk in the 1959 film, he works in media, not municipal government: a BBC news editor hungry to cut himself out of the anonymous pack of journalists in Broadcasting House. He does a smooth selling job on an even smoother publisher (David de Keyser) to write a history of the Suez crisis of 1956 — a revisionist project calculated to 'sell' the book to the Americans in the light of their own disastrous Vietnam interventionism. The time is spring 1982. As Pryce's progress takes him through the next few months, exploiting upper-echelon media people, denying his own *petit-bourgeois* upbringing, but ultimately being out-manoeuvred in creepiness by an even crawlier cynic (Tim Curry) from the Sunday newspaper world, the Falklands War erupts, peaks, is won and turned to the political advantage of much more eminent people with a similar interest in fabricating history. The climax arrives when Pryce (like Laurence Harvey) gains the material goods, but is left with an emotional blankness. It takes place at the 1982 Tory Party Conference: the first British film in which fictional characters mingle solidly with the famous faces they were covertly filmed among — Paul Johnson, for example, is apposetely caught in transit from left to right by the camera. Mrs Thatcher is seen and heard delivering her post-victory peroration to 'the spirit of Britain at her best . . . rediscovered in those spring days . . . but never really lost'.

It is just such an ironic resonance that made *The Ploughman's Lunch* the most politically conscious film for many years — one that in the run-up to the 1983 General Election might have made an impact on the voters, if only it had been more widely screened. For 'the spirit of Britain' as here exemplified, is simply part of the calculating 'self-service industry' which those on the make — and that includes almost everyone in it — never cease to manipulate. Pryce's girl-friend (Charlie Doré) is a spoilt, unfeeling bitch employed at London Weekend TV. ('I don't trust anyone: that's what comes of working in television,' she says. Replies her laconic lover: 'We're different in radio.') His pursuit of her is in the interest of self-advancement as much as pleasure, since her mother is a once-famous left-wing historian privy to the Suez secrets who now inhabits an affluent country-house surrounded by 'Keep Out' signs. 'The way to the daughter is through the mother, up the Suez Canal,' cracks the Iago-like Curry. But the older woman, like her counterpart in *Room at the Top,* proves the meatier bed-mate. Played by Rosemary Harris, she is the film's only character with any values. Inevitably, they are nostalgic ones for her Socialist past which Pryce's quest rekindles among the household comforts she enjoys in her bourgeois present. She venerates what she sees as his historial integrity, but ravishes his flesh — which is just as pliable as his mind. When both play her false, her self-hatred is almost as lethal as Simone Signoret's crashing to her death on the emotional rebound from *her* faithless lover.

But *The Ploughman's Lunch* was not just a film about betrayal. It was about the exploitative, fraudulent, manipulative skills of the Eighties encapsulated in the very title. For the 'ploughman's lunch', as explained by Harris's husband, an advertising agency executive (Frank Finlay), was the creation of a publicity campaign in the Sixties to get more people to eat 'pub grub' by associating it with the manly, rural virtues of an England-that-never-was. It is a fabricated lie: such as, it is suggested, the history of the Falklands War will become.

McEwan's original screen-play was inspired by Eyre's telling him the history of a 'ploughman's lunch'; so, as McEwan said, 'the idea of a false past was there before we knew what we were going to put in it'.* In retrospect, he could quote Milan Kundera: 'The struggle of man against tyranny is the struggle of memory against forgetting.' In the months following the film. Tam Dalyell's obsessive parliamentary pressurizing of the Prime Minister and her Cabinet members about the sinking of the Argentine warship, *General Belgrano*, at least served the same 'lest we

*Ian McEwan, quoted by John Wyver, *Stills*, July–August 1983.

forget' ethic that the film underwrote. As Eyre said; 'It is generally about bad faith. That you can think one thing and do another.' One of the most telling moments was when Pryce stumbled on a 'squat' outside an American air base which resembled the Greenham Common encampment, then a daily feature of the newscasts; even the radiant sincerity of its anti-nuke mothers and housewives, half day-crèche and half Doomsday warning, fails to stir his conscience into self-reproach. It was thus a pessimistic film, for it offered no hope of moral reformation and no avenue of escape from the closed circle of deceitfulness that constituted public life. Its nominally left-wing hero played along. For this reason, too, it was actively disliked by left-wingers: it was not an accident that it was omitted from the official list of films for British Film Year 1985–6.

But if one wishes to understand the snakes-and-ladders feel of Britain in the first years of the Eighties, it is to be found in the social scene portrayed by this subversive film, from publishers' parties in Bloomsbury (where hands rape the passing drinks trays, but scarcely a word is uttered about the book of the moment), through the 'power lunches' at Langan's Brasserie, the morning confabs in the BBC news-room which arrange the world's agenda with splendid superciliousness, the cocktail-shaker gossip at the Zanzibar, the 'conspicuous waste' of the spacious Barbican Centre betokening the last of the Seventies splurge before the Tory cut-backs came, right to the polytechnics where Atari video-games have been added to the furnishings of the academic mind.

It was odd, perhaps ominous, that the two films which dealt with contemporary issues, *1984* and *The Ploughman's Lunch*, should share the same basic fear of living in a society that re-wrote the past in terms of the present. The multi-cubicled scribes in Orwell's bureaucracy pasted the approved versions of history into the Party scrapbook: the media smoothies in the Eyre-McEwan picture re-wrote the past for their own advancement in the power game. Each film presented a different perspective, but it was of the same view — a Britain becoming ever more subordinate to the authoritarian view of things.

THE TAXMAN GIVETH, THE TAXMAN TAKETH

So much creative turbulence in the film industry in the early Eighties was not of course entirely due to the accidental conjunction of opportunity and talent: between these two ingredients, the connection was — money. It in turn had been made more available than it usually was by a change of the tax rules. Prior to 10 August 1979, money spent on making films was normally treated as deferred revenue expenditure. It was written off by agreement with the Inland Revenue over a period of years, starting with the release of the film. Lenders of production finance could not claim capital allowances: their advances would be allowed against revenues only if they were made for the purpose of a trade carried on by them. But in August the Inland Revenue changed the rules. Effective from 10 June 1979, film production expenses were eligible for capital allowances. The change of practice related to expenditure on production, not to loans; but the change was a huge fillip to film-making. Movies became 'plant' and could be treated as assets and written off in full in the first year. At first, only individuals were permitted to do this: in 1980 individuals were disqualified, but not companies. Profitable trading groups quickly began to show an interest in backing films; and leasing companies started to extend the same facility to films as they were used to extending to plant and machinery. In general, the City favoured leasing rather than investment: it lessened the risk and was cheaper than borrowing when bank interest was high.

Alan Stanbrook described how the game worked.* The bank buys the product — i.e., lays out the money that enables the producer to make the film — and is thus able to write off the cost in full against its own profits in the first year. The bank (or financing company) then leases the film back to the producer on relatively cheap terms, sharing the tax-avoidance benefits with him. The producer, or lessee, has already sold the film to the distributors on terms which made him a profit and cover the cost of leasing the film back. To avoid fluctuating interest rates, the investor buys a future at a price he initially pays, thus locking today's exchange rate into the money he will not be receiving for some time. Originally this applied to a wide range of films, by no means all of them British. As usual, a measure intended to help the *British* producer was used, and abused, so as to enrich still further the American film-maker. One case which became common knowledge, even inside the Inland Revenue, referred to a subsidiary company of one of the big British banks which actually bought a 'future' in $100m. of American-financed movies, including an American blockbuster then being made in Britain. The leaseback arrangement enriched both parties to the deal and the entrepreneur who acted as go-between is said to have received his 'finder's fee' of one per cent, which amounted to a useful million dollars.

Such cases are amplified by hearsay: they become industry legends. Unfortunately, they can become Inland Revenue talk, too; and this case, as well as other evidence of downright abuse by which several parties were each claiming 100 per cent 'write-offs', led to the exclusion of all films not registered as British. This still left a lot of pickings for the British-based Hollywood companies, who found the arrangements even more attractive than their share in the Eady Levy — whose total was

Stills, July–August 1983.

shrinking with the yearly drop in admissions, while its payout was now limited to £500,000 tops for any one British feature. Moves to abolish a jackpot that the British dispensed to those with the knack of operating the money machine were inevitable. On 9 March 1982, the Chancellor of the Exchequer announced that 100 per cent capital allowances would remain in force for two more years only. He later relented slightly and extended the deadline in 1987. Later still, in March 1984, he thought again and decided to reduce the permitted percentage in stages forthwith.

This was dispiriting news, except to that small community of people who are not themselves creative, but have the time and aptitude to find loopholes in legislation the world over that will benefit someone, somewhere — and themselves all the time. They simply started looking for new 'opportunities'. The actual film-makers were distraught. But the heaviest blow was still to come: in the middle of 1984 it fell on them like an Old Testament plague.

A hint of what was on the way had appeared in January 1983, when Iain Sproat announced the suspension of the 1927 quota that compelled cinemas to show a minimum percentage of British films. Losing the quota wasn't exactly ruinous: it was already ineffectual in protecting British cinemas from American domination — many cinemas in 1983 were desperate for more 'domination' from the people who had brought them *E.T.* and *Rocky III* — or dissuading British companies from investing abroad. Quota regulations were already worm-eaten by elaborate exemptions. Few would miss it. But when the Government announced, in July 1983, that it was starting a major economic review of the film industry, alarm bells began ringing. The Conservatives had made no secret — but rather boasted — of their intention to see subsidized undertakings pass into private hands. How ruthless they could be emerged one General Election, two Films Ministers and a great deal of fretful waiting later. In July 1984, Kenneth Baker's White Paper, *Film Policy*, effectively knocked down every structure that film-makers had sheltered under.

Away with the Eady Levy! It hadn't much life left in it, anyhow. But abolishing it meant cutting the slender lifeline that supported the NFFC — which was at that very moment in the middle of its biggest investment programme in years with six pictures in stages of production, underwritten by the regular Eady income that the Government had promised to dole out to it. It was now to be put out of business as a subsidized entity, only to be called back into being as a privatized one. 'Valuable work' . . . 'many notable films' . . . 'fostered talent'. . . . Mr Baker's praise of the NFFC in the Commons, on 19 July 1984, sounded like a coach who praises his swimmer for performance while holding his head underwater. The NFFC was to be replaced by a company financed jointly by Thorn-EMI, Rank, Channel 4 and the British Videogram

Association, a body representing video cassette companies which was to fail lamentably in its campaign to stop the insidious Video Recordings Act, passed in December 1984, which gave the British censor statutory power over the moving image for the first time in history. These four ill-assorted bodies had agreed to contribute £1.1m. annually for three years 'to part-finance low-budget feature films involving largely British talent' — a two-minute egg, if ever there was one! The Government also undertook to give £1.5m. a year for five years to co-finance films with the new company. This tatty arrangement with its short shelf-life was an earnest of official faith that the '[successor company] will preserve the positive functions of the NFFC, while at the same time being enhanced by the dynamic of private enterprise'.* This was the language of hypocrisy, not realism. To sweeten the deal further, the NFFC's assets — primarily income from past and current recent successes bringing in some £200,000 a year — would be made over to the new body.

And so it came to pass that Rank, which had pulled out of film production after failing so miserably in it barely five years before, and Thorn-EMI, which had expended so much British money vainly trying to 'crack' the US market, became two of the heirs to the longest-sustained and most honourable output of British film-making. The shamelessness of this manoeuvre was only enhanced by its timing. At the very moment Mr Baker was handling over the NFFC's patrimony, the Monopolies Commission's report on the supply of films to cinemas was repeating earlier criticism of the obstructionist attitudes of the Rank and EMI duopoly. In addition, Rank was even then defying the wishes of the Office of Fair Trading, which had asked it to take part in a six-month experiment designed to let popular films reach the screens of independent cinemas before the big circuits had sucked them dry of box-office life. But since the Government's 'privatization' proposals depended on financial goodwill from combines like Rank and Thorn-EMI, there was little either had to fear — and once more the issue of monopoly that had undercut the viable basis of an independent film industry was shelved.

To expect four companies like these to agree on a film production programme, even granted an independent chairman, was an improbable notion. Mamoun Hassan detected 'a massive opportunity for conflict of interest'. He asked 'what would stop the major companies who were investing in the NFFC's privatized successor from using money to support their own projects? And who would have the vital television distribution rights for the films which were part financed by the new company?'**

Film Policy, White Paper Cmd. 9319, July 1984.
**Mamoun Hassan, interviewed by Nicholas de Jongh, *The Guardian*, 26 July 1984.

Responsibility for the National Film and Television School was also shuffled off on to 'the dynamic of private enterprise' — i.e., a charitable hand-out from the BBC, the ITV companies and the cinemas of £600,000 a year for five years only. The BFI Production Board's Eady allotment of £125,000 a year 'should cease entirely at the end of 1984'. The board needn't now worry about keeping its budgets artistically low: the BFI's director doubted whether there would be any budgets at all in future.

Oddly enough, the White Paper proposed a modest increase, to £500,000 a year for five years, in the funds used as 'seed money' for budding film scripts administered by the NFFC's subsidiary, the National Film Development Corporation. This was considered by many to be an act of aberration rather than generosity: if it meant anything at all, it was that the money was there to pay for scripts, but not to turn the scripts into films.

Another rather unexpected beneficiary of this almost wholly quixotic policy was the Interim Action Committee on the Film Industry which Harold Wilson had set up seven years earlier. It had issued a number of useful informative reports on various aspects of films or, rather, 'moving images' as it had been forced to call them in its remit, since video was now a part of its discussions on the last Thursday of each month. To its surprise, the committee was promoted into the only body that would henceforth 'represent' the film industry, a non-statutory successor to the Cinematograph Films Council which became a victim in the frenzy of abolition gripping the Government. Many of Lord Wilson's members smiled cynically to themselves — this one included. For, over the years, they had had good reason to suspect that successive Film Ministers wished to see them cease to be. Indeed, at one time, a half-hearted attempt was made by Whitehall mandarins to 'starve' the committee of the few residual secretarial services it continued to enjoy after the retirement of the senior Civil Servant who had previously managed its agenda. It was a minor moment in the history of the committee, but one that deserves recording since it was so symptomatic of Whitehall's attitude, official and unofficial, towards films, when the young secretary from the Department of Trade looked up from his Minute-taking during a particularly pessimistic spell of heart-searching by members about their future. Surveying some fifteen of the most powerful people in politics, films, the BBC and ITV companies, the law, science and industry, he reminded them that without the minimal aid he was giving them, they would cease to exist in the eyes of his overlords. 'You're here because I'm here,' were his words. In the shameful tombola that constituted the White Paper on the future of British films, it seemed foolish to seek any deeper reason why some were spared and others were axed.

RENAISSANCE OR REMISSION?

At the very moment the Government was dismantling the British film industry, and putting only short-term, prefabricated structures in place of it, the industry itself announced that it was going to celebrate 'British Film Year'. It all looked like the last reel of an Ealing comedy. The brainchild of the Association of Independent Producers, the BFY, was officially scheduled to run from March 1985. The aim was to show a selection of British films in UK cinemas and overseas; and to get enough people going back into the cinemas to raise the admission figures by four per cent. A modest enough target: but when the 1984 drop in admissions was being projected at 34 per cent by *Screen Digest*, a piece of wish fulfilment of this nature did not look remotely like being fulfilled. The twenty-one films* chosen to represent what was dubbed 'The Revival Years' also caused dismay in some quarters — particularly among those left out. But they had a point. Not one film was included by any of those 'uncomfortable' directors noted for their highly critical look at today's Britain. No *Jubilee*, no *Britannia Hospital*, no *Babylon*, no *Ploughman's Lunch*; no woman director's work, though Sally Potter's *The Gold Diggers* was eligible; no truly low-budget work by an independent director except *The Draughtsman's Contract* — where was Terence Davies's autobiographical trilogy that the BFI had just honoured as the most original of all the films shown at the National Film Theatre in 1984? Excellence *was* represented, but not controversy. Thirteen were 'period' films — set before or during the Second World War — unlikely to cause any social, political or cultural upset if screened abroad. It seemed to some that the National Film and Television School, whose staff chose the list, should be in the business of training not young film-makers, but young fogeys.

In other respects, too, this ill-timed toast to the 'Revival Years' — the first five of the Eighties, it could be gleamed from internal evidence — sowed confusion where one might have hoped it would shed illumination. What a 'British' film was, is or should be was nowhere defined. But blame should not lie too heavily on anyone for that omission: it was exercising a lot of people in 1985 when the Government published a consultative Green Paper in February 1985, seeking views from interested parties on whether the sale and rental of audio and video copyright material should bear a levy; and, if so, how it should be distributed to copyright holders.

Film people saw hope here for making good the Government's depredations into their traditional sources of finance. Sums around

*The list comprised: *Another Country; Another Time, Another Place; Chariots of Fire; The Company of Wolves; The Dresser; The Draughtsman's Contract; Educating Rita; The Elephant Man; The French Lieutenant's Woman; Gandhi; Gregory's Girl; Greystoke; Heat and Dust; The Hit; Local Hero; The Life of Brian; The Long Good Friday; Merry Christmas, Mr Lawrence; Moonlighting; Pink Floyd – The Wall; Tess.*

£30m. were tantalizingly quoted as the potential yield from such a levy — the way that box-office estimates were mentally totted up before the film had even opened. If such funds could be used to finance 'British films', then the future wasn't so bleak after all. The trouble was, the copyright holder in most cases would turn out to be a production company not necessarily interested in recycling its coup among the deserving artists who made the film or even putting it back into a new film; and in many cases, it would be the British subsidiary of a Hollywood company — and so the old abuses of the Eady Levy would be resurrected and British tax-payers, rather than British film-goers, would be contributing to the greater financial comfort of Hollywood.

But wait — what if the levy were paid into a central fund and then doled out *only* to films that could confidently — well, plausibly — be categorized as indigenously British in look, attitude or content . . .? Where previously the only criterion recognized by the Department of Trade had been quantitative — the proportion of labour costs — the criterion would now be qualitative. Though the Treasury disliked recycled taxes and the film industry disliked artistic judgments, the future of independent film-making in Britain might come to depend on their acceptance of just such a plan.

Apart from the proposed successor company to the NFFC, and some of the newer groupings already noted, the power posts in film-making in Britain still rested in the hands of foreigners, mainly American though not exclusively so. The British offices of American majors were a source of finance that could flow bountifully, but also be turned abruptly off — as had happened in the Seventies. Goldcrest had entrusted its production roster to an American, Sandy Lieberson, valuing his proven 'international' outlook that was quickly reflected in his choice of subjects and stars: among them, *Revolution*, about the origins of the American War of Independence (with Al Pacino) which could certainly be said to have a British dimension; and *The Mission* (with Robert De Niro) about the Jesuits in the Spanish conquest of South America, which was rather more problematical although Robert Bolt had written the screen-play, David Puttnam was producing and Roland Joffé directing.

As the memory of its American disasters faded off the balance sheet, Thorn-EMI seemed set for a second attack. In March 1985 it announced a $175m. fund backed by twelve international banks to invest in twenty films annually aimed, said an executive, 'at the factory worker aged forty-two in Cincinnati.' The 'grand illusion' of 'cracking the American market' persisted! Another American, Denis O'Brien, seemed successfully set on cornering the market in British comedy, but could his HandMade company examine more contentious issues of British life?

Another large slice of the film industry which could have transformed the scene in earlier years passed into the control of two Israelis, Menahem Golan and Yoram Globus, whose fast-growing Cannon

Group paid £7m. in 1982 for the 128-screen of Classic cinemas that had been owned by Lord Grade's ACC for a short period before it hit the *Titanic* iceberg. Independents in the past had hankered for the cash flow that the Classics took: with that circuit as the basis for independent film financing and exhibition, they might have given Rank and ABC a battle for audiences. Now the chance was lost. Disposed by temperament and ambition to think in Hollywood terms, the Cannon bosses were hardly likely to contribute any 'revival years' to British cinema — it had not escaped comment that the Government's plan for the NFFC's successor had not been based on the premise that the ownership of this cinema chain, which might benefit from its future film production, should contribute to its liquidity. This was perhaps understandable. 'From a commercial angle (their) record seems more than acceptable,' wrote one commentator, '(but) scarcely any movie that Cannon has yet made will figure in any serious film history.'*

Another one-time asset of the independents had also changed hands. So many battles had been fought over the ownership of Shepperton Film Studios that it had come to seem like a national shrine rather than a dream factory. In 1984, Mills and Allen, the financial services and money-broking group, sold it to Lee Electric (Lighting), a film and TV company, for £3.6m. The NFFC's preference share, giving it a qualified say in Shepperton's future, would presumably accompany the rest of the NFFC's goods and chattels when they were bestowed on its successor company. But it was typical of the exhaustion reached by all who had had anything to do with the studio that had once spearheaded independent production in Britain, that the Government's White Paper did not get round to even mentioning this last, much-fingered card that the old NFFC had held.

So, as the decade neared its half-term, one could be forgiven for wondering whether one had been invited to attend a feast or a wake. A feast by the amount of talent in evidence: a wake by the amount of despondency. On the one hand, the industry was planning an official celebration: on the other, it was rending its garments and tearing its hair. Did the 'revival years' signify a true renaissance, or would they simply be a deceitful symptom of remission that would make the coming collapse even more bitter to witness? Britannia Hospital was still open for business: but that perpetual patient, the British film industry, needed to have a lot of faith in the doctors treating it.

*Alan Stanbrook, *Stills*, June–July 1984.

Industrial Chronology 1970 to 1985

An asterisk indicates that a film is made for a British, or preponderantly British, production company and distributor. Films unmarked indicate existence of American interests.

1970

Admissions fell in 1969 by over 22 million, but increase in box-office prices resulted in higher gross takings, up from £57.6m. in 1968 to £57.69m. in 1969. MGM announces its British studios will make between 10 and 12 films a year, but this does not allay rumours of imminent studio closure. Smaller American companies in Britain start slowing down production in response to 'ever changing market' and over-stocked Hollywood inventories.

Closure of MGM's British studio announced in April: MGM to link up with EMI's facility and guarantee annual £175,000 subvention. Call for NFFC to acquire MGM studios: but Films Minister announces it has no power to do so. British Lion's studios at Shepperton hard hit by American cut-back: profit reduced from £65,534 to £46,848.

NFFC proposes consortium in August to finance films on *pari passu* basis. ('Several merchant bankers are at the edge of the water, but haven't got their feet wet yet' — John Terry, NFFC managing director.) NFFC has functions extended till end of the decade and is promised £5m. to refresh kitty for loans to film-makers.

Government grant to British Film Institute rises to £524,004. In December Sir Joseph Lockwood, EMI chairman, says: 'I think we have got the situation under control. It's a little more risky than ordinary business. But we shall not allow ourselves to lose lots of money in film production.' Disagreement breaks cover at Elstree's EMI studios over kind (and profitability) of films produced by Bryan Forbes as production chief.

Despondency thickens as year ends. Although 70 films are in production in 1970, their budgets are smaller, their shooting schedules shorter, more are made on location. Columbia is only American major in Britain to maintain former level of production with six films; United Artists, only two; MGM, three; Paramount, two; Universal and Twentieth Century-Fox, none at all.

But outlook not so black for some: Rank Organization announces all time high in profits of £15,060,000 for year ending June 1970, increase of 31 per cent on 1969, most of it due to investment holdings in Xerox copiers.

British films premiered during the year included: *David Copperfield; The Looking Glass War; The Reckoning; Twinky; The Birthday Party; Spring and Port*

Wine; * *Anne of the Thousand Days; The Last Grenade; The Magic Christian; The Sea Gull; On Her Majesty's Secret Service; The Bed-Sitting Room; Entertaining Mr Sloane; Kes; Hamlet; The Walking Stick; Julius Caesar; The Adding Machine; The Executioner; Hoffman;* * *Leo the Last; Ned Kelly; The Virgin and the Gypsy;* * *And Soon the Darkness;* * *The Games; The Man Who Haunted Himself;* * *Cromwell; Fragment of Fear; The Buttercup Chain; Bronco Bullfrog,* * *The Sisters; The Body;* * *Figures in a Landscape; Scrooge; The Private Life of Sherlock Holmes; Ryan's Daughter; The Railway Children;* * *There's a Girl in My Soup; Perfect Friday;* * *Loot.* *

1971

Year opens on a patriotic note: *Battle of Britain* declared top British box-office film of 1970 'especially among men'. Pessimism soon restored: 67 films made in Britain last year, against 76 in 1969, 93 in 1968.

In February MGM in association with EMI announces it was prepared to spend $13m. (then worth £5m.) on film-making in Britain, part of last year's quid pro quo for closure of MGM British Studios.

New film censor, Stephen Murphy, appointed in March in succession to John Trevelyan. In same month Bryan Forbes resigns from £40,000 year job as production chief for EMI Films at Elstree after making 11 films at cost of £4m. Production fund revenue from Eady Levy now running at £4m. a year: British Film Institute grant from Government tops £750,000.

In June Films Minister, Nicholas Ridley, announces Government aim to withdraw from financing film production and allow NFFC only £1m. on condition private sources put £3 for every £1 from public funds. In the event, NFFC would obtain commitments from eleven private groups of only £750,000 to float its consortium.

British Lion showed net profits of only £61,259 against £171,051 in 1969–70. Overseas (i.e., US) investments in British films cut from £31.2m. in 1969 to £17.5m. in 1970. Profits of EMI collapse in year ending June 1971 down after tax from £10,515,000 in 1970 to £5,427,000, but film exhibition side contributes £4,146,000 against £3,875,000 in 1969–70.

National Film School opens at old Beaconsfield Studios in October with twenty-five students. In November Star Group tries to gain control of British Lion in reverse take-over: the bid was £9.5m. Cinema admissions in 1970 dip by 7 per cent to 198.7 millions, exactly the same percentage decline as in 1969.

British films premiered during the year included: *The Music Lovers; Murphy's War;* * *Performance; The Raging Moon;* * *Take a Girl Like You; 10 Rillington Place; Assault;* * *Percy;* * *A Severed Head; Bartleby;* * *Country Dance; Dad's Army;* * *Get Carter; Hotel Paradiso; Jane Eyre; The Last Valley; Tales of Beatrix Potter;* * *Up Pompeii,* * *Black Beauty; Melody;* * *Connecting Rooms;* * *Wuthering Heights; Sunday, Bloody Sunday; The Devils; Puppet on a Chain; The Abominable Dr Phibes; King Lear; Vanishing Point; Blind Terror; The Go-Between;* * *Unman, Wittering and Zigo; And Now for Something Completely Different; Doctor Jekyll and Sister Hyde;* * *Fright;* * *I, Monster;* * *Please, Sir!;* * *Straw Dogs; Gumshow; Mr Forbush and the Penguins;* * *Up the Chastity Belt;* * *Bloomfield; Villain.*

1972

EMI announces in January plans to spend £1.5m. on expanding num
screens in its ABC circuit. Deepening outcry over cinema violence as Kubrick's
A Clockwork Orange opens and embroils censor in public row: 'ultraviolence'
becomes the 'in' word.

Great despondency in the film studios: total of £8,440,000 invested in film
production in first quarter of 1972 compared with £39,220,000 in same period
previous year. Government grant to BFI running at £940,921. Government
decides to give NFFC £1m., even though private resources can muster only
£750,000. Lord Rank dies in March, aged 83.

Closure of Shepperton Studios rumoured, but averted when take-over tycoon
John Bentley makes bid of £5.45m. for British Lion, which shows a loss of
£1,064,638 for year ending March 1972. Bentley proposes sale of part of
Shepperton for property development.

Lord Longford's pornography report published in September and greeted
with mixed scepticism and derision. US investment in British films via UK
subsidiaries falls to £14m. Admissions in 1971 dipped to 176 millions.

British films premiered during the year included: *Living Free; Carry On at Your
Convenience;* * *Diamonds Are Forever; A Clockwork Orange; Dulcima;* * *Family Life;* *
No Blade of Grass; One Day in the Life of Ivan Denisovich; * *200 Motels; The Boy
Friend; Under Milk Wood;* * *Antony and Cleopatra; Doomwatch;* * *Steptoe and Son;* *
Mary Queen of Scots; The Nightcomers; Time for Loving; * *Welcome to the Club; Bleak
Moments;* * *Chato's Land; A Day in the Death of Joe Egg; Follow Me; Kidnapped;
Running Scared; Sitting Target; Vampire Circus;* * *All Coppers Are ...;* * *Carry On
Matron';* * *Catlow; Loving Memory;* * *Rentadick;* * *The Ruling Class; The Darwin
Adventure; The Moon and the Sledgehammer;* * *My Childhood;* * *Asylum; Baffled!;
Mutiny on the Buses;* * *Pulp; Tales from the Crypt; Young Winston; The Alf Garnett
Saga;* * *Endless Night;* * *Savage Messiah; Dr Phibes Rises Again; Dracula; Images;* *
Innocent Bystanders; The Ragman's Daughter; * *Neither the Sea nor the Sand;* * *The Triple
Echo;* * *Miss Julie;* * *Lady Caroline Lamb; The Amazing Mr Blunden;* * *Carry On
Abroad;* * *Alice's Adventures in Wonderland; The Pied Piper.*

1973

Michael Deeley and Barry Spikings, partners of Stanley Baker, join Lion
International to head new entertainment division in January. Rank group profit
increases by 37.6 per cent.

Vavasseur take over John Bentley's Barclay Securities in February, thus
gaining British Lion and Shepperton. Michael Deeley takes over as managing
director of British Lion in April, with Barry Spikings as board member,
announces intention to make British Lion first company producers turn to.

EMI, separated from MGM after financial differences, announces it will set
up own distribution arm in Britain and, in May, announces seven films in £5m.
package. Government grant to BFI increases to £1,360,000.

Only six films in production in Britain in July, a drop from sixteen during
first week of June 1972. Lew Grade announces he is expanding into film
production. In November film unions withdraw opposition to redevelopment of
Shepperton, including work-force cut by half.

Cinema admissions in 1972 reached a new low of 156.6 millions. Britain suffers power crisis at year's end with three-day week imposed, staggered electricity cuts and temporary closure of some cinemas.

British films premiered during the year included: *The Offence; Skin Flicker;* * *Fear Is the Key;* * *Ooh . . . You Are Awful; Our Miss Fred;* * *Adolf Hitler: My Part in His Downfall;* * *Baxter!;* * *The National Health; England Made Me;* * *That'll Be the Day;* * *The Day of the Jackal; A Doll's House* (Garland);* *Hitler, The Last Ten Days;* * *O Lucky Man!; The 14; A Doll's House* (Losey);* *Live and Let Die; Steptoe and Son Ride Again;* * *Voices;* * *The Hireling;* * *Night Watch; Don't Look Now;* * *The Final Programme;* * *Man At The Top;* * *Carry On Girls;* * *Digby; The Mackintosh Man; The Double-Headed Eagle.* *

1974

Year opens with bad news for exhibitors: United Artists preparing to lease first six Bond films to television for £850,000 ('largest sum yet involved in British TV deal'). Estimated that the films have taken more than £3m. in Eady Levy. Cinemas compensated during energy crisis by early close-down of TV transmissions and slight drift-back to movies. Rank announces 38 per cent pre-tax increase in group profits.

In February Vavasseur runs into cash-flow troubles, shares suspended, doubts gather over British Lion and Shepperton holdings. Government grant to BFI rises to £1,537,000.

In June Barry Spikings named chairman of reconstructed Shepperton. Vavasseur also 'reconstructed'. Bernard Delfont knighted in June for 'services to charity'. Threats of wealth tax being introduced cause prominent film people to start packing their bags. Admissions fall to 134.2 millions in 1973.

NFFC loses £457,244 on previous year's business, second highest deficit in its history: only one film (*Stardust*) approved for production out of 134 scripts submitted. Lew Grade announces multi-million dollar production programme. Shepperton loses £469,000 (including redundancy costs of £360,000) in past trading year: Elstree said to be losing £900,000 a year.

British films premiered during the year included: *Soft Beds, Hard Battles;* * *The Optimists of Nine Elms; Swastika;* * *Frankenstein and the Monster from Hell;* * *Mahler;* * *Swallows and Amazons;* * *Zardoz; Dead Cert; Venom; The Tamarind Seed; Carry on Dick;* * *11 Harrowhouse; Gold; Confessions of a Window Cleaner; The Internecine Project;* * *Percy's Progress;* * *Stardust;* * *Vampira; Can You Keep It Up for a Week?;* * *Murder on the Orient Express;* * *My Ain Folk;* * *The Odessa File.*

1975

Stephen Murphy resigns as film censor after four years, compared with predecessor's thirteen. Shepperton Studio losses much diminished, but Rank group profits fall and Elstree cuts work-force by 49 per cent. All three major studios are without films shooting at end of January. Agreement so sell British Lion to Deeley and Spikings. Admissions rose to 138.5m. in 1974.

In May second enormous package of films is announced by Lew Grade. British Lion becomes wholly independent outfit from end of June. James

Ferman appointed as film censor in June. Huge emigration of stars and other key production executives to avoid effect of Denis Healey's new taxes.

Prime Minister Harold Wilson sets up working party to report on ways of reviving film industry. Government increases BFI budget to £1,862,000. In December British Lion and EMI go into partnership with Columbia for *Nickelodeon* production: first venture to co-producing in American-made movies.

In December Prime Minister's working party reports and advises immediate cash injection and a British Film Authority. Lew Grade announces production-distribution link with General Cinema Corporation of Boston.

British films premiered during the year included: *The Abdication; Akenfield;* * *All Creatures Great and Small;* * *Blue Blood;* * *The Land That Time Forgot; Little Malcolm and His Struggle Against the Eunuchs;* * *Ransom;* * *Alfie Darling;* * *Bedtime with Rosie;* * *The Wilby Conspiracy; A Bigger Splash;* * *Brother, Can You Spare a Dime?;* * *Monty Python and the Holy Grail;* * *Paper Tiger;* * *Tommy; The Stud;* * *Brannigan; Knots;* * *Out of Season;* * *The Return of the Pink Panther; The Rocky Horror Picture Show; Royal Flash; Confessions of a Pop Performer; Hennessy; Overlord;* * *Mister Quilp; The Moon Over the Alley;* * *The Romantic Englishwoman; Lisztomania;* * *Great Expectations; Inserts;* * *Autobiography of a Princess;* * *Barry Lyndon.*

1976

Year opens with knighthood for Richard Attenborough. Reaction to report of P.M.'s working party on the film industry is mixed: 'Abysmal' — Michael Winner; 'Good as far as it goes' — David Puttnam.

In February Rank reports a slump of £2m. in film profits from over £3m. in 1974 to under £1m. in 1975 in production and exhibition, Pinewood Studios and even group's film laboratories; cinema interests outside London's West End described as producing 'virtually nil' and attendance at Rank cinemas down by 8.4 per cent. Bingo and dance halls, on the other hand, showed £3m. profit.

Association of Independent Producers holds first meeting in February: founded in January by Richard Craven and Simon Perry 'to encourage production . . . and to broaden the base of finance and exhibition'. In March Sir Harold Wilson announces NFFC to be given £2.37m. immediately. AIP calls for all of it to be spent on 'realistically budgeted' films: 'It would make possible fifteen medium-budgeted pictures a year.' Cinema admissions fell to 116 millions in 1975. Government grant to BFI rises to £2,514,000.

By April studios beginning to exhibit signs of general resurgence of American-financed film-making in Britain. Huge Hollywood-made hits (e.g., *The Godfather*) held partly responsible for renewed overseas investment, but also collapse of pound Sterling to $1.82. Elstree fully booked with *Star Wars* and *Valentino* to follow; *The Pink Panther Strikes Again* being shot at Shepperton; Pinewood shooting *Space 1999* and *The Avengers* mini-series.

In May it is announced EMI are to buy British Lion and Deeley and Spikings are to join the board of EMI Film Distributors 'effectively ensuring the succession to Nat Cohen, chairman and chief executive'. Peerages announced in May for Sir Bernard Delfont and Sir Lew Grade, knighthood for John Terry.

In August EMI formally takes over British Lion; Lord Grade tells ACC shareholders that company's film future is 'excellent'. In August it is announced ex-P.M. Sir Harold Wilson will chair Interim Action Committee on the Film Industry.

Decline in cinema audiences gathers momentum — down to 55.86 millions in first six months of 1976 as against 68.10 millions in same period of 1975. Britain slumps to sixth place in overseas markets for Hollywood films. In December Barry Spikings leaves for Hollywood to firm EMI investment plans in American production.

British films premiered during the year included: *Carry On Behind;* * *Conduct Unbecoming;* * *Man Friday; The Homecoming; In Celebration; Luther; The Maids; The Man Who Fell to Earth;* * *Winstanley;* * *It Shouldn't Happen to a Vet; The Likely Lads;* * *Shout at the Devil; The Slipper and the Rose;* * *Aces High;* * *Bugsy Malone;* * *Sweeney;* * *Carry On England;* * *Sebastiane;* * *The Ritz; The Incredible Sarah.*

1977

Statistics show number of films registered as 'British' in 1976 fell to 64, as against 65 in 1975. One hundred and twenty-seven American films were registered — twice as many as in 1975. In February EMI announces multi-million dollar programme of films to be shot in the USA.

Cinema admissions in 1976 fell to new low of 103 millions. Government grant to BFI rises to £3,480,000. EMI announces Michael Deeley will leave for Hollywood to oversee its film production there, Barry Spikings remaining in London. In April David Puttnam leaves for Casablanca Film Works, Hollywood, to produce films there under $12m. rolling production fund. *Superman,* a $25m. production officially registered as 'British', moves into Pinewood Studios: great rejoicing at the return of the Americans.

In April AIP proposes all Eady Levy money should be paid into central fund and shared out among investors, with producer's share being credited to next film: no notice taken. Interim Action Committee on the Film Industry, chaired by Sir Harold Wilson and comprising eighteen members, is named in April. Goldcrest Films constituted in the same month.

Lord Grade announces new $125m. production package at Cannes Film Festival in May. Obscene Publications Act is extended in July to bring film exhibition and distribution under its jurisdiction. In August NFFC announces that of the £2.37m. unfrozen by the Government the previous year, nothing now remains for financing films due to repayment of interest debt and prior commitments. Remainder will be frozen until April 1978. Sir Michael Balcon dies in October. First rumours of Lord Grade's film-making running into difficulties begin to be voiced in November.

EMI reports group profits up by over 26 per cent before tax: pre-tax profits from film division up from £5.6m. to £7.2m. Company gives £5,000 to AIP to help reduce latter's £25,000 overdraft: sum to be paid over two years.

In December first rumours break of EMI running into financial difficulties with bodyscanning machine in USA. Partnership between Lord Grade's ACC and General Cinema Corporation of Boston dissolved in same month.

British films premiered during the year included: *The Squeeze; Emily;* * *Hedda; Eclipse;* * *Not Now Comrade; The Brute;* * *The Butterfly Ball;* * *Jabberwocky; James Dean — The First American Teenager;* * *Joseph Andrews; A Bridge Too Far; The*

Cassandra Crossing; Nasty Habits; The Spy Who Loved Me; Confessions from a Holiday Camp; * *Black Joy;* * *Equus; March or Die; Portrait of the Artist as a Young Man; Valentino; Before Hindsight;* * *The Duellists;* * *Voyage of the Damned.*

1978

Year opens with announcement that, due to increased tax burdens, no principal photography on *Moonraker*, the next Bond film, will be done in the United Kingdom. Wilson Interim Action Committee publishes first report, recommending establishment of British Film Authority to absorb representative industry bodies and NFFC financing functions.

American majors now back in force: Twentieth Century-Fox announces big British programme, including *Star Wars* sequel, *The Omen*, *Julia*, etc., representing £18m. investment. Lord Grade sets up ITC Entertainment to distribute his films in Britain. EMI group profits suffer disastrous drop in first half of 1977 — down to £8,599,100 for first six months, compared with £16,578,000 for corresponding period of 1976: but film and leisure division doing well.

Lord Delfont refuses to finance *The Life of Brian* on grounds of possible blasphemy. Cinema admissions in 1977 were 103 millions, the same as for 1976: box-office gross rose with inflation from £79m. to £89m. Government grant to BFI rises to £3,900,000. In April Michael Meacher, Films Minister, announces Government not yet ready to set up British Film Authority.

Lord Grade announces his customary multi-million dollar ($120m. this time) film programme at Cannes, including *Raise the Titanic*. Sir John Terry, managing director of NFFC, announces his retirement in June. Rumours thicken over EMI's future American film investments: Deeley and Spikings deny in August any intention to quit EMI. David Puttnam, who had returned to Britain from USA and was completing Casablanca Film Works contract, turns down post as Columbia Pictures European Production chief.

Don Boyd, backed by Roy Tucker's Rossminster group, announces ambitious film package in September, including *Honky Tonk Freeway* to be made in USA for EMI. John Schlesinger returns from America to shoot *Yanks*, first film in Britain in eight years, but backed by American and German money. Director Alan Parker and producer Alan Marshall sign three-picture deal with Twentieth Century-Fox.

Cubby Broccoli, shooting *Moonraker* in three Paris studios, denounces British tax penalties. ('They're throwing people out of Britain.') In September Barry Spikings quoted as saying his future with EMI is 'a long-term one'. Michael Deeley rumoured to be on point of leaving EMI. ('Something may happen in the New Year: we shall have to wait and see about it.')

Death in September, aged 61, of George 'Bud' Ornstein, inspirer of many American-backed British New Wave films of the Sixties: see *Hollywood, England*. In October Lord Delfont announces Michael Deeley will be moving to a 'more flexible' position after March 1979, as an independent producer. EMI's profits crash to £25.9m. before tax compared to £64.7m. previous financial year. Sales of bodyscanner machines account for loss of £13m. Company position rumoured to be precarious.

In November EMI and ACC announce link-up to distribute films in USA through Associated Film Distribution Corp: chairman, Lord Grade; vice-chairman, Lord Delfont. Mamoun Hassan appointed in November as managing director of NFFC. Much hope pinned on Government's new Films Bill to re-finance NFFC to tune of £5m.

British films premiered during the year included: *East of Elephant Rock;** *Jubilee;** *The Four Feathers;** *Tomorrow Never Comes; Hamlet;** *Pressure;** *The Stud;** *The Hound of the Baskervilles;** *The Medusa Touch; Midnight Express; The Shout;** *The Wild Geese;** *International Velvet; The Big Sleep; Revenge of the Pink Panther; A Walk Through H;** *Death on the Nile;** *My Way Home;** *Carry on Emmanuelle;** *Stevie; The Thirty-Nine Steps;** *Force Ten from Navarone; Who?; The First Great Train Robbery; Superman.*

1979

Details of Eady Levy made public for the first time: *The Wild Geese* scoops up £138,984. NFFC pinning its hopes of funds on Government's Film Bill currently passing through Commons committees. In February Lord Delfont begins production of *SOS Titanic* to the annoyance of brother Lord Grade and his film *Raise the Titanic*. Lord Grade's ACC buys Classic cinema chain (141 screens) for £12,690,000 to give his films exhibition outlet. Admissions rose in 1978 to 127 millions. Government grant to BFI rises to £4,724,000.

February Eady Levy breakdown reveals British-made short *Hot Wheels*, distributed with *Grease* and wholly owned by British subsidiary of Hollywood major, has taken £98,135 to date (It would eventually gross £200,000). Rank announces profits in March held to almost the same level as previous year: £123m. as against £124.8m. Leisure division jumps from £6.3m. to £10m., of which cinema interests account for £3.7m.

In March EMI announces a $50m. film production programme. In May NFFC-backed films, *The Europeans* and *Black Jack* representing Britain at Cannes Festival while Films Bill, which former Labour Government had almost completed, languishes in wake of Conservative victory at May General Election. Department of Trade announces a review of all Government film policies, creating apprehension and further delay in re-financing NFFC.

Virgin Films makes its production debut in June with *The Mike Oldfield Space Film*. June sees second report, on film financing, by Wilson Interim Action committee. Barry Spikings succeeds Lord Delfont in June as chairman and chief executive of EMI Films and Theatre Corporation, the holding company for all EMI entertainment. Lord Delfont becomes chief executive of EMI.

Cash crisis in EMI and consequent offer to sell half of music division to Paramount for £70m. much-needed cash flow for new investment after 18 months losses in medical, electronics and record divisions. NFFC is granted a reprieve in July with promise to write off its debt and give it annual funding from Eady Levy in return for eliminating dependence on Government funding.

August brings good news: a film is now to be considered 'plant' by Inland Revenue, entitling makers to qualify for 100 per cent capital allowance write off. Peter Beale appointed managing director of EMI Films Ltd., in August, ('I think it is the best job in the British film industry.')

EMI crisis in September as offer to sell half of music division to Hollywood major falls through. Disastrous profits fall announced in October: EMI group results for year ending June 1979, reveal profits crashed from £25,973,000 to £10,822,000. Music division down by 22 per cent. Only leisure division (including films) shows increased profit. Lord Delfont reaffirms film production not affected by cash crisis. EMI rejects October bid by Thorn Electrical of £147m. (Thorn profits in 1978 were £117m.) In November, EMI caves in and accepts Thorn take-over bid of £169m. Take-over officially completed by June 1980.

British films premiered during the year included: *The Passage;* * *The Riddle of the Sands;* * *Tarka the Otter;* * *The Water Babies; The Class of Miss MacMichael; Firepower; The Lady Vanishes;* * *That Summer; Escape to Athena; The Muppet Movie; Eagle's Wing;* * *Hanover Street; Alien; The Bitch;* * *Quadrophenia;* * *Scum;* * *Yanks; Monty Python's Life of Brian; Radio On.* *

1980

EMI's *Honky Tonk Freeway* begins shooting in the USA in February. *The Jazz Singer*, another EMI-backed American film, reported hitting budgetary troubles. Ceiling of subsidy that any single film can draw from Eady Levy fixed at £500,000 in February.

In March Department of Trade guarantees bank loans to NFFC of up to £1m., enabling it to continue trading until restructuring promised for 1981. Rank reports rise in group profits from £122m. to £131m., but film division shows slump. Cinema admissions fell in 1979 to 112 millions. Government grant to BFI rises to £5,829,000. Interim Action Committee's third report, on cables and video, presented in March focuses attention on satellite broadcasting. Chancellor of Exchequer, in March budget, extends to companies the capital allowance privileges hitherto enjoyed by individuals: a film is henceforth classified as 'plant' — great fillip given to domestic production.

Films Bill published in April (becomes law in July) extending life of NFFC, writing off debt, giving it an annual subvention of £1.5m., or 20 per cent of Eady Levy, whichever is the greater. EMI follows ACC lead in making films available to TV after three years instead of the five hitherto required by exhibitors' associations.

Rank announces at Cannes Festival in May it is increasing its investment in feature films by £12m. Lord Grade announces further films at Cannes amidst reports of *Raise the Titanic* hitting serious financial difficulties. Monopolies and Mergers Commission announces in May that it intends to probe supply of films to Rank and EMI circuits to determine whether lack of competition is against public interest.

In June Rank surprises film industry by announcing it is pulling out of film production. (*The Economist* reports story under headline, 'Copier Company Quits Films'.) In July Peter Beale, deputy to Barry Spikings, quits job one year short of contract expiry to return to independent production. EMI's $20m. production *Can't Stop the Music* one of biggest recent flops at American box-office.

Eight films released by AFD in America between 1979–80 gross $42m., of which all but $4m. came from *The Muppets Movie. Raise the Titanic* opens in US at end of August to disastrous business. Lord Grade granted salary increase of £12,646 in August, making total of £207,854 annually. ACC's borrowing up by almost £46m. on previous year, part of it due to purchase of Classic cinema circuit from Laurie Marsh's Inter-european company for nearly £13m.

In November Lord Delfont relinquishes office as head of EMI's entertainment and leisure division. In December, Department of Fair Trading refers supply of films for UK exhibition to Monopolies and Mergers Commission. Feature film production in UK falls to 38, against 61 in 1979: investment also shows fall from £94m. to £70m.

British films premiered during the year included: *The Human Factor; Bad Timing;* * *Rising Damp;* * *Black Jack;* * *The Custard Boys;* * *Rude Boy;* * *Silver Dream Racer;* * *SOS Titanic; The Tempest;* * *Hussy;* * *Sweet William;* * *Breaking Glass;* * *The Great Rock 'n Roll Swindle;* * *The Secret Policeman's Ball;* * *McVicar;* * *Prostitute;* * *The Awakening;* * *Babylon;* * *The Shining; That Sinking Feeling;* * *The Dogs of War; Flash Gordon; Sir Henry at Rawlinson End; The Falls;* * *Little Lord Fauntleroy; The Mirror Crack'd; The Long Good Friday.*

1981

Lord Grade denies in January that boardroom manoeuvres in ACC are forcing him to take a back seat or that film plans will be hit by low half-year profit forecast. ('Our commitment to production remains as strong as ever and anybody who surmises otherwise is an idiot.') Same month sees re-shuffle at Rank, ending with departure of Ed Chilton who had brought Rank back into short-lived, unprofitable film production. Gloom is deepened by sliding Rank profits — down to a pre-tax £111.2m. against £131.2m. — attributable in part to pull-out from film production.

In March AFD is officially closed down in US: all product to be distributed by Universal. Lord Grade quoted as saying: 'I am absolutely delighted . . . we feel that the contribution of AFD's extensive programme of films along with the experience (of Universal) will result in great success to us all.' Cinema admissions for 1980 fall to 96 millions. Government grant to BFI rises to £5,829,000.

In April 21 film-makers (including Schlesinger, Boulting Brothers, Forbes, Losey, Lester) sign a 'Save Our Industry' open letter after figures show the fewest British movies ever playing in cinema — 32.4 per cent of cinema programmes in 1980 was devoted to British or EEC-related movies, as against 36.8 per cent in 1979.

EMI announces a $60m. production programme in May, mostly American-made movies. In July Goldcrest Films International spawns Goldcrest Films and TV Ltd., production company with Jake Eberts as head. Jack Gill, Lord Grade's 'heir apparent', departs ACC suddenly in September: Lord Grade speaks of company's 'exciting future' in the 'revolution that's sweeping the country' — i.e., cable, Pay TV, video, satellites. . . .

Brian North, mens-wear executive, appointed managing director of EMI Films: quoted as saying he cannot remember when he last saw a movie. Lord Grade sells his last six movies (some as yet unproduced) to Universal for reported £20m.: they include *A Man from a Far Country; On Golden Pond; Barbarossa; The Last Unicorn; Dark Crystal;* and *Sophie's Choice.*

In November Lord Grade closes ITC international selling and UK distribution arms, both ACC subsidiaries. Australian tycoon Robert Holmes à

Court buys 50 per cent of ACC non-voting shares for £6m. ('Well, it shows he has got great faith in the company' — Lord Grade.) *Screen International* comments that Grade empire has gone from 'vertical integration to virtual disintegration'. In December Barry Spikings speaks of his 'five-year plan' for Thorn-EMI film-making.

British films premiered during the year included: *Superman II; Chariots of Fire; Green Ice; Tess;* * *The Disappearance; Gregory's Girl;* * *Clash of the Titans; Quartet;* * *For Your Eyes Only; Time Bandits;* * *The French Lieutenant's Woman; Memoirs of a Survivor;* * *An American Werewolf in London; Absolution; Lady Chatterley's Lover; Maeve;* * *Priest of Love;* * *Venom.*

1982

Lord Grade compelled to relinquish control of ACC as Holmes à Court prepares take-over bid. Holmes à Court's bid challenged by Gerald Ronson of the Heron Corporation: law suits and counter-bids drag on for weeks. In March budget, film leaseback deals are dealt a death blow by Chancellor Sir Geoffrey Howe who cancels 100 per cent write-off. Later, relents slightly and permits a two-year transitional period.

Great jubilation as *Chariots of Fire* wins four awards at April 'Oscars' — 'The British are coming', vows its screen-writer Colin Welland. Cannon Group buys ACC's Classic cinema circuit for £7m. in April. At end of month Lord Grade ceases to be director of ACC, now owned by Holmes à Court, and only remains deputy chairman of ITC Entertainments.

Alarmed by media campaigns against video 'nasties', British Videogram Association in association with British Board of Film Censors plans self-censorship scheme to ward off parliamentary action. Plan falls through and Video Recordings Act of 1984 will establish first legally backed censorship in Britain for video cassettes.

In July Lord Grade, having finally quit ACC, begins at Embassy Communications International's London operation as chairman and chief executive. Jerry Perenchio, co-founder (with Norman Lear) of Embassy says: 'Some people are old at 40. He is ageless.' ACC's new group managing director Bert Reuter says: 'We are staying in the business but doing it in a more disciplined way.' Films Minister Iain Sproat vows wide-ranging review of all film legislation going back for 70 years. Admission fell to 83 millions in 1981. Government grant to BFI rises to £6,520,000.

Goldcrest announces that before Oscar award to *Chariots of Fire*, in which it has pre-production money, it had approached 73 City institutions to raise film funds without success: a second whip-round after the awards now raises £9.4m. With £13.1m. from parent company Pearson Longman, chairman James Lee expresses optimism for future plans.

Increasing unease about Government's intentions: 'The British film industry is under threat,' says NFFC annual report. New film censorship certificates introduced in autumn imposing bars at age limits 15 and 18 and introducing PG (parental guidance) rating. In October Euston Films production chief Verity Lambert to join EMI Films as production chief. Barry Spikings's contract a year still to run.

Commons Report on Public Funding of the Arts recommends grouping all arts, including films, under a single Minister of Cabinet rank: absolutely no notice taken of it. Channel 4 starts transmissions in November 1982. As year ends, industry is shocked by reports of Government's intention to abolish NFFC, Cinematographic Films Council and Eady Levy. Apocalypse now!

British films premiered during the year included: *The Secret Policeman's Other Ball;* *Victor/Victoria; Evil Under the Sun;* *Friend or Foe;* *Britannia Hospital;* *Remembrance;* *Burning an Illusion;* *Pink Floyd — The Wall; Moonlighting;* *Brimstone and Treacle;* *Who Dares Wins; The Draughtsman's Contract;* *Privileged;* *Scrubbers;* *Gandhi; Hero;* *Giro City;* *Trail of the Pink Panther.*

1983

Barry Spikings departs Thorn-EMI in January 'by mutual agreement'. Verity Lambert, brought over from Euston Films, tipped to assume charge of EMI production programme. Goldcrest announces it has $70m. commitment to TV and films.

Rank's pre-tax profits in 1982 fall from 1981 high of £102m. to £61.5m. due largely to reduced yield from share in Xerox. Film division and Pinewood Studios do well. Hopes for sales to US, given fillip by American cable TV, suffer set-back with news of discontinuance of the Entertainment Channel in February. Thorn-EMI announce production slate in February of six films, four for UK production, two for US. ('We're going to be making films in Britain, but they've got to have themes and subjects which are international.' — Verity Lambert.)

Ban called for on video 'nasties'. In March AIP demand levy on all media showing films in order to raise estimated £35m. annually for film production. In April Embassy Communications buys video and TV rights to *Gandhi* 'in perpetuity' for North American market. *Gandhi* wins eight 'Oscars' in April awards ceremony.

Government gives go-ahead for 12 pilot schemes in cable TV. Gary Dartnall appointed executive chairman of Thorn-EMI Films and Thorn-EMI Video. Cable enthusiasm high: in June Goldcrest joins in rush to 'cable up' Britain. Monopolies and Mergers Commission's report opposes 'banning', but expresses unwillingness to divest Rank or EMI of substantial number of cinemas to form 'third circuit' as 'impractical'. AIP call report 'too weak, too late and totally inadequate'.

· Virgin Films establish claim to be mini-major with £14m. production programme in August. Cinema admission in Britain fell to 60 millions in 1982. Government grant to BFI rises to £7,014,000 (plus supplementary grant of £1,456,000). Thorn-EMI combines films and video divisions to form a 'united front'. NFFC steps up investment in September with six new pictures: *Loose Connections; Another Country; Secret Places; The Company of Wolves; Dance With a Stranger; Defence of the Realm.* Investment of £4.5m. became possible because other commitments had not been picked up. ('For the first time we can invest in a portfolio of films, not just one at a time.' — NFFC managing director Mamoun Hassan.)

AIP proposes a 'Year of the British Film' to start in 1984. In November Graham Bright MP introduces Video Recordings Bill to curb so-called video 'nasties' by requiring all videos to be licensed, including estimated backlog of 6,000 titles. Bill gets first reading in December.

Jake Eberts leaves Goldcrest to join Embassy International in December with intention of expanding production by a further four to six films a year. Sandy Lieberson, formerly Ladd Company's chief in London and ex-partner of David Puttnam, replaces Eberts at Goldcrest.

British films premiered during the year included: *Looks and Smiles;* * *Heat and Dust;* * *The Return of the Soldier;* * *The Dark Crystal; The Missionary;* * *Party, Party;* * *Privates on Parade;* * *Enigma; Local Hero;* * *Eureka; Merry Christmas, Mr Lawrence;* * *Ascendancy;* * *Educating Rita; The Wicked Lady; Monty Python's The Meaning of Life; The Ploughman's Lunch;* * *Octopussy; Another Time, Another Place;* * *Superman III; Betrayal;* * *Bullshot;* * *Oliver Twist; Krull; Never Say Never Again; Biddy.* *

1984

Forty-two films shot in UK, or British-crewed, in 1983, compared with 52 in 1982. Excluding three films with blockbuster (American) budgets (*Never Say Never Again; Greystoke* and *Octopussy*) total investment was £180m. compared with £230m. in 1982. Rank group pre-tax profit for 1983 up by 12 per cent at £69.3m.

Bombshell dropped in March with Budget announcement of immediate phasing out of capital allowances for films: from 100 per cent to 75 per cent from 14 March to 50 per cent from April 1985; to nil after April 1986. Flurry of activity results to take advantage of last ten days at 100 per cent. ('A savage blow . . . will snuff out the reviving confidence in the production of British films' — AIP.)

In March Michael Deeley, formerly EMI production chief, joins Consolidated Productions (films and TV) as chief executive officer. Growing anxiety manifested in April at Video Recordings Bill's possibilities of extending video censorship to cinemas. Cinema admissions rose in 1983 to 64 millions. Government grant to BFI rises to £7,128,000.

Industry collects its forces in late April, engages a professional parliamentary lobbyist, prepares to persuade Government to 'think again' on abolition of capital allowances. In May Goldcrest Film and TV ceases to be subsidiary of S. Pearson, becomes independent entity and raises £22m. on market to double output: makes first profit of £900,000.

Plans for British Film Year unveiled at Cannes festival: Government to give £250,000. Mamoun Hassan resigns from NFFC in June over Government's plans to dismantle and privatize film industry. Hopes being pinned on Prime Minister's intervention on behalf of industry to modify Treasury's tax changes.

Further blows in July with publication of 18-page White Paper abolishing Eady Levy, privatizing NFFC. Levy yielded £4.8m. in 1983 and contributed £2.7m. of this to makers of British-registered films. Government action ironically attributed to success of Channel 4 in stimulating independent production! Shepperton Studios sold in August to Lee International for £3,675,000. Rank Organization refuses to take part in non-barring experiment requested by Office of Fair Trading (in light of recent Monopolies Report).

Disenchantment running high by September with Government's plans for cable — due to publication of much tighter than anticipated regulations. No 'licence to print money' this time round. In October Goldcrest announces $75m. production slate; Virgin announces a $20m. production budget.

In December Thorn-EMI offers investors opportunity to participate in five upcoming features by issuing £36m.-worth of shares in them: films are *A Passage to India; The Holcroft Covenant; Dream Child; Morons From Outer Space; Wild Geese II*. Will repeat plan, if successful. Fifty-three features made in UK in 1983, increase of 11 on previous year.

British films premiered during the year included: *Champions; Curse of the Pink Panther; Almonds and Raisins;* * *The Dresser; Loose Connections;* * *Yentl; The Gold-Diggers;* * *Bloodbath at the House of Death;* * *The Country Girls;* * *Fords on Water;* * *Greystoke — The Legend of Tarzan Lord of the Apes; Reflections;* * *Secret Places;* * *Another Country;* * *Mehmed my Hawk; Supergirl; The Bounty; The Hit;* * *Laughterhouse;* * *The Company of Wolves;* * *The Bostonians; Cal;* * *Electric Dreams;* * *P'Tang Yang Kipperbang;* * *Those Glory Glory Days;* * *Forever Young;* * *A Private Function;* * *A Christmas Carol; Give My Regards to Broad Street; The Killing Fields;* * *1984;* * *Success Is the Best Revenge.* *

1985

Films Bill, dismantling Government subsidies to industry, comes under all-party attack as it progresses through Parliament. Films Minister Norman Lamont implacable, believing British film-makers will welcome 'free market'. Levy on old movies on BBC and ITV also officially opposed. Green (consultative) Paper issued on whether to exact levy on blank and pre-recorded video-tapes in order to compensate copyright holders for home copying. Film industry spokesmen welcome idea if levy money used to fund British film production: otherwise, 'copyright holders' will turn out, in many cases, to be British-based American companies and worst features of abolished Eady Levy will continue.

In March Thorn-EMI announce planned $175m. fund to finance about 20 features annually, backed by 12 international banks. Target audience stated to be 'the factory worker aged 42 in Cincinnati'. British Film Year officially launched mid-March by Variety Club luncheon at luxury hotel amid allegations of British-based American companies not contributing their share. Government has to inject extra £75,000 to permit plans for overseas screening of films in 'Revival Years' section.

Rank reports surprise 65 per cent December-February increase in admissions; Thorn-EMI likewise state attendance up by 51 per cent in the same period. Increase attributed mainly to American blockbuster films *Gremlins*, *Ghostbusters* and *Beverly Hills Cop*, as well as strong if limited showing of successful British comedy *A Private Function* and British-made social drama *Dance With a Stranger*. Government grant to BFI rises to £7,810,000.

Industry braces itself for expected Department of Trade announcement that admissions in 1984 have fallen to all-time low of 55 million. Only five per cent of population now goes to cinema once monthly. Number of cinemas now 700 comprising some 1,200 screens.

Video Trades Association announces in April it favours levy on blank and pre-recorded tapes if money is used to fight video pirates. Lord Wilson's Interim Action Committee (soon to be renamed British Screen Advisory Council) favours levy provided copyright owners — i.e., mainly American companies — will agree to funds forming general pool for British film-makers.

Video Recordings Act 1984 still not functioning due to failure to work out agreed machinery with British Board of Film Censors in advance of 'scare' legislation: estimated 10,000 video cassettes awaiting classification.

In April House of Lords votes surprise amendment into Films Bill to permit levy to be raised on movies shown by BBC and ITV. Jubilation tempered by announcement that amendment will be deleted when Bill returns to Commons. May opens with BFY celebrations in Leicester Square, including plan for stars to affix personal prints in wet concrete *a la* celebrated 'Sidewalk of the Stars', Los Angeles.

Nicolas Roeg's *Insignificance* selected at Cannes Film Festival as British entry starring Tony Curtis and Gary Busey as two of 'four American icons — the Actress, the Senator, the Actress and the Ballplayer . . . thrown into the melting pot of a New York night'.

In June, Verity Lambert, production chief at Thorn-EMI Screen Entertainment in succession to Barry Spikings, reported 'changing the nature of her relationship' with TESE — probably turning independent producer within group.

The Coca Cola Company acquire the former Lear-Perenchio Embassy Communications divisions, including London-based company headed by Lord Grade and lately production base of Jake Eberts, formerly of Goldcrest.

Goldcrest announces pre-tax profit of £1.6m. on turnover of almost £14m. in first year since company became independent group. Features provided 75 per cent of all revenues, with *The Killing Fields* and *Gandhi* heavy contributors, but 'too many productions failed to live up to expectations'. Chief executive James Lee admits 1985–6 results heavily dependent on performance of Hugh Hudson's *Revolution*, already over budget. ('Hopefully, this will be the last year we find ourselves quite as vulnerable to one particular film' — Lee.)

British films premiered during first half of year include: *The Shooting Party;* * *Brazil; Dance with a Stranger;* * *Wetherby;* * *Scream For Help; A Passage to India;* * *Every Picture Tells a Story;* * *Morons from Outer Space;* * *Agatha Christie's Ordeal by Innocence;* * *Not Quite Jerusalem;* * *Number One;* * *Wild Geese II;* * *Steaming;* * *A View to a Kill; She'll Be Wearing Pink Pyjamas;* * *The Chain.* *

INDEX